Gentility and the Comic Theatre of Late Stuart London

When Adam delved and Eve span
Who was then the gentleman?

Mark S. Dawson's approach to this riddle is not to study the lives of those said to belong to early modern England's gentry. He suggests we remain sceptical of all answers to this question and consider what was at stake whenever it was posed. We should conceive of gentility as a mutable process of social delineation. Gentility was a matter of power and language, cultural definition and social domination. Neither consistently defined nor applied to particular social groups, gentility was about identifying society's elite.

The book examines how claims of gentility were staged at London's theatres (1660–1725). Employing a rich assembly of sources, comedies with their cits and fops, periodicals, correspondence of theatre patrons and polemic from its detractors, Dawson revises several of social history's conclusions about the gentry and offers new interpretations to students of late Stuart drama.

MARK S. DAWSON completed postgraduate studies at the universities of Auckland (New Zealand) and Cambridge. He is currently associate lecturer in early modern history at the Australian National University, Canberra.

Cambridge Social and Cultural Histories

Series editors:

New cultural histories have recently expanded the parameters (and enriched the methodologies) of social history. Cambridge Social and Cultural Histories recognises the plurality of current approaches to social and cultural history as distinctive points of entry into a common explanatory project. Open to innovative and interdisciplinary work, regardless of its chronological or geographical location, the series encompasses a broad range of histories of social relationships and of the cultures that inform them and lend them meaning. Historical anthropology, historical sociology, comparative history, gender history and historicist literary studies – among other subjects – all fall within the remit of Cambridge Social and Cultural Histories.

Titles in the series include:

1 Margot C. Finn *The Character of Credit: Personal Debt in English Culture, 1740–1914*
2 M. J. D. Roberts *Making English Morals: Voluntary Association and Moral Reform in England, 1787–1886*
3 Karen Harvey *Reading Sex in the Eighteenth Century: Bodies and Gender in English Erotic Culture*
4 Phil Withington *The Politics of Commonwealth: Citizens and Freemen in Early Modern England*
5 Mark S. Dawson *Gentility and the Comic Theatre of Late Stuart London*

Gentility and the Comic Theatre of Late Stuart London

Mark S. Dawson
Australian National University, Canberra

CAMBRIDGE
UNIVERSITY PRESS

CAMBRIDGE UNIVERSITY PRESS
Cambridge, New York, Melbourne, Madrid, Cape Town, Singapore, São Paulo

Cambridge University Press
The Edinburgh Building, Cambridge CB2 2RU, UK

Published in the United States of America by Cambridge University Press, New York

www.cambridge.org
Information on this title: www.cambridge.org/9780521848091

First published 2005

Printed in the United Kingdom at the University Press, Cambridge

A catalogue record for this book is available from the British Library

Library of Congress Cataloguing in Publication data

ISBN-13 978-0-521-84809-1 hardback
ISBN-10 0-521-84809-1 hardback

For Holly, *in memoriam*
Both because she was a breed apart and because the author cannot trump Hogarth's memento of his own companion in the attempt to capture London life.

Contents

Illustrations

Acknowledgements

In keeping a weather eye on a broad range of material while at the same time trying to maintain a close focus on a group of texts that historians are (still) not given many opportunities to consider, there are bound to be moments of critical astigmatism. Here I acknowledge the people who have done their very best to help me see clearly, though, at the same time, I accept full responsibility for any errors and misconceptions that remain.

For richer or poorer, the present study is a product of dualities of form, place, time and academic discipline. It has now had two incarnations, as this book and as a doctoral dissertation (with principal funding in the form of a Prince of Wales Cambridge Commonwealth Trust scholarship), and been worked on, and lived with, in different hemispheres since mid-1998. That it has not succumbed to the fatigue of these transitions, and still may have something worth saying to both socio-cultural historians and critics of early modern drama, is due largely to its having two mentors who guided and encouraged my work in different but always complementary ways. That they have both continued in these roles, so long after the research for this particular book was done, also deserves special mention. Sincerest appreciation, then, to Keith Wrightson as supervisor at Cambridge and now editor from New Haven; Barry Reay as advisor and, once again, commentator in Auckland.

In crossing disciplinary boundaries, as well as datelines over an extended period of time, it is a pleasure to recall the names of various people who offered encouragement, suggestions and constructive criticism of various kinds along the way: Donna Andrew, Helen Berry, David Cressy, Howard Erskine-Hill, Erin Griffey, Tim Hitchcock, Mac Jackson, Larry Klein, Michael Neill, Steve Snobelen and Sophie Tomlinson. From different perspectives, four anonymous readers as well as the editors for Cambridge University Press also offered valuable advice on extending a dissertation into a book.

Every effort has been made to secure permission from the authors of doctoral dissertations to refer to their unpublished work. I thank those who not only responded, but also were interested in my own research and were willing to entertain contrasting interpretations. For taking the time to help with certain references and queries, I am also grateful to several 'virtual' colleagues:

Tom Foster, Richard Gorrie, Ralph Houlbrooke, Mark Knights, Tim Meldrum, Linda Pollock, Alexandra Shepard, David Turner and subscribers to the Internet groups 'H-Albion' and 'C18-L Interdisciplinary Discussion'. Annette Fern, on behalf of the Harvard Theatre Collection, and Susan North, for the Victoria and Albert Museum (Department of Textiles and Dress), provided helpful pointers on certain details midway through the project. Judith Milhous and Robert D. Hume are to be lauded for their willingness to make their ongoing revision of *The London Stage (Part II)* available in draft. My thanks also go to the archivists and staff of the British Library and Museum; the respective university libraries of Cambridge and Auckland; the Beinecke at Yale and the Houghton at Harvard; the Folger Shakespeare Library and US Library of Congress in Washington, DC.

Even if they were not quite sure what I was researching or why, my research in these different locales would not have progressed very far at all were it not for the reassurance and support of family and friends in New Zealand.

Abbreviations and note on the text

ELH	*English Literary History*
ELR	*English Literary Renaissance*
Evelyn	E. S. de Beer (ed.), *The Diary of John Evelyn*, 6 vols. (Oxford, 1955)
HMC	Historic Manuscripts Commission (London)
HWJ	*History Workshop Journal*
Pepys	R. C. Latham and W. Matthews (eds.), *The Diary of Samuel Pepys 1660–1669*, 11 vols. (London, 1970–83, reprint 1995)
PMLA	*Publications of the Modern Language Association*
PP	*Past & Present*
RES	*Review of English Studies*
SEL	*Studies in English Literature*
Spectator	D. F. Bond (ed.), *The Spectator*, 5 vols. (Oxford, 1965)
Tatler	D. F. Bond (ed.), *The Tatler*, 3 vols. (Oxford, 1987)

Dates

Years are 'new style', understood to begin on 1 January. However, days and months will be those used by diarists and correspondents themselves. Most, written in England, will therefore be 'old style'.

Newspapers and periodicals

Where these carry no systematic pagination, in either their original or modern editions, I refer to the first page recto of each issue as '[1]', what was technically the verso as '[2]', and so on. Pertinent details of changed titles and interrupted sequences are explained in the relevant section of the bibliography.

Plays

I have departed from standard dramatic citation practices in several respects. When quoting dialogue, I have given the speaker's name in full to avoid any confusion that might have resulted from using the original abbreviations found in some first editions. I reference by act and page number only. So 'ii, 3' would refer to act ii, page 3, of the playbook in question.

I have refrained from citation by scene and line number for two reasons. First, the first editions consulted usually make no systematic attempt to mark their scripts, particularly the line numbers, in this way. Any attempt to do so on my part would not have been productive. Second, many of these first editions are now available as searchable digital transcripts. The active reader can easily pinpoint a particular citation and its context by entering a key phrase into the database, *Literature Online*. I have used first editions whenever possible. Later editions have been consulted when they compensate for lacunae in the originals and are footnoted accordingly. Readers should also bear in mind that the year of a playbook's publication does not necessarily match the date of its first performance.

Serial publications

For long-lived organizations (for example, the Camden Society) that have published several 'series', every effort has been made to retain consistent numeration of individual volumes. However, in the event of discrepancy, readers should refer to the year of publication.

Introduction
Early modern society, drama and cultural history

> We see nothing more frequently galls a Man, than baseness of Birth, when in Reputation or Honour; nor nothing more elevates him, than the empty Title of a **Gentleman**, which duely considered in its Rise, Progress, and End, is but a *Non ens.*
>
> W. Ramesey, *The Gentlemans Companion* (1672)

If the research behind this book has a single intention it is to contribute towards the reassessment of one of the most important and persistent distinctions for early modern English society: its cleaving in two by the constant identification of a 'gentle' elite and, as a corollary, a 'simple' majority.[1] To those familiar with current historiography, this aim may appear out of step with the abiding concern to recover the histories of the marginalized and subordinated. Yet, for all its gains, this preoccupation has had unfortunate side-effects. Research on that oxymoronic subject, a ruling minority, goes largely unpursued because its modern relevance remains open to debate. Surely not another study of the gentry is the implied query, the tacit assumption that decades of political and then related social historiography have largely exhausted a narrow field of inquiry. Recent work has also reached the point where it denies the usefulness of viewing early modern society as divided in two, genteel and non-genteel or elite versus plebeian. Having completed this book I was not surprised to find a sophisticated collection of essays prefaced by the claim that it would put aside a 'simple dichotomy' riddled with problems.[2]

Yet however crude or ultimately untenable this dichotomy may have been, the fact remains that a genteel/non-genteel divide made a persistent if contingent difference in the lives of countless people who fell on either side for diverse reasons and with varied consequences. To give but a handful of random instances

[1] Use of the term 'gentle' itself implied another non-elite group, but occasionally contemporaries did explicitly juxtapose a second term for the 'other' group. Uses of 'gentle' and 'simple' may be found in 'The Maids Call to the Batchelors', in W. G. Day (ed.), *The Pepys Ballads* (Cambridge, 1987), vol. V, 194; Anon., *The Whitsun-tide Ramble* (?1720), 6.

[2] M. J. Braddick and J. Walter, 'Introduction. Grids of Power: Order, Hierarchy and Subordination in Early Modern Society', in M. J. Braddick and J. Walter (eds.), *Negotiating Power in Early Modern Society. Order, Hierarchy and Subordination in Britain and Ireland* (Cambridge, 2001), 3.

here, consider that identification as 'gentle' or 'simple' could quite possibly determine privileges as a university student;[3] capacity for government office;[4] marriage prospects;[5] course of debate in the House of Commons;[6] tax liability;[7] perception of professional skill;[8] ability to serve on a jury;[9] success in foreign diplomacy;[10] severity of criminal prosecution and punishment;[11] interment.[12]

Readmitting the elite to our agenda does not need to be at the expense of the plebs, or to come at the price of reinstating the condescension of posterity. Far from it. In the same way that historians of gender are realizing they can no longer take the history of dead (white) males as written, but must interrogate masculinity if they are to understand the complexities of both femininity and questions of relative subordination, the first main premise of this study is that we

[3] For example, Thomas Dixon to Sir Daniel Fleming, 24 July 1678, HMC, *Le Fleming* 25, 1 (1890), 147 (reports on the status of Fleming's son and his lodgings at Queen's College, Oxford). Daniel Woolf's *The Social Circulation of the Past. English Historical Culture 1500–1730* (Oxford, 2003), 73–98, offers further treatment of this issue and other social privileges associated with genteel heredity.

[4] Peter to Thomas Wentworth, 24 September 1714, in J. J. Cartwright (ed.), *The Wentworth Papers 1705–1739* (London, 1883), 422 (concerning the uncertain status of new appointments made by George I).

[5] Robert to his merchant father Thomas Pitt, 30 December 1703, HMC, *Fortescue* 30, 1 (1892), 9ff. (on the possibility of his marriage: 'alliance with the greatest families in England is as much to your credit'). See also several of the legal case-studies presented in L. Stone, *Uncertain Unions. Marriage in England 1660–1753* (Oxford, 1992); Stone, *Broken Lives. Separation and Divorce in England 1660–1857* (Oxford, 1993).

[6] HMC, *Manuscripts of the Earl of Egmont. Diary of Viscount Percival afterwards First Earl of Egmont. Volume I: 1730–1733* 63, 1 (1920), 65–77 (entry for 26 February 1730 reports socially invective Commons debate over the East India Company).

[7] *Pepys*, 20 March 1667, vol. VIII, 120 (Pepys was rated as esquire for the poll tax); Rev. Robert Stubbes to Dr William Trumball, ?May 1678, HMC, *Downshire* 75, 1 (1924), 11 (complains that gentlemen of the cloth are exempt from certain levy).

[8] For example, in the early 1660s Lady Gardiner considered the reliability of an oculist and his treatment stemmed directly from the superior pedigree of the man. See M. M. Verney (ed.), *Memoirs of the Verney Family from the Restoration to the Revolution 1660 to 1696* (1899), vol. IV, 97.

[9] Peter to Thomas Wentworth, 15 July 1731, in Cartwright, *Wentworth Papers*, 466 (reports delay in a trial while it was reckoned who were gentlemen and, therefore, able to constitute a special jury).

[10] John Vanbrugh to his mother in London, 30 October 1691, HMC, *Finch* 71, 3 (1957), 294 (on the matter of his imprisonment in the Bastille he instructs her that a certain individual cannot help them because he is a 'man of no birth').

[11] For instance, Edmund Thaxter *et al.* to Lord Yarmouth, 29 September 1676, HMC, *Sixth Report* 5, 1 (1877), 380, report on a search of the Herald's Office in order to establish whether a case against Bowers the coffee-man, who claims gentility, can proceed; when detained at Cork in the wake of the Rye House Plot, Elizabeth Freke recalled that she and her husband received consideration that was only proper on account of their higher status. See R. A. Anselment (ed.), *The Remembrances of Elizabeth Freke 1671–1714* (Camden Society, London, fifth series, 2001) vol. XVIII, 50, 221 (entries for 29 July 1683); Dr Joseph Browne to Robert Harley, 30 May 1706 at 1 o'clock, HMC, *Portland* 29, 8 (1907), 229 (pleads that 'your honour's generosity will not let a gentleman suffer so much shame' in the pillory).

[12] Anselment, *Remembrances of Elizabeth Freke*, 247–51 (in relation to the burial and memorials for both her grandson and her husband, 1706).

can better comprehend the experience of the socially marginalized if we know more of how they were dominated and why certain people came to presume power over others.

What follows has no immediate quarrel with the notion that early modern inequality was far more complex than a single cleft separating the haves from the have-nots. This is not as contradictory an assertion as it might appear. Although the present work concurs in seeing early modern social differentiation as elaborate, plural, contingent and processual, we have still to explain how and why premodern people expended so much energy trying to uphold a divide that was obvious, singular and unchanging. Granted this separation was persistently being undermined in both large and small ways, even to the point of near-collapse. Yet gentility (in company with its implied opposite) retained an enduring if not entirely consistent presence and we have a way still to run before we understand this distinction's meanings and their implications for contemporaries. While it is fashionable to read normative social distinctions against the grain, as evidence that the early modern majority lived largely opposed to them and their socio-cultural experience thereby refuses easy categorization, to concede the existence of the normative is itself tacit recognition that perennial efforts were also made to realize a simple, stable and definitive ordering of society. However partial their success these attempts had consequences, immediate or postponed, major and minor, for diverse aspects of early modern life.

The second working premise of *Gentility and the Comic Theatre* is that by studying London's comic stage of the later seventeenth and early eighteenth centuries, it should be possible to recover significant aspects of the complex socio-cultural process that was gentility. In isolation, this suggestion may not seem particularly novel. For scholars of early modern theatre have long been aware of its social politics, even though they may disagree over its precise modulations and importance. However, the current study aims to address both audiences, social historians and drama critics alike. Situated at the intersection of two disciplines, this brief introduction of current thinking in social history for literary scholars, and of literary criticism for the historian, sometimes runs the risk of stating the obvious as it tries to reconcile not always mutual or familiar points of view. Fundamentally however, these disciplines share the endeavour of understanding the cultural, the networks of meaning shaping and shaped by past societies. In the course of this book we will find that the comic theatre was a prominent example of such a network for London society in the early modern period; that gentility gave particular meaning to power in this society and, conversely, to define gentility was itself a question of power.

Studies of England's gentry in the early modern period are subject to paradox. On the one hand, their authors are prone to confess that the identity of their subjects, the gentlemen and -women whose history they are telling, remains inherently uncertain. On the other, they persist in the idea that it is possible to chart the fortunes of these people as a discrete social group over time. For instance, the introductory chapter to a perceptive synthesis of this research by Felicity Heal and Clive Holmes is in the curious position of ending with the statement: 'At the risk of tautology we therefore must conclude that the gentry were that body of men and women whose gentility was acknowledged by others.'[13] The rest of their book is spotted with similar concessions, some drawn from contemporary texts. Yet as that study draws to a close we find 'gentility triumphant', a conclusion seconded by its definitive title of '*The* Gentry . . .'.[14] Apparently we *are* meant to know precisely who the gentry were, what gentility comprised, after all. A similar tension can be seen in a concise survey of gentility across four centuries. Penelope Corfield concludes that the 'definition of gentility remained disputed . . . It signified not stasis but flexibility.'[15] But this kind of conclusion is counter-intuitive, for it assumes an *a priori* stability against which flexibility can be gauged.[16] It also suggests that our paradox is largely self-inflicted, the result of a not always rigorous conceptualization of the phenomenon under investigation. We need to ask anew: how are we to define gentility and who were the gentry during the seventeenth and eighteenth centuries? Problems with periodization, the incomplete conceptualization of the relationship of culture to social stratification, and underrecognition of the complexities of cultural change and transmission, all suggest that current historiography does not approach these questions with the rigour they deserve.

What was 'gentility'; what did it mean to be 'genteel' and 'generous', or to identify someone as a 'gentleman' or 'gentlewoman', and a member of the 'gentry'? What did these words signify? The answer often assumed by studies of 'the gentry' is that they comprised part of the 'language of social description' and so alluded to social structures.[17] This is the first mis-step. The second is to reason from the first that it is the historian's task to excavate these structures, that with a little effort she or he can uncover the material, objective reality behind the façade of language. Arguably, the majority of studies of gentility in the early modern period are liable to this kind of reductionism. Furthermore, it remains a given that the language of gentility reflected a material, class position in the last instance. Although the gentry's class consciousness has long since been rejected as a remnant of 'vulgar' marxism, early modern gentlemen and gentlewomen

[13] F. Heal and C. Holmes, *The Gentry in England and Wales, 1500–1700* (Stanford, 1994), 19.

[14] *Ibid.*, 382; also G. E. Mingay, *The Gentry. The Rise and Fall of a Ruling Class* (London, 1976), cf. 53 and 57ff.

[15] P. J. Corfield, 'The Rivals: Landed and Other Gentlemen', in N. Harte and R. Quinault (eds.), *Land and Society in Britain, 1700–1914. Essays in Honour of F. M. L. Thompson* (Manchester, 1996), 22–3.

[16] See also, for instance, Mingay, *Gentry*, 10; Heal and Holmes, *Gentry*, 9, 11–12.

[17] Corfield, 'The Rivals', 20.

still comprise a ghostly class-in-itself.[18] Much as recent studies of England's gentry reject description of the gentry as a 'class', they cannot stop thinking of it as one. For example, Corfield diligently avoids any mention of class in her discussion of gentility until the final paragraphs, where it is suggested that gentility's malleability is indicative of the 'opacity of class definitions'.[19] Her essay then comes full circle. Denials notwithstanding, materialist and positivist assumptions have driven the interpretation from the beginning. Those who owned a sizeable amount of land over a number of years, that is, a country estate inherited through several generations of the one family, were 'gentlemen'; 'gentlewomen' were their mothers, sisters, wives and daughters. Collectively these people were the 'gentry' and gave expression to their common social position by way of their 'gentility', variously described by historians as their lifestyle, manners or culture.

It is this assumption that 'generous language' referred to England's larger landowners which permits contradictory claims that the 'definition of gentility' was contracting or expanding at different times and for various reasons.[20] The historiography for our chosen period is no exception, maintaining that gentility was undergoing substantial change. As just one example, Peter Borsay writes that

> in mid-seventeenth-century Britain birth was probably still the principal factor in defining a gentleman, and the ownership of a rural estate the most common method of sustaining this honour. In the years after the Restoration this traditional model of gentility was seriously eroded. Though ancestry remained an important qualification and land a valuable support, the critical definition of a gentleman increasingly became a *cultural* one.[21]

And what was the main effect of this cultural shift which some have described as involving the advent of a '*cult* of gentility'?[22] The most obvious consequence, it has been argued, was the rise of individuals usually referred to by historians as the 'pseudo-gentry'.[23] In other words, a growing number of people claimed to be 'gentlemen' and 'gentlewomen' without fitting the established profile of ancient landownership. These 'pseudo-gentry' are usually characterized as having been urban in both their origin and their means of livelihood. And were it not for the so-called culture of gentility, a further assumption is that we should otherwise describe these 'pseudo'-gentlemen and gentlewomen as ambitious

[18] See the first studies of the gentry produced by the new social history; a position summarized by Mingay, *Gentry*, 3.

[19] Corfield, 'The Rivals', 23.

[20] I use the phrase 'generous language' as shorthand for the various cognates of gentility.

[21] P. Borsay, *The English Urban Renaissance. Culture and Society in the Provincial Town, 1660–1770* (Oxford, 1989), 226. *Emphasis added.*

[22] L. Stone and J. C. F. Stone, *An Open Elite? England 1540–1880* (Oxford, 1984), 410. *Emphasis added.*

[23] For this term see A. Everitt, 'Social Mobility in Early Modern England', *PP* 33 (1966), 56–73.

members of the upper-middling sort (or 'class'). Lawrence and Jeanne Stone speak for many when they suggest that

> what makes the rise of this middling sort so crucial is their attitude towards their social superiors. Instead of resenting them, they eagerly sought to imitate them, aspiring to gentility by copying the education, manners, and behaviour of the gentry . . . This attitude thus provided the glue which bound together the top half or more of the nation by means of an homogenized culture of gentility that left elite hegemony unaffected.[24]

There are problems with this model of social development. Several important shades of grey in the social landscape have largely escaped comment, passed over in favour of black-and-white explanation. There are obvious discrepancies in the timing of the alleged transition from a 'true' to a 'pseudonymous' gentry, the reduction or 'debasement of gentility'.[25] The reputed collapse in the integrity of a genteel social identity, as it came to be culturally defined, seems always to be on the agenda of early modern social change. Some see it as a notable feature of the Restoration era (1660–*c*.1685);[26] others trace it to the early years of the eighteenth century or perhaps delay its onset until 1750 and beyond.[27] Still others have observed a similar phenomenon much sooner, by the opening decades of the seventeenth century.[28]

It is even more difficult to explain the perceived nature of the change in question: the implicit but all too common notion that at some point, and quite suddenly, the social certainty of being one of the gentry gave way to cultural uncertainty over exactly who was, or was not, one of the elite. It is by no means clear to whom or what the concept of a 'culture of gentility' is meant to refer. For surely England's gentlemen and -women had always had a culture: shared values, beliefs (including faith in their superiority) and the symbolic forms in which these found expression? How is it that at a particular point in the early modern chronology this culture assumes characteristics vaguely reminiscent

[24] Stone and Stone, *Open Elite*, 409. See also, for example, M. L. Bush, *The English Aristocracy. A Comparative Synthesis* (Manchester, 1984), 9, 76, 128–9; D. Castronovo, *The English Gentleman. Images and Ideals in Literature and Society* (New York, 1987), 14–19; J. Barry, 'Introduction', in J. Barry and C. Brooks (eds.), *The Middling Sort of People. Culture, Society and Politics in England, 1550–1800* (London, 1994), 19; R. Grassby, *The Business Community in Seventeenth-Century England* (Cambridge, 1995), 117, 378–85, 390–1 (but cf. 118, 386–8, 391–3).

[25] P. Langford, *A Polite and Commercial People, England 1727–1783* (Oxford, 1989), 66.

[26] J. S. Morrill, 'The Northern Gentry and the Great Rebellion', *Northern History* 15 (1979), 73; Heal and Holmes, *Gentry*, 7–8.

[27] Langford, *Polite*, 67–8; L. E. Klein, 'Politeness for Plebes. Consumption and Social Identity in Early Eighteenth-Century England', in A. Bermingham and J. Brewer (eds.), *The Consumption of Culture 1600–1800. Image, Object, Text* (London, 1995), 362; Klein, 'The Political Significance of "Politeness" in Early Eighteenth-Century Britain', in G. J. Schochet (ed.), *Politics, Politeness, and Patriotism. Papers Presented at the Folger Institute Seminar* (Washington, DC, 1993), 95–6.

[28] K. E. Wrightson, 'Estates, Degrees and Sorts: Changing Perceptions of Society in Tudor and Stuart England', in P. J. Corfield (ed.), *Language, History and Class* (Oxford, 1991), 37–41.

of some portrayals of modern-day mass culture, inducing a numbing social consensus among its consumers? Broadly speaking, the answer would seem to lie in lingering traces of the *marxisant* notion of cultural superstructure as a function of distinct socio-structural groups (classes, once again).

Finally, and paradoxically, it is becoming clearer that distinctions between social groups were far more contingent than we once assumed. Indeed, there are grounds for arguing that historians have misused the very term 'pseudo-gentry'.[29] Early modern Londoners appear never to have employed this compound word either in the sense or to the degree that modern historiography has. Instead they recognized that the language of gentility was itself contested. As Guy Miège conceded when trying to write his own definition of the term 'gentleman' in the 1690s: 'But Use has so far stretched the Signification of this Word, both high and low.'[30]

In sum, we need to understand more of how and why this 'stretching' was possible (bearing in mind that it might involve contraction as well as expansion). Evidently there was nothing 'pseudo' about it. If we continue to think of the gentry as an identifiable social group with a discrete culture then we end up playing a zero-sum game, recognizing that gentility was highly significant, full of meaning(s), for early modern people but largely meaningless to us. All are agreed that gentility was a definition; but of what and why? To use the words 'gentleman' or 'gentlewoman' was to make an identification, but of whom?

There is a way out of this conceptual cul-de-sac. We need to acknowledge that with the advent of history 'from below', studies of elites, social groups like England's gentry, became unfashionable. To a large extent they remain so and, as a consequence, those studies which do emerge often fail to engage with the rethinking of the social which has been pursued predominantly with regard to the histories of subordinate, non-elite groups.[31] In fact, the broader outlines of this reconsideration can help us to make better sense of the babble of voices disputing gentility in the early modern period; to escape the tautology and paradox which dogs much historiography. The reconsideration that follows will essentially contend that gentility *always* comprehended a cultural and political dynamic.

29 In my research I happened across only one contemporary instance but with connotations quite unlike those implied by Everitt *et al.* See *Universal Spectator*, no. xxxviii (28 June 1729), [1], where the term is associated with gambling and con-men, not the prosperous urban upstart.

30 G. Miège, *The New State of England* (1691, fourth edition 1702), part ii, 153–4.

31 In British history see the reconsideration, by Patrick Joyce, of those once confidently described as the 'working class' in his *Visions of the People. Industrial England and the Question of Class 1848–1914* (Cambridge, 1991); Joyce, *Democratic Subjects. The Self and the Social in Nineteenth-Century England* (Cambridge, 1994). For a conceptually similar reassessment of the 'middle class', see D. Wahrman, *Imagining the Middle Class. The Political Representation of Class in Britain, c.1780–1840* (Cambridge, 1995). A useful introduction to the wider issues involved may also be found in the opening chapter of Kathleen Wilson's *The Sense of the People. Politics, Culture and Imperialism in England, 1715–1785* (Cambridge, 1995), which, as the title implies, aims to deconstruct the idea of 'the people'.

A rhetorical disposition of power constantly in progress, gentility delineated society's most powerful grouping, thereby structuring and rationalizing social inequality.[32]

Social structures (relationships of difference or inequality) are no longer considered immanent and impersonal sets of cast-iron roles lived out by human beings. Instead, they are deemed to be as much the product of cultural agency because individuals give meaning to material experiences in a ceaseless and dialectical process, a process which Anthony Giddens labels 'social structuration'.[33] As material experience is shaped by culture, so culture, as the giving of meaning, has a material presence. Therefore, inherited social roles structure life but the contingency of experience means that we typically cannot describe these roles as permanently structured, static and embedded within society. In other words, as people learn the social roles they are to play, certain conditions make for smaller improvisations within or even beyond what culture and history might otherwise seem to dictate. Improvisation makes for accretions of new meaning that eventually recast the role's subsequent performance.

This constant process may be described as subjective in three respects. First, if the structure of society is partly a matter of interpretation then people have multiple views of society ('where' or 'how' they and others fit; what roles they are to play) and these may change over time and place. Second, whilst these interpretations are necessarily varied, some become more persuasive or dominant. Differences of power are as much a matter of culture as they are of material experience. Third, both rulers and ruled are subject to, or constrained by, prevailing cultural conventions. This means that if certain individuals in early modern England were powerfully dominant as society's elite, possessing social prominence, political influence and sprawling acres, then they were equally powerful by way of their ability to impose a prevalent view of themselves as elites – gentility – on society at large. However, at the same time, they themselves had also to be seen to 'live out' or impersonate that identity in order for it to carry conviction. In sum, social history has taken a cultural or linguistic turn. There is a greater recognition that social structure and relationships, along with

[32] What follows also finds itself in general sympathy with the positions taken by three recent studies. First, an excellent micro-history of the Phelips family, Tudor–Stuart claimants of gentility, by R. W. S. More, 'The Rewards of Virtue: Gentility in Early Modern England', unpublished PhD dissertation, Brown University (1998), 24–30, 79–80, 196. Second, a revisionist stance is evident in a study of gentility from the perspective of the Anglo-Atlantic world during the eighteenth century by M. J. Rozbicki, *The Complete Colonial Gentleman. Cultural Legitimacy in Plantation America* (Charlottesville, 1998), 17, 34, 38, 70, 80, 170, 178 (cf. 6, 20, 75, 129). Third, and more generally, see D. M. Posner, *The Performance of Nobility in Early Modern European Literature* (Cambridge, 1999), 4, 15–18, 110–15, 207–10.

[33] A. Giddens, *The Class Structure of the Advanced Societies* (London, 1973, second edition 1981), *passim*.

the resulting identities and groups, are not simply inherent to a given society. They are not waiting somewhere 'out there' to be discovered by the historian, nor were they transparently described or perceived by contemporaries.[34] Rather they were inscribed by language, organized in discourse.

It was suggested above that 'gentility' and its various cognates were ultimately social signifiers, they limned a social distinction. The discourse of gentility comprehended the forging of an unequal relationship, apprehended a process of differentiation, or, in short, a creation and distribution of power in early modern society. Naming the 'gentleman' or 'gentlewoman' ineluctably identified those who were *not* 'gentlemen' and 'gentlewomen', split dominant from subordinate. Generous language constructed a differential network of power rather than simply commenting on or always reflecting independent, pre-existing differences. If gentility comprehended a process, the structuring of inequalities, then in an important sense it preceded 'the gentry' as early modern society's dominant social stratum. Individuals then lived out these linguistic strictures by (re)creating the distinctions achieved in discourse as 'structuring' experience, as a ceaseless dialectic of the discursive and the material. Gentility was a set of cultural claims about power in early modern society that sought to order this world in terms of itself.[35]

With this recognition of the historical and cultural contingency of social stratification also comes the realization that it is multi-dimensional, for want of a better term. 'Social strata' are interpretations of power, power being simultaneously and recursively a combination of the economic (situations of exchange and ownership, or 'class' in a broadly Weberian sense), the political (in terms of institutional authority or 'command'), the social ('status') and the discursive.[36] Gentility was nothing more nor less than one construction, one gloss, on power. Like all such constructions, gentility tended to privilege one element of power

[34] What follows therefore finds itself in general agreement with the work of D. Cannadine, *The Rise and Fall of Class in Britain* (New York, 1999), 1–58. However, it should be said that the current study conceives of power (the 'political') more broadly and places greater emphasis on the inscriptive rather than simply descriptive nature of social discourse. Accessible introductions to these much-debated developments and the issues involved include the discussions triggered in their respective journals by L. Stone, 'History and Post-Modernism', *PP* 134 (1991), 217–18; D. Mayfield and S. Thorne, 'Social History and Its Discontents: Gareth Stedman Jones and the Politics of Language', *Social History* 17, 2 (1992), 165–88. For a useful prospectus on the politics of social history, see K. E. Wrightson, 'The Politics of the Parish in Early Modern England', in P. Griffiths, A. Fox and S. Hindle (eds.), *The Experience of Authority in Early Modern England* (London, 1996), 31–7.

[35] See G. Eley, 'Is All the World a Text? From Social History to the History of Society Two Decades Later', in T. J. McDonald (ed.), *The Historic Turn in the Human Sciences* (Ann Arbor, 1996), 218–20.

[36] Especially useful in my formulation have been M. Mann, *The Sources of Social Power. Volume I: A History of Power from the Beginning to A.D. 1760* (Cambridge, 1986), 1–33; J. Scott, *Stratification and Power. Structures of Class, Status, and Command* (Cambridge, 1996).

but at the same time attempted to account for the others. The resulting social strata were comprehended, often by means of a moral vocabulary, as being natural, legitimate and self-sustaining rather than as cultural constructs dependent on language. However prominent, however important, gentility was but one understanding of power such that both its meaning and its priority might be overridden, even controverted, by rival figurations. Consequently, individuals inhabited multiple relationships of domination and subordination, plural but overlapping subject positions, at one and the same time. What follows will, therefore, comment on gentility's interfacing with constructions of gender and sexuality.

Looking more closely at gentility we can suggest that it privileged status, social power, which was defined in terms of blood lineage or one's belonging to a particular pedigree. Normatively, the individuals comprehended by generous terminology were being identified as the 'well-born' or 'well-descended';[37] of 'good' 'blood', 'birth', 'name', 'family' or 'descent';[38] of relatively higher 'degree',[39] 'quality',[40] and, rather oxymoronically, 'descent';[41] or, more unusually, said to be of 'ancient bloud', 'stock' or 'ancienity',[42] when compared with the rest of society who were, relatedly and relatively, 'obscure' and 'meane';[43]

[37] **i.** Sir Robert Southwell to the earl of Ormonde, 9 April 1681, HMC, *Ormonde* 36, 4 (1906), 586 (of the young Lord Courcy). **ii.** G. Mackenzie, *Moral Gallantry. A Discourse* (1685), 28 (trying to distinguish masters from servants).

[38] **i.** Southwell to Ormonde, 10 January 1681, HMC, *Ormonde* 36, 4 (1906), 583 (of a wife for Lord Courcy). **ii.** F. Tyrer and J. J. Bagley (trans. and ed.), *The Great Diurnal of Nicholas Blundell of Little Crosby, Lancashire. Volume I: 1702–11* (Record Society of Lancashire and Cheshire, Liverpool, 1968), no. CX, 114 (entry for 9 July 1706, describing coach passengers). **iii.** Anselment, *Remembrances of Elizabeth Freke*, 50 (entry for 29 July 1683, see n.11 above). **iv.** *Evelyn*, 13 July 1675, vol. IV, 69 (of James Graham, soldier and politician). **v.** [E. Haywood], *Bath Intrigues in Four Letters to a Friend in London* (1725), 16 (on the perception of pedigree at this leisure resort); Dr William Denton to Sir Ralph Verney, 8 July 1682, HMC, *Seventh Report* 6, 1 (1879), 497 (reporting a duel).

[39] See, for example, J. Logan, *Analogia Honorum* (1677), part i, 155 (explaining the situation of well-born apprentices); P. Ayres, *Vox Clamantis* (1684), 20–1 (promoting temperance 'above the ordinary sort of people'); B. Smithurst, *Britain's Glory and England's Bravery* (1689), 83–4 (elaborating the place of gentlemen in the hierarchy of honour).

[40] For instance, ?John Heys to Roger Kenyon, 26 February 1695, HMC, *Kenyon* 35, 1 (1894), 377 (in relation to the appointment of some justices of the peace); *Spectator*, no. 219 (10 November 1711), vol. II, 352 (an essay by Addison on superiority).

[41] H. Woolley, *The Gentlewomans Companion* (1673, third edition 1682), 134 (in the context of marrying properly).

[42] **i.** J. Dare, *Counsellor Manners* (1673, second edition 1676), 3 (*italics reversed*; advice on behaviour). **ii.** *Evelyn*, 7 December 1680, vol. IV, 233 (of Lord Stafford currently on trial). **iii.** John Laws to the earl of Oxford, 14 June 1711, HMC, *Portland* 29, 5 (1899), 7 (on the latter's elevation to an earldom).

[43] **i.** A. Browning (with M. K. Geiter and W. A. Speck) (ed.), *Memoirs of Sir John Reresby. The Complete Text and a Selection from His Letters* (London, 1936, second edition 1991), 406 (of a former associate of the family). **ii.** *Evelyn*, 22 March 1675, vol. IV, 56 (commenting on the humble parentage of Sir William Petty).

of 'obscure name';[44] of 'no', 'ordinary', 'ill' or 'mean(e) extract(ion)';[45] of 'noe' or 'mean birth';[46] of 'low degre[e]',[47] and 'base(ly) born'.[48] Therefore, if we must have a working characterization of 'the gentry', we should say that they were society's predominant status grouping.[49] The gerund is used deliberately to suggest a continual process of ordering, a constant but contingent making of social meaning. But since these individuals, 'gentlemen' and 'gentlewomen', simultaneously inhabited situations of economic and political power, so, in other contexts, competing social idioms or rival figurations of power might overwrite the language of gentility. For example, the 'gentry' could just as easily metamorphose into the 'better sort' (as opposed to the 'poorer', 'meaner' or 'ordinary' sort)[50] and people said to be of 'condition', 'fortune' or 'estate' (the 'of' implying a juxtaposition to those with *no* condition, fortune or estate).[51] As much

44 George to Henry Savile, 1 March 1680, in W. D. Cooper (ed.), *Letters to and from Henry Savile, Esq.* (Camden Society, London, 1858), vol. LXXI, 144 (of an opposing litigant whom he thinks a barber by trade).

45 **i.** Thomas to Peter Wentworth, *c.* August 1710, in Cartwright, *Wentworth Papers*, 133 (of a ministerial rival). **ii.** Browning, *Memoirs of Sir John Reresby*, 392. **iii.** J. Priestley, 'Some Memoirs Concerning the Family of the Priestleys, Written, at the Request of a Friend, By Jonathan Priestley, Ano. Domini 1696, Aetatis Suae 63', in Anon. (ed.), *Yorkshire Diaries and Autobiographies in the Seventeenth and Eighteenth Centuries. Volume II* (Surtees Society, Durham, 1886), vol. LXXVII, 12 (of his uncle's unfortunate first marriage). **iv.** *Evelyn*, 7 March 1700, vol. V, 393 (noting the status of the cuckolder of the duke of Norfolk, now divorced from his wife); A. Jessop (ed.), *Lives of the . . . Norths* (1890), vol. I, 196 (of Sir William Scroggs as the son of a butcher).

46 **i.** Browning, *Memoirs of Sir John Reresby*, 90 (of a prominent lawyer). **ii.** Woolley, *Gentlewomans Companion*, 5 (of the ideal governess for elite children).

47 John Muddyman to Rochester, September 1671, in J. Treglown (ed.), *The Letters of John Wilmot, Earl of Rochester* (1980), 71 (in relation to Rochester's brief affair with an upstart woman of the Court); Dare, *Counsellor Manners*, 43 (in relation to correct modes of address).

48 A. Behn, *Town-Fopp* (1677), ii, 21 (regarding courtship and marriage); R. Gould, 'Jack Pavy. A Satyr', in his *The Works* (1709), vol. II, 317 (line 555) (of actors mixing with their elite patrons).

49 Particularly supportive of this argument is the case-study by H. R. French, '"Ingenious & learned gentlemen" – Social Perceptions and Self-Fashioning among Parish Elites in Essex, 1680–1740', *Social History* 25, 1 (2000), 46–7, 65–6.

50 **i.** C. Cibber, *Careless Husband* (1705), prologue. **ii.** *Tatler*, no. 148 (21 March 1710), vol. II, 337 (discussion of status, taste and diet). **iii.** Sir Thomas Browne to his son, 22 August 1680, in G. Keynes (ed.), *The Letters of Sir Thomas Browne* (London, 1931, second edition 1946), 179 (on the hard work of a gentleman turned physician); J. Locke, *Some Thoughts Concerning Education* (1705), in J. L. Axtell (ed.), *The Educational Writings of John Locke* (Cambridge, 1968), 171 and 227 (on exposure of elite children to those in their parents' employ). **iv.** W. Matthews (ed.), *The Diary of Dudley Ryder 1715–1716* (London, 1939), 68 (entry for 3 August 1715, of company at a dance).

51 **i.** Priestley, 'Some Memoirs', 1 (for the contrast between quality and condition); [E.P.], *The Gentleman's Library, Containing Rules for Conduct in All Parts of Life* (1715), 51 (how the rich should improve their minds not their dress); *Weekly Journal*, no. 274 (25 January 1724), 1628 (of the company at a masquerade); *ibid.*, no. 300 (25 July 1724), 1872–3 (how consumer society encourages wealthy people to dress above their status). **ii.** 'The Northamptonshire Knight's Daughter', in Day, *Pepys Ballads*, vol. V, 176; Anne to Sir James Clavering, 8 August 1710, in H. T. Dickinson (ed.), *The Correspondence of Sir James Clavering (1680–1748)* (Surtees Society, Durham, 1967), vol. CLXXVIII, 89 (in relation to courtly place-seeking). **iii.** Anselment,

as the still current meanings of 'estate' and 'fortune', the terms 'sort'[52] and 'condition'[53] resonated with associations of exchange and ownership.[54] Their predicated use announced the economic power which the language of gentility otherwise worked to occlude.[55] For we shall see that to be 'gentle' was partly to claim that one was above relations of exchange, positioned beyond the marketplace. Alternatively, subjects of the language of gentility might be differentiated as people of 'rank',[56] 'distinction'[57] and 'station',[58] thereby suggesting the lion's share of political authority or, in this case, power which gentility construed as a natural inheritance legitimated by lineage and selflessly exercised for the good of society.

If gentility typically traced one configuration of power, there was little to prevent its terms being misused to reckon another. If generous language was meant to project social power (status), we will see in the following chapters that much of the debate surrounding gentility had to do with its linguistic integrity, its attempted appropriation as a means to gloss inequalities which

Remembrances of Elizabeth Freke, cf. 62 and 230 (3 November 1694, her reprieve of the only son of an 'estated (gentle)man' from the gallows).

52 See Ayres, *Vox*, 21, 84 (supra n.39, cf. later comment on tradesmen); Smithurst, *Britain's Glory*, 90–1 (of those below the gentry); Anon., *The English Theophrastus* (1706), 4 (how playwrights have now to play to different tastes for profit); *Review of the State of the English Nation*, no. 2 (3 March 1705), book 4, 8 (advertisement); Anon., *Whitsun-tide Ramble*, 4.

53 For incidences of this term which make the following connection clear, see Henry to George Savile, 28 February 1680, in Cooper, *Savile Correspondence*, 142 (of a marriage proposal); Smithurst, *Britain's Glory*, 82 (supra, n.39); Browning, *Memoirs of Sir John Reresby*, 174–5 (of providing for his children); *Review of the State of the English Nation*, no. 83 (19 December 1704), book 2, 346 (on the state of trade); Anon., *English Theophrastus*, 76 (of revenue versus title); J. Graile, *An Essay of Particular Advice to the Young Gentry, for the Overcoming the Difficulties and Temptations They May Meet With* (1711), 135–9 (of pride); Anon., *A Discourse Concerning the Character of a Gentleman* (Edinburgh, 1716), vi, 12 (constancy of mind whatever his situation); HMC, *Egmont. Diary of Viscount Percival. Volume I*, 246 (entry for 23 March 1732, in relation to the Land Qualification Bill and property requirements for entry into the House of Commons).

54 Thus John Evelyn rejected a suitor to one of his daughters on account of the fact that their fortunes did not match, 'he being in no condition sortable to hers', *Evelyn*, 27 July 1685, vol. IV, 462.

55 Of course this does not mean that such terms were always used with relations of exchange in mind. However, it can be argued that this was the dominant association of the language of 'sorts' by the later seventeenth century. See K. E. Wrightson, '"Sorts of People" in Tudor and Stuart England', in J. Barry and C. Brooks (eds.), *The Middling Sort of People. Culture, Society and Politics in England, 1550–1800* (London, 1994), 43–5.

56 [F. Brokesby], *A Letter of Advice to a Young Gentleman at the University* (1701), 3 (of leading by example); Lady Rachel Russell to the earl of Rutland, 14 April 1702, HMC, *Rutland* 24, 2 (1889), 171–2 (part of a description of Rutland himself).

57 H. Sutton to Robert Pitt, 16 September 1723, HMC, *Fortescue* 30, 1 (1892), 71 (complains of certain 'gentlemen, persons of rank and distinction' not acting as they should).

58 Graile, *Essay of Particular Advice*, xii (of virtuous behaviour by the well-born who rule); *British Journal*, no. 26 (13 July 1728), [2] (the natural order sees the nobility rule); *Universal Spectator*, no. 'xlx' (20 September 1729), [1] (of the education proper for the gentleman, as opposed to the tradesman); *ibid.*, no. lxxi (14 February 1730), [1] (virtuous rule is better than ancient pedigree).

privileged economic (class) and political (authority) power instead. Arguably it was this reinterpretation which prompted William Ramesey to announce that the 'gentleman' was a '*Non ens*', an identity without inherent, self-evident meaning, but then to speak in less than two pages of: a 'Gentility of Birth' (status); 'his Gentility, or Revenues' (class); gentlemen who 'rise by force' (authority).[59]

Instead of trying to establish definitively who were the 'gentle' in early modern society, it would seem more profitable to investigate gentility as a socio-cultural dynamic and, therefore, its implications as a discourse of social differentiation. A person's identification as 'gentle' or 'genteel' put the seal on a hermeneutical process. It capped an act of interpretation that here was a dominant, relatively powerful individual. Answering the historical questions 'what was gentility' or 'who was the gentleman' relies on our recognizing that we are about to interpret a culturally and historically conditioned process of social interpretation *per se*.

If gentility comprehended a contingent (because disputable) making of meaning, we need to question established narratives of change and should forego attempts at charting any linear development. As we saw earlier, it has become a commonplace that the importance of lineage to claims of gentility declined during the later seventeenth century, with gentility becoming increasingly 'cultural' or a matter of refined manners and such like instead.[60] We have no way of proving the first proposition absolutely – certain sources could be selected to argue the exact opposite – and the catch-cry that gentility became culturally defined during our period of main interest makes little sense. Gentility was always a cultural matter, a way of apprehending or seeing society. At most the forms, the signs, for articulating that vision multiplied. Understanding gentility as refined manners, the 'less tangible' or the 'elusive quality' of the gentry, is to misconstrue the nature and import of what was involved.[61] These gestures, these 'genteel' behaviours, were as much signifiers as the very appellations of 'gentleman' and 'gentlewoman'. All were a part of the constant process of elite social ordering, not simply a secondary reflection of a definitive social group heading an already established social hierarchy. Indeed, as the most deceptively 'natural' aspect of gentility, lineage itself was a cultural construct. Claims that an individual was innately superior on the basis of birth were not as transcendent, beyond culture, as they pretended. A person's pedigree was as much culturally

59 W. Ramesey, *The Gentlemans Companion; or a Character of True Nobility and Gentility* (1672), 2–3.

60 Heal and Holmes, *Gentry*, 38ff.; J. M. Rosenheim, *The Emergence of a Ruling Order. English Landed Society 1650–1750* (London, 1998), 29. Woolf, *Social Circulation*, 73–137, offers a more subtle account of changes in both the relative importance of pedigree to elite social standing and the perception of that pedigree.

61 Heal and Holmes, *Gentry*, 17; Mingay, *Gentry*, 3.

elaborated as it may have been naturally embodied. For at a time when one's parentage could not be proved absolutely, bloodlines verified, the well-born had constantly to act as if they were manifestly and precisely that; to body forth or impersonate their superior but always less than fully transparent origins.[62] We should therefore collapse the binary of birth versus culture that underwrites much existing research. No matter how often they attempted to erase their basis in culture, elite pedigrees were necessarily and irresolvably rhetorical. Institutions mandated to arbitrate rival claims of genteel descent can be found in operation at both the opening and the closing of our period, demonstrating not just that lineage remained central, but, further, that it was always open to interpretation as a matter of culture.[63]

To conceive of gentility as a singular social endpoint to be striven for and to then explain its apparent dilution in terms of 'social mobility' (that is, picturing more and more individuals scaling a socio-economic ladder and crowding this position of pre-eminence) probably simplifies the situation.[64] Our impressions of social movement and change may equally be the result of the manipulation and multiplication of meanings achieved by the rerouting of 'genteel' signifiers. In other words, not so much the result of more people becoming 'gentlemen' and '-women' in any objective and quantifiable sense (for example, purchasing country estates), but the effect of gentility's inherent malleability. The same generous language was appropriated to inscribe variations on the one constant, the familiar theme of power and justification of its (supposedly) ideal distribution. The ability to (re)define society's dominant ordering was itself power because at least half the battle was to wrest control over the representation of society. The persistent but varied use of the same language gives a false impression of calm totality and continuity, masking instability and disputed hegemony.

By reconsidering gentility as a socio-political rhetoric we need, in turn, to be more critical of texts customarily used to study 'the gentry'. As we have seen, historians of 'the gentry' must eventually concede that they cannot overcome the deadweight of subjectivity, the conflicting interpretations and rival ascriptions, and reach objectivity. Indeed, we shall find it is precisely at the point of contention, the failure to achieve consensus in defining genteel subjects, that gentility's early modern dynamic becomes most visible to us. Conclusions about

62 For just two detailed accounts of disputed parentage, and so possibly spurious lineage, see HMC, *Egmont. Diary of Viscount Percival. Volume I*, 400 (entry for 12 August 1733); HMC, *Manuscripts of the Earl of Egmont. Diary of the First Earl of Egmont (Viscount Percival). Volume II: 1734–1738* 63, 2 (1923), 224 (entry for 21 January 1736).

63 See, for example, newsletters reporting the proceedings of the Court of Chivalry in 1687, HMC, *Downshire* 75, 1 (1924), 270–4; or accounts from 3 March 1732 onwards in *Gentleman's Magazine*.

64 For instance, Mingay, *Gentry*, 8–10; Heal and Holmes, *Gentry*, 40–2. Cf. Wrightson, 'Estates, Degrees and Sorts', 40, 52.

early modern society which rely on data culled from university matriculation or guild apprenticeship records, for example, tend to take references to gentility at descriptive face-value, eliding the fact that some entries of 'gent.' or '*generosus*' were claims to identity and power which may have been questioned and even controverted in other contexts. But if official documents prove more opaque than first thought, what reason is there to believe that staged fiction will permit any sharper insight? Caught in post-structuralist eddies similar to those responsible for history's cultural turn, the 'return to history' now evinced by literary criticism is a much-debated development.[65] Here, the objective is simply to trace the basic features of recent critical practice which seem most pertinent to an explanation of why comic theatre should be of any use to the study of elite social structuration in early modern London. For the sake of convenience we may label this practice 'new historicism', bearing in mind that its practitioners often part company over narrower philosophical, theoretical, methodological and political issues which need not directly concern us.

Much of the novelty of new historicism as critical practice derives from its recognition of the textuality of past reality. Acknowledging that the past is only ever retrievable by indirect means, via textual traces, which make for plural interpretations, or histories rather than History, has allowed for a reappraisal of early modern literature's importance and meaning. New historicism rejects formalist criticism that treats literature as the aesthetic embodiment of universal truths unmediated by the material and historical circumstances of its creation. The predication of this historicist orientation as 'new' is equally important. New historicism distances itself from interpretation that conceives of literature as the reflective expression of an underlying historical context: namely, criticism based on the assumption that history is recoverable via so-called 'non-literary' or 'factual' sources which provide prior, unfettered access to a societal past, thereby serving as the unequivocal grounding for the subsequent interpretation of 'fictional' works. A new historicist orientation, by contrast, recognizes context to be as much the product of interpretation as the reading of allegedly singular literary works, or just plain 'texts' as they have become known.

Since historians have become more attuned to the fictive properties of what were once described as 'documents', there has been something of an interdisciplinary rapprochement. Historical document has met literary text at the crossroads of representation, on the common ground of culture. The shared

[65] The body of work examining the 'return to history' by literary criticism is considerable and still growing. Recent reviews, attempts at some degree of critical synthesis, expositions on the current state of play, include J. H. Zammito, 'Are We Being Theoretical Yet? The New Historicism, the New Philosophy of History, and "Practicing Historians"', *Journal of Modern History* 65, 4 (1993), 783–814; C. Colebrook, *New Literary Histories. New Historicism and Contemporary Criticism* (Manchester, 1997); J. Brannigan, *New Historicism and Cultural Materialism* (London, 1998); C. Gallagher and S. J. Greenblatt, *Practicing New Historicism* (Chicago, 2000).

assumption is that a text as artefact captures a process, the weaving together of meaning, which results from the complex negotiation between socio-historical conditions ('reality') and cultural conventions ('language'). As a result, new historicist practice gives equal attention to questions of how 'literary' texts activate rather than simply mimic socio-historical processes: the 'social presence to the world of the literary text', as one of the leading exponents of this critical praxis phrases it.[66] And if historians are being encouraged to rethink the existence of social collectivities, the nature of social categories once taken for granted, then new historicists have pursued a sceptical anti-humanism on the individual level: subjectivity writ small. Individuals construe and are constructed by discourse such that what appear, at first, to be the most enduring aspects of their identities (part of a timeless, transcendental human nature) prove on closer examination to be culturally conditioned, constantly asserted and contested, performed and reiterated.

Whether our disciplinary starting point is history or dramatic criticism, the shared enterprise is not so much the resolution of what certain texts mean but the recovery of how they gave meaning(s) to the world for contemporaries in an incessant interchange of experience and interpretation. Texts derive meaning from social relationships and these relationships are, at the very same time, influenced by their cultural (re)presentation in the form of texts. This critical reorientation gels with our proposed reassessment of gentility, the recovery of how and why individuals might be recognized as elite (or not). When faced with two designations of 'gentleman', for the sake of argument an admissions register of the Middle Temple and the dramatis personae in a playbook, common sense might tell us that the identity of the gentleman-templar had a validity and consequence beyond that of the actor merely impersonating a genteel figure for a few hours. Yet our interest lies not with determining the 'truth' of either identity but with resurrecting the nature and rationale of this identification as part of an intensive socio-cultural process, a discursive action, of which the designation 'gentleman' is merely a textual end fragment.

To recover this process of identification we need to have some understanding of the socio-cultural network that first made this generation of meaning possible. We can arrive at a fuller comprehension of the nature and significance of claims of gentility if we pay careful attention to how and why they were made and received, the 'social presence of the world in the literary text'.[67] Compared with trying to unravel the socio-cultural processes behind the deceptively definitive notation of 'gentleman' in a matriculation register, tracing the comedy's discursive formation, coming to terms with its representation of gentility, is conceivably an easier task. This is because London's early modern comic theatre

[66] S. J. Greenblatt, *Renaissance Self-Fashioning. From More to Shakespeare* (Chicago, 1980), 5.
[67] The quote is the other part of Greenblatt's formulation, *ibid.*, 5.

possesses the twin virtues of having itself been an intensely social experience and of having left a sizeable textual footprint. The theatre was a space where multiple claims of gentility, or elite social placement, were simultaneously and routinely produced *and* consumed, accepted *and* rejected – behind the scenes, on the stage and in the auditorium amongst writers, players, spectators. The late seventeenth-century playhouse buzzed with social interaction for, on any given evening, hundreds of people had literally to take their places before the show could begin. The book's structure aims to recapture something of this dialogue, not only interpreting the most commonly staged re-enactments of claims and counter-claims for social superiority as gentility, but also turning about to demonstrate how their presentation and reception were most probably preconditioned, both socially and discursively, for their original audiences. The beauty of the late Stuart stage is precisely that contemporaries gave ongoing, reflexive attention to the theatre as a social occasion of the first order.

If we cannot follow its patrons into the playhouses as often as we might like, we can at least listen in on them by reading traces of their conversations and debates at the coffee-house, around the tea-table, from the pulpit, and perhaps even in their closets. To achieve this, extensive use has been made of periodical essays, anti-theatrical tracts, conduct books, correspondence and diaries, whilst all the time keeping in view the fact that these texts, like the comedies themselves, had their own discursive axes to grind as they represented London's theatre as both a social experience and a (re)presentation of the social. Rather more selective reference has also been made to prose fiction and poetry, particularly that written in a satirical vein. Whilst these literary genres often rehearsed very closely the same issues and characters already familiar on the comic stage, the non-dramatic context compelled them to make explicit features which performance could take as read (or rather watched).

Clarification of some of the terminology employed, followed by explanation of the decision to comment mainly on comic drama from the period *c.*1690–1725, would seem in order. 'Late Stuart' is used as shorthand for the whole period from *c.*1660 to 1725. 'Restoration' refers to the span of years from 1660 to the later 1680s, '(post-)revolutionary' to the period from 1688 onward. These terms are used as basic markers and are not intended to prejudge questions of social, cultural or theatrical continuity and change. Nevertheless, they do capture the point that drama of the later seventeenth and early eighteenth centuries was preoccupied with specific questions of power.

Why not address late Stuart comedy comprehensively, from at least 1660 to 1725? Speaking in strictly relative terms, comedy from the second half of this period has been poorly served by scholarship in recent years and, as a consequence, hardly touched by newer interpretive perspectives. Despite its democratic implications (all texts are potentially created equal), the irony is that new historicist praxis remains preoccupied with canonical texts dating from the Renaissance and more lately the Restoration. Critics would seem to have trod lightly over the early eighteenth century on the basis that its comic drama is – aesthetically speaking – second- or even third-rate when compared with the golden and silver ages of Shakespeare, Jonson, Beaumont and Fletcher; Wycherley, Etherege or Dryden. Ending the study at *c.*1725 also allows us to embrace a fairly distinct generation of theatre, largely spanning the careers of key playwrights (William Congreve, Richard Steele, Susanna Centlivre, John Vanbrugh, George Farquhar, Mary Pix and Colley Cibber); prominent players (Robert Wilks, George Powell, Colley Cibber, Thomas Doggett, Elizabeth Barry, Anne Bracegirdle or Anne Oldfield); theatre critics of all stripes (from Jeremy Collier to John Dennis to Richard Steele); even playhouses and their audiences (the later 1720s would see moves to circumvent the duopoly of Drury Lane and Lincoln's Inn Fields, something of a revival in Court patronage).

However, this concentration should not imply that the theatre was simply made anew in the wake of the Glorious Revolution. Although the aforementioned individuals came to prominence after 1688 they carried the legacy of the Restoration years. This same, often ambiguous legacy helps explain many of the complexities, and indeed controversies, surrounding comic theatre from *c.*1690 and beyond. London's theatre in this period was so vibrant precisely because the Revolution was not as clear a political, social or cultural caesura as hoped or later portrayed. There was a web of uncertain transitions and conflicting imperatives: a newly constituted political regime badgered by the possible resurrection of the old; a booming yet precarious wartime commerce; moral revival amid consumer decadence; cultural innovation versus tradition and even censorship.

Readers can therefore expect some general observations on the Restoration years and the associated scholarly literature which typically emphasizes the earlier period, *c.*1660–85. Such comment seemed especially appropriate when tracing what seemed to be significant continuities or attempting to assess the degree of change for certain aspects of the post-revolutionary dramatic experience. The end result, a chronologically elongated yet more impressionistic narrative, means that this book is sometimes in the uncomfortable position of indicating how a feature of the early eighteenth-century theatre is incompatible with assumptions made by scholarship of the Restoration stage. Such criticism serves more as a plea to avoid the blindspots that can be imposed by adherence to overly rigid divisions in chronology; as an agenda for future reconsideration and research by those who take *c.*1660–85 for their preferred territory and, it should be noted, without whose labours the current study would not have been possible.

No apologies are made, then, for a certain degree of unevenness in the depth of coverage. In the final analysis, the book is not intended to survey formally the entire body of late Stuart comic drama (conceivably from 1660 to 1714 if one chooses a chronology pegged to dynastic events; to 1737 if one goes by the institutional deadline of the theatrical Licensing Act, or, if one prefers a looser and more conspicuously political endpoint, to 1745 and the last hurrah of the Stuart cause). This would have been a task beyond the patience and skills of the present author. I did begin by listening for a social chorus across the full range of late Stuart comedy but the final production is rather less ambitious and more selective in its scope. I trust, however, that the study has still achieved two things: first, homing in on and interpreting several interesting chords, largely as they resonated in post-revolutionary comedy; second, treating them as echoes of broader but bygone processes of both social and cultural composition. I would further hope that different readers at least find particular aspects thought-provoking. Social and political historians may want to test the main theses against other kinds of material to see if they ring true beyond the playhouse. Theatre and literary scholars may find that closer attention to individual texts adds finer or corrective layers of detail to the interpretations offered in the following pages. Both audiences might contest the study's conclusions when applied to earlier or later periods.

It now remains to outline how the study will proceed. The first half of the book (parts I and II) takes up our earlier points that gentility was fundamentally to do with the delineation of power and that this constant process was most often visible when it faltered, when genteel identifications were advanced only to be disputed.

What must surely have been the most rehearsed contest for gentility, the configuration of superiority on the late Stuart stage, contrasted London's upper-middling citizenry and landowners of established, well-born families. Part I undertakes a close rereading of the scenario that indelibly associated cuckoldry with the wealthy and politically powerful City.[68] Usually interpreted by modern critics as a quite straightforward representation of bourgeois mobility cum class conflict, this scenario is found to have had a more intricate and lasting socio-cultural significance than previously recognized.

We begin where many critics finish: with Richard Steele's *Conscious Lovers* (1723) as alleged rejection of a once-vibrant City comedy tradition and presumed acceptance of the London merchant's upward social mobility. By surveying the City comedy tradition as it had played for much of the seventeenth century, the first chapter contests the notion that *The Conscious Lovers* amounted to a new departure. Finding noteworthy continuity from the 1660s right the way through to the 1720s compels us to reconsider received explanations of the cit cuckold stereotype. In particular, the chapter suggests we abandon the tidy assumption that occasional social disruption, the rise of a

[68] The City here refers to the area under the charter of the Corporation of London, the commercial and financial heart of the larger metropolis.

middle class, corresponds with perceived discontinuities in the frequency of the figure's staging.

Our recovery of the cit's enduring importance for its original spectators pivots on an underremarked feature of the stereotype, its similarity to the punitive social ritual known as skimmington or charivari. Understanding the cultural logic of this ritual and its rehearsal on the early modern London stage proves a crucial step in reading the cuckolded cit as the expression of an abiding social anomaly. As chapter 2 explains, that sense of anomaly stemmed from an inability to reconcile the London citizen's conspicuous material success and a less than illustrious descent, on the one hand, with the well-born landowner's impecuniosity on the other. Did the contrasting sources of their power cancel each other out and make both 'gentlemen'? Accustomed to having the reins of power held by those who were 'gentle', or self-evidently superior on account of their pedigree, late Stuart Londoners found the meanly born but powerfully prosperous citizen hard to place in the traditional ordering of society. Drawing analogies from early modern physiology, especially the critical combination of vital bodily fluids (humours) and their role in reproduction, the comedy tested to see whether blood and wealth would mix and the citizen's social position could be resolved. Most plays returned a negative result, putting the cit in his proper place as less than a gentleman and unable to sire a reputable lineage. However, the comedy's reassertion of a natural hierarchy was, in fact, far from confident or undisputed. This much is suggested by a near-compulsive need to repeat the test and purge society of its ill ease, until the next performance of a similar disparagement. Whilst people remained caught in the ongoing, incomplete transition from a society configured mainly and ideally by birth (status) to one perceived as defined according to wealth (class), the rehearsal of an apparently decisive resolution would continue to provide only a temporary release.

The third and last chapter of part I explores some of the elaborate plays on the basic cit cuckold plot which occurred in the course of this constant enactment and re-enactment. It does so by acknowledging a political factor that was often at work in the early eighteenth-century scripting of City comedy. For defining gentility was political, in both the broad sense of power's contestation and the narrowly factional way of leadership. The 'gentry' were a social elite but also claimed a right and ability to govern. So even if the comedy could put aside or see beyond the citizen's economic importance it had still to confront the issue of whether that importance entailed an authority normally understood to be the preserve of 'gentlemen'. As social debate and partisan polemic blurred together, so London's playhouses increasingly favoured rival factional interests and distinctly partial representations of the cit and his cuckolding. Social uncertainty and satiric utility made for a volatile blend that further served to question the citizen's capacity for virtue and, therefore, his eligibility to be considered genteel.

Foregrounding contemporary conditions of theatrical reception, part II turns to investigate how and why the comic drama could have made such social knowledge possible. Arguing that the theatre's producers used various means, including the auditorium space, to discourse a well-ordered audience of superior, genteel status, chapters 4–6 demonstrate how such efforts were being constantly but partially countermanded by the situation of London's theatres in a competitive leisure market. Variously implicated in the theatre as a commercial venture, the comedy's spectators may well have had first-hand experience of contestable social positioning, disputed or competing claims of 'genteel' superiority, and contradictory lines of social differentiation – all while at the playhouse. In retracing these conditions, the study modifies our understanding of the late Stuart theatre's audience profile. The usual audience was rather more exclusive than once thought. This relatively refined atmosphere made the playhouse prone to social combustibility, in terms both of the meanly born successfully mixing it up as if they were genteel and of the pedigreed individual failing to concede that others might have had an equal stake in gentility.

In the second half of the book, parts III and IV, the emphasis shifts to consideration of the problems inherent to gentility as a subjective social process given cultural expression, and how these problems were themselves, in their turn, articulated by London's theatre.

Chapter 7 argues that the role of the stage fop or beau was to send up the idea that the 'gentleman' was self-evidently superior by virtue of his lineage, not satire directed at an upwardly mobile or sexually deviant individual as previous readings maintain. The fop's rehearsal posed a riddle: if the gentleman's ancestry makes him inherently and truly superior why does he need the likes of fashionable clothes or an exquisite salute to announce what should be always already apparent, the obviously anterior reality of his 'good birth'? The unsettling answer was that people could not proffer conclusive evidence of descent but must, instead, be seen to impersonate or embody their parentage. This still left further, lingering doubts. How did one tell apart the well-born impersonating their gentility and those imposing a genteel behaviour but spurious pedigree on the rest of society?

The next chapter focuses on how comedy gave expression to this angst by means of extended sexual metaphor. Earlier interpretations have been eager to take the sexually suspect fop or sodomitical beau as demonstration that the third gender, the effeminate male homosexual, had finally arrived at the forefront of early eighteenth-century cultural consciousness. *Gentility and the Comic Theatre* suggests that this reading is usually wide of the mark; that we ought not to presume a connection between the stage fop's 'effeminacy', 'hermaphroditism' or 'sodomy' and any broader changes in gender identities or understandings of sexual behaviour which may have been occurring at this time. Instead, chapter 8 contends that these sexually transgressive terms were a well-established way to pose searching questions about the nature and inevitability of the inherited social distinctions of *both* gentleman and -woman. Briefly, the beau did not reflect a new gender identity but was a reflection on the relationship between culture and selfhood, identity and discourse. The character did not lambast a new kind of socially or sexually deviant man (the upwardly mobile bourgeois; the homosexual) so much as it pondered the fundamental contingency of recognizing an essential, elite identity.

In considering the reasons for the fop's late Stuart rehearsal, chapter 9 attends to its strongly partisan and domestic undercurrents. Therefore the study parts company with readings which view the character as an expression of a particular inter-class cum international antipathy. The fop character was more a matter of England's gentry telling themselves to put their own houses in order rather than elite derision of upward social mobility, bourgeois criticism of an effete aristocracy or xenophobic reaction to France's absolutism and expansionist ambitions. The chapter shows that the political effects of the British monarchy's own dynastic uncertainties were amplified into a broader questioning of a natural social ordering by birth. The common issue was how does premodern society discern a true birthright? The cultural medium for consideration of this question was rehearsal of the gentleman-as-foppish beau.

The fourth and final part of the study opens with a short reassessment of the turn-of-the-century anti-theatrical controversy sparked by Jeremy Collier. It argues that his crusade was preoccupied with the socially and politically subversive potential of the theatre's enactment of gentility. In particular, the successful 'personation' of an inherited social superiority by base-born players implied that gentility was not inimitable, wholly innate, after all. It was this potential which impelled tabloid-like revelations of the actors' private lives and condemnation of the theatre as licentious. Lurid tales were told about the players in the hope that lines of difference and social inequality would be that much clearer and, seemingly, inevitable. As chapter 11 shows, previous readings of these stories have tended to treat them as a documentary monologue on the nature of late Stuart theatre, accounts of the subjection and sexual commodification of the performer before the all-powerful gaze of the spectator. The fundamental problem is that these tales comprised *representations of* people representing or performing, not an untrammelled record of possibly titillating spectacle which allows for recovery of the original experience of watching actors at the London playhouse. Instead, these rumours mainly constituted a didactic dialogue or corrective commentary on acting. Implicitly they taught spectators how to look or what to see in future; to construe the next performance of a Lord Foppington or Beau Wildair as nothing more than an inferior, 'nasty' imitation of true superiority otherwise known as gentility. So, at one and the same time, these stories excoriated the player but also disciplined spectators to discriminate between supposedly true and false impersonations of gentility.

The final chapter considers how claims of gentility were used to bolster the authority of comedy, its quality and originality, as part of a cultural institution that was increasingly capitalized and politicized from the later seventeenth century onward. Examining John Dennis's and Richard Steele's assessments of *Sir Fopling Flutter* and *The Conscious Lovers* we find their respective understandings of comedy, favouring the satirical versus the sentimental, split on the shoals of 'what' was gentility.

Part I

Gentility and power

1 The citizen cuckold and the London repertoire

> Again you cry, the City is expos'd,
> And Secrets of domestick Wrongs disclos'd;
> Cuckolds are made, and wealthy Knights abus'd,
> And Ladies of dishonest Joys accus'd;
> The careful Merchant is a Scoundrel made,
> A Balk to Business, and a Slur on Trade.
>
> *Muses Mercury* (July 1707)

On a winter's evening in 1722, London's *beau monde* streamed to the Theatre Royal in Drury Lane for the premiere of *The Conscious Lovers*, the long-awaited comedy by Sir Richard Steele. Rumour as to the play's novelty had been rife. Listening for this gossip we catch a hint that elite London fully anticipated the new comedy to be about gentility, dubbing the play 'The (Fine) Gentleman' prior to its first public performance.[1] This anticipation was understandable. Over the previous ten years Steele had been writing about gentility and about how he thought comedy ought to be written, mostly in the form of some very successful periodical essays. By contrast, he had produced nothing for the stage during the last decade and a half. *The Conscious Lovers* was evidently scripted and rescripted over a similar period. For Steele it proved worth the wait. His comedy held the stage for an unprecedented eighteen-night stretch before entering the repertoire, a sign, at least as far as most modern critics of early eighteenth-century drama are concerned, that expectations of genteel novelty had been satisfied.

In modern criticism and historiography of late Stuart comedy and society, Steele's play is held to epitomize a more moralistic drama which, responding to the rise of bourgeois sensibilities, presented upper-middling Londoners with an uncompromisingly positive representation of themselves and their social

[1] Anticipation of the play was the stuff of both public print and private correspondence. See, for example, *(Applebee's) Original Weekly*, 21 November 1719; J. Dennis, 'A Defence of Sir Fopling Flutter, a Comedy Written by Sir George Etheridge' (1722), in E. N. Hooker (ed.), *The Critical Works of John Dennis* (Baltimore, 1943), vol. II, 250; George Berkeley to Sir John Percival, 26 January 1713, HMC, *Seventh Report* 6, 1 (1879), 238. Cf. also 'Copyright Agreement between Richard Steele and Jacob Tonson for The Conscious Lovers', fMS Eng 760(19), Houghton Library, Harvard.

position. Gone were the condescension and smutty innuendo of the earlier, 'courtly' Restoration theatre. Yet it is the argument of this chapter that there are considerable difficulties with this narrative of socio-cultural change and that inconsistencies in chronology imply deeper interpretive problems. Careful recontextualization of both *The Conscious Lovers*' production and its reception will show that Steele had not delivered exactly what he may once have seemed to promise. Yet the larger portion of responsibility for wrongly billing Steele's comedy as a resounding innovation in its depiction of social groups rests with twentieth-century literary scholars. Whilst they quite properly consider early modern comic drama to have been socially informed, there is a need for a more rigorous historicization of the theatre's participation in processes of social structuration. In particular, the comedy's delineation of late Stuart London's 'gentle' and 'simple' was both more complex and more enduring than many commentators have assumed. As a result, the citizen cuckold cannot be viewed as the expression of incidental social mobility or sporadic class conflict.

In order to test whether our central period of interest, *c.*1690–1725, may have witnessed a transformation in the representation of claims of gentility by upper-middling Londoners, it is important for us first to know something of the proximate dramatic tradition with which Steele *et al.* were faced. Outlining some signal features of the Restoration stage's typical middling milieu at its reputed cynosure will permit assessment of the degree to which the later comedies really did articulate changing ideas about the contours of London society.

The purpose of this very brief excursus is twofold: to identify the most common character types and plot-lines for those readers not already familiar with them, and to establish a point of reference whence any later innovations by Steele and his contemporaries may be charted. Given the wider argument being made, we need not examine particular plays in their entirety or account explicitly for all comedy written in this period (*c.*1660–90). Detailed overviews of the Restoration repertoire are readily available in any case.[2] Nor, given the limited space available, will an extended reading of the key features be offered here. Interpretation will take place in the context of considering their post-revolutionary rehearsal as part of chapters 2 and 3.

In Restoration comedy, the majority of characters representing those of middling degree are linked to London's trade and finance. In relation to the former, they range from domestic retailers, like the Salewares, traders in silk, from Aphra Behn's *Debauchee* of 1677, the Essences, milliners in Thomas Rawlins's comedy from the same year, and the vintner Mr Dashit featured in Behn's *Revenge*,[3] to the likes of Alderman Whitebroth, Mr Pett, Sir Patient Fancy, and

[2] R. D. Hume, *The Development of English Drama in the Late Seventeenth Century* (Oxford, 1976); D. Hughes, *English Drama 1660–1700* (Oxford, 1996).

[3] A. Behn, *Debauchee* (1677), i, 8 and 10 (adapted from R. Brome's *Madd Couple Well Matcht*, first performed *c.*1638); T. Rawlins, *Tom Essence* (1677), i, 6; A. Behn, *Revenge* (1680), i, 3.

both Wiseacres and Doodle in Edward Ravenscroft's *London Cuckolds*, who all deal internationally.[4] Although they collectively outnumber trading types, rather less attention is given to the precise economic background and associations of the financiers. They tend to clump together as usurers. The origin of their substantial levels of speculative capital remains undisclosed, despite occasional hints that we should think of them as one-time merchants and domestic traders. The main focus tends to be their future earnings as mortgagors of country estates, like the Gripe character from both William Wycherley's *Love in a Wood* and Thomas Shadwell's *Woman-Captain* or the not so fortunate Sir Cautious Fulbank in Behn's *Luckey Chance*, and moneylenders akin to Sir Arthur Twilight in *The Rambling Justice* or Security from *Cuckold's-Haven*.[5] There are, by comparison, few representations of middling professionals pursuing a career in either medicine or law. With instances of the latter there are usually connections to commercial enterprise – take the brokering attorney, Docket, and speculating scrivener, Bramble.[6]

As the stigma of usury implies, the plays in question take a decidedly dim view of material success. Regardless of whether the citizen did engage in moneylending, his wealth was considered the ill-gotten spoils of sharp business practice. Thus Francisco, the middling character in *The False Count* from 1681, is described as a 'Shoo-maker, Which he improv'd in time to a Merchant, and the Devil and his Knavery helping him to a considerable Estate, he set up for, a *Gentleman*'.[7] *The London Cuckolds*' Dashwell, brother to a Hamburg merchant, is a 'Blockheaded City Attorney, a Trudging, Drudging, Cormuging, Petitioning Citizen, that with a little Law, and much Knavery has got a great Estate'.[8] This last quote, with its forceful tricolon of trudging, drudging, cormuging, is full of spiteful rejection and disputes any claim of social superiority as somehow tainted by money, ink or laboriously 'greasie' effort.[9]

Yet, at the same time, the majority of mercantile types are by no means denied enjoyment of an affluent authority in their later years, often holding office in the senior echelons of London's municipal government by virtue of their membership in one of London's companies. This last aspect is, after all, what identified

4 Respectively J. Wilson, *Cheats* (1664), iii, 34; E. Revet, *Town-Shifts* (1671), ii, 18; A. Behn, *Sir Patient Fancy* (1678), ii, 15; E. Ravenscroft, *London Cuckolds* (1681), ii, 17.

5 W. Wycherley, *Love in a Wood* (1672), iii, 50; T. Shadwell, *Woman-Captain* (1680), i, 6; A. Behn, *Luckey Chance* (1687), i, 4; J. Leanerd, *Rambling Justice* (1678), ii, 17; N. Tate, *Cuckold's-Haven* (1685), i, 6 (itself a farcical adaptation of *Eastward Hoe* from 1605, variously attributed to Ben Jonson, George Chapman and John Marston).

6 Anon., *Woman Turn'd Bully* (1675), i, 4; Tate, *Cuckold's-Haven*, ii, 21.

7 A. Behn, *False Count* (1681), i, 3.

8 Ravenscroft, *London Cuckolds*, i, 8. See also ii, 14.

9 This last quote is made with reference to the character Sir Davy Dunce (see also pp. 80ff below), from T. Otway, *Souldiers Fortune*, 1681, i, in J. C. Ghosh (ed.), *The Works of Thomas Otway* (Oxford, 1932), vol. II, 104.

them as 'citizens', or 'cits' as comedy preferred to call them, in the first place.[10] There is, in fact, a marked preference for bestowing aldermanic honour on these figures, meaning they had been or were possible contenders for the City's mayoralty. Along with several of the characters already mentioned, we might add the right worshipful Muchworth, Paywell, Sir Feeble Fain-wou'd and, if we count political analogies, Paulo Camillo, the Neapolitan *podestà* (chief magistrate) from John Crowne's *City Politiques*.[11] Even the few scripts that encumber their citizens with more parochial responsibilities tend to conjecture similar power for the future.[12] It is also noteworthy, with one significant exemption, that no City figure exhibits the remotest links with national office. None has designs to become a member of parliament (much less a royal functionary), except in the extreme case of republican government. Several Restoration comedies are set against the mid-seventeenth-century backdrop of the interregnum, with a fairly predictable stress on the unprecedented authority this offered London's citizens.[13]

If there is a single, defining trait of the citizen in Restoration comedy it is that he is portrayed as socially maladroit and out of place, notwithstanding his prosperity and authority. This ineptitude is nowhere more clearly indicated than by the disordered state of the citizen's household. As we shall see, the inability to form, maintain or perpetuate its existence lies at the heart of the citizen cuckold scenario. Most obviously, as the foregoing label suggests, his comic staging customarily involved the depiction of the citizen's failure to prevent his wife's adultery. Such is the fate of the merchants featuring in Ravenscroft's triplicate City plot, *The London Cuckolds*, and the relevance of the ironic answer made to Sir Arthur Twilight's rhetorical proposition in John Leanerd's *Rambling Justice*:

SIR ARTHUR TWILIGHT: I am out of Breath with running, a pox of Matrimony if this be the fruits on't, was ever Gentleman made a Cuckold before?

BRAMBLE: Yes Sir, especially Citizens; 'tis an Hereditary possession belonging to the Court of Aldermen, and scarce one scapes it, if their Wives are either Young or Handsome.

[10] For an interesting discussion of the tensions surrounding the term 'citizen' in the seventeenth century, its connotations of both autonomy and subjection, see C. Condren, *The Language of Politics in Seventeenth-Century England* (London, 1994), 91–114. Condren argues that the term 'citizen' carried negative and derisive associations of inferiority. However, he also notes that this meaning was sometimes challenged and the term then assumed a positive connotation. Perhaps the variation of 'cit' as diminutive was, in turn, a means to counter this second possibility, in which case see *Tatler*, no. 25 (7 June 1709), vol. I, 197.

[11] E. Ravenscroft, *Careless Lovers* (1673); T. Rawlins, *Tunbridge Wells* (1678); Behn, *Luckey Chance*; J. Crowne, *City Politiques* (1683). All these characterizations are readily evident from the respective dramatis personae.

[12] See, for example, the ambitious churchwarden Gotam from J. Wilson, *Projectors* (1665), i, 11.

[13] J. Tatham, *Rump* (1660); A. Cowley, *Cutter of Coleman Street* (1663); R. Howard, *Committee* (1665); A. Behn, *Roundheads* (1682); T. Durfey, *Royalist* (1682). For a ready introduction to their immediate political context, see S. J. Owen, 'Restoration Drama and Politics: An Overview', in Owen (ed.), *A Companion to Restoration Drama* (Oxford, 2001), 126–39.

SIR ARTHUR TWILIGHT: I would mine had been neither, I would she had not been a Woman, rather than I should thus be made a Cuckold; but 'tis done, 'tis done, I am all over Horns that's certain, and shall be counted a greater Monster than the Elephant.[14]

Other citizens are, at the very least, in imminent danger of this disgrace, unable to satisfy sexually insatiable spouses yearning to bear children, like the Fribbles or Paywells who trip to fashionable spas hoping that the chalybeate waters or good air will put them in the family way.[15]

Several variations on the cuckolding scenario were made possible by both pro- and retrospective framings of the plot. Some plays featured citizens who were, in effect, cuckolded even before the banns were read or vows exchanged. Either they are like Sir Feeble Fain-wou'd, unable to seal what would have been a socially advantageous match, or, as in the case of Treat-all, Rash and Docket, they find themselves wed to a froward, meanly born maidservant or cast mistress rather than the demure gentlewoman whom they thought they had espoused.[16] Alternatively, the City wife as harridan foreshadowed the likelihood that the subdued and often uxorious husband would become a cuckold, as we find with the Gotams, Bibbers, Strikers or the aptly named Turbulents.[17] City fathers might also be confronted by disobedient children. Here conflict pivoted on incompatible marital expectations held by parents and guardians, on the one hand, and daughters or genteel wards affined to the male cit on the other. Thus we find comedies where: a guardian arranges a marriage for City lucre (or not if he wishes to keep control of her estate) only to have his ward wed a gentleman equal to her own, higher status; the City daughter, wanting to marry anyone of superior quality rather than further enrich her money-grubbing father by a marriage of economic convenience, unwittingly marries a humble individual masquerading as ennobled gentleman; parental attempts to compel marriage solely in pursuit of higher status are foiled by romantic elopement.[18] Finally, there is even the occasional suggestion of cuckoldry come full

[14] Leanerd, *Rambling Justice*, v, 53–4.

[15] T. Shadwell, *Epsom-Wells* (1673), ii, 28; Rawlins, *Tunbridge Wells*, i, 5. See also the figure of Old Monylove in Rawlins's *Tom Essence*, ii, 19.

[16] Behn, *Luckey Chance*, v, 67–8 (the nephew and heir of the banker Sir Cautious Fulbank also ends up married to a chamber-maid); A. Behn, *City-Heiress* (1682), v, 61; J. Leanerd, *Country Innocence* (1677), iv, 45; Anon., *Woman Turn'd Bully*, v, 80. See also the fates of the former mercer, Farendine, in Rawlins, *Tunbridge Wells*; the young citizen, Mr Gillet, in E. Ravenscroft, *Dame Dobson* (1684).

[17] Wilson, *Projectors*, i, 12; J. Dryden, *Wild Gallant* (1669), i, 5–6; T. Shadwell, *Humorists* (1671), i, 10; Anon., *Factious Cit* (1685), i, 9 (a re-release of *Mr. Turbulent* from 1681).

[18] **i**. Anon., *Woman Turn'd Bully*, i, 4–5; Anon., *Factious Citizen*, i, 4–5; Ravenscroft, *Careless Lovers*, iii, 32–3. **ii**. Behn, *False Count*, dramatis personae (or without the genteel impostor, see W. Wycherley, *Gentleman Dancing-Master* (1673), dramatis personae and i, 2). **iii**. E. Ravenscroft, *Citizen Turn'd Gentleman* (1673), i, 10.

circle and the possible irony that the citizen's child, now grown, is not his own.[19]

Before addressing the issue of what this kind of familial disharmony may have been trying to say about elite social structuration, it is important that we critique the received chronology of its prevalence on the post-revolutionary stage (i.e. after 1690). Discrepancies here will suggest weaknesses in previous readings of the scenario's meaning, compelling a reconsideration of its significance for late Stuart audiences.

The established critical trajectory for the citizen cuckold's appearance on the London stage is long-standing. In the 1950s, John Loftis argued that our period witnessed a fundamental shift in comedy's depiction of the citizen, marking the turning of the tide at 1710 or thereabouts. Objection to the stereotype, like that expressed in the verse which serves as this chapter's proem, had presumably reached critical mass. For Loftis, comedy from the late seventeenth to early eighteenth centuries 'reflected' rather nondescript tensions between wealthy businessmen and establishment gentry (understand landowners). As society adjusted in various ways to these tensions, so Loftis maintained, stage satire directed at the citizen decreased markedly in the frequency of its rehearsal. Indeed, social resolution gradually made for the 'literary enfranchisement of the merchant class' with the result that comedy like Steele's *Conscious Lovers* depicted merchants as 'not cuckolded aldermen but family-proud gentlefolk'.[20]

Despite fundamental shifts in literary theory and the burgeoning of socio-historical research, these conclusions remain essentially unchallenged by scholars of early modern drama. The sustained reluctance of early modern historians to engage rigorously with 'fiction' means that their contribution to advancing our understanding has been negligible. Indeed, scholars of the drama have been left in the unenviable position of offering new 'literary' interpretations on the basis of some quite dated historiographical paradigms. Thus, in the most recent and exhaustive study of cit cuckolding on the Restoration stage, J. Douglas Canfield takes it for granted that his chosen topos rises and falls with the Stuart monarchy.[21] In attempting to trace correspondences between generic and social shifts, Laura Brown considers *The Conscious Lovers* to be the exemplar of a newly moral and emphatically pro-bourgeois drama.[22] Some have read even further against the grain, dating the genteel acceptance of the merchant citizen in drama earlier than the 1710s and 1720s. For instance, Rose Zimbardo argues that Mary Pix's *Innocent Mistress* from 1697 upholds the ideological

19 Wycherley, *Love in a Wood*, i, 6; Crowne, *City Politiques*, iii, 38.

20 J. Loftis, *Comedy and Society from Congreve to Fielding* (Stanford, 1959), 38, 84.

21 J. D. Canfield, *Tricksters & Estates. On the Ideology of Restoration Comedy* (Lexington, 1997), 74.

22 L. Brown, *English Dramatic Form, 1660–1760. An Essay in Generic History* (New Haven, 1981), 167–73.

position of a 'new gentry' or 'ruling class' and a 'decidedly merchant-class value system. Gone are the literary stereotypes of the *senex iratus*.'[23] A similar claim has been made on behalf of the 1691 comedy from the pen of William Mountfort, *Greenwich Park*. The main citizen character, Mr Raison the London grocer, apparently comprehends a 'complete inversion of the old Restoration stereotype.'[24]

Surveys of the manner in which merchants and new wealth are represented in early modern literature concur in seeing the first half of the eighteenth century as the time of most positive attitude. Sometimes granting fictive representation more influence in shaping society than Loftis was prepared to concede, these surveys argue that acceptance of the merchant allowed Daniel Defoe, Joseph Addison and Richard Steele to lobby for the merchant's place in the sun and, vice versa, commercial success made for affirmative portrayal. Hence John McVeagh maintains that Steele's play amounted to a 'social restitution' as it and other literature elevated the merchant to 'heroic status'.[25] Even the most nuanced revision of the issues involved in the literary representation of commercial enterprise and early modern urban society considers that in drama the 'benevolent verdict was clearly dominant' by the first decades of the eighteenth century.[26] In other words, Steele's play is again cited as definitive proof that the prosperous upper-middling citizen was deemed on a social par with the well-born landowner, the 'gentleman': a conclusion that related social historiography tends to take on board with scarcely a murmur of dissent.[27]

23 R. A. Zimbardo, 'Toward Zero/Toward Public Virtue: The Conceptual Design of Dramatic Satire before and after the Ascension of William and Mary', *Eighteenth-Century Life* 12, 3 (1988), 63–5. The term *senex iratus* translates as 'angry old man' and, as we shall see, is a fitting way to describe the citizen cuckold. See also Hughes, *English Drama*, 420.

24 M. W. Walsh, 'The Significance of William Mountfort's *Greenwich Park*', *Restoration and 18th Century Theatre Research* 12, 2 (1973), 36.

25 J. McVeagh, *Tradefull Merchants. The Portrayal of the Capitalist in Literature* (London, 1981), 22.

26 N. McKendrick, '"Gentleman and Players" Revisited: The Gentlemanly Ideal, the Business Ideal, and the Professional Ideal in English Literary Culture', in N. McKendrick and R. B. Outhwaite (eds.), *Business Life and Public Policy. Essays in Honour of D. C. Coleman* (Cambridge, 1986), 109.

27 See also W. A. Speck, *Society and Literature in England 1700–60* (Dublin, 1983), 60; R. W. Bevis, *English Drama. Restoration and Eighteenth Century, 1660–1789* (London, 1988), 166; R. D. Hume, *Henry Fielding and the London Theatre 1728–1737* (Oxford, 1988), 20; R. Russell, 'Dramatists and the Printed Page: The Social Role of Comedy from Richard Steele to Leigh Hunt', unpublished DPhil dissertation, Oxford University (1995), 25. Social historians, who adduce literary evidence as part of their argument for the existence of such a shift during the late Stuart period, rehearse similar assumptions. For example, P. J. Corfield, 'The Rivals: Landed and Other Gentlemen', in N. Harte and R. Quinault (eds.), *Land and Society in Britain, 1700–1914. Essays in Honour of F. M. L. Thompson* (Manchester, 1996), cf. 7, 17; P. Gauci, *The Politics of Trade. The Overseas Merchant in State and Society, 1660–1720* (Oxford, 2001), 194. Compare also N. Rogers, 'Money, Land and Lineage: The Big Bourgeoisie of Hanoverian London', *Social History* 4, 3 (1979), 446, and Rogers, 'A Reply to Donna Andrew', *Social History* 6, 3 (1981), 367, with D. T. Andrew, 'Aldermen and the Big Bourgeoisie of London Reconsidered', *Social History*, 6, 3 (1981), 363.

While there may have been some refinement of the stereotype, the basic plot of male citizen confronted by insubordinate and unfaithful women continued to have a considerable presence on the London stage for the duration of the late Stuart period. Although there was an occasionally positive word for the citizen, particularly the thriving overseas merchant, this sympathetic voice was drowned out by more of the same mocking chant of citizen cuckold that had echoed throughout the seventeenth century. On closer examination the argument of declining incidence, that London's patent theatres rehearsed this highly popular figure less and less during the early eighteenth century, simply cannot be sustained. This stricture applies whether we are considering all comedies performed from 1690 to 1725, all new comedies scripted during the same period or even the individual work of an otherwise innovative playwright like Steele.

Studies of early eighteenth-century drama tend to treat comedy as another literary genre, essentially ignoring the performative aspects of their texts by confining their attention to new plays appearing in print. This interpretive perspective misses the importance of repertoire, an underlying continuity. London's playhouses were not only showcases for new texts, new messages.[28] In any given theatre season, running from about October to June, the majority of offerings were usually 'old' plays. Perhaps they were part of the theatre's current stock, a piece by George Farquhar or Susanna Centlivre, which had first played several years earlier. Equally, they might have been revivals of plays from the Restoration, those we have just surveyed, or perhaps early seventeenth-century pieces from the pens of still popular and influential playwrights like Ben Jonson. Of course it was Jacobean drama that had firmly established the basic conventions of satire on the City, cuckolding included.[29] Little account of this scheduling of old alongside new has been taken when critics have charted the novelty of the social messages articulated by the late Stuart stage.

Even when we confine our attention to the first performances of new plays, we find little support for the arguments of those who would follow Loftis's lead. In round figures, at least eighty of the 160-odd comedies known to have debuted at London's patent theatres from 1690/1 to 1725/6 featured citizen cuckold plots.[30] Dismissing these works out of hand, as somehow 'second rate'

[28] The strongest argument for the importance of repertoire comes from R. D. Hume in *The Rakish Stage. Studies in English Drama, 1660–1800* (Carbondale, 1983), 64–74. For an overview of the early eighteenth-century repertoire, see G. W. Stone, jr., 'The Making of the Repertory', in R. D. Hume (ed.), *The London Theatre World, 1660–1800* (Carbondale, 1980), 194–9.

[29] See W. Griswold, *Renaissance Revivals. City Comedy and Revenge Tragedy in the London Theatre 1576–1980* (Chicago, 1986). This is not to say, however, that the cit cuckolding tradition did not have an even earlier history, prior to its dramatic articulation and consolidation.

[30] I concede that this ratio is not equivalent to the frequency of actual appearance on stage. To arrive at a percentage, one would have to factor in the different runs of each of the 160 comedies in question then compare totals with those evenings when another type of comedy or drama was being offered. However, I am prepared to estimate that the figures would still be high. As we shall see, even those nights featuring a tragic mainpiece might work in one-liners about the cit during the course of the evening's entertainment.

because they continue to play on the cit stereotype, simply will not suffice.[31] For the most successful and well-regarded playwrights perpetuated the idea that cits could not control their womenfolk. And authors did so with scripts that have been earmarked by modern critics as demonstrating a positive attitude to the London citizen's place in English society. For example, Pix's *Innocent Mistress*, cited above by one critic as abandoning the stereotype of the irascible City elder, nevertheless features a West Indies merchant character who rails at his wife and, therefore, points directly to Pix's own variation on the cuckold scenario:

MR FLYWIFE: Is it so, thou worst Offspring of thy Grannam *Eve*? but I'll stifle my Rage, lest without further Proof she wheedles me into a Reconciliation, take another Coach and follow her, catch her amongst her Comrades, without the possibility of an Excuse, cut her Windpipe, and send her to Hell, without the possibility of a Reprieve: Damn her, damn her.[32]

We are faced with a similar anomaly when it comes to Richard Steele, the supposed doyen of London's bourgeois, mercantile lobby. As we shall see, Steele's vaunted social rehabilitation of the merchant was purposefully ambiguous.

While he was drafting *The Conscious Lovers*, Steele gave various indications that his forthcoming comedy would be different. In his periodical essays he attempted to avoid, even counteract, the City merchant pasquinade. In an early number of *The Spectator*, Steele congratulated himself by having his merchant figure, Sir Andrew Freeport, praise the work of the authorial eidolon, Mr Spectator, in the following terms:

[He] had done great Good in the City, and that all their Wives and Daughters were the better for them: And further added, That the whole City thought themselves very much obliged to me for declaring my generous Intentions to scourge Vice and Folly as they appear in a Multitude, without condescending to be a Publisher of particular Intrigues and Cuckoldoms. In short, says Sir ANDREW, if you avoid that foolish beaten Road of falling upon Aldermen and Citizens, and employ your Pen upon the Vanity and Luxury of Courts, your Paper must needs be of general Use.[33]

Steele's first periodical, *The Tatler*, critiqued a performance of Ravenscroft's *London Cuckolds* by beginning with the observation that the audience 'were extremely well diverted with that Heap of Vice and Absurdity'.[34] He used this review essay as a vehicle for self-promotion, at the same time recognizing the interpenetration of gentility and theatre:

The Amendment of these low Gratifications is only to be made by People of Condition, by encouraging the Presentation of the Noble Characters drawn by *Shakespear* and others, from whence it is impossible to return without strong Impressions of Honour and Humanity . . . If a Thing painted or related can irresistibly enter our Hearts, what

[31] Loftis, *Comedy and Society*, 81–2. [32] M. Pix, *Innocent Mistress* (1697), iv, 38.
[33] *Spectator*, no. 34 (9 April 1711), vol. I, 142. [34] *Tatler*, no. 8 (28 April 1709), vol. I, 72–3.

may not be brought to pass by seeing generous Things perform'd before our Eyes? . . . recommending the apt Use of a Theatre, as the most agreeable and easie Method of making a Polite and Moral Gentry.[35]

By means of a shorter-lived periodical enterprise, Steele sketched the kind of comic plot he believed would bring both respectability and revenue to the early eighteenth-century playhouse. His contemporaries would have found his subtle but firm rejection of a 'cit' scenario unmistakable when he wrote of the ideal comedy that the 'daughter may be agreeable and blooming, though the mother is at the same time discreet, careful, and anxious for her conduct. No necessary imperfections, such as old age, and misfortune, shall be the objects of derision and buffoonery.'[36] With his last broadsheet project, designed to advance his legal claim on a share of the management and profits for the Drury Lane theatre as well as advocate the drama's moral reclamation, Steele suggested the formation of an audience advisory committee. He gave fictive biographies of likely candidates, hoping that an East India merchant, Mr Sealand, would represent London's substantial citizens and be elected 'for his Thoughts and Sentiments against the unworthy Representations of Citizens on the Stage, [which] may highly contribute to the Abolition of such ridiculous Images for the future'.[37]

Yet all these protestations of best intent were to no avail. Both *The Tatler* and *The Spectator* redacted the comic cuckold in newsprint and when *The Conscious Lovers* finally made it into production the script clearly signalled Steele's rehearsal of the same stereotype.[38] Its merchant figure, also called Mr Sealand, plans to marry his daughter, Lucinda, into the landed family of Sir John Bevil. However Mrs Sealand has another suitor in view, proving to be anything but concerned for her daughter's happiness. Wilfully contradicting Mr Sealand, she earns the proverbial description that intimated how cuckoldry was on the cards if the husband did not regain control of his unruly spouse. For the Sealands' servant remarks: 'In that Family the Grey Mare is the better Horse.'[39]

Those readers familiar with the precise actions of *The Conscious Lovers* will perhaps object that Steele's play is a far cry from the breeches-round-ankles romp visited upon the luckless cits from *The London Cuckolds*, for instance. Although Mrs Sealand is not depicted as committing adultery, the difference

[35] *Ibid*., 73–4. [36] *Town Talk*, no. 6 (20 January 1716), ed. J. Nichols (1789 edition), 99.

[37] *Theatre*, no. iii (9 January 1720), ed. J. Loftis (Oxford, 1962), 12.

[38] See, for instance, *Tatler*, no. 136 (21 February 1710), vol. II, 284–6 (although the dénouement here is ultimately positive for the citizen); *Spectator*, no. 450 (6 August 1712), vol. IV, 81–6; *ibid*., no. 527 (4 November 1712), vol. IV, 377–80.

[39] R. Steele, *Conscious Lovers* (1723), i, 8. The proverb was very much a commonplace. See, for example, L. B. Wright (ed.), *The Prose Works of William Byrd of Westover. Narratives of a Colonial Virginian* (Cambridge, MA, 1966), 344, 408.

is one of degree rather than kind.[40] As we saw in our review of Restoration comedy, the variation of a shrewish wife who verbally or physically lashes her upper-middling husband was well established prior to Steele's use of it. Moreover, it was a commonplace that men who could not master their wives' tongues would, sooner or later, be unable to control the rest of their bodies. This unspoken assumption allowed Steele to claim that London's stage had cleaned up its act but also to perpetuate the reputation of City women for transgressive socio-sexual behaviour.

A contemporary pamphlet, in the form of a mock dialogue between Steele and one of *The Conscious Lovers*' first spectators, leaves little doubt that early eighteenth-century audiences had picked up on the play's deployment of the cuckold stereotype. Ironically reviewing its standard features, *The Censor Censur'd* admonished Steele and asked of Mr Sealand:

> Why, then, must this Gentleman be treated as an humble, insignificant, despicable Wittal? – a Cully, to be led by the Nose at the Will of a termagant, senseless Wife? – despised by Sir *John*, even while he's treating with him about a Match for his Son with *Sealand's* Daughter? – and the Laughing-stock of a sneering Footman? . . . I would fain know, which End of Comedy this Character answers. – *Instruct* it cannot, for Vertue's despised; *Please* it cannot, because the Behaviour does not answer to the Character given: Therefore 'tis absurd and monstrous.[41]

How is it possible to reconcile Mr Sealand's domestic troubles with those very important lines by which modern-day commentators judge the play a ringing endorsement of London's middle classes? Addressing Sir John Bevil, the gentleman patriarch, Steele's merchant figure observes:

> Sir, as much a Cit as you take me for – I know the Town, and the World – and give me leave to say, that we Merchants are a Species of Gentry, that have grown into the World this last Century, and are as honourable, and almost as useful, as you landed Folks, that have always thought your selves so much above us; For your trading, forsooth! is extended no farther, than a Load of Hay, or a fat Ox – You are pleasant People, indeed; because you are generally bred up to be lazy, therefore, I warrant you, Industry is dishonourable.[42]

Attempting to treat issues of elite social structuration, Steele's comedy, like so many before and since, had little say in the matter of the citizen's cuckoldry. This was because suspect sexual behaviour, even if only suggested in dialogue rather than explicitly enacted, was 'good to think' questions of gentility (as cultural anthropologists might put it). As this chapter will elaborate, cuckoldry was a

40 Cf. A. Dharwadker, 'Class, Authorship, and the Social Intertexture of Genre in Restoration Theatre', *SEL* 37 (1997), 478.
41 Anon., *The Censor Censur'd* (1723), 42–3. Dialogue attributions omitted.
42 Steele, *Conscious Lovers*, iv, 62–3.

means to address discrepancies in social structuration like those evidenced by the last two quotes that, together, identify Mr Sealand as *both* a gentleman and a citizen.

Before we unravel the stereotype's socio-cultural significance, it is just as well to highlight, in advance, two additional features of which any interpretation needs to be aware. First, we should always keep in mind the issue of the comedy's bias. Currently, there is little indication that London's upper-middling males were any more likely than the rest of the metropolitan population to be victims of adultery in 'real life', branded as cuckolds in narratives deposed before the capital's courts for instance.[43] Discussion of cuckoldry in print often made the point that this fate awaited every man foolish enough to marry.[44] A recent study by David Turner has shown that representations of cuckoldry were highly diverse, particularly in terms of the social position of the husbands and their alleged reactions to marital infidelity.[45] Yet the stage rather obsessively entertained this predicament for a particular sort of man, insisting that cuckoldry could be nothing other than humiliating and dishonourable. So, just who was the comedy's citizen seething with jealousy and why was he so often mocked?

Second, the hapless citizen character was long-lived. He appeared onstage for a good century and a half, that is, from the turn of the seventeenth century and well into the next.[46] While it is important to take into consideration the smaller modifications made to the citizen's comedic portrait during the late Stuart period, it is equally necessary for us to remember that such persistence is itself significant and needs to be allowed for in any reading of the character. That the figure had an imminently extendable stage-life was sometimes quite obvious, at least to certain playwrights who presented new comedies cobbled together from the old. Hence George Powell's *Very Good Wife* (1693) borrowed from, among others, Richard Brome's *City Wit* (first performed *c.*1630); or John

43 L. Stone, *The Road to Divorce. England 1539–1987* (Oxford, 1990), 38–9, 427. The same might be tentatively concluded for other familial dysfunctions associated with the cuckolding such as widely disparate ages at (re)marriage on the basis of the data, but not the general conclusions, in R. Grassby, *Kinship and Capitalism. Marriage, Family, and Business in the English-Speaking World, 1580–1740* (Cambridge, 2001), 58ff., 137ff. See pp. 70ff below.

44 See, for example, *British Gazetteer*, no. 20 (11 September 1725), [1].

45 D. M. Turner, *Fashioning Adultery. Gender, Sex and Civility in England, 1660–1740* (Cambridge, 2002), 83–115.

46 Key studies of the earlier drama and London society include T. B. Leinwand, *The City Staged. Jacobean Comedy, 1603–1613* (Madison, 1986); D. Bruster, *Drama and the Market in the Age of Shakespeare* (London, 1992); J. Haynes, *The Social Relations of Jonson's Theatre* (Cambridge, 1992); L. Manley, *Literature and Culture in Early Modern London* (Cambridge, 1995), esp. 431–77. See too the suggestive recent essays of I. Clark, *Comedy, Youth, Manhood in Early Modern England* (London, 2003), which treat related issues from the 'gentry' viewpoint.

Shirley's *Gamester* (first performed *c.*1633) was recycled in Charles Johnson's *Wife's Relief* (1712). While the case has been made for substantial revision, it is still important to note the close resemblance between the social calculus of old and new scripts.[47] For example, in the Shirley–Johnson pairing a wealthy citizen is prepared to pay good money to have his nephew earn his spurs by braving it about town with a group of genteel hectors. As Shirley's citizen, the prospective alderman Barnacle, explains:

> . . . we that had
> Our breeding from a Trade, cits as you call us,
> Though we hate gentlemen our selves, yet are
> Ambitious, to make all our children gentlemen,
> In three generations they returne agen,
> We for our children purchase Land, they brave it
> I'th Countrie, begets children, and they sell,
> Grow poore, and send their sonnes up to be Prentises:
> There is a whirle in fate, the Courtiers make
> Us cuckolds; marke, we wriggle into their
> Estates, poverty makes their children Citizens;
> Our sonnes cuckold them, a circular justice,
> The World turnes round, but once more to the purpose.[48]

Barely modifying the syntax and splitting the dialogue with one of the hectors, Volatil, Johnson's knighted alderman explains to the bullish gentleman the social paradox affecting his nephew and why he, Sir Tristrum Cash, could not 'train him up a Citt, in the Road of [my] Family':

SIR TRISTRUM CASH: Why, we Citts, as you call us, tho' we hate Gentlemen, are proud to breed our Children so – but in three Generations they always come back into their Shops – as thus, – We Purchase Land, our Gentlemen Children live high and Mortgage, the Grand-Children Sell, and the Great-Grand-Children are always Prentices again –

VOLATIL: This is a whirl of Fortune quite round her Wheel; or take it thus, Sir *Tristrum*; we Courtiers make you Cuckolds, you wriggle into our Estates; Poverty makes our Children Citizens, and you Cuckold us again; a Circular Justice, the World turns round.[49]

Rather more obliquely, for those not already attuned to the social punning, Powell's play (*Very Good Wife*, 1693) commented on the position of a young City widow rumoured to be worth at least 10,000 pounds:

[47] Paulina Kewes has made the case for such revision by Powell, also outlining the multiple sources for his borrowings. See P. Kewes, 'The Politics of the Stage and the Page: Source Plays for George Powell's *A Very Good Wife* (1693) in their Production and Publication Contexts', *Zagadnienia Rodzajów Literackich* 37, 1–2 (1994), 41–52.

[48] J. Shirley, *Gamester* (1637), i, sig. B3$^{r–v}$.

[49] C. Johnson, *Wife's Relief* (1712), i, 6–7.

VENTURE: Like enough, he may aim at her, but she will be hit by none but a Gentleman; that I hear too; oh she's a fierce Ambition to be of Quality, tho' her first Husband was but a Tanner.

BONAVENT: A Tanner! Plague on't, I shall be loath to venture on her, she'll kill me, or any Man, at her Husband's Occupation, before I shou'd be able to make her Hide gentle.[50]

As with Johnson's borrowing, there is the slightest of alterations regarding the speech dynamic between characters and the status reference points, inasmuch as the widow from Brome's original of 1630 has designs on a 'ladyship'.[51] This aside, Powell evidently believed that his late Stuart audience would appreciate the faintly bawdy and misogynistic pun about tanning the meanly born skin of a presumptuously wealthy and sexually wayward woman, a pun that was now some three generations old. Such supple and perhaps not so subtle longevity would seem, in fact, to restrict our explanation of the cit figure. It would appear to rule out the type of cause so often advanced as the reason behind the figure's obvious currency during particular theatrical eras, treated separately in convenient isolation. In other words, discussions of Jacobean, Restoration and early eighteenth-century comic theatre, each wanting to explain the citizen's trouncing in their seemingly unique slice of dramatic history, resort to the same *deus ex machina*, the middle class and its rise. That the same device is always being trundled out, the bourgeoisie always seem to be ascending, should give us pause. In fact, on closer inspection we will find that this concept does not pull the critical weight needed both to recover the original meaning of citizen cuckoldry and to resolve its prolonged popularity.

As with our consideration of the stereotype's continuity over time, critique of the class paradigm will take place in the immediate context of the post-revolutionary comedy (1690 and beyond). Yet, once again, the revision that is offered for the late Stuart drama should also prove applicable, in its essentials, to the Jacobean and Restoration plays. Given the near-continuous appearance of the cit figure, this long-term applicability is one test for any reading of the character. By the same token, we should caution that applicable does not suppose a numbing theatrical sameness. Playwrights were capable of numerous smaller variations on the character. Therefore, a further breaking point for our interpretation will be versatility, its ability to explain this lateral improvisation within a very well entrenched tradition.

Earlier interpretations of the comic cit's cuckolding seem to combine to form a paradox. At one and the same time, the citizen cuckold is an expression of the rise of an English bourgeoisie, a self-conscious middle class which challenges the aristocracy, and satire on the middling Londoner's desire to escape his or her very middleness by emulating, and in some fashion becoming, the elite.

[50] G. Powell, *Very Good Wife* (1693), ii, 15. [51] R. Brome, *City Wit* (1653), ii, sig. C^r.

The shared assumption is that the cit figure articulates movement of some kind between discrete social groups, not always consistently or accurately defined by his modern interpreters.[52]

Yet it so happens that the cuckolds of the comedies under investigation here are, in some important ways, not obviously mobile. As represented onstage they often do not conform to the established criterion for upward social mobility into the elite. They purchase or possess no land in an attempt to claim genteel status. There has been considerable disagreement amongst historians as to how many flesh-and-blood urban middling families acquired a landed estate complete with country seat during our period. H. J. Habakkuk suggests that a prominent minority did so, while Lawrence and Jeanne Stone dismiss such ideas and instead characterize their incessant repetition by contemporaries as self-perpetuating myth.[53] We are faced with the observation that comedy of the late Stuart era largely falls between these two historiographical stools, neither reflecting the existence nor continuing the myth of an open elite. Few of our citizen cuckolds, some 5 to 10 per cent from the eighty or so new comedies featuring them between 1690 and 1725, are concerned with the deliberate accumulation of land, as either a means to gentility or merely an investment for surplus capital.[54] In this respect, another noteworthy feature of the citizen comedy is the sparse use made of terms that contemporaries would have associated with outright social mobility or social conflict, opprobrious words and phrases like 'upstart', 'mushroom' or 'dunghill cock'.[55] *En masse*, the adopted perspective of late Stuart comedy seems to have been not so much one of a socially superior landed gentry looking down the social hierarchy and seeing the newly wealthy rushing up to meet them, but, instead, one registering the abiding presence of powerful urban individuals. Some cit characters even announce that they are simply building

[52] Even one of the most up-to-date collections of essays on later Stuart theatre has not overcome this vagueness which stands in marked contrast to a much more subtle treatment of gender, sexuality and politics. See, in particular, J. Munns, 'Change, Skepticism, and Uncertainty', in D. Payne Fisk (ed.), *The Cambridge Companion to English Restoration Theatre* (Cambridge, 2000), 145–7; S. J. Owen, 'Drama and Political Crisis', in *ibid.*, 164; P. Gill, 'Gender, Sexuality, and Marriage', in *ibid.*, 191–2.

[53] H. J. Habakkuk, *Marriage, Debt, and the Estates System. English Landownership 1650–1950* (Oxford, 1994), 403ff.; L. Stone and J. C. F. Stone, *An Open Elite? England 1540–1880* (Oxford, 1984), *passim.*

[54] Some texts make the social background of their citizen figures decidedly contradictory or uncertain when it comes to this issue. 'Open elite' figures appear in T. Doggett, *Country-Wake* (1696); D. Crawfurd, *Courtship à la Mode* (1700); W. Walker, *Marry, Or Do Worse* (1704); N. Rowe, *Biter* (1705); W. Taverner, *Female Advocates* (1713). 'Possibles' include T. Southerne, *Sir Anthony Love* (1691); R. Bourne, *Contented Cuckold* (1692); P. Motteux, *Farwel Folly* (1707); S. Centlivre, *Artifice* (1723).

[55] See, for instance, R. Gould, 'To Madam L.', in Gould, *The Works* (1709), vol. I, 109 (line 59); J. Disney, 'The Institution of the Gentleman In a Letter to a Young Gentleman upon his remove from Cambridge to the Temple', *c.*1699, in his 'Essays', f.110, Osborn Shelves b 346, Beinecke Library, Yale; W. A. Speck, *Literature and Society in Eighteenth-Century England. Ideology, Politics and Culture, 1680–1820* (London, 1998), 49.

on the metropolitan affluence and power achieved by their forefathers, much as 'gentlemen' who inherited country estates claimed from their own ancestors.[56]

These features weaken any interpretation that considers the cit stereotype to be either a cultural expression of class struggle or ridicule of social mobility fuelled by new money. Roger Thompson, for example, maintains that cuckoldry in early modern literature symbolizes a 'sexual battle of the classes' following on the heels of the 'rise of the urban middle class and individualism'.[57] Elaborating this basic thesis to considerable length, J. D. Canfield suggests that the grasping citizen is out to overturn gentry dominance: the bourgeoisie challenges aristocratic power by acquiring their real estate. Specifically, Canfield offers the reading that the citizen's wife is symbolic of land. Extra-marital sexual conquest by a gentleman-libertine therefore serves as a metaphoric means of repossession; a gradual reassertion of gentry superiority which had been seriously compromised (he claims) during the upheavals of the mid-seventeenth century.[58]

On closer inspection, this is an oversimplified reading on at least three counts. First, sexual intercourse was often described metaphorically using terms from agricultural discourse in contexts where land was not the actual issue. Equally prevalent, as we shall detail in the next chapter, were similes that relied on terms borrowed from the domestic milieu or urban workplace.[59] Second, a number of the examples interpreted by Canfield ignore the obvious textual presence and importance of status defined as blood lineage.[60] Third, the 'class conflict' frame has a hard task explaining apparent exceptions to the 'middling male bested by superior gentleman' plot, particularly those comedies where the victim is himself a well-born individual. These exceptions are typically swept aside as signs of intra-class conflict. Before we know it, classes and their conflicts proliferate out of hand, beyond the pale of contemporary (and current historiographical) understandings of the early modern social order.[61]

56 See, for example, T. Baker, *Tunbridge-Walks* (1703), iv, 43.

57 R. Thompson, *Unfit for Modest Ears. A Study of Pornographic, Obscene and Bawdy Works Written or Published in England in the Second Half of the Seventeenth Century* (London, 1979), 108, 101; also D. Hughes, *English Drama 1660–1700* (Oxford, 1996), 31. A similar argument continues to hold sway in the interpretation of the stereotype's non-dramatic articulation. See, for example, S. L. Maurer, *Proposing Men. Dialectics of Gender and Class in the Eighteenth-Century English Periodical* (Stanford, 1998), 72ff.

58 Canfield, *Tricksters & Estates*, 2, 8.

59 See T. Meldrum, 'London Domestic Servants from Depositional Evidence, 1650–1750: Servant–Employer Sexuality in the Patriarchal Household', in T. Hitchcock, P. King and P. Sharpe (eds.), *Chronicling Poverty. The Voices and Strategies of the English Poor 1640–1840* (London, 1997), 59; B. Reay, *Popular Cultures in England 1550–1750* (London, 1998), 19.

60 Canfield, *Tricksters & Estates*, 84, 91–5, for instance. This is not to say that Canfield ignores status entirely, but he does underestimate the complex modulation of status with class and how the plays participate in social stratification.

61 *Ibid.*, 3. See also, for example, how Canfield's treatment of Behn's *False Count* must introduce the terms 'petite and haute bourgeoisie' in order to make the dramatic action fit the class frame,

What of the related argument that the cit character gave expression to an abiding hostility towards capitalist accumulation? Citizen figures were certainly depicted as ambitious individuals, frequently to the extent of being avaricious and predatory in their business dealings, and commercial exchange sometimes became usurious exploitation onstage. Although ethical disquiet went into the satirical mix, it can be argued that this was not the primary motivation for the derision directed at the harried citizen. For instance, Steele's Mr Sealand is a model of commercial propriety but henpecked none the less. Looked at from the opposite perspective, Jonathan Swift's *Examiner*, which in many of its clearly partisan issues had little time for the City or its citizens,[62] came to the conclusion that the

> *Stage*, which carries other Follies and Vices beyond Nature and Probability, falls very short in the Representations of *Avarice*; nor are there any Extravagances in this Kind describ'd by ancient or modern Comedies, which are not outdone by an hundred Instances, commonly told, among our selves.[63]

The prevalence of the cit comedies is difficult to reconcile with this remark, unless many spectators did not consider these plots to be mere morality tales about usury and greed. Such is also the case with Eliza Haywood's claim from 1724 (towards the end of our period) that her new comedy's cit figure was one of 'Novelty' because the plot hinged on the figure's unusual rapacity.[64] As far as explaining the significance of the citizen cuckold scenario is concerned, this commentary suggests that we need to make a distinction between attitudes to commercial activity *per se* and attitudes towards the perceived social ramifications of this activity.[65] We tend to find that it was invariably when dramatic discourse tried to delineate the citizen's place in the social order that even the most favourably disposed pictorial of perfectly legitimate commerce was attracted to the paradigm of sexual (im)propriety.

Incidentally, a corresponding discrimination would also prove fruitful in relation to current explanations of wider generic change. Critics of late Stuart drama have grown accustomed to thinking in terms of a shift from satiric to sentimental comedy, a gradual and complex improvement in ethical tone and social purpose for the theatre. Typically this cultural transition is taken to correspond directly with societal change: a move away from a predominantly amoral aristocracy towards an upstanding middle class as allegedly represented by the likes of *The*

ibid., 180–2; or, similarly, in relation to the character of Mr Rich from Pix's *Beau Defeated*, see Canfield, 'Restoration Comedy', in S. J. Owen (ed.), *A Companion to Restoration Drama* (Oxford, 2001), 223.

62 See, for example, *Examiner*, no. 29 (24–28 August 1713), vol. IV, (1–2).

63 *Ibid.*, no. 28 (1–8 February 1711), vol. I, [1].

64 E. Haywood, *Wife To Be Lett* (1724), epilogue spoken by the author.

65 Cf. T. N. Corns, W. A. Speck and J. A. Downie, 'Archetypal Mystification: Polemic and Reality in English Political Literature, 1640–1750', *Eighteenth-Century Life* 7, 3 (1982), 12–13, 16.

Conscious Lovers.[66] Yet just as there may well have been an improvement in attitudes to commercial activity, so the slow but certain lifting in the comedy's moral tone does not mean that we should infer the comedy was eliminating the customary social categories too. Even if a new type of sentimental comedy did come to chide 'aristocratic' or 'genteel' standards of behaviour and offer something more improving in its place, we must not assume either an equally straightforward, parallel rejection of aristocracy or gentility as *social* concepts or, conversely, that any improvement correlates with a clearly defined and alternate social group (i.e. a bourgeoisie) becoming newly prominent as both theatrical producers and spectators. Attempts to modify and therefore rescue this alleged correspondence between generic change and social location by arguing for a partial but progressive combination of landed nobility and merchant class also prove unsatisfactory. Why? Fundamentally because they assume that early modern theatre affected particular social groups when a strong case can be made for late Stuart drama *effecting* social groups, for it comprehending complex and incomplete processes of social differentiation.

Current readings interpret their early modern texts according to a preconceived social grid when, in fact, the comedies were attempting to establish social co-ordinates for late Stuart Londoners using something other than modern axes of class. The following pages will attempt to understand this process of social configuration on its own terms, as represented by the comedy.

The interpretations critiqued thus far rely on *a priori* dichotomies, aristocracy versus bourgeoisie and feudalism versus capitalism in particular. The cuckold scenario articulates not so much group conflict within an established social hierarchy as the dislocation of the hierarchy itself, a testing of the constant process of social ordering which distinguished between 'gentle' and 'simple'. City cuckolds were figures of lingering social anomaly, of the difficulty in reconciling the socio-political rhetoric of the dominant, the gentry so-called, with social experience. Cits were chastised onstage because they refused to fit established social definitions. Rather than serve as an expression of animosity towards defined social groups, their cuckolding expressed anxiety at the failure of social structuration, an inability to identify definitively who belonged where and why in the first instance. To put it rather crudely, the comedy did not simply represent cits plodding up the rungs of a social ladder in order to be pushed brusquely back down again but interrogated the ladder's very construction instead.

The citizens' representation rehearsed the ways in which their power was deemed inconsistent with the dominant configuration of power known to contemporaries as gentility. It is the contemplation of this inconsistency, not the

66 For the most recent and nuanced elaboration of this thesis, see K. Combe, 'Rakes, Wives and Merchants: Shifts from the Satirical to the Sentimental', in S. J. Owen (ed.), *A Companion to Restoration Drama* (Oxford, 2001), 291–308.

coincidence of a perpetually rising, newly self-aware middle class, which explains *both* the durability of the basic scenario in early modern London's playhouses and the smaller shifts of emphasis, variations that are themselves indicative of rival opinions concerning precisely how or why the cit might be considered out of place. The work of the next chapter will be to show how the theatre as discursive event got this message across or, more precisely, how it interrogated the citizen's ambiguous social position.

2 Confronting ambiguities of genteel birth and city wealth

From careful brows, and heavy downcast eyes,
Dull cits, and thick-skulled aldermen arise.
J. Addison, *The Playhouse* (1688/9)

Tracing the precise manner in which the citizen's domestic troubles were encoded within the drama reveals much more about contemporary perceptions of elite social structuration and its possible failings than previously acknowledged by modern commentators. Late Stuart theatregoers were frequently active participants in what was, ultimately, a representation of *a representation* of cuckoldry. As a consequence, we need to alter our perception of how the citizen was portrayed on the early modern stage. For he was not only the cuckolded husband, but also the ridden victim of a punitive ritual known as skimmington. This distinction is subtle yet vital. Recognizing that citizen comedy could be ritualistic in nature takes us to the heart of its socio-cultural meaning and the way in which cits and their onstage treatment served as synecdoche for problems over social stratification and power.

It is helpful if we first turn to newspapers and periodicals in order to trace how late Stuart comedy's first spectators might have reacted in 'real life' to the presence of an adulterous wife or henpecked husband in their community,[1] undoubtedly a topic of rumour and gossip, talked about in doorways, on the street, at the local coffeehouse. Fingers were pointed at the infraction of order and the failure of patriarchy represented by female insubordination. If the threat to social order was deemed serious enough, further action might be taken and the transgressors subjected to a shaming rite known in its varied but overlapping forms as 'skimmington', 'riding' and 'rough music', or 'charivari' as historians have preferred as a collective label. The key to this ritual was performance, the symbolic re-enactment of the disharmony brought to the neighbourhood

[1] See the work of M. J. Ingram, 'Ridings, Rough Music and the "Reform of Popular Culture" in Early Modern England', *PP* 105 (1984), 79–113; 'Ridings, Rough Music and Mocking Rhymes in Early Modern England', in B. Reay (ed.), *Popular Culture in Seventeenth-Century England* (London, 1985), 166–97; 'Juridical Folklore in England Illustrated by Rough Music', in C. Brooks and M. Lobban (eds.), *Communities and Courts in Britain, 1150–1900* (London, 1997), 68–75. Also E. P. Thompson, *Customs in Common* (London, 1991), 468–530.

and the public 'outing' or identification of the offenders. For example, a man considered to have been too passive in the day-to-day life of his household might well be played by a neighbour clothed in a petticoat or his termagant wife portrayed as wearing the male's breeches.

The comic staging of the citizen cuckold bore obvious resemblance to charivari. Particular features warrant emphasis for the modern reader. Key symbols were appropriated by the stage and playwrights seem to have fashioned several ironic devices to integrate the ritual with the overall plot. Instances of the serenading, beating and cross-dressing of citizen figures were common. For example, Thomas Shadwell's *Scowrers* subjects Sir Richard Maggot, an alderman, and his new wife, a widowed gentlewoman, to a raucous 'house-warming'.[2] A case of mistaken identity has William Burnaby's Sir Lively Cringe, City alderman turned Court hanger-on, and his wife serenaded by an unlucky suitor in place of the intended gentlewoman.[3] The drunken revels of Hector, son of the merchant Gripeall in David Crawfurd's *Love at First Sight*, pass for rough music and introduce the idea that Hector is actually the illegitimate son of a gentleman, Sir John Single.[4] Sometimes the beating of drums was replaced by the pummelling of bodies. Arriving at the genteel leisure resort of Hampstead Heath in search of his wayward wife, Deputy Driver is the victim of vigorous slapstick.[5] The audience would have appreciated the irony of a play written by the actor Thomas Doggett, who specialized in performing cit roles, that featured Sir Thomas Testie, a citizen-purchaser of a country estate, 'shedding my Blood' in an affray with a group of 'Rustich Rogues'.[6] Perhaps part of the fun was that Doggett played one of these rogues and not the citizen character. Transgression was also figured by transvestism. Attempting to keep a close watch on his spouse, a retired businessman dresses as a woman selling gloves in John Dryden (jr.)'s *The Husband His Own Cuckold*.[7] In the case of *The Female Fortune Teller* it is the wife who assumes the breeches. Disguised as a soldier, she deserts her husband.[8] Similar humiliation awaited merchant figures in plays by George Farquhar and Mary Pix.[9] Other emblems of charivari were more often invoked with words or by gesture. This was typically the case with the animal horns that pointed to cuckolding. Finally, it was even possible for the citizen to be quite literally ridden onstage. One of the most popular devices of comic epilogue, which included jibes at the 'cits' in the audience, was the delivery of the satirical final verse by the celebrated Joe Haynes whilst seated on the back of a donkey (see Figure 1). This practice may explain a punch-line

[2] T. Shadwell, *Scowrers* (1691), iii, 25. [3] W. Burnaby, *Modish Husband* (1702), v, 67.
[4] D. Crawfurd, *Love at First Sight* (1704), i, 11–12.
[5] T. Baker, *Hampstead Heath* (1706), ii, 25–7. [6] T. Doggett, *Country-Wake* (1696), iv, 49.
[7] J. Dryden, jr., *Husband His Own Cuckold* (1696), iv, 45.
[8] C. Johnson, *Female Fortune Teller* (1726), iv, 81.
[9] Smuggler in G. Farquhar, *Constant Couple* (1700), iv, 40; Mr Draul as an essence woman in M. Pix, *Different Widows* (1703), i, 8.

1 From a penny broadsheet (*c.*1710) depicting Joe Haynes's 'ridden' delivery of an epilogue, a practice he initiated in the 1690s

in Burnaby's *Reform'd Wife*. Here it is suggested to a poor young gentleman that by becoming an actor he might get to play a rich alderman, to which the reply is: 'I'd rather be his Horse.'[10] It certainly sheds light on the comment of another character, in a comedy by Thomas Southerne from the mid-1680s, that he hoped to avoid being like the 'common, ridden Cuckold of the Town; Stag'd to the crowd on publick Theatres'.[11]

As soon as the cit and his wife were introduced onstage the audience presumed cuckoldry. It was as if the actual cuckolding had occurred before the staged adultery the audience was now witnessing, such that the comedy itself became like a riding, a mock rehearsal of the original sin. With some scripts this was precisely the case. For instance, the *widow* of a City banker, Mrs Rich, cannot shake the rumour of adultery in *The Beau Defeated*.[12] That prior knowledge (as it were) of a City character's predicament may have been at work is not surprising given a rate of repetition which itself approached ritualistic levels. We have already noted how every second new comedy recited the citizen's denigration. This heavy flow became a deluge that not even an occasional playgoer in turn-of-the-century London could easily avoid. If one preferred the more sober fare of tragedy there was still a good chance that the prologue or epilogue would

[10] W. Burnaby, *Reform'd Wife* (1700), i, 4.
[11] T. Southerne, *Disappointment* (1684), iii, 22.
[12] M. Pix, *Beau Defeated* (1700), ii, 14.

make some wisecrack about the City. For instance, the preliminary verses to John Bancroft's *Henry II* imagined what would happen if the citizens' womenfolk met the same fate as the play's heroine, Rosamond:

So may you thrive, your Wagers all be won;
So may your Wise Stock-jobbing Crimp go on;
So may your Ships return from the *Canaries*,
And stoln *French* Cargoes in your *Johns* and *Maries*.
Stand Buff once for a Mistress: Think what Lives
Some of you daily lead with scolding Wives.
And though she fell by Jealous Cruelty,
For Venial Sin 'twas pity she should die.
Ah! should your Wives and Daughters so be try'd,
And with her Dose their Failings purify'd,
Lord! What a Massacre wou'd mawl *Cheapside*![13]

In like fashion, following the stoic calamity of John Dennis's *Appius and Virginia* the epilogue perversely contrasted modern London with ancient Rome:

That 'tis far otherwise with us is plain,
While City Captain here makes short Campaign,
In *Bunhill*-Fields subduing *France* and *Spain*.
How oft has Courtier maul'd both Wife and Daughter?
Yet no such bloody Business follow'd after.[14]

Many kinds of literature replayed the 'cit com' in printed type. For example, all four of the intrigues narrated by the novella *Art of Cuckoldom* (1697) were about luckless middling tradesmen. There was even a handsome frontispiece depicting London's most famous citizen. Paralleling the typically 'senior' citizen cuckold of the stage, Dick Whittington was featured with not just his cat but also the gout and a fool's cap resembling the cuckold's horned forehead. A satiric survey of visitors to Bath in 1725 toyed with its readers' expectations concerning the cuckoldry of a citizen holidaying there with his genteel spouse, only to present an even more elaborate variation on the stereotype just a few pages later.[15] The unlucky cit was grist for broadsheet ballads like *Advice to the Ladies of London, In the Choice of their Husbands* and *The Cuckold's Calamity: Or, The Old Usurer Plunder'd of his Gold by his Young Wife For the Supply of her Gallants*.[16] The horns of urbane cuckolding also cropped up at multiple points in collections of witticisms and poetry.[17]

[13] J. Bancroft, *Henry the Second* (1693), prologue. *Italics reversed.*

[14] J. Dennis, *Appius and Virginia* (1709), epilogue. *Italics reversed.* Similar remarks concluded C. Gildon, *Love's Victim* (1701), epilogue written by Mr Burnaby; C. Johnson, *The Victim* (1714), epilogue written by Mr Cibber.

[15] [E. Haywood], *Bath Intrigues in Four Letters to a Friend in London* (1725), 24, 28–30.

[16] W. G. Day (ed.), *The Pepys Ballads* (Cambridge, 1987), vol. IV, 85; *ibid.*, vol. V, 256.

[17] Anon., *Cambridge Jests* (1674), 26, 73, 123; E. Ward, *Nuptial Dialogues and Debates* (1723), vol. I, 178–84.

2 'Skimmington-Triumphs, Or the Humours of Horn-Fair', *c.*1720

If the audience had not previously experienced skimmington at first hand (it was evidently still frequent enough to be encountered personally by one European tourist visiting London in the 1690s),[18] its enactment as street theatre particularly common to London was further popularized and elaborated on by the metropolitan press (see Figure 2). For instance, correspondence to the editor of *The British Gazetteer*, dated from the City's Royal Exchange, began:

SIR, IF Sh—en Luck be Good Luck, I don't know but Sh—en Stories may be Good Stories: An eminent House-keeper in our Neighbourhood having Occasion some Days ago, to have the Lumber of Nature bore off the Premises, (vulgarly miscall'd a Wedding) some arch Apprentices in the Neighbourhood laid their Heads together, and sent the Musick the next Morning, to facilitate the honest Inhabitants, and give him Joy; who being exasperated to have his Rest broke, and be Banter'd into the Bargain, leap'd out of Bed, and saluted the Manufacturers of Ca[t]s-Gut and Rozin, with a brimming Close-Stool-Pan, discharg'd on their Musical Noodles.[19]

A letter to *The Weekly Journal* had aimed to forestall such action by sending, this time from Linendrapery Row in the City's Cornhill district, a 'fair Warning to all Drummers under what Denomination soever, that if they entertain me with their rough Musick under my Window, I am resolved not to give them one Doit . . . they may beat *Round about Cuckolds*, or what Round they please, I am resolved in that they shall not displease'.[20] Among the studied responses offered to readers' questions in the periodical *The Athenian Mercury* we find one querist, unidentified by his printed submission, asking if he was still a cuckold now that his unfaithful first wife had died and he was remarried. The response hazarded a rather familiar estimation of the correspondent's identity:

Once an *Alderman* and *ever an Alderman*, is a common saying indeed: But what's that to *Cuckolds*? . . . That the *Whore* being *dead*, which made the poor Querist a *Cuckold*, he ceases to bear that *opprobious name*, and becomes as *Honorable a Citizen* agen as any in all the Ward he lives in.[21]

Whilst we must concede that the aforementioned ritualistic gestures and symbols do not always have an obvious presence in the surviving playbooks, we should recall theatre as a lived cultural event. Although a script might not expressly cue rough music, given what we know about theatregoing it seems entirely legitimate to suggest that contemporary audiences could take matters into their own hands. Appropriate gestures, clapping, pointing, hissing,

[18] Mr Ozell (trans. and ed.), *M. Misson's Memoirs and Observations in His Travels over England* (1719), 129.
[19] *British Gazetteer* [unnumbered] (19 August 1721), 2006.
[20] *Weekly Journal*, no. 94 (27 September 1718), 561. See also a report of skimmington on account of a virago in *British Gazetteer*, no. 10 (3 July 1725), [4].
[21] *Athenian Mercury*, no. 11 (4 October 1692), vol. VIII, question 4. See H. M. Berry, *Gender, Society and Print Culture in Late-Stuart England. The Cultural World of the* Athenian Mercury (Burlington, VT, 2003).

stamping of feet, snapping of fans, and most obviously mocking laughter, may all have been applied at the climax of a play's City affair.

An up-market audience that liked to consider itself genteel was a guarantee neither of polite decorum nor of elite separation from popular culture.[22] Some playhouse spectators seem to have come quite prepared to effect disruption. One of the Steele–Addison periodical essays was dedicated to the noisemakers known as 'catcalls' brought by some patrons, 'so many Persons of Quality', to the theatre.[23] Indeed, Henry Higden discovered this custom to his cost at the 1693 debut of his first and only comedy. He complained in the printed edition of *The Wary Widdow* that the theatre had been 'by Faction transformed into a Bear-Garden', with 'hissing, mimicking, ridiculing, and Cat-calling', and he contemplated why 'these Gentlemen (whom we must allow good Criticks in dressing) shall assume to vent their ill grounded Fury'.[24] Higden came to the conclusion that his play had been judged to pale in comparison with William Congreve's *Old Batchelour*, which had premiered a typical 'cit com' subplot immediately before Higden's own effort hit the boards, because it did not script an entirely routine action for its citizen figure. Higden's scripting was overridden by the audience, though how much of the ensuing serenade was directed at the character and how much at its author's misjudgement is uncertain. It only remained for the piqued playwright to launch into his own diatribe against the established conventions of late Stuart comedy, providing us with a catalogue of recent City roles in the process:

What does it import if *Parson Spintext* have a wicked design on the Alderman's wife? What harm was it if his agreable Impudence revenged the City cheats upon the Aldermans head, and exalted his horns above the rest of his Brethren? There cannot be a taking Play without some Limberham or fumbling Alderman, or keeper to expose. Let the fair Gilt ingage her Gallant like a Spider in her own cobweb, before her poor Nickapoops face, unbar the sluces, that her kindness may run down in a mighty stream; let the lightning of Courtship melt his Daughters maidenhead in the scaboard, or chopping of that *Hidra's* Head of barren Virginity, let twins sprout up in their stead and let the Family of love be propigated quite through the City.[25]

22 See B. Reay, *Popular Cultures in England 1550–1750* (London, 1998), 198–223; cf. Ingram, 'Juridical Folklore', 81–2.

23 *Spectator*, no. 361 (24 April 1712), vol. III, 349–53. See the reported use of the catcall by several gentlemen at Lincoln's Inn Fields on the evening of 9 May 1715 in J. H. Wilson, 'Theatre Notes from the Newdigate Newsletters', *Theatre Notebook* 15, 3 (1961), 84; HMC, *Manuscripts of the Earl of Egmont. Diary of Viscount Percival. Volume I: 1730–1733* 63, 1 (1920), 216, entry for 16 January 1732.

24 H. Higden, *Wary Widdow* (1693), preface, sig. [A3^r]; dedication to the earl of Dorset, sig. A2^r.

25 *Ibid.*, preface, sig. [A3^v]. Parson Spintext featured in Congreve's *Old Batchelour* (1693) as the fake identity used by the gentleman gallant to rendez-vous with the spouse of banker Fondlewife; Limberham was from John Dryden's *Kind Keeper* (1680); 'Nickapoops' references 'Deputy Nicompoop, Deputy of a Ward, a softly sneaking uxorious Citizen, Husband to L[ady] Addle-plot', from T. Durfey, *Love for Money* (1691), dramatis personae.

In deploying the symbols of charivari and in riding the citizen, early modern playgoers and playwrights were thinking about gentility as elite social structuration, a rhetoric of socio-political identification, and thinking about it in a very particular way. Heavy with irony, an exchange printed in a 1709 issue of the question-and-answer paper *The British Apollo* hints as much. Evidently, exposure in print tended to have something of the same effect as riding the citizen onstage:

> Q. Apollo, *be it known to you, that I am a* Cuckold, *an Egregious* Cuckold. *My* Horns *Sprout, Terribly Sprout, insomuch that they are grown far too large to put in my Pocket. 'Tis true I am a Tradesman, and so appear not such a* Monster, *as if I were a Gentleman; however they grow Burdensome. Now Honest, Good Humour'd* Apollo, *what Comfort can you give me under my Whimsical Circumstances* [?]
>
> A. To lessen your *Horns* or even prevent their further growth, we know no Remedy, for they are an odd sort of a Plant which not only grow as long as the Bearer Lives, but also Sprout after his Decease. However we will give you some Crums of Comfort . . . shou'd a Civil War happen between the Cuckolds and those not Dignify'd and Distinguish'd, you will not only have a Powerful Army on your side, but also such as are strongly Arm'd for Assaults and Defence.[26]

The query of Apollo's suppliant is double-edged. He makes the apparently definitive claim that he is not a 'gentleman', but, at the same time, a lingering uncertainty regarding his social position underwrites the piece as a whole. Consider the following points. Having identified himself as a tradesman in 'truth' the very mention of gentility is redundant, unless, of course, there is more to it. The item is spotted with terms related to and punning on social differentiation ('sort', 'dignify'd', 'distinguish'd', perhaps even 'egregious'). Apollo's response suggests that the problem will only get worse. By claiming the horns will continue to grow after his death the inference is that the tradesman will only become 'more' of a monster and, therefore, 'more' like the gentleman he refers to. Finally, the black humour may extend to those citizens who tried to seal their gentility, resolve their status as elite in death if not in life, by bequeathing substantial fortunes to their heirs and by having funerary monuments, complete with heraldic devices, erected in their own names.

Even more forthcoming on the significance of the citizen's 'horning' during the 1720s was Daniel Defoe. In the second volume of his conduct book for the tradesman, Defoe posed some rather sharp questions of his subject:

> How is it when he comes among Gentlemen? when sallying out from his Sphere, in which Nature circumscrib'd him, and for which alone he was fitted, (if fit for any Thing,) he comes out, and calls himself *a Gentleman*? . . . How should he be the Agent upon himself, metamorphise himself . . . from a conceited Purse-proud Shop-Keeper turn

[26] *British Apollo*, supernumerary paper, no. 2 (May 1709), vol. II, 4.

himself into a Gentleman? Much easier might he get an *Actaeon* set upon his Shoulders, than a Stock of Brains put into his Head, *Modesty* upon his Face, or *Manners* upon his Behaviour.[27]

Defoe's reference to Actaeon is a classical allusion posing as the author's own refinement, an awkward expression of the desire to distance himself somehow from popular culture and its cit comedy yet at the same time manipulate this tradition for effective meaning. Strictly speaking, Actaeon was a mythological figure and not an object as Defoe's syntax might imply. In Greek legend the hunter Actaeon offended the goddess Artemis by daring to look upon her whilst she bathed. She exacted revenge by transforming the mortal into a stag and then having his hounds tear him to pieces.[28] Defoe is therefore branding his tradesman for daring to make a claim for gentility, violating the natural order of things. Citizens on London's stage were described in equally monstrous terms, as 'men-brutes', with Farquhar's *Constant Couple* making use of the same mythological allusion in dialogue.[29] Paying close attention to the logic behind this horning provides important clues as to why the citizen and his social position were considered anomalous. In other words, the ritualistic medium helped shape the message.

The citizen's charivari was concerned with the transgression of hierarchy. Despite first impressions, it was not about a simple inversion where 'high' became 'low' and 'low' became 'high', or, applying concepts used in previous modern commentary, 'bourgeois' becomes 'aristocrat' or 'upper class' is figuratively usurped by a 'lower cum middle class'. Instead this dramatic play on a very familiar ritual expressed the confusion, the failure, of the principles which distinguished high from low, low from high in the first instance.[30]

Charivari has typically been considered an early modern expression of gender transgression, the simultaneous re-enactment of a failure for patriarchal hierarchy and its reaffirmation as a relationship of power where domination is masculine and subordination feminine.[31] Here the ritual is not so much the

27 D. Defoe, *The Complete English Tradesman* (1727), vol. II, part i, 246–7.

28 The myth was evidently common currency in our period. See, for instance, *Gentleman's Journal* (February 1691–2), 24–5.

29 Farquhar, *Constant Couple*, i, 2; Farquhar, 'A Discourse upon Comedy, in Reference to the English Stage', in his *Love and Business* (1702), 138. For citizens as 'brutes', see Pix, *Beau Defeated*, iv, 28; S. Centlivre, *Beau's Duel* (1702), ii, 16; R. Estcourt, *Fair Example* (1706), i, 12.

30 For a succinct statement of this distinction, see S. Hall, 'For Allon White: Metaphors of Transformation', in A. White (ed.), *Carnival, Hysteria, and Writing. Collected Essays and Autobiography* (Oxford, 1993), 8.

31 D. E. Underdown, 'The Taming of the Scold: The Enforcement of Patriarchal Authority in Early Modern England', in A. J. Fletcher and J. Stevenson (eds.), *Order and Disorder in Early Modern England* (Cambridge, 1985), 116–36; M. J. Ingram, '"Scolding women cucked or washed": A Crisis in Gender Relations in Early Modern England', in J. Kermode and G. Walker (eds.), *Women, Crime and the Courts in Early Modern England* (London, 1994), 48–80. See also the

expression of struggle or conflict between defined groups for power (in this case, 'men' and 'women') as the cultural processing or the structuration of power (arising from sexual difference) and the legitimation of unequally powerful groupings. In other words, this use of the ritual refigured males and females as men and women by defining the masculine and the feminine.

Our sudden diversion into a discussion of gender may seem puzzling, but there would have been no disjunction for early modern audiences for two reasons. First, as gender was a power relationship, so too with gentility. Our stage charivaris figured people as 'gentle' or 'simple' by defining gentility, by structuring power arising from status, class and command situations as we argued in the Introduction. Of course the problem was that power proved, in reality, to be multivalent and diffuse. In configuring domination and subordination there were those who refused to fit, blurring the ideal order by claiming too much power. Charivari reinscribed order at the same time as it called attention to its anomalies. Second, as gender is an ideal relationship of power, so other early modern power relationships were inextricably gendered. The gentry's power was ideally in the hands of gentle-*men* and gentility worked primarily to distinguish superior from inferior males. Given that a fundamental measure of male power was the subordination of women, so the latter became symbols of the relative empowerment and disempowerment of men.[32] In failing to master their womenfolk, the comedy's male citizens were being disempowered and their claims for gentility disavowed.

The affluent London City household is depicted in late Stuart comedy as a hotbed of sexual intrigue. Familial dysfunction in this period continued to be a powerful symbol of perceived disorder within society at large.[33] City women are portrayed as having an abundance of sexual energy, or 'heat', which needs to be released by an adulterous liaison (in the case of wives) or by a clandestine marriage (in the case of daughters). The City wife's lust is contrasted with her husband's failed virility, the longings of a nubile daughter compared to the lack of vigour exhibited by the rich old City bachelor chosen as suitor by her genteel parents. As a consequence of such physiological

apt consideration of charivari which appeared after this chapter was completed, J. G. Turner, *Libertines and Radicals in Early Modern London. Sexuality, Politics, and Literary Culture, 1630–1685* (Cambridge, 2002), 47–73.

32 A point clearly registered by Margaret Cavendish in her 'Oration against a Foolish Custom', or charivari, from *Orations of Divers Sorts, Accommodated to Divers Places* (1662, second edition 1663), 221–2. See also the likes of *Spectator*, no. 212 (2 November 1711), vol. II, 330. Particularly pertinent treatment of these general issues may be found in J. W. Scott, *Gender and the Politics of History* (New York, 1988). Their importance for the early modern period has been highlighted by S. H. Mendelson and P. Crawford, *Women in Early Modern England 1550–1720* (Oxford, 1998), 345–430.

33 Cf. S. D. Amussen, *An Ordered Society. Gender and Class in Early Modern England* (Oxford, 1988), 33. However, this view has since been revised by R. J. Weil, *Political Passions. Gender, the Family and Political Argument in England 1680–1714* (Manchester, 1999).

disparity, City women are attracted to more full-blooded and often younger males.

In its simplest rendition, differences in bodily heat make for varying degrees of sexual energy and mark a perceived inequality of social power (status)[34] which was deemed reliant on the relative purity, the 'degree' or 'quality', of one's blood.[35] The lust of City wife and lover is strongest because they are judged well-born and descendants of established 'gentry' pedigree. The hapless husband or senile suitor does not ordinarily enjoy such status. The blood flowing through his veins is considered inferior and this inferiority is signalled, via a humoral physiology, as some kind of sexual inadequacy, some type of deficiency or imbalance involving the blood.

Early modern medical discourse, comprising overlapping but not entirely compatible theories of reproduction, held that a mixture of 'spirits' and blood was needed for copulation. Thus the low-born citizen might simply be depicted as 'feeble', devoid of the requisite blood and heat altogether, and unable to initiate conjugal relations. For instance, it is said with reference to the merchant figure from Francis Manning's *All for the Better*:

> But when that Nourishment is gone, and the Lamp can give no more Light, its consuming Fury vanishes with the Flame; whereas Old Men rage the more for the loss of that supply of Spirits; and being Conscious of their Weakness, They are jealous of their Wives, whom they can't please.[36]

Similarly, the wealthy City barrister, Serjeant Wrangle, is dismissed as 'too demure; he has no heat'. This heat is later specified as 'Genial warmth', with 'genial' suggesting a perfection transmitted by descent, through the *gens* of the landed elite.[37]

Alternatively, the citizen might be portrayed as able to 'raise his spirits' but remain childless no matter how much he tried. This contradicts a recent claim that early modern medical discourse did not understand that men could have intercourse yet be infertile.[38] Blood was held to be both the means of circulatory arousal and the principal matter that was distilled by the body into semen. One of the most published turn-of-the-century tracts on human reproduction explained

34 Cf. Mendelson and Crawford, *Women in Early Modern England*, 27.

35 For a detailed account of how early modern physiology as a 'hierarchy of heat and perfection' made the body a discursively shaped, plastic microcosm of society, see T. Laqueur, *Making Sex. Body and Gender from the Greeks to Freud* (Cambridge, MA, 1990), 25–62. A useful, broader survey may also be found in M. Healy, *Fictions of Disease in Early Modern England. Bodies, Plagues and Politics* (London, 2001), 1–49. For consideration of similar issues more closely related to the socio-cultural context under discussion here, see G. K. Paster, *The Body Embarrassed. Drama and the Disciplines of Shame in Early Modern England* (Ithaca, 1993), 1–22; Paster, 'The Unbearable Coldness of Female Being: Women's Imperfection and the Humoral Economy', *ELR* 28, 3 (1998), 416–40.

36 F. Manning, *All for the Better* (1703), i, 7.

37 J. Drake, *Sham-Lawyer* (1697), i, 11; ii, 16.

38 E. A. Foyster, *Manhood in Early Modern England. Honour, Sex and Marriage* (London, 1999), 70.

how 'impotence' also comprised the insufficient quantity or inferior quality of the male seed: 'If some Humours happen to come out in the amorous agitations, 'tis only a little serosity, which has not all the qualities requisite for generation. The Woman . . . will never make any thing of a Humour that wants disposition for Nature['s] great work.'[39] As this exchange between Raison the grocer in *Greenwich Park* and his well-born wife shows, sterility intimately represented a perceived social disparity:

MRS RAISON: We'l think on't, Bungler. I long for a Coach, and I will have a Coach; and you may spare it out of Clarret, you So[t]; since you can get no Children to Inherit what you have, I'le spend it; and thou shalt never live an easie hour till I have a Coach; and so think on't, thou Associate of Drunkards, eternal Tobacco Funker; must I be contented with a Beast that stinks perpetually, sits up till two or three of the Clock in the Morning, and knows nothing but his Bottle some times a Week together? The World shall know what a Bed-fellow thou art, that snores all night, and art sick in the morning; thou Debilitated Booby, thou sapless trunk. [*Exit*]

RAISON: What will become of me? Beat her I can't, hate her I can't, turn her away I dare not. If I could complain of her, I must not, for my own Reputation suffers in't; besides, she has such a bloody crew of Relations, that would murder me, if I should do any of these things: A Pox of all Fools that marry poor Gentlewomen, for you wed their whole Family, and entail a Plague upon your Posterity.[40]

Or, as the scrivener Moneytrap in *The Confederacy* is sharply reminded, rich City husbands in the bedchamber are like a 'Bag without Money – an empty Bottle – dead Small-Beer'.[41] In other words, they may prosper in terms of their wealth but they are disappointed when trying to conceive a male heir who would potentially, on the basis of the citizen's superior fortune, pass for genteel. However, a relatively weak distillation of blood might still achieve an 'inferior generation', that is, result in the conception of a girl.[42] If the citizens depicted onstage are fathers, their children are usually female.[43] In the few cases where they have sons, paternity is in doubt and the inference that City wives had formerly cuckolded their husbands and then fallen pregnant by a well-born and more virile lover.[44]

[39] [N. Venette], *The Mysteries of Conjugal Love Reveal'd* (1703, eighth edition 1707), 423. Cf. R. Porter and L. Hall, *The Facts of Life. The Creation of Sexual Knowledge in Britain, 1650–1950* (New Haven, 1995), 33–90.

[40] W. Mountfort, *Greenwich Park* (1691), i, 3.

[41] J. Vanbrugh, *Confederacy* (1705), ii, 26.

[42] [Venette], *Mysteries*, 381–2. See too Merryman's comment from C. Sedley, *Bellamira* (1687), iii, 31; the discussion in D. Cressy, *Travesties and Transgressions in Tudor and Stuart England. Tales of Discord and Dissension* (Oxford, 2000), 35–47.

[43] Of course, in social terms, City or middling blood was always *already* inferior and the bodies of any offspring assumed less than perfect when compared with those of the well-born. For this connection, see the likes of E. Ward, *The Dancing-School with the Adventures of the Easter Holy-Days* (1700), 6. I hope to examine this reputed contrast in genteel/non-genteel physiology at greater length in future work.

[44] For example, the character of Hector in David Crawfurd's *Love at First Sight*; the irony at work in Anon., *War Horns, Make Room for the Bucks with Green Bowes* (1682), 9.

In one way or another, then, male citizens are represented as incapable of ensuring their posterity, unable to sire sons and so establish an honourable lineage. If the citizen's body was 'dull', his well-born rival was the one with all the natural vigour and this potential made for the fictive correction of society's bloodlines, its disposition of power. Frequently implicit in the citizen comedy is the social *frisson* that the husband might never discover his wife's affair, which could, in turn, result in her pregnancy and their raising of another (gentle)man's son who will one day inherit from his surrogate City father.[45] What might at first seem an overextended reading of the comedy's possible social purview finds confirmation in non-dramatic retellings of the citizen's tale which engaged in just this kind of fantastic, wish-fulfilling projection. Hence a broadside ballad took cruel delight in forecasting an eventual settlement of social scores, a future resolution of the anomaly we have been discussing, when it observed:

> But yet these Citts are subtile Slaves,
> Most of them Wits, and knowing Knaves;
> We get their Children, and they do,
> From us get Lands, and Lordships too:
> And 'tis most [apt] in those affairs
> The Lands should go to the right h[e]irs.[46]

In this regard we might also note here that the popular etymology of the word 'cuckold' derived it from 'cuckoo' and, more specifically, that the City wife's cuckolding of her husband was known by the cant phrase 'mending his breed', refining the family's stock by surreptitiously grafting a superior strain to it.[47] Of course the comedy is typically preoccupied with the dynamics of the original cuckolding and, given dramatic strictures regarding the unities of time and place, was not always in a position to impersonate potential, future consequences (to represent the 'taking' of the graft; the growth of a son to maturity).

The City son's putative inheritance comprised not necessarily land but economic power *per se*. This wealth was something that the boy's actual father had lacked. Although the cuckolder was well-born, his purse was empty. He was often described as a younger brother who did not stand to inherit a landed estate from his genteel forebears, and thus match economic power (class) with his gentle blood (status). An added attraction of bedding a City woman was the chance to gain from the greater wealth of her husband. Hence the young gentleman denied an allowance by his father says of his affair with Mrs Raison:

45 See, for instance, the prologue to W. Congreve, *Double-Dealer* (1694).

46 Anon., *The New Courtier* (?1700), Early English Books Tract Supplements, Reel A5 (Ann Arbor, 1998). For the opposite point of view, cf. Anon., *The Academy of Pleasure* (1656), 26–7.

47 For the popular definition of cuckoldry see *Athenian Mercury*, no. 20 [1691], vol. I, question 8; *ibid.*, no. 11 (7 May 1695), vol. XVII, question 4. For this characterization of citizen cuckoldry see, for instance, E. Ward, *A Step to the Bath With a Character of the Place* (1700), 14.

''Tis an Intrigue of a pretty long standing, and tho' it be somewhat scandalous to receive more Favours from Women than one, my necessity has oblig'd me to comply; for ever since your Travels she has been my Father.'[48] Similarly, Sir Vanity from *Kensington Gardens* prefers 'Citizens Wives: They pay best.'[49] Thanks to related satiric exposés, like the following verses, spectators would have well understood the dense social ambiguity signalled by this brisk witticism of a poor gentleman who had slept with the spouse of a rich but humbly born cit:

> There never was a Squire,
> That could the least out-vie me;
> Long Wigg and rich Attire,
> I can afford to buy me:
> For while the Merchant walks the *Change*,
> I can in his little Warren range,
> And freely play the Game,
> Which I forebear to name;
> And when the sport is o'er,
> There's a reward in store,
> Bright Ginneys half a score,
> Thus I, I have ever more a full supply.[50]

Far from being a headlong clash of opposed classes, the typical cit scenario should more properly be viewed as the representation of tension between status *vis à vis* class power, the expression of an abiding inconsistency in early modern society.[51] The well-born man was supposed to be equally well-heeled; his social and economic power ideally corresponded and were configured as gentility. The base-born citizen was meant to be relatively powerless in *both* social and economic terms. What to do when the citizen's economic power outstripped his ascribed (i.e. low-born) status and matched or surpassed the wealth of those who claimed the superiority of 'gentlemen'?

Defoe, for one, exulted: 'In how superior a port or figure (as we now call it) do our tradesmen live, to what the middling gentry either do or can support!'[52] Likewise a newspaper of about the same time made use of the phrase, '*Middle Sort of Gentry*'.[53] These particular uses of 'middling' terminology are tantalizing, evidence of a lingering uncertainty. They suggest that when primacy in

48 Mountfort, *Greenwich Park*, ii, 18.   49 J. Leigh, *Kensington Gardens* (1720), iv, 61.

50 Anon., *The London-Libertine* (?1700), Early English Books Tract Supplements, Reel A3 (Ann Arbor, 1998).

51 Although this study does not necessarily concur with all its terms of reference or wider conclusions, the idea of status inconsistency was first suggested by a quite perceptive reading of the early modern social order and the latter's presence in literature, M. McKeon's *The Origins of the English Novel 1600–1740* (Baltimore, 1987).

52 D. Defoe, *The Complete English Tradesman* (1726), vol. I, 215.

53 *British Journal*, no. ccxiv (22 October 1726), [1], *italics reversed; ibid.*, no. lxxxviii (23 May 1724), [1]. See too *British Gazetteer*, [unnumbered] (10 April 1725), [1], which describes

his social positioning is given to wealth ('sort') instead of birth, the prosperous upper-middling trader achieves a standing parallel to that of the landed man who has, inversely, more pure blood but relatively less wealth. They prompted the question: if the second individual is identified as a 'gentleman' then why not the first? The City comedy, and this related tendency to place once distinct social terms like 'middling' and 'gentry' into apposition, contributed to a persistent apprehension that those outside the reputedly charmed circle of genteel pedigree were achieving more than their fair share of prosperity and, impertinently, wanting admission to this circle as part of the bargain. Or, rather, they were attempting to shuffle the criteria for membership as a way to resolve their precise social position and thereby account for the novel power which their excessive wealth gave them.

So many texts, ranging from prolix, scribbled correspondence to terse printed reportings of nuptials and obituaries for upper-middling London,[54] registered perceptions of an anomalous prosperity and an attendant social dislocation that it can prove a difficult exercise to separate fact from fiction. We simply cannot determine whether theatrical comedy merely reflected or mainly triggered these bouts of anxiety concerning the citizen's precise social position. To trace but one instance in detail. During the early 1700s Lady Isabella Wentworth developed quite a penchant for relaying news of some rich 'seteson' or other. She moved from something approaching awestruck envy, when asked to stand as godparent with two merchants worth in excess of 100,000 pounds apiece, to a barely disguised pique when reporting the intermarriage of the pedigreed (but relatively insolvent) with the meanly born (but crassly rich). Surely the extent of both the latter's fortune and vulgar ostentation was inflated each time the news passed from newspaper column to private epistle and back again during 1709.[55] With a delicious sense of irony and inevitability, life began to imitate art as Lady Wentworth reported the undoing of one of these same marriages less than three years later, in 1712. Of a City husband and his well-born wife

'metamorphos'd Tradesmen' who think 'because they have got Money, they have all the necessary Qualifications of Gentility'; *Prompter*, no. xiii (24 December 1734), [2]: 'If the *Middling Gentry* and *Trades-Folks* should follow their Example . . .'.

54 See, for instance, Alice to Christopher Hatton, 3 February 1687, in E. M. Thompson (ed.), *Correspondence of the Family of Hatton* (Camden Society, London, new series, 1878), vol. XXIII, 63, on the marriage of Lord Colrain's son to a merchant's daughter; the reaction of Montagu North, himself a former merchant from gentry stock, when he found in 1697 that the cost of apprenticing his nephew to the eastern trade was prohibitively expensive and so 'fitt onely for rich cittyzons sons or elder brothers sons in to[w]n' (Add. MS 32,500, f.168r., British Library); the examples cited in H. J. Habakkuk, *Marriage, Debt, and the Estates System. English Landownership 1650–1950* (Oxford, 1994), 193ff.

55 Isabella Wentworth to her son Peter, 23 December 1707 and 23 April 1709, in J. J. Cartwright (ed.), *The Wentworth Papers 1705–1739* (London, 1883), 62, 84. Such comments became quite ironic in light of Thomas Wentworth's marriage to the daughter of a shipbuilding magnate in 1711. See I. H. Tague, *Women of Quality. Accepting and Contesting Ideals of Femininity in England, 1690–1760* (Woodbridge, 2002), 78 and *passim*.

living it up at Bath, Lady Wentworth whispered: 'Mr. Gore desired her to goe no more into that company, but she told him she would and if citizens pretend'd to marry Quality they must take it for their pains.'[56] Yet we should pause to ask how much of this might be too good to be true, as much art intimating too much about what had really happened between the Gores. After all, Lady Wentworth had more than equal motive and opportunity to embellish this rumoured marital *contretemps* by appropriating the common currency of the dramatic cit com. Although like her peers, well-born and pressured by the newly prosperous yet obscurely descended, Wentworth also had affinity with Thomas Wentworth, the earl of Strafford who had, for all intents and purposes, been sent to the block in 1641 because of the then militant politics of London's citizenry.[57]

We shall return to the partisan dimensions of the cit figure's performance in the next chapter. For now, we will concentrate on how the repeated representation of ridden London merchants was an often visceral expression of ill-ease at this inconsistency between wealth and birth, this contradictory positioning in society. Irresolvable social disjunction made for persistent disparaging. That such disjunction was sufficient to perpetuate the belittling remedy of the comedic charivari may be seen in an eerily prescient item of related correspondence. Relaying gossip about high-society marriages in 1709, Anne Clavering mentions the possibility of cuckoldry: 'I wish the former disappointed or a pair of horns on his head. He's dealt rudely with an agreable young woman in this neighbourhood.' Did this remark and the close association of cuckoldry with London's affluent citizenry prompt Anne, in the very next sentence, to recount a recent instance of *mésalliance*; that 'Lord Northampton['s] second dau[ghter], the Town says, certainly marries Mr. Gore a citticen who has £5000 per annum'?[58] Given the implicit socio-cultural tensions which surrounded such alliances of 'quality' with 'condition', ancient pedigree and modern affluence, it seems more than coincidence that (alleged) cuckoldry resulted not for the rude, unnamed suitor but instead, if Lady Wentworth's later, post-nuptial intelligence from Bath is anything to go by, for the very same City heir who was certainly married to the daughter of a peer.

The spirit of contradiction that dogged the citizen household may be read as an attempt to deny (at the very same time as it registers) the persistent disjunction

56 Isabella to Peter Wentworth, 4 December 1712, in Cartwright, *Wentworth Papers*, 219. Mr Gore was William, the eldest son of Sir William Gore. He had married the daughter of George Compton, fourth earl of Northampton.

57 At least this was Lady Wentworth's perception. London's citizenry were far from united and their role in the mid-century crisis was complex. See R. Brenner, *Merchants and Revolution. Commercial Change, Political Conflict, and London's Overseas Traders 1550–1653* (Cambridge, 1993).

58 Anne to Sir James Clavering, 19 February 1709, in H. T. Dickinson (ed.), *The Correspondence of Sir James Clavering (1680–1748)* (Surtees Society, Durham, 1967), vol. CLXXVIII, 26.

between the experience of power, on the one hand, and its cultural configuration on the other. Both the cit comedies and wider discussions of alleged marital dysfunction among citizens bear subconscious signs of anxiety at a lingering status–class rift in the social fabric. They signal an inability to reach a socially definitive conclusion, to reconcile whether the prosperous 'middling' individual was or *was not* a citizen on account of his birth; *was* or was not a gentleman because his wealth surpassed that of the landowner. The social dislocation represented by the cit would endure as long as the transition from a status- to class-envisioned hierarchy was incomplete and gentility caught between these competing lines of social inequality. Yet perhaps this dislocation was especially acute during our period, amid the turbulent undercurrents of a prosperous yet fragile global economy; political innovation dogged by faction and possible counter-revolution at home and abroad; relentless growth of a metropolis ever more closely integrated into an urbane social network by means of an effusive print culture and more efficient carriage of both people and ideas.

Bearing in mind the difficulty of trying to define and discuss individuals whose very social identity and grouping were questionable, we will highlight some common traces of this abiding uncertainty and their place in the staged pageant of the cit's cuckolding. For while the comedy's message was typically meant to be one of obvious humiliation and social resolution, the ritualistic medium betrayed the ambiguity prompting the need for its repetitive performance.

Playwrights have their middling characters use a rather strange label to praise, or equally to condemn their women. Finding his wife with another man, Scribblescrabble, the City lawyer in Nicholas Rowe's *The Biter*, brands her a 'cocatrice'.[59] The cit figure from Pix's *Deceiver Deceived* employs the same term when his daughter refuses to marry into a rich mercantile family, favouring an impoverished gentleman instead.[60] Uxorious City husbands use the related diminutives of 'Cocky' and 'Keecky' as ironic terms of endearment.[61] To modern readers these puns are rather opaque. The association of the term 'cockatrice' with City women may not have been dwelled upon even by the playwrights themselves, phonically similar as it was to the masculine expletive of 'cuckold'. But, in fact, context sometimes made clear that the cockatrice was a monster (part bird, part serpent), remarkable because it was both a part of the heraldic lexicon, used to blazon hereditary genteel identity, and an emblem of miscegenation. A heraldic compendium of the day described the cockatrice and its ilk in the following terms: 'Monstrous Animals, such as are exorbitant from the general course of Nature either for Quality or Essence; and of these there

[59] N. Rowe, *Biter* (1705), ii, 37.
[60] M. Pix, *Deceiver Deceived* (1698), iii, 25. Also see S. Centlivre, *Mar-Plot* (1711), ii, 2.
[61] Sir Anthony Loveman, financier, in Pix, *Different Widows*, i, 5, and *passim*; Sago, the drugster, in S. Centlivre, *Basset Table* (1706), ii, 24.

3 'A satirical coat of arms', late seventeenth century

are divers Sorts, as Amphibia, that is, such as live sometimes as if they were Water Creatures, and other times as if Land Creatures.'[62] The resonance with Defoe's Moll Flanders and her 'amphibious Creature', her '*Land-water-thing*' of a '*Gentleman-Tradesman*', is unmistakable.[63] So too the echoes of different languages of social stratification.

Some texts made an analogous play out of the popular symbol of the cuckold, his horns, since antlered beasts also figured among the emblems of social superiority. Yet, at the same time, bestiality connoted unbridled lust and a concomitant confusion or absence of social order.[64] Citizens fear being 'dubbed' cuckolds in the way that the monarch or the heralds bestowed symbolic recognition of elite status.[65] A rare turn-of-the-century woodcut managed to tell the story of the citizen's cuckolding at the same time as its format underscored the tale's meaning (see Figure 3). Quartered like a coat of arms, it featured a gentleman

62 R. Blome, *The Art of Heraldry* (1685, fourth edition 1730), 214.

63 D. Defoe, *The Fortunes and Misfortunes of the Famous Moll Flanders* (Wordsworth edition, Ware, 1993), 55.

64 See, for example, the main quote in Weil, *Political Passions*, 134.

65 See, for instance, the ironic comment of the City knight, Sir Anthony Thinwit, in C. Molloy, *The Perplex'd Couple* (1715), v, 62, and, for those citizens who did marry well-born women, Heartwell's comment from W. Congreve, *The Old Batchelour* (1693), i, 7.

(and goat) on the left gesturing the citizen's horning.[66] The same gentleman features in the upper left quadrant kissing the citizen's wife. The two canines at upper right imply sexual intimacy. The gentleman reappears in the lower left quarter, behind the City wife presenting her new-born to a man (possibly her husband) carrying a stave as symbol of municipal authority. The last quadrant apparently depicts the citizen's rejection of his wife and her bastard. The female figure on the right border seems intended as a study in contrast. Wearing plainer clothes (not the fashionable headdress of the genteel City dame) and accompanied by a sow, she symbolizes an unquestioned but inferior status, a humble yet respectable and domesticated maternity. With a little more subtlety an item from *The Weekly Journal*, in describing those attending a masquerade ball, referred to a citizen with 'Ensigns on his Forehead'.[67] 'Ensigns' initially suggested the gentleman's proud armorial bearings but was really a backhanded way of saying that the citizen was thick-skulled, a wearer of antlers. Finally, a passing reference to the citizen's horning in a Restoration pamphlet (promoting colonial resettlement of all things) serves to demonstrate the longevity and prevalence of the stereotype. Hinting at their root cause, the Londoner's anomalous prosperity, it represented the customary horns as 'well drest and tipt with silver'.[68] A later description favoured gold.[69]

Calls for the theatre's reform occasionally objected to the disgraceful treatment meted out to the thriving citizen, sometimes citing the well-known example of Congreve's Fondlewife.[70] In response to this criticism, Elkanah Settle read the cuckold scenario at face value and disingenuously claimed that Fondlewife's fate was a 'true Poetick Justice, to expose the unreasonableness of such Superannuated Dotage'.[71] In other words, the significance of the cit comedy was simply to teach the moral that the old should not marry the young. Settle was deliberately trying to deny that the comedy and theatre had any further significance or power. His interpretation was obviously tongue-in-cheek for two reasons. First, as an experienced writer Settle was quite familiar with the far

[66] For the everyday, common use of this non-verbal sign, one that may well have been used onstage, see R. Adair, *Courtship, Illegitimacy and Marriage in Early Modern England* (Manchester, 1996), 159; R. Trumbach, *Sex and the Gender Revolution. Volume I: Heterosexuality and the Third Gender in Enlightenment London* (Chicago, 1998), 37; A. Fox, *Oral and Literate Culture in England 1500–1700* (Oxford, 2000), 327.

[67] *Weekly Journal*, no. 276 (8 February 1724), 1639. In physiognomy the forehead was considered the seat of shame.

[68] G. Alsop, 'A Character of the Province of Maryland' (1666), in C. C. Hall (ed.), *Narratives of Early Maryland 1633–1684* (New York, 1946), 378.

[69] T. Brown, *Amusements Serious and Comical, Calculated for the Meridian of London* (1700), quoted in A. M. Nagler (ed.), *A Source Book in Theatrical History* (New York, 1952), 250.

[70] See n. 25 above, and J. Collier, *A Short View of the Immorality, and Profaneness of the English Stage* (1698), 24; [G. Ridpath], *The Stage Condemn'd* (1698), 93; J. Swift, 'A Project for the Advancement of Religion' (1709), in H. Davis (ed.), *The Prose Works of Jonathan Swift* (Oxford, 1939), vol. II, 56.

[71] E. Settle, *A Defence of Dramatick Poetry* (1698), 88. For a broadly similar interpretive move, see also Anon., *The Stage Acquitted* (1699), 80–1.

from politically innocent workings of the citizen character. He was to employ elements in his own *City-Ramble* of 1711. Second, Settle gives the game away in the conclusion to his argument about 'May and December' relationships when he writes:

And if an Author would pick out such a Character for a little Stage Satyr, where can he meet with it but amongst the City or Court Quality? Such Inequality of Marriages are rarely to be found, but under the Roofs of Honour, for so Antiquated a Lover . . . must bring a Coach and Six, to carry off such a Young Bride.[72]

The passing references to 'quality' and 'honour' (i.e. birth, inherited social position) actually spoke volumes about how the scenario tried to resolve questions of social parity and domination or difference and subordination; to reconcile new money with ancient pedigree.[73]

A last set of telltale indications of the social dis-ease manifested by London's comic theatre may be found in the printed playbooks themselves. For instance, the playbook for Charles Johnson's *Generous Husband* features Carizales, a West Indian merchant, trying to make the best out of what he believes is proof of marital infidelity. Addressing his wife, the compositor of the quarto has the citizen say: 'When I am gone, I command you to espouse that young Fellow, whom the grey Heirs [read 'Hairs'] of this unfortunate old Man never yet offended.'[74] In referring to a citizen's occupation, rather than his genteel and leisured retirement, another playbook termed it his 'bas[i]ness' instead of his business.[75] Trifling as these thin quartos may seem, they were typically dedicated to elite individuals in the hope of material reward or some other patronage. Dedicatees ranged from the monarch down to plain gentlemen and often included descriptions of the person's virtues, a thumbnail sketch of their gentility. Amongst our comedies there are a few books dedicated to prominent London citizens. Three features of these epistles stand out. First, in addressing a citizen, the playwright is manifestly subscribing to (even inscribing) the individual's gentility, putting the merchant on a par with or literally placing him in the same position as the well-born landowner. Thus Susanna Centlivre's dedication to Sir Henry Furnesse (apprenticed to a hosier as the son of a bankrupt grocer he had since become an eminent financier, Flanders merchant, war contractor, one-time sheriff of London and baronet[76]) made particular play of his

[72] Settle, *Defence*, 89.

[73] Cf. D. M. Turner, *Fashioning Adultery. Gender, Sex and Civility in England, 1660–1740* (Cambridge, 2002), 97–102.

[74] C. Johnson, *Generous Husband* (1713), v, 59. A recent study of the early modern importance of male facial hair as a 'marker of procreative potential' would tend to support the alternate reading that this was a quite deliberate pun. See W. Fisher, 'The Renaissance Beard: Masculinity in Early Modern England', *Renaissance Quarterly* 54 (2001), 174.

[75] W. Walker, *Marry, Or Do Worse* (1704), ii, 18.

[76] G. S. De Krey, *A Fractured Society. The Politics of London in the First Age of Party 1688–1715* (Oxford, 1985), 145–6; Habakkuk, *Marriage*, 427.

'Honour' as a 'Worthy Citizen'.[77] In like manner, Thomas Durfey commended Sir William Scawen (merchant, Bank director, member of parliament, purchaser of a country seat, brother to a London alderman[78]) for his 'generous Actions'.[79] Second, the writer is at pains to distance those he or she would honour from the associations of the cuckold stereotype. Recalling ideas which we will examine more closely in the next chapter, Durfey therefore commended Scawen's 'harmonious Disposition . . . the rugged Cares and Disturbance that publick Affairs brings with it, which does so vexatiously affect the Heads of other great Men of Business, &c. does scarce ever ruffle your unclouded Brow so much as with a Frown' (or the imagined horns of a cuckold?). Third, and most obviously, the dedications discussed here are for plays where the cit's riding is not given a full dress rehearsal.

Paradoxically, then, conjectured or staged adultery was meant to mend adulteration of the social hierarchy, or deal to its 'disturbing wild cards' as one historian has recently termed them.[80] Hence a scene from David Crawfurd's *Courtship à la Mode* attempts a resolution by comparing the count of the gentleman's generative matter with the citizen's cash surplus. Yet it ultimately ends up short as the gentleman, Freelove, has 'spent' (slang for 'climaxed') too often:

SIR JOHN: Is the Goldsmith's Wife lost too, *Jack*?

FREELOVE: Yes faith, after a Month's Tryal, she weigh'd me in the Scales with (that massy lump of ill-shap'd Clay) her Husband, and finding I was some grains too light, she threw me aside.

NED: Would she not take thee for Bullion?

FREELOVE: No, your married women are always for ready Coyn; and my stock being exhausted, she wou'd not bargain; for the old Fox, her Husband, cou'd lend but little to my assistance.

CAPTAIN: . . . I hope thou hast got a Mint of thy own.

FREELOVE: A large Treasury may soon be spent, when 'tis in the Hands of an Extravagant Master.[81]

Furthermore, the stress on the imagined virility of the gentlemen-lovers, as opposed to the alleged infertility of the male citizens, may have spoken to the rather unnerving perception that both the size of elite families and the chances for a perpetuated lineage were in decline during the late Stuart period.[82]

[77] S. Centlivre, *Perplex'd Lovers* (1712), sig. A2[r].
[78] P. Gauci, *The Politics of Trade. The Overseas Merchant in State and Society, 1660–1720* (Oxford, 2001), 83, 92; De Krey, *Divided Society*, 145.
[79] T. Durfey, *Modern Prophets (*1709), epistle dedicatory to Sir William Scawen, Baronet, unpaginated. The dedication also prompted discussion in *Tatler*, no. 43 (19 July 1709), vol. I, 306–8.
[80] S. E. Whyman, *Sociability and Power in Late-Stuart England. The Cultural World of the Verneys 1660–1720* (Oxford, 1999), 31.
[81] D. Crawfurd, *Courtship à la Mode* (1700), i, 7.
[82] B. McCrea, *Impotent Fathers. Patriarchy and the Demographic Crisis in the Eighteenth-Century Novel* (Newark, 1998); Whyman, *Sociability and Power*, 44–5, 123.

Meanwhile, other texts rehearsed the social calculus and resulting discrepancy in more subtle ways. For example, when dedicating her play *The Different Widows* which featured a financier (Sir Anthony Loveman) in the typical predicament of the citizen, Mary Pix praised the widowed countess of Salisbury for her marital fidelity which ensured that her husband's name and power would pass to their son and down on through the generations.[83] From the opposite angle of view, *The Man of Manners* insisted that it was not seeking to deprecate the 'trading part of the People, which is so infinitely superior in Number and Wealth, to the Families who call themselves Gentry', when warning such commercial types about boasting of their birth 'if they have got a little elevated'. But with a knowing, ironic wink and extended word-play it continued: 'Indeed, some have been so obscure, that they can give no more Account of their Origin, than an old Fellow of his young Wife's Transactions, when he trusts her with a brisk young Fellow to a Play.'[84] In other words, their humble parentage cannot be reconciled to their current commercial success, a prosperity that allows their spouses the socially dubious (and sexually suspect) pleasure of attending the theatre in the company of the well-born, the self-proclaimed genteel (see chapters 4–6).

There was always something special about the citizen's cuckolding. Illicit sexual behaviour was at once the great leveller but also what distinguished the prosperous and powerful citizen as socially '(in)-distinguishable'. Thus a verse description of London's famed Horn Fair singled out 'ten thousand Cits [who] might lead the Van, | With Coat of Arms of marry'd Man', transforming it into a parody of the Lord Mayor's parade.[85] Conversely, it is interesting to observe precisely what happens to this logic when the elite male of pedigree and landed estate is depicted as the victim of marital infidelity. William Ramesey's *Gentlemans Companion* described the victim's position as heralded not by horns but by the wearing of '*Acteons* Livery', livery being the distinctive costumes of bound labour (whether referring specifically to the offices of London City companies or the drudgery of servanthood it is not entirely clear).[86] In a similar vein, research by Tim Meldrum into the lives of servants in the metropolis during the late Stuart period has uncovered a fascinating case where a footman not only had an affair with his mistress, but also attempted to perform a skimmington in front of his former master's (John Dormer, Esq.) London residence. The errant footman evidently knew how to rub salt into the wound for he was alleged to have shouted: 'Room for cuckolds, here comes a company! Room for cuckolds, here comes my lord mayor!'[87] In other words, gentlemen-cuckolds

[83] Pix, *Different Widows*, epistle dedicatory, sig. A2^{r-v}.

[84] E. Jones, *The Man of Manners* ([third edition], 1737), 55–6. Thanks to Tim Hitchcock for drawing this title to my attention. Cf. Turner, *Fashioning Adultery*, 113.

[85] *British Gazetteer*, no. 26 (23 October 1725), [4].

[86] W. Ramesey, *The Gentlemans Companion* (1672), 97.

[87] T. Meldrum, 'London Domestic Servants from Depositional Evidence, 1650–1750: Servant–Employer Sexuality in the Patriarchal Household', in T. Hitchcock, P. King, and P. Sharpe (eds.),

were further humiliated by being notionally degraded to the level of base commoners, whereas the fictive cuckolding of cits *raised* the issue of their gentility for prosperous 'middling' men.

Problems of power were inherited by the successful citizen and those who attempted to represent him. We should now be in a better position to understand the seemingly inappropriate, often awkward injection of sexual impropriety into contexts where it initially appears incongruous, unwarranted and even unfathomable to modern eyes. For instance, while their political ambitions will be the subject of the next chapter, we can at least begin to comprehend the logic behind a satire which included these *ad hominem* remarks about two former sheriffs of London, now knights, Sir Charles Duncombe and Sir Edward Willis:

> Has often try'd in vain to mount the Stage:
> Profuse in Gifts and Bribes to God and Man,
> To ride the City-Horse, and wear the Chain
> . . .
> A Knighted Booby Insolent and Base
> '*Whom Man no Manners gave, nor God no grace.*
> The Scorn of Women and the Shame of Men,
> Matcht at Threescore to innocent Fifteen;
> Hag-rid with jealous Whimsies let us know
> He thinks he's Cuckold '*cause he should be so.*'
> His vertuous Wife exposes to the Town,
> And fears her crimes because he knows his own.[88]

Similarly, we may grasp the reasoning behind the quip of *The London Spy* on viewing the dedication of a charity hospital: 'As many Names were Pencill'd out upon the Walls, as if there had been the Genealogy of the Twelve Tribes, or a publick Register of all the Topping Cuckolds in the City.'[89] Occasionally, we can even see how the fictive cit helped contemporaries make playful sense of their own ambivalent situation. Thus Nathaniel Harley, a younger son apprenticed to the East India Company, wrote to his brother from Aleppo describing the shifting fortunes of their family in the following terms: 'Pray Sir inform your clark who superscribes your letters that no merchants are wrote Esqs. but fools, coxcombs,

Chronicling Poverty. The Voices and Strategies of the English Poor 1640–1840 (London, 1997), 59. Intriguingly, Lawrence Stone's discussion of the related court action also makes the claim that it was Mrs Dormer, not her husband, who was of humble origin. See L. Stone, *The Road to Divorce. England 1539–1987* (Oxford, 1990), 271, and related contemporary comment in Cartwright, *Wentworth Papers*, 329–30.

88 D. Defoe, *Reformation of Manners* (1702), 13–14. See also F. H. Ellis (ed.), *Poems on Affairs of State. Augustan Satirical Verse. Volume VI: 1697–1704* (New Haven, 1970), 409–10. As a tory MP Duncombe had been impeached by the Commons but went on to become a London alderman and sheriff. Willis, at the age of fifty, had had the recent but ambiguous fortune to marry the eighteen-year-old daughter of Sir Thomas Cuddon.

89 *London Spy* (March 1699), part v, 15 (printed as '51').

and cuckolds.'[90] And, finally, it is abundantly clear why Richard Steele was compelled to introduce a domineering wife into his exemplary comedy. For the well-born Mrs Sealand tries to overrule her husband in choosing a son-in-law in order to 'keep the Blood as pure, and as regularly descended as may be', to rectify the anomaly of her having married a merchant.[91] On the other hand, Mr Sealand's 'riding' tacitly assumed that he had a half-plausible claim to gentility, to power, to begin with. He had to have a certain something to lose in order to be potentially dishonoured since honour was 'only truly challenged in a direct confrontation between social *equals*'.[92] (And Steele further fudged the issue, suggesting that Mr Sealand was a once bankrupt younger brother of gentry stock re-established in London incognito.)

In contrast to its repetition by other texts, when represented at London's patent theatres the citizen's horning was quite finely and deliberately pointed. Other discursive spaces, especially the law-courts with their narratives of adultery as part of proceedings for slander, libel or extra-marital fornication, and other media, particularly ballads, chapbooks and periodicals, often found the City wife in a compromising position which receives very little attention in late Stuart comedy. Beyond the theatre it was something of a cliché that the wayward City wife would first turn her attention to her husband's male servants, particularly the household's young apprentice.[93] As the ballad *Advice to the Ladies of London, In the Choice of their Husbands* wryly recommended:

> But above all, the rank Citizen hate;
> the Court or the Country chuse rather;
> Would you have a Blockhead that gets an Estate
> by [the] Sins of the Cuckold his Father?
> The [sne]aking Clown intreaging does mar,
> the Prentices huffing and canting,
> Cit puts on his Sword, when without *Temple-Bar*
> and goes to *Whitehall* a Gallanting.[94]

While it was not impossible for that apprentice to be well-born, the drama seems to have avoided this particular scenario in order to stress that a tightly defined

90 Nathaniel to Edward Harley [the Auditor], 6 September 1712, HMC, *Portland* 29, 2 (1893), 255.

91 R. Steele, *Conscious Lovers* (1723), iii, 46.

92 R. Cust, 'Honour and Politics in Early Stuart England: The Case of Beaumont *v*. Hastings', *PP* 149 (1995), 76.

93 On court proceedings see notes 96–8 below. For cheap print compare the findings of J. Wiltenburg, *Disorderly Women and Female Power in the Street Literature of Early Modern England and Germany* (Charlottesville, 1992), 152–7; further examples may be found in Anon., *Cambridge Jests*, 12–13; *London Spy* (January 1699), part iii, 5; *London Terraefilius*, no. ii (1707), 12–15; *Female Tatler*, no. 85 (18–20 January 1710); *British Gazetteer*, [unnumbered] (20 August 1720), 1689; Anon., *The Honest London Spy, Discovering the Base and Subtle Intrigues of the Town* (?1725), 87–100; Anon., *The Crafty London Prentice* (?1730).

94 See n. 16.

and unambiguous social superiority, blood lineage, was at stake.[95] Rather than fumble behind the shop counter with a beardless youth who may himself have been of common status, City wives in comedy typically leave the domestic sphere, their husbands' workplace, and rendez-vous with their gentlemen-lovers in spaces of leisured resort. The only dramatically developed example of this first narrative from our period is James Drake's *The Sham-Lawyer* (1697), which finds the gentleman, Friendly, fraudulently signing on as an attorney's clerk in order to have access to his former mistress, now the attorney's wife.

Reports of legal proceedings for alleged sexual impropriety also show up an instructive point of similarity with the comic drama. Study of the war of words in London's streets has demonstrated how sexual slander was deployed as a weapon when no adultery had actually occurred.[96] Instead, vituperative oaths of 'whore' and 'cuckold' (even allegations of scolding *per se*[97]) expressed tensions arising from a diverse range of problems. From the evidence of court records, David Turner describes cuckoldry as a 'pungent means of voicing rivalries, expressing social grievances and undermining status and authority, as well as offering opportunities for wit and social display'.[98] Such narrative dexterity further reinforces the idea that late Stuart playgoers would have quite easily read the staged cuckoldings for what they were; at once having everything and ultimately nothing to do with actual bodily transgressions.[99] This said, the intimate nature of the citizen's humiliation is consistent with arguments that the reputations of early modern men did indeed extend to sexual honour. Furthermore, casting aspersions on a man's patriarchal authority has recently been shown to have been common currency among males disputing rival claims for social precedence. One axis of social structuration interfaced with another.[100]

It is therefore missing the point to argue that plays like Ravenscroft's *London Cuckolds* 'lack any particular anger and trade on what almost all writers . . . discerned as a taste for farce and meaningless debauchery' and, at best,

95 For the well-born apprentice, see also chapter 7. For an example of contemporaries using this comedic situation to make sense of their own place in society, see A. Jessop (ed.), *The Lives of the . . . Norths* (London, 1890), vol. I, 407.

96 See especially L. Gowing, *Domestic Dangers. Women, Words, and Sex in Early Modern London* (Oxford, 1996); Trumbach, *Sex and the Gender Revolution*, 25–49; B. Capp, *When Gossips Meet. Women, Family, and Neighbourhood in Early Modern England* (Oxford, 2003), esp. 185–266.

97 Ingram, '"Scolding women cucked or washed"', 66.

98 D. M. Turner, '"Nothing is so secret but shall be revealed": The Scandalous Life of Robert Foulkes', in T. Hitchcock and M. Cohen (eds.), *English Masculinities 1660–1800* (London, 1999), 188–90.

99 However, by the same token, this characterization of the cit stereotype should not be taken to imply that late Stuart comedy did not, or could not, comment meaningfully on sexual behaviour and morality. For an introduction to these other dimensions of sexuality and the drama, see M. E. Novak, 'Libertinism and Sexuality', in S. J. Owen (ed.), *A Companion to Restoration Drama* (Oxford, 2001), 53–68.

100 A. Shepard, *Meanings of Manhood in Early Modern England* (Oxford, 2003), 152–85.

'reflected . . . debates on marriage'.[101] Similar but incomplete assessments of Ravenscroft's most popular piece, and the tradition it came to epitomize for late Stuart audiences, include the judgement that it is 'morally and socially unreflective', or 'rollicking good fun with no ulterior point whatever. It is often considered a "political" play . . . but there is no serious attack on the cuckolds, and indeed the play was staged annually on the Lord Mayor's Day especially for the cits'.[102]

Instead, this chapter confirms that whilst the cit's chastisement does seem to have aimed at achieving a pleasantly contrived solution or, at least, a soothing but temporary release from social dislocation and ambiguity, it was, for this very reason, neither mindless nor without an underlying socio-cultural significance. By taking a closer look at some of the more complex variations on the cit scenario, the next chapter will further demonstrate that late Stuart comedy was, in fact, persistently satirical and political. When the distribution of power in society was contested, and when this same contestability helped fuel formal partisan division and polemic, the comedy could hardly fail to be otherwise.

101 S. Staves, *Players' Scepters. Fictions of Authority in the Restoration* (Lincoln, NE, 1979), 168.

102 D. Hughes, *English Drama 1660–1700* (Oxford, 1996), 230; R. D. Hume, *The Development of English Drama in the Late Seventeenth Century* (Oxford, 1976), 355. Cf. S. J. Owen, 'Restoration Drama and Politics: An Overview', in Owen (ed.), *A Companion to Restoration Drama* (Oxford, 2001), 126–39.

3 Genteel authority and the virtue of commerce

> *Tradesmen* grumbling at the *Taxes*, *Merchants* at their *Losses*, most Men complaining for want of *Business*, and all Men in *Business*, for want of *Money*: Every Man upon *Change* looking with as peevish a Countenance, as if he had unluckily stumbled upon his *Wife's Failings*, and unhappily become a witness to his own *Cuckoldome*.
>
> E. Ward, *A Trip to Jamaica* (1698)

Late Stuart dramatists varied the basic cit cuckold scenario. Hence we cannot claim all late Stuart City comedy represented gentility, the defining of society's superiors, simply as the configuration of class and status power, where status as lineage had priority over wealth. In quite a number of instances this would provide an incomplete reading of the plot on offer, misinterpreting the comedy's articulation of the complex nature of both gentility and elite London society. There was often more to the cuckold plot because it figured gentility in a more intricate manner. How, for instance, are we to account for performances which conclude with no actual cuckoldry, despite the citizens' suspicions that their wives are unfaithful or their daughters promiscuous, and those comedies which choose to 'horn' the well-born male?

The solution traced in the present chapter is that the aforementioned variations on the standard scenario not only involve the thinking through of inconsistency between the power situations of status and class, but also factor in a third element of political command. For 'the gentry' were not just a socio-economic elite. They were also early modern society's governors.[1] Some citizen comedies therefore put into play the question of political power, resulting from the exercise of authority, in addition to the already complex interrelationship of status (birth) and class (wealth). Thus we will trace how discourses of sexuality and gender further contributed to the presentation of gentility as a superiority which claimed to be not only natural but also above relations of economic exchange and ownership, thereby entailing the right to hold the larger share of political power. Indeed, the impetus behind many of these plays on the cit

[1] For extensive treatment of the broader conceptual and historical issues, see M. J. Braddick, *State Formation in Early Modern England, c.1550–1700* (Cambridge, 2000), 9–100.

cuckold setpiece was itself political, the product of partisan divisions which criss-crossed both the City and the metropolis during the later seventeenth and early eighteenth centuries.

It is crucial to make a prefatory comment on the meaning of a central term encountered in our texts, namely, 'virtue'. Although it bore obvious ethical and religious connotations, when used in relation to social structuration virtue usually conjured ideas of the even-handed exercise of political authority on the basis of the possession of a certain kind of socio-economic power, that is, the inherited country estate. Women in the City comedies stand as figures of the potential for virtue on the part of their menfolk. If virtuous, the men will be accorded the title of 'gentleman'. Given the previous two chapters, it almost goes without saying that the drama persistently tested this assumption.

In representing possible adultery (or perhaps nothing more than the disobedient or domineering female), some reworkings of the basic City scenario focus as much on the failure of authority, the inability to achieve legitimate patriarchal rule over social inferiors, as they do the matter of lineage. Normatively, a gentleman's loss of command within his household was believed to render him unfit to exercise authority in society at large, 'make their Private Character an Obstruction to their Publick' as one periodical essay explained on behalf of some '*honest Gentlemen*' standing for parliamentary election late in the reign of Queen Anne.[2] By dint of social rule a gentleman accrued virtue to his name as self-perpetuating proof of his generosity, his inherited superiority. Conversely, the relinquishing of authority, the fall from virtue, compromised that inheritance. Gentlewomen, and their chastity in particular, stood as emblems of their fathers' and husbands' virtue: the ability and right to authority as guaranteed by a particular status–class nexus, that of the inherited country estate. In this way, female bodies symbolized male (dis)empowerment.

This much is evident from one of the few early eighteenth-century comedies with a rural *mise-en-scène*. Charles Johnson's *Country Lasses* finds two gentlemen lost in the countryside. One of them, Heartwell, falls in love with the ward of an impoverished gentleman turned yeoman farmer. Heartwell voices his intention to marry the young woman but is ridiculed by Modely in the following terms:

MODELY: . . . He that purchases an Estate where all the World take a Right of Common may build Churches for Atheists, and Alms-Houses for Misers.

HEARTWELL: But a little legal Inclosure is for the Comfort of our Lives, when the Land has been carefully and virtuously cultivated.

[2] The quote comes from *Examiner*, no. 20 (20–24 July 1713), vol. IV, [1]. Similar thinking is readily evident, for instance, in W. Ramesey, *The Gentlemans Companion* (1672), 183, 199. See also R. Cust, 'Honour and Politics in Early Stuart England: The Case of Beaumont *v*. Hastings', *PP* 149 (1995), 57–94; the essay series in *Transactions of the Royal Historical Society*, sixth series, 6 (1996).

. . .

MODELY: Indeed? Ah pretty Doe, Doe, fling two thousand Pound a Year away upon a Cottage *Marian* – Take the Refuse of a Bumpkin to your Marriage-Bed, and after that be the Cuckold of a Plowman.

HEARTWELL: How! What!

MODELY: Ay, ten to one but some Sinewy Thresher, who has warm'd her brisk Blood at a Mop or a Wake, steps into your Place, and delivers down a Posterity of young Flail-drivers, known by the Name of *Heartwell*' –

HEARTWELL: Fie *Modely*, no more of this; you know her Virtue is unsully'd as her Beauty; besides, her Education has been above these Clods.[3]

Cuckoldry, the potential fate of those who engage in commerce and later buy land, is rejected on the grounds of female chastity as the playwright later reveals his virtuous heroine to be the blue-blooded heiress to a substantial country estate. In other words, the chaste and well-born wife will free her spouse for the performance of his civic duty, the exercise of political authority. He remains in command of his wife and landed estate. Both are benignly husbanded, ensuring his independence and right to authority in wider society and therefore underwriting his identification as 'gentleman'. He is at once empowered but ideologically positioned above relations of exchange as the steward of his acres. Likewise, his wife's virtue situates her body beyond the sexual marketplace as the unquestioned possession of the gentleman, intended for the begetting of heirs and the continuation of an equally virtuous line of gentlemen and -women.[4]

Gentility incorporates and mystifies particular class situations, those of agrarian capitalism, configuring them as a natural and inherited superiority (status). Simultaneously, it validates the claim of the well-born landowner to exercise political authority for the larger public good on the grounds that his inherited position is, ideally, what ensures that the 'gentleman' will not fall victim to the corrupting and selfish interests of economic exchange but remain virtuous, a just and selfless governor.

By contrast, of course, the London citizen has no such luck. The body of the citizen's wife assumes a decidedly negative position in gentility's socio-political configuration. Like the gentlewoman of *The Country Lasses*, the City woman's chastity also stands for 'virtue'. But, as we might now anticipate, that virtue is persistently compromised. While their husbands engage in commercial enterprise, accruing economic power to equal or trump that of the well-born landowner, the citizens' wives are represented as trading in commodities of their own, selling their bodies, sullying their chastity, and, in a crucial extension, the

[3] C. Johnson, *Country Lasses* (1727), iv, 44–5.

[4] For the discursive negotiation of the gentleman as paternal steward and market-driven improver, see A. McRae, *God Speed the Plough. The Representation of Agrarian England, 1500–1660* (Cambridge, 1996).

virtuous potential of their menfolk.[5] John Vanbrugh's *Confederacy* features two women who each scheme to charm money out of the other's spouse. One husband, the scrivener Gripe, grows impatient at his wife's gallivanting which is described in terms of the marketplace:

GRIPE: . . . Have I not reason to be in a Passion? tell me that.
CLARISSA: You must tell her for what, my Life.
GRIPE: Why, for the Trade you drive, my Soul.
FLIPPANTA [their maid]: Look you, Sir, pray take things right. I know, Madam does fret you a little now and then, that's true; but in the Fund she is the softest, sweetest, gentlest Lady breathing: Let her but live entirely to her own Fancy, and she'll never say a word to you from Morning to Night.
GRIPE: Oons, let her but stay at home, and she shall do what she will. In reason that is.[6]

Time and again the comedies resort to this conflation of commercial exchange and the discrediting of female chastity (indicated here by a pun on 'fund'), the male citizen's inability to ensure his woman's virtue representing the market's corruption of any political authority he might otherwise wield.

In the following dialogue, for instance, a financier's instruments of credit are associated with female virginity.[7] Both relied on elusive notions of reputation to maintain their value in their respective markets, commercial and marital. Ultimately the greedy cit figure, Caprice, is portrayed as being more concerned about the strength of his credit than the virtue of his daughter, courted by the genteel Bellamy who, when discovered, pretends that he was only after one of the household servants and not the maiden Julia:

CAPRICE: Ha, what is this Rogue doing; endeavouring to get in there? O the Thief! He has found out the very Room where all my Bills and Money lies: I wish I had my Gun . . . Pray, Sir, what are you doing there?
BELLAMY: What, surpriz'd! What the Devil shall I say now!
CAPRICE: I say, Sir, what was your Business there?
BELLAMY: Business! Why, Sir, I had no Business at all, only to, to, to – that is, I thought it had been the Way out.

. . .

Well, Sir, since you have found me out, I'll tell you the whole Truth. I took this for one of your Maids Bed-Chambers; so without telling you my Design, you may guess what it was. I confess my self to blame, for offering any thing like this in your Family: But as you were once Young your self, I hope you'll make some Allowances for this Warmth of Blood.

5 Admittedly some comedies were not too concerned about the precise details of the transactions, featuring City women who paid gentlemen lovers for their services and not the other way around.

6 J. Vanbrugh, *Confederacy* (1705), iv, 51–2. 'The Funds' were government stocks instituted to finance England's war efforts, but in the singular (as here) the term also suggests the lower body.

7 A similar equation was made by Daniel Defoe: 'A tradesman's credit and a virgin's virtue ought to be equally sacred from the tongues of men', in his *The Complete English Tradesman* (1726), vol. I, 133. See S. Sherman, 'Lady Credit No Lady; or, the Case of Defoe's "Coy Mistress," Truly Stat'd', *Texas Studies in Literature and Language* 37, 2 (1995), 185–214.

CAPRICE: And had you no Design upon any thing more substantial than a Maiden-head?
BELLAMY: I own my Design was upon that very Transitory Thing.
. . .
CAPRICE: How he stammer'd for an Excuse; I believe he has not been a Thief long, for he scarce knows his Trade yet.[8]

In similar fashion, the wife of the war profiteer in William Burnaby's *Reform'd Wife* refers to her flirtations with other men as 'ventures'.[9] Occasionally some of our texts pulled no punches and featured their citizens as wittols, husbands who connived at or naively ignored their wives' indiscretions in the hope of material gain.[10]

As the ultimately uncontrollable and mysterious forces of the market were often feminized – for example as the imperious goddess Fortune or fickle Lady Credit – so too were City women anthropomorphic miniatures of the new economy held to rule England as it ascended to global power.[11] For example, William Chetwood's *Stock-Jobbers* features three brokers conversing as follows:

SIR JOHN WEALTHY: . . . this Fall of the *South-Sea* Stock vexes me confoundedly.
BEAU NOODLE: Ay, Mr. *Wealthy*, that and your Neice happen'd to be of a Mind; they both fell *backwards* at the same Time.
SIR JOHN WEALTHY: Right, Sir: Look ye, Mr. *Moneywise*, what need you make such a Splutter about a Fall in my Neice's Stock? It's what's common with us Citizens. If my Neice make a Cuckold of you before she has you, this damn'd *South Sea* makes a Cuckold of me after I had laid out all my Estate upon her, and that's the Devil.[12]

The City woman's possible incontinence figures the market's perceived instability. The jealous husband's (or suspicious father's) lack of mastery makes for an equally unbalanced socio-political personality incapable of exercising reasoned authority or ensuring virtue. This authority is instead secured by the rational integrity of the owner of inherited acres who, supposedly, has the material means to be above sordid exchange and can therefore guarantee both his women's chastity and his virtue, or, in a word, their 'gentility'.

Citizen figures jealously doubt their wives' chastity, forecasting that they will eventually discover their women are unfaithful (for in a number of comedies they turn out not to be promiscuous yet it is the father's or husband's suspicion for the first four acts which is more important). The male citizen's domestic

[8] C. Molloy, *Coquet* (1718), iii, 52–4. [9] W. Burnaby, *Reform'd Wife* (1700), v, 38.
[10] See Dick Stockjobb in T. Durfey, *Richmond Heiress* (1693); Sordico in [G. Bowes], *Love the Leveller* (1704); Graspall in E. Haywood, *Wife To Be Lett* (1724).
[11] See, for example, *Spectator*, no. 3 (3 March 1711), vol. I, 14–17. See also the contrasting interpretations of Sherman, 'Lady Credit'; J. F. O'Brien, 'The Character of Credit: Defoe's "Lady Credit," *The Fortunate Mistress*, and the Resources of Inconsistency in Early Eighteenth-Century Britain', *ELH* 63 (1996), 603–31.
[12] [W. R. Chetwood], *Stock-Jobbers* (1720), iii, 36.

angst serves as metaphor for involvement in speculative commercial relations, or what Edward Harley came to refer to as the 'machine of paper credit supported only by imagination' and had allowed Thomas Burnet to juxtapose

> a mind at Leisure in the Country, than to one that's hurryed here in Town, where Confusion is the only thing one regularly meets with. For the Merchant is in a Confusion for fear Trade shoud be ruined, the Stockjobber for fear the Funds shoud be paid with a Spunge.[13]

As the cit falls victim to whispers, opinions and appetites, he envisages an outcome of intercourse (or exchange) and, ultimately, possible bastardy (uncertain profit). Hence Sir Miles Cook could comment facetiously during the deflationary recoinage of 1696, 'the golden citizens padlock their guineas as they do their wives', or, at much the same time, Ned Ward could refer to 'most Men complaining for want of *Business*, and all Men in *Business*, for want of *Money*: Every Man upon *Change* looking with as peevish a Countenance, as if he had unluckily stumbled upon his *Wife's Failings*, and unhappily become a witness to his own *Cuckoldome*.'[14]

In other words, the citizens' wealth is notional. It exists largely on paper and is perceived as being a matter of insubstantial fiction (or 'jealous Whimsies' as Defoe described it, see p. 66), rather than in the apparently solid and inherited form of real estate which guarantees the landowners' independence, incorruptibility and continued socio-political pre-eminence as 'gentlemen'. William Stratford captured this distinction for his patron at a crucial time for the nation's economy:

> I hope this will find you safe at Welbeck and full of the satisfaction of viewing some of the noblest manors in the world which you now call your own. A more solid as well as more honest estate, than any got in the extravagant acquisitions of the South Sea.[15]

The True Conduct of Persons of Quality put it this way: 'Being always submissive to the Decrees of Providence', the providence by which the gentleman had inherited his particular socio-economic position, 'his Consolation is lodged in his own Virtue; and as nothing is able to ravish from him that precious

[13] Harley [the Auditor] to the earl of Oxford, 25 June 1720, HMC, *Portland* 29, 5 (1899), 599; Burnet to George Duckett, 18 March 1714, in D. N. Smith (ed.), *The Letters of Thomas Burnet to George Duckett, 1712–1722* (Roxburghe Club, London, 1914), 59. See also W. Bulstrode, *Essays* (1724), 15–16.

[14] Cook to Sir G. Treby at Cambridge, 13 August 1696, HMC, *Fitzherbert* 32, 1 (1893), 42; E. Ward, *A Trip to Jamaica With a True Character of the People and Island* ([third edition], 1698), 6. See also a similar jibe noted by Pepys following the Great Fire in *Pepys*, 20 October 1666, vol. VII, 333 and related comments reported in *ibid.*, 13 September 1667, vol. VIII, 435; 18 May 1668, vol. IX, 204.

[15] Stratford to Edward Harley, 19 June 1720, HMC, *Portland* 29, 7 (1901), 276.

Treasure which is included in himself, so nothing has power enough to render him unhappy'.[16]

The citizens' 'interest' (the term often used as a negative reference to the relations of exchange in which the citizen was mired) prevents their independence because they are placed at the mercy of market considerations or 'riches . . . fluent and mutable', thus spoiling their claims to the virtuous and independent exercise of socio-political rule, to gentility.[17] Once again, the represented male physiology could function as barometer for this socio-political disqualification. Here the citizen is depicted as choleric, or perhaps melancholy, but certainly never sanguine.[18] Sometimes sour and quietly resentful, more often passionately distracted and mad with suspicion, he worries about the state of his credit which could, of course, depend on the presentation of an image of domestic harmony to the world.[19] Not surprisingly, in the wake of the boom-and-bust of the South Sea Bubble of 1720, satirists found it especially easy to link speculative mania with social instability, political confusion and bodily chaos:

> What Numbers of upstart Figures we meet
> Set up by Stockjobbing in every Street?
> They're so fond of their *Arms* when they come to approach
> They can hardly for Staring, get into their Coach;
> But when we examine their true Pedigree,
> We trace their Original from the *South Sea.*
> . . .
> It is such as no other Sea yet ever had,
> Instead of preventing, 'twill make People mad.
> Distracting their Reason to such a Degree,
> That head-long they throw themselves in the *South Sea.*[20]

Returning to the comedy *The Confederacy*, we find that the scrivener Gripe is not at all reassured by his wife's pledges of meek and mild constancy and he begins to doubt his own place in society:

16 N. Rémond des Cours, *The True Conduct of Persons of Quality* (1694), 5. For further statement of a similar logic, see [W. Darrell], *A Gentleman Instructed in the Conduct of a Virtuous and Happy Life* (1704, fourth edition 1709), 53.

17 [B.B.], *The Young Gentlemans Way to Honour in Three Parts* (1678), 97.

18 Although there was never a total consensus, popular opinion often ranked the humours to the extent that sanguinity was considered the tendency of the well-born whilst the meaner sort possessed constitutions dominated either by choler or melancholy. Forthcoming work will examine this issue at greater length than possible here, and see too the account of how age, sex and status were believed embodied, in A. Shepard, *Meanings of Manhood in Early Modern England* (Oxford, 2003), 47–69.

19 C. Muldrew, *The Economy of Obligation. The Culture of Credit and Social Relations in Early Modern England* (London, 1998), 148–72, 298–303.

20 Anon., *The South Sea Ballad, Set by A Lady* (1720). Early English Books Tract Supplements, Reel A6 (Ann Arbor, 1998).

GRIPE: I don't know what I can ask, and yet I'm not satisfy'd with what I have neither, the Devil mixes in it all, I think, Complaisant or Perverse, it feels just as't did.

FLIPPANTA: Why, then your Uneasiness is only a Disease, Sir, perhaps a little Bleeding and Purging wou'd relieve you.[21]

By nervously questioning his wife's chastity because its absence will ruin his credit, the citizen reveals how concern for his interest pre-empts virtue. It comes as little surprise when we later find the suggestion that Gripe's passionate engrossment makes for excessive heat which not only incapacitates any ability to exercise a social duty of reasoned control, but also unfits him for the begetting of 'Family' and the 'blessing' of a male heir.[22] As his wife says with mock sincerity: 'But don't swear and curse thy self at this fearful rate, don't my Dove: Be temperate in your Words, and just in all your Actions, 'twill bring a Blessing upon you and your Family.'[23] Even Steele's exemplary Mr Sealand is described as a 'moody old Fellow' to whom 'there's no offering Reason . . . especially when [they are] Rich'.[24]

At this point we should note too that the apparent emphasis on a certain hot-headedness is not as contradictory of the cit's lack of manly vigour, the absence of a virile heat, discussed earlier. The cit's passion or moroseness is linked causatively to exertion and exhaustion in the course of his business, on the one hand, and the further stresses brought on by his troubled marriage to a domineering or wayward woman on the other. As a result, the cit's economy of bodily fluids, already deficient in terms of his humble birth, is in overdraft: an excess is consumed worrying about his credit and inhibits his generative potential, or the transformation of blood into seed. This tendency to allude specifically to the cit's cerebral 'melt-down', rather than manual fatigue, was entirely in keeping with Hippocratic and then Galenic influences on early modern notions of procreation and the pivotal role which they assigned to the brain in the concoction of semen.[25] Hence, to offer one particularly pointed example, Ned Ward's poem *Character of a Covetous Citizen* explained the ultimate marital consequence of the cit's angst-ridden preoccupation with business: 'No Nights endearments does the Churl dispense. But kills her with the want of due Benevolence.'[26]

Therefore, to the early modern spectator, the citizen's jealousy was not exclusively psychological but physical, social and political too; a means to figure his

[21] Vanbrugh, *Confederacy*, iv, 54.

[22] See also John Graunt's assessment of London's health, quoted in A. Wear, *Knowledge and Practice in English Medicine, 1550–1680* (Cambridge, 2000), 164.

[23] Vanbrugh, *Confederacy*, v, 69. [24] R. Steele, *Conscious Lovers* (1723), i, 16.

[25] For a suggestive overview of classical understandings of the 'economy of bodily pleasures', see M. Foucault (trans. R. Hurley), *The Use of Pleasure. Volume 2 of The History of Sexuality* (New York, 1985), 125ff; and, *The Care of the Self. Volume 3 of The History of Sexuality* (New York, 1986), 105ff.

[26] E. Ward, *The Character of a Covetous Citizen* (1701), 7.

lack of gentility. Considering the problem of jealousy in marriage, *The Gentlemans Companion* incidentally reached a conclusion about the deeper significance of such passion with an extra twist, namely that it was the 'weakest thing a man can possibly be guilty of, especially a *Gentleman*. And extremely discommendable, in that it argues he has either an ill Opinion of her, *or himself*.'[27] *The Censor* elaborated:

> I conceive it an Infirmity arising from a Poorness of Spirit. That which is *Distrust* in the Breast in point of *Commerce*, is *Jealousy* in point of *Love*: Now to suppose a Man *must* defraud me, because he *may*, is a Suspicion low and ungenerous . . . So, to suspect a Woman will be careless of her Honour, because she has a Power of playing false with me, is not only encouraging a base Fear, but carries with it a *tacit Confession of my own Want of Merit*.[28]

The socio-political rhetoric of gentility, further fuelled by a revival of classical ideas of civic humanism, held that the gentleman had a born duty to sacrifice his self-interest for the benefit of state and society. Ideally, virtue was the price paid for the inheritance of a privileged and dominant position in society. It is in this figuring of the capacity for gentlemanly virtue that we find the explanation for the variations of the standard scenario noted earlier. These include plays which find the citizen wife represented as neither well-born (a young gentlewoman married to an older middling man as we saw earlier), nor unfaithful to her spouse even though her husband speculates that she will be at some point in the future. Variation was possible because the related question of authority, figuring who belonged to the *ruling* elite, was of more immediate concern than the initial problem of identifying a socially superior grouping; the cuckold scenario no longer just a matter of reconciling status and class power (or wealth with blood).

The obverse of such elaboration was the cuckold who presented as well-born but was none the less lacking in virtue, the reasoned authority supposedly assured by a landed estate. In this case, the well-born male's once-refined 'spirits', his inherited potential for virtue or honour, are corrupted by the speculative passions and anxieties held to be a part of the new credit economy.[29] His gentility is abrogated as he degenerates to the same position as the base-born citizen: irrational, jealous, childless and virtueless. In the context of the gentleman's economic situation *The Gentleman's Library* cautioned, for example, that a 'continual Load of *Cares* depresses the Vigour of the Mind, dulls the Inclination, and clouds the Chearfulness of the Spirits . . . *Covetousness* governs, the

[27] Ramesey, *Gentlemans Companion*, 95. *Emphasis added.* For similar comment, see Anon., *A Letter of Advice to a Young Gentleman of an Honourable Family, Now in His Travels Beyond the Seas* (1688), 33–4; Anon, ['By a Person of Quality'], *A Discourse Concerning the Character of a Gentleman* (1716), 12.

[28] *Censor*, no. 16 (16 May 1715; second edition 1717), vol. I, 115. *Emphasis added in final phrase.*

[29] For a useful introduction to the early modern significance of the 'passions', see A. Johns, *The Nature of the Book. Print and Knowledge in the Making* (Chicago, 1998), 397–408.

Appetite is ty'd up, and Nature is put under Penance.'[30] Such thinking gelled with imagery which likened the free circulation of money to the vigorous pulsing of the body's blood.[31] The hoarding of wealth violated the genteel credo of liberality and was thought to contradict the best interests of a commonweal ruled by a gentle elite. So amongst our comedies we find, for instance, the stock-jobbing, well-born Sir Feeble Dotard from *The Female Advocates* who courts the daughter of a rich City acquaintance, Sir Charles Transfer. To avoid this arranged marriage the daughter plagues her suitor with demands for an expensive and independent way of life. Sir Feeble, whose generosity has been supplanted by 'Phlegmatick Notions of Thrift', figured morphologically as a 'dry, wither'd Carcass', is finally incapacitated and literally consumed by a penurious concern for his pelf:

SIR FEEBLE: Oh, *Feeble, Feeble*! That ever thou should'st have a Colt's Tooth in thy Head! Thou Witch, thou Succubus! I am worse ridden by thee, than ever I was by the Night-Mare – Thou art a Daughter of Darkness, and the Devil do thy Guardian good with thee.

...

SIR CHARLES: I protest I can't conceive the Reason of the Distraction, except it should be the sudden Fall of Stock, by which he lost considerable. He told me he miss'd being let into the Secret, which he never used to fail of.[32]

Further instances of distracted men of extraction turned commercial types can be found in the form of the aptly named Sir David Fancy from William Taverner's *Maid the Mistress* (1708), Morecraft from Charles Molloy's *Perplex'd Couple* (1715) or Bondi in Mary Pix's *Deceiver Deceived* (1698).

Before turning to explore how political discourse derived polemical gain from the citizen's anomalous position, or, perhaps more accurately, from *positioning* the cit in ambiguous ways, let us summarize Part I's argument thus far. The citizen's representation articulates not so much the idea of two conflicting ways of gaining wealth, rival class ideologies or 'aristocracy versus bourgeoisie', as it comprises an attempt to come to terms with newer forms of capitalist endeavour in a society where one's property (class) shaped one's social personality (status) which, in turn, served as qualification for the exercise of political power (command).[33] As J. G. A. Pocock has argued, English society at the turn of the seventeenth century was confronted by novel forms of mobile property resulting

30 [E.P.], *The Gentleman's Library, Containing Rules for Conduct in All Parts of Life* (1715), 200–1.

31 N. A. F. Glaisyer, 'The Culture of Commerce in England, 1660–1720', unpublished PhD dissertation, Cambridge University (1999), 168ff.

32 W. Taverner, *Female Advocates* (1713), iii, 36–7.

33 J. G. A. Pocock, *Virtue, Commerce, and History. Essays on Political Thought and History, Chiefly in the Eighteenth Century* (London, 1985), 103–15; Pocock, *The Machiavellian Moment. Florentine Political Thought and the Atlantic Republican Tradition* (Princeton, 1975), 431–505.

from capitalist development, specifically those derived from the rapid expansion of finance capitalism as England found itself on an almost perpetual war footing which could only be sustained by the development of the fiscal-military state.[34] Questions then arose. Should people empowered by England's burgeoning commerce exercise authority; could they manifest a civic virtue in society which was broadly commensurate with the governance exercised by the 'naturally' wealthy landowners, those customarily recognized as 'gentlemen'?[35] As *The Examiner* elaborated forcefully: 'Should some Rich *Modern* with a portable Estate, his whole Fortune in his *Pocket-book*, contend . . . that it would be as wise a Confidence to trust him with the Lives, Liberties and Fortunes of a Nation, as any *Landed Representative*, whose Stake in the Publick, was as immoveable as the Mountains?'[36] Variation on the basic cit com plot attempts to ask and answer these queries.

We should recall at this point that our stage cits are not just economically powerful. They also lay claim to some kind of metropolitan political authority. We find urban justices of the peace (Scrapeall in John Coyre's *Cure for Jealousie*, for instance), members of the City militia (several are linked to the revolutionary years of Oliver Cromwell, for example Hackwell Senior in Thomas Shadwell's *Volunteers* or Driver in Baker's *Hampstead Heath*), officious councilmen, deputies, aldermen and, at least in 'non-dramatic' texts, even lord mayors. For those watching from the vantage points of either the Court at nearby St James or parliament at Westminster, perhaps the provincial country seat, these individuals collectively represented the quite unsettling authority of the semi-autonomous City. Thus the citizen comedy of the early eighteenth century could just as easily figure the disqualification of the citizen from a genteel virtue, suggesting that the commercial-financial capitalist did not possess the means or right to the exercise of authority possessed by the 'gentry' (whom modern historiography has nevertheless shown to have been heavily implicated in the same relations of exchange).[37]

On balance, the satire of the citizen comedies is increasingly directed against those men involved in specific kinds of enterprise. Most are not profiled as simply turning over a modest amount of capital in local trade of various kinds.

[34] For a detailed synopsis of these developments, see J. Brewer, *The Sinews of Power. War, Money and the English State, 1688–1783* (London, 1989).

[35] For discussion of these issues in non-dramatic literature of the period, particularly civic humanism, see C. E. Nicholson, *Writing and the Rise of Finance. Capital Satires of the Early Eighteenth Century* (Cambridge, 1994).

[36] *Examiner*, no. 2 (30 October–6 November 1712), vol. III, [2].

[37] For example, R. Grassby, *The English Gentleman in Trade. The Life and Works of Sir Dudley North, 1641–91* (Oxford, 1994); S. E. Whyman, 'Land and Trade Revisited: The Case of John Verney, London Merchant and Baronet, 1660–1720', *London Journal* 22, 1 (1997), 16–32; Whyman, *Sociability and Power in Late-Stuart England. The Cultural World of the Verneys 1660–1720* (Oxford, 1999), 76–84.

Such a portrayal would have made them much more like the early seventeenth-century comedic cit, a domestic retailer, even a master artisan or one-time farmer who really did get his hands dirty.[38] Instead, some three generations later, the citizens (perhaps earning their original principal in an unremarkable way) make both their capital and that of other investors work for them in international commercial ventures and the rather novel forms of shares, loans and futures. The irony of our early eighteenth-century citizen, and quite possibly a good part of the hostility directed towards him, is that he was perhaps meant to be only nominally 'of the City'. A persistent bone of contention in late Stuart London's municipal politics was that the integrity of the traditional corporate structure was crumbling for two conflicting reasons. For some, too few merchants were assuming the 'freedom': pursuing their civic duty by becoming members of the chartered livery companies and then being elected to City government.[39] This was particularly the case for religious dissenters who were technically disqualified from holding office, their religious sympathies marked by allusions to the Cromwellian era (i.e. old dissenting merchants were once young London puritans).[40] In contrast, successful merchants were seen by others as buyers of prestige or interlopers in the civic *cursus honorum* which, at its higher levels, was an urban oligarchy.[41] Both trajectories were often perceived to rest on self-interested speculation that diverted capital from honest trade and, therefore, the public interest for which 'gentlemen' were ideally responsible.

Sometimes the political implications of representing those who were ambivalently positioned in London's socio-political economy were very thinly disguised, the comedy apparently musing about the actual careers of eminent citizens. *The Refusal* of 1721 christens its merchant financier, who is made to confess that 'money won't do every thing, I am uneasy at home for all this', Sir Gilbert Wrangle. Contemporaries would surely have identified the stage figure with the magnate Sir Gilbert Heathcote. The original prologue made the identification quite obvious in any case. Possibly the audience thought of Thomas Papillon, a well-known former director of the East India Company, when laughing at Sir Timothy Tallapoy, the merchant obsessed with things Chinese in *The Biter* from 1705.[42]

[38] The earlier comparison of Brome's *City Wit* with Powell's *Very Good Wife* captures something of this transition.

[39] N. Rogers, *Whigs and Cities. Popular Politics in the Age of Walpole and Pitt* (Oxford, 1989), 1–45.

[40] See also Samuel Johnson's comment on Congreve's character of Fondlewife, in R. Montagu (ed.), *Samuel Johnson. Lives of the English Poets* (London, 1965), 252.

[41] For the late Stuart increase in the purchase of membership, a practice known as 'redemption', see C. Brooks, 'Apprenticeship, Social Mobility and the Middling Sort, 1550–1800', in J. Barry and C. Brooks (eds.), *The Middling Sort of People. Culture, Society and Politics in England, 1550–1800* (London, 1994), 65.

[42] Which is to say that the character was a composite caricature, see B. Orr, *Empire on the English Stage 1660–1714* (Cambridge, 2001), 228.

In some instances these representations followed along the shifting fractures of metropolitan party politics. Playwrights on the lookout for patronage exercised the expediency of trying to laud some groups of citizens at the same time as they acknowledged the tradition of the cit's riding. Of course, late Stuart London's mercantile interests had quickly become linked in the public mind, if not entirely in fact, with whiggish politicos. The whigs, in turn, were branded new men, corrupt money-grubbing parvenus. However, the citizen figure had been on the scene well before the arrival of party.[43] Late Stuart partisanship merely added further colour, each party attempting to appropriate the figure as a kind of anti-mascot. For example, once he had switched political loyalties, Thomas Durfey made sure to depict his cits as tory-jacobites.[44]

This factional expediency may also help to explain the observation by contemporaries that London's citizens themselves requested performances of the cuckold scenario. In particular, it became customary for a presentation of Ravenscroft's eponymous version of the satire to coincide with Lord Mayor's Day, a celebration that epitomized both the City's power and its contestation.[45] By locating the stereotype within a contingent and complex socio-political process, one spectator's comment after he had attended a production of *The London Cuckolds* resolved the paradox of citizens wanting to watch cits onstage: 'When this play is given, there are always prodigious crowds; it is not that everyone wishes to see how it is represented . . . but that everyone fits the cap to his neighbour and not to himself.'[46] Since theatregoing was largely promoted as a genteel activity (see part II), attending to laugh at the cit might well serve as self-congratulatory assurance that 'you' were not one of 'them'. Very probably those citizens not sharing the ruling partisan position of the Corporation in any given year, or the interests of rival companies then dominating both trade and office, boycotted the City's formal pageantry in favour of the playhouse's anti-theatre.[47] Featuring in satiric verse, the personification of a Catholic saint contrasted the official civic parade with the anti-papist protests of the late 1670s yet, simultaneously and rather snidely, also likened the new mayor's feting to a comedic riding:

[43] Cf. E. Burns, *Restoration Comedy. Crises of Desire and Identity* (London, 1987), 103–4, 118, 235; S. J. Owen, *Restoration Theatre and Crisis* (Oxford, 1996), 5, 104–6, 170–2.

[44] See the characters of Deputy Nicompoop in *Love for Money* (1691) and Dick Stockjobb in *Richmond Heiress* (1693), also the prologue to T. Shadwell, *Scowrers* (1691).

[45] For example, *Review of the State of the English Nation*, no. 71 (7 November 1704), book 2, 299; R. Gould, 'The Play-House', in his *Works* (1709), vol. II, 232, [lines 149ff.].

[46] W. H. Quarrell and M. Mare (trans. and eds.), *London in 1710 from the Travels of Zacharias Conrad von Uffenbach* (London, 1934), 38. The 1681 debut of the *London Cuckolds* itself concluded with a politically loaded epilogue.

[47] Associated with this were cheap broadsides and ballads, conceivably part of a pamphleteering campaign or protest cum street theatre. See the likes of Anon., *The London Cuckolds. An Excellent New Song, to an Old Tune &c.* (1682).

Some offer gorgeous robes, which serve to wear
When I on holy days in state appear;
When I'm in pomp on high processions shown,
Like pageants of Lord May'r, or Skimmington.[48]

The wider point may also be demonstrated with reference to performance patterns. London's two patent theatres, Drury Lane and Lincoln's Inn Fields, rapidly established reputations for favouring rival party interests during the early eighteenth century.[49] Analysis of performance schedules reveals occasions when it was tit for tat: Drury Lane offering pro-whig polemic, Lincoln's Inn scrambling to reply for tory interests. For example, when Drury Lane premiered Colley Cibber's *Non-Juror* in early December 1717 its virulent attack on tory-jacobite non-jurancy drew a direct, studied response in the form of *The Perjuror*, a farce. For the intervening week, the rival theatre filled the gap with the likes of *The London Cuckolds* and *The Fair Example*. To state the obvious, both featured several cits in their classic dilemma. However, at the same time, there seems to have been an awareness that this political colouring could be misinterpreted, might misrepresent complex policies. For example, in the months that *The Conscious Lovers* was in vogue at Drury Lane, Lincoln's Inn replied with productions of Thomas Betterton's *Amorous Widow* and Ravenscroft's *London Cuckolds*, two of the most revisited City satires available. However, it cannot be said that their overall message anathematized London's merchants as despicable representatives of capitalist exploitation, or was purely a matter of anti-mercantile polemic fuelled by partisanship. In fact, it would appear that Lincoln's Inn made a concerted effort to complicate their message and to show support for commercial endeavour *per se*. This was achieved by presenting a version of *The Royal Merchant*, an early seventeenth-century piece attributed to the pens of John Fletcher and Francis Beaumont. The play tells the tale of a prince disguised as a merchant in order to eulogize the benefits of trade and laud the efforts of those involved in commercial enterprise. This kind of nuanced juxtaposition (which was, of course, also at work within the text of Drury Lane's *Conscious Lovers*, see p. 69) serves as a further caution against assuming that the praise of trade, on the one hand, impelled social acceptance of traders, on the other.

48 J. Oldham, 'Satires upon the Jesuits: Satire IV' (1678–81), in E. F. Mengel, jr. (ed.), *Poems on Affairs of State. Volume II: 1678–1681* (New Haven, 1965), 71, [lines 82–5].

49 Perhaps the stock contemporary account of the theatre's potential for partisanship is provided by the description of the Haymarket theatre found in *Spectator*, no. 81 (2 June 1711), vol. I, 346–9. For related material see [Unknown correspondent] to Abigail Harley, 21 June 1690, HMC, *Portland* 29, 3 (1894), 448, reporting how 'Tory wickedness' had used a fake playbill as a party squib; the contest that developed over the partisan meaning of Joseph Addison's *Cato* as remarked by George Berkeley to Sir John Percival, 27 March 1713, HMC, *Seventh Report* 6, 1 (1879), 238; Lord Castlecomer to same, 28 April 1713, *ibid.*, 246.

At this point it may be wise to conclude by stating what our reading of the cit cuckold scenario's political inflection should *not* imply, thereby making the overall position of part I more explicit. Staking out a new argument at the expense of current scholarly literature may seem uncharitable, particularly when that work has much else to recommend it. Yet the end purpose is to demonstrate how coming to terms with gentility through the eyes of contemporaries, as we have started to do in the preceding pages, prompts further rethinking of established lines of dramatic interpretation. In particular, we should revisit certain readings of the cit's satiric meaning as well as revise our understanding of attitudes towards the City merchant in late Stuart society.

The foregoing paragraphs should not suggest that the cuckold scenario was nothing more than the plaything of high political debate, that the disorders of the merchant citizen's household can be explained solely as the satirical, expedient creation of partisan politicking. This is the position adopted by a very detailed reading of late Stuart drama and literature.[50] Richard Braverman considers that the drama was preoccupied with the question of the nature of political legitimacy during a period which saw challenge after challenge to authority justified on the basis of genealogical inheritance (specifically the Crown's). He argues the 'best comedies . . . were attuned to historical and political preoccupations despite the fact that they were *displaced to the social sphere*' where dynastic questions were figured as sexual liaisons.[51] The suggestion is that various rival theories of the monarch's authority are explored and debated by means of synecdoche and metaphor; that the fictional society presented on the stage can be reduced to the political 'facts' beyond the playhouse in a one-way correlation. This is a problematic assumption. Most obviously, Braverman's argument of displacement assumes a separation of public-political as against private-social spheres when we have shown (and will detail further in the course of part III) how they interpenetrated. Social hierarchy was itself a political live-wire.

The notion of displacement is also common to readings of the City comedy that highlight its economic dimension. In this view, concerns about the unsettling potential of capitalist exchange were projected on to City women, figured as sexual behaviour which transgressed notions of a 'bourgeois' femininity, as part of a misogynistic, patriarchal tradition.[52] A 'class' structure is assumed,

[50] R. Braverman, *Plots and Counterplots. Sexual Politics and the Body Politic in English Literature, 1660–1730* (Cambridge, 1993).

[51] *Ibid.*, 212. *Emphasis added.*

[52] J. K. Mandy, 'City Women: Daughters, Wives, Widows, and Whores in Jacobean and Restoration City Comedy', unpublished PhD dissertation, Lehigh University (1996), 5, 40ff. Similar arguments have been made for both early Stuart cit comedy (K. Newman, *Fashioning Femininity and English Renaissance Drama* (Chicago, 1991); S. Miller, 'Consuming Mothers/Consuming Merchants: The Carnivalesque Economy of Jacobean City Comedy', *Modern Language Studies* 26, 2–3 (1996), 73–95) and late Stuart literature in general (L. Mandell, 'Bawds and Merchants: Engendering Capitalist Desires', *ELH* 59 (1992), esp. 107–13; L. Brown, *Ends of Empire. Women and Ideology in Early Eighteenth-Century English Literature* (Ithaca, 1993)).

eliding both the partisan dimension first noticed by Braverman and the social issues identified in the current study. Unnoticed is the persistent failure of the citizen's *man*hood as metaphor for the ill-effects of new credit mechanisms. It is also important not to give the impression that the scenario's interrogation of elite structuration was entirely novel, as many literary studies do, by coupling a profound shift from feudalism to capitalism with seismic social consequences like the proverbial rise of a middle class.[53] At most, our period witnessed a new phase of capitalism's development, the rise of finance.[54] The conspicuous success of this particular transition (or equally its spectacular failure towards the end of our period in the form of the South Sea Bubble) brought certain issues to the fore, including those of social stratification. As the longevity of the cuckolded citizen plot itself demonstrates, earlier capitalist expansion had also prompted social questioning: generally similar bouts of uncertainty about gentility's exact configuration and application.[55] And later eighteenth-century developments would be accompanied by the persistence of the cit com narrative. In 1735, *The Prompter* was still asking '*whose* Reproach shou'd it be, to a Nation of Trade, that *Citizen*, and *Cuckold*, are Synonymous Terms, in our Comedies?'[56] And during the next ten years, William Hogarth presented his own visual plays on the narrative in both the *Times of Day* and the *Marriage à la Mode* print series.[57] The comedy tended to maintain a focus on those perceived to be at the sharper end of commerce during a particular stage within capitalism's growth. Shifting its sights to target those types of citizen seemingly most out of place at a given time, those who were in a social no-man's land, the precise triggers for a salvo varied, but as we shall see presently, the ammunition, gentility, remained the same.

In light of our criticism of explanations which reduce the citizen cuckold stereotype to a matter of 'class' or 'politics', it is as well to stress that we neither exaggerate the actual extent of the status anxiety facing London's urbane population beyond the playhouse nor generalize too quickly about how that anxiety then unleashed a humorously cathartic counter-strike. Suggesting that

[53] A fairly obvious feature of the studies already mentioned, most recent are D. Hughes, *English Drama 1660–1700* (Oxford, 1996), 19ff.; J. D. Canfield, *Tricksters & Estates. On the Ideology of Restoration Comedy* (Lexington, 1997), *passim*. Cf. D. M. Turner, *Fashioning Adultery. Gender, Sex and Civility in England, 1660–1740* (Cambridge, 2002), 101–2.

[54] For the classic account of these developments, see P. G. M. Dickson, *The Financial Revolution in England. A Study in the Development of Public Credit, 1688–1750* (London, 1967).

[55] Although it does not address citizen comedy specifically, see the pioneering work by L. C. Stevenson, *Praise and Paradox. Merchants and Craftsmen in Elizabethan Popular Literature* (Cambridge, 1984), esp. 7ff. However, the current study does not agree with Stevenson's argument that the likes of Steele and Defoe easily resolved such problems by subscribing a distinctly 'middle class' point of view during the early eighteenth century, 128ff.

[56] *Prompter*, no. xxxviii (21 March 1735), [1].

[57] In relation to *Times of Day*, see S. Shesgreen, *Hogarth and the Times-of-the-Day Tradition* (Ithaca, 1983), 112–14; for *Marriage à la Mode*, see R. L. S. Cowley, *Marriage-A-La-Mode. A Review of Hogarth's Narrative Art* (Manchester, 1983), 103ff.

the stereotype was merely a knee-jerk reaction to anomalies in status would be equally reductionist. The social dislocation in question was, just as often, deliberately rigged to explode. As we saw in the case of *The London Cuckolds* on Lord Mayor's Day, there was a quite intentional playing with fire in the hopes of wounding the opposition.

We should view the late Stuart rehearsal of the comic cuckold as a significant intervention in a complex, ongoing dialogue which had power *per se* as its subject and 'gentility' as its common but disputed language. In other words, the cit stereotype was not singularly an expression of party faction (authority), about involvement in relations of exchange (class), or the presence and absence of lineage (status), but intricate figurations of all three at once. What our comedies shared was that they were fundamentally political in the broadest of senses. They contemplated the dynamics of power, its delineation as social relationships of domination and subordination that were comprehended by the rhetoric of gentility. To deny gentility was to deny superior power, to refuse its legitimacy. So when it came to recognizing who was (or was not) gentle, or identifying early modern society's more (or less) powerful subjects, gentility reached neither a point of static definition nor entirely consistent application to particular persons and groups.[58] And, by the same token, the balance of factors (social, economic, political) compelling gentility's (re)definition was different every time.

Gentility was, therefore, a cultural weapon with which to carve out power. As a consequence it was fought over, disputed between the trading cit and his shrewish wife as well as contested by the theatre's spectators as cultural consumers and producers. This conclusion is at odds with work that has posited increased respect and influence for the London trader during the post-revolutionary years. Perry Gauci aims to assess how perception of international merchants, both their self-image and wider society's view of them, was impacted by shifts in their economic function during this period. He concludes that there was mounting approval for these men on account of modernizing commercial attitudes (i.e. more people understood that trade was in the public interest) and their ability to achieve incremental success on what he terms the 'real proving-ground', the field of politics and, especially, the floor of the House of Commons, without alienating a majority of the landed classes.[59] His study

[58] For the ways in which the rhetorical purposes of trade discourse, particularly that of extra-parliamentary lobbyists, kept the issue of the merchant's social position undecided, see L. M. Harteker, 'Steward of the Kingdom's Stock: Merchants, Trade, and Discourse in Eighteenth-Century England', unpublished PhD dissertation, University of Chicago (1996). For a related case-study that further illustrates many of the broader points being made here, see J. Walter, 'Public Transcripts, Popular Agency and the Politics of Subsistence in Early Modern England', in M. J. Braddick and J. Walter (eds.), *Negotiating Power in Early Modern Society. Order, Hierarchy and Subordination in Britain and Ireland* (Cambridge, 2001), 123–48.

[59] P. Gauci, *The Politics of Trade. The Overseas Merchant in State and Society, 1660–1720* (Oxford, 2001), 194, 277.

also attempts to quantify how many merchants had genteel ambitions, assuming that these can be correlated with the rate of application to the heralds for coats of arms and the like. Recovering only small percentages, Gauci reasons that his merchants were not much interested in upward mobility. Most 'did not hopelessly pursue an amorphous "gentility"'.[60] In fact, he implies that this relative immobility assisted in both the maintenance of political harmony with the gentry so-called and the improvement of the traders' relative position in the Commons. Since that harmony was sustained amid both the tough realities of commercial achievement and parliamentary politicking, there is, for Gauci, no more rigorous measure of how much attitudes towards the City merchant had improved. Yet the tendency to separate society from politics, to downplay the social snobbery of literature in favour of a concentration on the (supposedly) more tangible and objective experience of politics in the debating chamber, is to elide crucial aspects of the merchant's persistently ambiguous position.[61]

This chapter's reading of his comic representation suggests that the merchant citizen was as much pursued or targeted by gentility owing to the fact that gentility, as a constant process of social structuration, was fundamentally political and a matter of subjective impressions. These impressions not only shaped and were shaped by parliamentary debate (what of Walpole's sturdy beggars?), but were also heavily implicated in related socio-political fora like the playhouse.[62] It might seem we are simply trying to argue that perceptions of the merchant remained negative and hostile into the eighteenth century, yet this would be missing the wider point. Ultimately, the last three chapters should demonstrate that these perceptions were always unstable; that it is redundant to try and characterize views of the merchant as either good or bad and impossible to prove final acceptance of the merchant as gentleman. Instead, we need to consider the question of why this malleability was possible, enduring and sometimes quite deliberately perpetuated. The second part of this study will investigate specifically how and why the theatre's discursive imperative often worked to heighten – even create – awareness of the disputatious nature of elite social structuration as a constant cultural process.

[60] *Ibid.*, 94. [61] *Ibid.*, 13, 194. [62] Cf. *ibid.*, 277.

Part II

The social microcosm of London's playhouses

4 Stratifying the playhouse

> The Country Client stares; the Comedian is waggish, the Ladies look grave, the Pit is merry, the Side-Boxes Ogle, the Middle Gallery Claps, and the Upper Gallery Roars – the Criticks have the Spleen – Rakes Intrigue, Drunkards Snore, Men of Punctilio Quarrel, and Men of Mettle Tilt; Young Fops are Noisie, and the Old ones Touchy, and damnably Powder'd . . . So good Acting being little minded, our Gains decay, and the Audience now make the most sport for one another.
>
> P. Motteux, *Farwel Folly* (1707)

Why should London's theatre have been concerned with the predicament of the citizen who had economic and political power to outstrip that of the 'gentleman' yet lacked the established lineage which some insisted was the key to elite social standing? How is it that late Stuart comedy became so preoccupied with the (re)negotiation of gentility, the delineation of superiority? The raucous intervention of catcalls provides a clue. The mere act of attending the theatre was an inveterately social experience and, as we shall see, an experience of a particular cast.

Critics and historians of early modern drama have tried to anatomize this social experience for the simple reason that the audience is viewed as having been a crucial factor in the theatre's original creation of meaning.[1] Dramatic texts were not self-contained monologues consumed by passive spectators but the product of transaction: active interpretation performed by and, indeed, *of* the audience.[2] For if the meaning of the comedy was conditional, so too was that of the theatre's wider social text. The dramatist never knew exactly how his or her work would be received because it was partly a matter of speculation as to who would be watching and interpreting the entertainment. These

[1] The position adopted, for instance, by two important studies of drama for our period, P. Holland, *The Ornament of Action. Text and Performance in Restoration Comedy* (Cambridge, 1979); J. Milhous and R. D. Hume, *Producible Interpretation. Eight English Plays 1675–1707* (Carbondale, 1985).

[2] A point lucidly conceptualized by A. R. Botica, 'Audience, Playhouse and Play in Restoration Theatre, 1660–1710', unpublished DPhil dissertation, Oxford University (1985), 193ff.; L. A. Freeman, *Character's Theater. Genre and Identity on the Eighteenth-Century English Stage* (Philadelphia, 2002), 3–5.

circumstances have led one scholar to describe the experience of early modern theatre as amounting to a 'cognitive and therapeutic instrument'.[3] In other words, London's playhouses were places where the audience, by telling stories to themselves about themselves, discovered certain 'truths' concerning wider society. Implicitly, it was the generation of a particular social knowledge which brought audiences back for more of this reflexive confrontation or dialogue: to what Lady Rakelove breathlessly refers to in *The Gentleman Cully* as 'that Microcosm, that representative of the great World, the Play-house'.[4]

If the early eighteenth-century playhouse can be thought of as a social laboratory, it was in the best interests of the playwrights and theatre managers to try to rig the theatre's experimenting to their advantage or, at the very least, achieve some semblance of control. In fact, order was a legal requirement of the licences granted to the proprietors by the Crown. The order which the licensees agreed on and aimed for was nothing more nor less than the imposition of distinction by status on to the auditorium space and the people enclosed by it. Marked by certain contours, divisions and points of social reference, to which the audience was exhorted to pay close attention, the playhouse was not merely an empty space into which London society spilled. A range of texts built a social grid which fairly shouted status, from the verse that introduced and concluded the main performances (prologues and epilogues) and the bills that advertised them, to the spatial nomenclature of the theatre's interior and the bawling door- and box-keepers. Our task here is to show how the playhouse discoursed, and was negotiated by, the spectators, to explore the dialectic of experience and interpretation conditioning the possible social meanings of the comic drama for the later seventeenth-century audience.

But first a cautionary word about the sources used and the broader interpretive perspective adopted in part II. Much of the extant material describing the theatre space and audience is considered suspect. The 'rhetorical stratagems' of prologue writers and satirists who 'crib from earlier models' are not the stuff of transparent and definitive conclusions about who comprised the later Stuart audience or what the theatre's social scene was really like.[5] The following takes such warnings to heart. However, it suggests that a good deal might still be learned from these representations if we treat them as prescriptive (not descriptive) texts. Hence the aim is not so much to recover the composition

[3] L. Montrose, *The Purpose of Playing. Shakespeare and the Cultural Politics of the Elizabethan Theatre* (Chicago, 1996), 40. Also suggestive of this approach in relation to the theatre of the early seventeenth century is J. Dillon, *Theatre, Court and City, 1595–1610. Drama and Social Space in London* (Cambridge, 2000), 6ff.

[4] C. Johnson, *Gentleman Cully* (1702), v, 42.

[5] H. Love, 'Who Were the Restoration Audience?', *Yearbook of English Studies* 10 (1980), 24; also D. Roberts, *The Ladies. Female Patronage of Restoration Drama 1660–1700* (Oxford, 1989), 27ff.; A. Dharwadker, 'Restoration Drama and Social Class', in S. J. Owen (ed.), *A Companion to Restoration Drama* (Oxford, 2001), 142–6.

of a 'typical' audience but to concentrate on tracing the contours of the target audience wanted by the managers and playwrights, particularly on the make-or-break opening night referred to by many of our texts. We can then examine how the audience's social character might have shaped, and been shaped by, particular aspects of the very entertainment it had assembled to watch.

Comedy in late Stuart London had two main venues that together will be our principal concern, those in Drury Lane and Lincoln's Inn Fields. The situation was slightly complicated because a second troupe was neither continuously operative (there was only one licensed, regular company from 1682 to 1695) nor in the same location for the whole of our period. At different times the Lincoln's Inn company played in a converted tennis court and Sir John Vanbrugh's new building at the Haymarket, before settling into more suitable premises of its own. There were other theatre spaces to which we will occasionally make reference. These include the ageing Dorset Garden; the Haymarket's novel design which rendered it much more suitable for the acoustics of opera rather than drama; two new buildings constructed in Covent Garden and Goodman's Fields towards the end of our period of main interest.[6] There would have been some smaller architectural variation between the theatres as physical spaces (and any contrast in their geographic situation will be examined below), but the socio-structural grid which each attempted to maintain was similar in outline and function.[7] It was this grid which proved crucial for the comedy's enactment of gentility, both onstage and in seats.

Let us begin our survey of the playhouse with the boxes that formed the pinnacle of the theatre's socio-spatial hierarchy. The position of these partitioned sets of seats is shown in Figure 4. The most important box was that reserved for the monarch and his or her courtiers. However, from about the early 1680s, direct patronage by the Court of London's commercial theatres could no longer be taken for granted. Political crises tended to keep its leading figures occupied and then, post-revolution, a combination of moral scruple, financial exigency and personal preference started to bite. Analysis of royal household records from after 1690 shows that members of the royal family attended the playhouses infrequently, if at all.[8] It was only slightly more common for a theatre company to be commanded to appear at Court, ostensibly making the performance a quite different social occasion from that experienced at the commercial venues. Research suggests that royal attendance gradually picked up with the

6 For a critical account of the institutional vagaries of London's theatres in the late Stuart period, see R. D. Hume, *Henry Fielding and the London Theatre 1728–1737* (Oxford, 1988), 1–61.

7 For an overview of London theatre buildings in the Restoration and Georgian eras, see the essay by E. A. Langhans in R. D. Hume (ed.), *The London Theatre World, 1660–1800* (Carbondale, 1980), 35–65.

8 R. O. Bucholz, *The Augustan Court. Queen Anne and the Decline of Court Culture* (Stanford, 1993), 241ff.

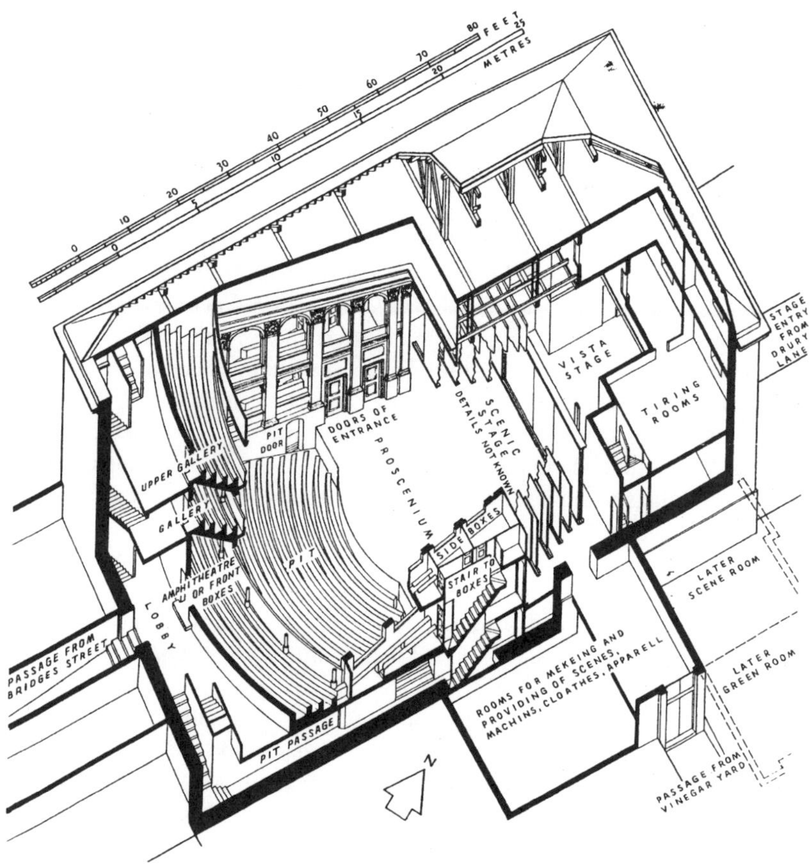

4 A reconstruction of the Drury Lane theatre as it would have looked from 1674, after the rebuilding directed by Sir Christopher Wren

installation of the Hanoverian regime in 1714, but, even so, the theatres could not fully restore the courtly patina seen during the 1660s and 1670s.[9]

In addition, early eighteenth-century drama faced mounting competition from other entertainments, most notably clubs, opera, musical concerts and masquerades. The fashionableness of the latter meant the theatre often had its work cut out keeping the attention and patronage of London's *beau monde*. Historians of the theatre are accustomed to argue in terms of the growth of certain sections of the audience during the late Stuart period. It is perhaps just as important to think

[9] H. W. Pedicord, *'By Their Majesties' Command'. The House of Hanover at the London Theatres, 1714–1800* (London, 1991).

about attrition.[10] At least as far as the comedy is concerned, prologues make relatively few direct appeals to titled spectators as inhabitants of the boxes. Rather than 'my lords and ladies' it is the more inclusive gesture of 'gentlemen . . . ladies'.[11] For much of our period, attendance by the Court was a newsworthy event because it did not happen very often. The patronage of the Court was infrequent even though control of the theatres was the Crown's prerogative, routed through the lord chamberlain's office.[12] Compared then with the situation during the Restoration, the boxes in the early eighteenth century were, generally speaking, intended as the preserve of the genteel, not just the courtly or ennobled.

Division by sex as well as status was operative. Addresses to the front boxes, those facing the stage, were to gentlewomen. This left the side-boxes for gentlemen (sometimes known as 'fops' and 'beaux', the subjects of part III). However, throughout our period, and despite several attempts to prohibit the practice, gentlemen also claimed the privilege of standing or sitting on the outer limits of the acting area itself.[13] When theatre management, anticipating a full house, went so far as to construct temporary boxes onstage then the presence of gentlewomen was more likely. For instance, the very first *Tatler* reported a sell-out benefit night for the actor Thomas Betterton and observed how the 'Stage it self was cover'd with Gentlemen and Ladies, and when the Curtain was drawn, it discovered even there a very splendid Audience'.[14] Similarly, Lady Hervey noted of a packed performance of Joseph Addison's *Cato* 'which I am to go to this day with [the] Dutchess of Cleveland, Lady Ann Hervey & Lady Thomond; we shall be free from the croud by being in [the] stage box, els I durst not have venterd'.[15] Yet it was predominantly the elite male spectator who staked out this prominent space and, in so doing, became the most visible spectator within the theatre. On at least one occasion, having been denied such liberty, some of these men made the newspapers. Early in the 1718 season, three gentlemen were said to have 'pelted the Players in a shameful Manner' with apples and then, with their swords, torn down the scenes for the Lincoln's Inn production

[10] For this point, in relation to aristocratic attempts at achieving an alternative to the Court in the form of a socially exclusive subscription opera, see H. Knif, *Gentlemen and Spectators. Studies in Journals, Opera and the Social Scene in Late Stuart London* (Helsinki, 1995), 217–34.

[11] For example, the epilogue to J. Vanbrugh, *Relapse* (1697).

[12] M. J. Kinservik, 'Theatrical Regulation during the Restoration Period', in S. J. Owen (ed.), *A Companion to Restoration Drama* (Oxford, 2001), 36–52.

[13] L. Hughes, *The Drama's Patrons. A Study of the Eighteenth-Century London Audience* (San Antonio, 1971), 21ff.

[14] *Tatler*, no. 1 (12 April 1709), vol. I, 19. See also C. Cibber, *Provok'd Husband* (1728), i, 3.

[15] Lady Hervey to her husband John, 14 April 1713, in S. H. A. Hervey (ed.), *Letter-Books of John Hervey, First Earl of Bristol* (London, 1894), vol. I, 359. Also, Lady Pembroke to the duchess of Marlborough, ?1710–11, in Blenheim Papers, vol. CCCLVI, Add. MS 61,456, f.150^r, British Library.

of *The Fair Quaker of Deal* as a protest against their exclusion from a vantage point onstage.[16]

Occupants of the boxes spilled over into the pit, a space which one late seventeenth-century visitor to London, Henri de Valbourg Misson, was to describe as encompassing 'Men of Quality, particularly the younger Sort, some Ladies of Reputation and Vertue, and abundance of Damsels that hunt for Prey, sit all together in this Place, Higgeldy-piggledy, chatter, toy, play, hear, hear not.'[17] Although Misson's narrative shows that the presence of gentlewomen was not unheard of, and perhaps more likely if they had a suitable male escort for the evening, the crush of people amid the benches, not to mention the company of working women (prostitutes but also the refreshment sellers), seems to have made the pit more of a male preserve. Hence a character from John Crowne's *English Frier* stressed that when belles entered the auditorium, grabbing the attention of the gentlemen already there, the 'whole Pit turns round as mov'd by an Engine'.[18] Typically, groups of gentlewomen were supposed to make use of the socially decorous boxes behind the pit, thereby leaving any ruffling of dress or composure to the backward-glancing male playgoer.

Two additional features of the theatre's social space need emphasis at this juncture. First, the theatre space was well-lit for the duration of the evening's entertainment. Sitting in the privacy of darkness was unthinkable and would have been a serious hindrance to the social imperatives which motivated theatregoing.[19] Despite the risk of fire, a selling point seems to have been each theatre's candle power. The greater the number and diligence of each company's candle-snuffers and the more inches of mirror glass, its placement and reflective properties boosting illumination and spectatorial range, so much the better. Hence the epilogue to Colley Cibber's *Woman's Wit* addressed the gentlemen of the side-boxes:

> I'll swear a Frown wou'd spoil their pretty Faces.
> Dear Sirs be kind, and let this Play but pass,
> We'll stop at nothing to deserve the Grace,
> We'll hang our Stage all round with Looking-Glass.[20]

And a contemporary claimed that the interiors of London's theatres were by far the brightest in Europe.[21] Second, with the exception of those who chose

[16] *Weekly Journal*, no. 96 (11 October 1718), 573.

[17] Mr Ozell (trans. and ed.), *M. Misson's Memoirs and Observations in His Travels over England* (originally published in French in 1698; London, 1719), 219.

[18] J. Crowne, *English Frier* (1690), iii, 24.

[19] J. L. Styan, *Restoration Comedy in Performance* (Cambridge, 1986), 12ff.

[20] C. Cibber, *Woman's Wit* (1697). Similar comment was made by the opening verses of Cibber's *Xerxes* (1699), prologue spoken by Mr Betterton.

[21] J. Macky, *A Journey through England* (1714, second edition 1722), 171. Compare Lady Montagu's complaint to Alexander Pope about the darkness of the Viennese playhouse,

to disport themselves on the stage, it is important to bear in mind the uneven nature of some of the primary lines of sight encouraged by the theatre's social grid. The occupants of the boxes and pit, amounting to some 400 out of about 600 possible spaces,[22] could look across, back and forth, at each other.[23] Thus *Greenwich Park* referred to ladies in the boxes bestowing 'many favours . . . by the Way of Ogle, Fan, the Language of the fingers' on gentlemen.[24] These people could be seen by the rest of the audience, the 200 or so more patrons whom we shall address shortly, but not so much looked at face-to-face. For what those not in the prime positions tended to see were the backs of heads, the tops of wigs, side profiles at best. They did not usually have the privilege, once the performance began, of directly holding the gaze of the theatre's first, genteel spectators.[25]

These features alone make for the working conclusion that genteel London was meant to claim the spaces closest to the onstage action, where they could see the players and, most importantly, themselves much more clearly. This was particularly true of the side-boxes, whence viewing the audience was often easier than watching the play being acted onstage. The less privileged, those of inferior status, were meant to sit towards the back and higher than the gentlemen and -women who positioned themselves up front and lower down. For above the front boxes came the galleries, long, unpartitioned and elevated rows of seating, and it was about here that the line between genteel and non-genteel was crossed – at least as far as the social map drawn by comedic texts, prologues, epilogues and other censorious descriptions of the playhouse interior were concerned.

The initial puzzle to solve about the galleries is how many there were. Descriptions sometimes speak of 'the gallery' as if there were only one such

14 September 1716, in R. Halsband (ed.), *The Complete Letters of Lady Mary Wortley Montagu. Volume I: 1708–1720* (Oxford, 1965), 264.

22 Advertisements for performances where the boxes and pit were to be combined and tickets sold at elevated prices typically claimed that no more than 400 would be available for sale. See, for example, a billing from the *Daily Courant* (20 January 1703), in A. Jackson, 'Play Notices from the Burney Newspapers 1700–1703', *PMLA* 48 (1933), 839.

23 Exact capacity is unknown but does not appear to have much exceeded 600 before the very end of our period. Even those who argue for slightly higher numbers concede that total capacity for all sections of the playhouse was rarely achieved. See H. W. Pedicord, *The Theatrical Public in the Time of Garrick* (New York, 1954), 15ff.; Holland, *Ornament*, 16–17. Tom Brown refers to 'daily Matter of Fact, of which there are a Thousand Witnesses', *The Stage-Beaux Toss'd in a Blanket* (1704), 47. This suggests an average of 500 spectators per venue, a position incidentally supported by a comment of G. Farquhar, 'A Discourse upon Comedy, in Reference to the English Stage', in his *Love and Business* (1702), 151.

24 W. Mountfort, *Greenwich Park* (1691), iv, 42.

25 See, for example, R. P. Bond, *Queen Anne's American Kings* (Oxford, 1952), 4. Bond cites contemporary observation that in late April 1710 'the Mob' of the upper gallery stopped the entertainment to insist that four Native American visitors to London, known as the 'Indian Kings', be moved from their front box to the stage so the entire audience might watch them.

space.[26] Rather more common are references to a 'middle gallery' such that some modern commentary has assumed there were as many as three galleries; middle gallery implying that it was sandwiched by a further two, one on top and one underneath.[27] Yet it seems clear enough that there were two galleries, an upper and a lower.[28] In order to cut through the conceptual tangle that has resulted from this shifting terminology, we should explain why the lower gallery could be known, at the same time, as 'the', 'the first', and 'the middle' gallery.

Reference to a 'middle gallery' demonstrates how status-conscious the late Stuart theatre space could be, for it was at this level more than any other that the theatre's status imperative actually overwrote the architectural structure. In other words, what was the lower or first gallery in terms of its relative shape, dimensions and position became socially encoded as 'middle' because it was designed for London's middling sort when they attended a performance.[29] Viewed from onstage, audience members in the so-called 'middle gallery' were sitting above the spatially dissimilar boxes and pit, that is, a divided series of enclosed or grounded spaces, rather than over another gallery, a gallery being a long, open, undivided and raised platform. Having to defer socially to elite spectators who sat at ground level in the boxes and pit, and at the expense of registering properly the actual disjunction in the architecture, the first/lower gallery of the pair (not trio) was conjectured as 'middle' in an attempt to maintain relative social distinctions.[30]

Apposition of the terms 'middle' and 'gallery' was socially rather than spatially fitting. Thus the epilogue to one of Susanna Centlivre's comedies surveyed the auditorium by pretending that its speaker had found a *billet-doux* dropped or thrown on to the stage by a member of the audience. The lines move directly from the 'middle' gallery to the pit, pausing only to present the image of hypocritical citizens who bargain with the nightwalkers in the narrow streets about the playhouse after they have vacated their assigned places:

[26] See, for instance, R. Gould, 'A Satyr against the Play-House', in his *Poems, Consisting Chiefly of Satyrs and Satyrical Epistles* (1689), 167; *Female Tatler*, no. 29 (9–12 September 1709), [1]; *Tatler*, no. 182 (8 June 1710), vol. II, 487; *Weekly Journal*, no. 232 (6 April 1723), 1363.

[27] Problems with locating the middle gallery appear in C. Gallagher, *Nobody's Story. The Vanishing Acts of Women Writers in the Marketplace, 1670–1820* (Berkeley, 1994), 11; E. Howe, *The First English Actresses. Women and Drama 1660–1700* (Cambridge, 1992), 6; H. C. Knutson, *The Triumph of Wit. Molière and Restoration Comedy* (Columbus, 1988), 29.

[28] Readily evident from newspaper advertisements promoting performances and the prices of the different seats. See J. Milhous and R. D. Hume, 'Revision of *The London Stage. Part II 1700–1729*', 7 April 1709 (Drury Lane); Ozell, *Misson*, 219–20. This conclusion is supported by the work of Alistair Potts on the early Restoration playhouses, 'The Development of the Playhouse in Seventeenth-Century London', unpublished PhD dissertation, Cambridge University (1999), 183–4, 198–9.

[29] For the basic equation see, for instance, R. Burridge, *A Scourge for the Play-Houses* (1702), 4.

[30] For discussion of similar issues in relation to Restoration London see C. Wall, *The Literary and Cultural Spaces of Restoration London* (Cambridge, 1998), 4ff.

Nor can I think it from the Middle fell;
For I'm afraid – as few of them can Spell:
Beside, their Haggling Passions never gain,
Beyond the Passage-walking Nymph[s] of *Drury-Lane*:
And then the Pit's more stock'd with Rakes and Rovers,
Than any of these senseless, whining Lovers.
The Backs o'th' Boxes too seem mostly lin'd
With Souls, whose Passion's to themselves confin'd.
In short, I can't perceive, 'mongst all you Sparks,
The Wretch distinguish'd, by these bloody Marks.[31]

A similar socio-spatial elision is implicit to the terms of a legal agreement between two playhouse proprietors. In 1691, Alexander Davenant conceded that Christopher Rich was to have the authority to gift 'two places in the Boxes every Month or else ffower places in the Pitt or Six places in the Middle Gallery'.[32] Several representations elaborated on this arrangement, seating the cits in this last section of the theatrical arena. For instance, as Sir Solomon Empty in William Burnaby's *Reform'd Wife* outlines his idea for a successful play he is told: 'You have forgot one Range, what wou'd you do for the Cits in the Middle?'[33] The epilogue for *Love's Last Shift* made hopeful reference to 'Kind Citty-Gentlemen, o'th' middle-Row',[34] whereas the verses exchanged by William Mountfort and Charlotte Butler at the conclusion of Thomas Durfey's *Love for Money* were far more dismissive:

Mountfort:
. . . A rampant Wife is well expos'd to view,
And not ill drawn, a sneaking Cuckold too.
I can't imagine where that Satyr hooks,
I can find no such Cuckold here by's looks;
. . .
Yes fifty in that upper Row Gadzookes.
Rich Goldsmiths, Mercers, Taylors, Brewers, Bakers,

Butler:
And what are these
[*Pointing to the Pit*]

Mountfort:
Oh these are Cuckold makers,
Who o'er that Tribe still bear preheminence,
For you must know there's as much difference
Between the Horner and the hen-peck'd Drudge
As is between a Tipstaffe and a Judge.[35]

31 S. Centlivre, *Man's Bewitch'd* (1709). *Italics reversed.*
32 The agreement dates from 26 March 1691 and is quoted from J. Milhous and R. D. Hume (eds.), *A Register of English Theatrical Documents, 1660–1737* (Carbondale, 1991), vol. I, 283–4.
33 W. Burnaby, *Reform'd Wife* (1700), i, 5.
34 C. Cibber, *Love's Last Shift* (1696), epilogue spoken by Miss Cross. *Italics reversed.*
35 T. Durfey, *Love for Money* (1691), epilogue. *Italics reversed.*

The 'upper gallery' topped the 'middle gallery'. The attention this space received in prologues and epilogues vacillated from total silence to complete verses. When the upper gallery got no attention it was almost as though it did not exist. And so it was that the lower cum middle gallery came to be referred to as 'the gallery', discursively but not architecturally singular. This verbal game of hide-and-seek was heavily conditioned by the main prescribed occupants of the second and uppermost gallery, liveried servants, particularly footmen, whose job it was to secure their employers' position at the theatre as well as conduct them to and from the venue.[36] Ideally the main plebeian section of the audience, for what was intended as a refined occasion, was conditional upon the presence of the theatre's first spectators, with servants receiving the perquisite of free admission on the basis of their masters' and mistresses' attendance from the mid-1690s.[37] Or as the satirist Tom Brown complained: 'And then the Vulgar Rascals share with Quality in the Diversion; the very Footmen in the Upper Gallery will judge of the Plays as well and louder than their Masters.'[38]

Yet as this last comment suggests, servants might act up and their presence would then become a sufferance. If they could not be seen they could certainly be heard and perhaps felt by their superiors, the result of chanting, vibrations passing through the floor, or being hit by falling debris from refreshments.[39] Sir John Reresby remembered being man-handled by a page, whilst William Byrd noted, after an evening at Lincoln's Inn in December 1718, that he 'had a quarrel with several footmen about wearing their hats'.[40] Byrd's statement is both intriguing and incomplete. It is incomplete in that Byrd does not tell us precisely how he came to argue with the footmen. Probably they first drew his attention because they did not doff their hats to him. Byrd, a well-established planter from Virginia whose immediate family origins in England can be traced to the City, moved about London seemingly sure of his elite status. The failure by servants of other gentlemen and -women to give him what he considered due deference may very well have sparked Byrd's words of rebuke. Finer details aside, the general

36 For an overview of the situation of servants at the eighteenth-century playhouse, see J. J. Hecht, *The Domestic Servant Class in Eighteenth-Century England* (London, 1956), 136–9.

37 For this development, see J. M. Evans (ed.), *Apology for the Life of Mr. Colley Cibber, Comedian* (New York, 1987), 135.

38 Brown, *Stage-Beaux*, 8. See also *Female Tatler*, no. 67 (7–9 December 1709), [2].

39 Terse objections about their unruliness were typically voiced in prologues and epilogues. See, for instance, C. Beckingham, *Scipio Africanus* (1718), epilogue spoken by Mrs Bullock. For extended treatment of the noise made by the footmen, see *Spectator*, no. 235 (29 November 1711), vol. II, 413ff.; for an instance of the problem of stray orange peel, see the case of the wayward servant of the singer Mrs Tofts cited from the *Daily Courant* (8 February 1704), in Milhous and Hume, *Register*, vol. I, 378. See too [J. Lawson], *The Upper Gallery. A Poem. Inscribed to the Rev. Dr. Swift, D.S.P.D* (1733).

40 A. Browning (with M. K. Geiter and W. A. Speck) (ed.), *Memoirs of Sir John Reresby. The Complete Text and a Selection from His Letters* (London, 1936, second edition 1991), 30; L. B. Wright and M. Tinling (eds.), *William Byrd of Virginia. The London Diary (1717–1721) and Other Writings* (New York, 1958), 209, entry for 19 December 1718.

principle remained operative as status demands chartered playhouse space. Need it be said, a good deal of the motivation for risking the unruly behaviour of those in livery was that servants advertised their employers' gentility to the audience at large. Hence the 'widow' Brumpton from *The Funeral* contemplates the end of her year's mourning:

What Pleasure 'twill be when my Lady *Brumpton's* Footman's called (who kept a place for that very purpose) to make a suddain Insurrection of Fine Wigs in the Pit, and Side-Boxes. Then with a pretty sorrow in one's Face, and a willing Blush for being Star'd at, one ventures to look round and Bow, to one of one's own Quality.[41]

Lady Brumpton's desire to look about and have one's quality acknowledged by an appropriately deep (or reciprocally, shallow) gesture of deference indicates it is precisely the theatre's status demands that so often explain why we have any references at all to the playhouse scene from the pens of early modern audience members. For the main business of a great many of these descriptions was to inscribe the writer's position within the auditorium's status arrangement. Noting 'from where I sat' became second nature because it was important. Next to going to church, the late Stuart theatre was one of the most common means for the upper reaches of London society to take routine, social stock of itself. An early issue of *The Female Tatler* expressly compared the two spaces for this very reason. So did other texts, though more briefly since the status-ridden nature of both venues was proverbial.[42] Hence John Evelyn, for instance, wishing to disparage the excessive social preening and scrutiny that occurred in London on the sabbath, could refer knowingly to the metropolis's 'Theatrical Churches'.[43]

One's social position found subjective measure within the theatre space. During the early Restoration, Samuel Pepys, a civil servant of urban middling origin, gauged his social standing and progress on a fairly regular basis whilst at the playhouse. As just one example of the process of social evaluation that he went through, he mused:

Which is the first time I ever sat in a box in my life. And in the same box came by and by, behind me, my Lord Berkly and his Lady; but I did not turn my face to them to be known, so that I was excused from giving them my seat. And this pleasure I had, that from this place the Scenes do appear very fine endeed and much better then in the pit.[44]

Later spectators seem to have made similar assessments of their own, the theatre's social grid (if not its precise demographic) retaining its basic contours

41 R. Steele, *Funeral* (1702), i, 8. Also Anon., *Letters of Love and Gallantry. Volume II* (1694), 155–6.

42 *Female Tatler*, no. 7 (20–22 July 1709), [2]. See E. Settle, *A Defence of Dramatick Poetry* (1698), 8; *Tatler*, no. 3 (16 April 1709), vol. I, 32; J. Ralph, *The Touch-Stone* (1728), 141.

43 *Evelyn*, 18 July 1703, vol. V, 542.

44 *Pepys*, 19 October 1667, vol. VIII, 487. Similar references include *ibid.*, 19 January 1661, vol. II, 18; 16 December 1661, vol. II, 234; 1 January 1668, vol. IX, 2; 6 January 1668, vol. IX, 12.

well into the eighteenth century. For instance, Dudley Ryder, when penning the extant months of his diary in the mid-1710s, expressed satisfaction at being able to mix successfully in fashionable London society. He noted quite specifically the times he was able to view a play (or part thereof) from a front or side-box, sometimes making related social comments about the quality of those around him such as: 'At the play there were the ladies that I danced with at Ironmongers' Hall in the first row of the front box and one of them extremely fine. She is married as I believe.'[45] Byrd seemed to take a seat in the boxes for granted, allowing him to concentrate intently on the degree of his proximity to the *beau monde*'s leading lights. For example, after attending a benefit night for the actress Mrs Porter, he noted that he 'sat by my Lady Buck'. Perhaps sitting near the wife of a baronet was now run-of-the-mill since, earlier that season, he 'had an occasion to do a civil thing to the Duke of Buckingham'.[46] Even the likes of John Byrom, a gentleman from the North who usually disparaged either the quality or the utility of the theatrical diversions he witnessed whilst resident in London during the later 1720s and early 1730s, still made a point of noting in his diary or letters where he had been placed in the social arena of the theatre; whether 'behind the scenes' (i.e. on the stage) or in the pit.[47]

This habit of mind also found encouragement in comic dialogue itself. For example, the eligible young gentlewoman from *Kensington Gardens* dismisses a novice attorney as a possible suitor saying, 'I have no notion of a Man who is but just arriv'd at the Bar from seeing no more than the two last Acts of a Play in the Eighteenpenny-Gallery.'[48] Eighteen pence was the sale price for a seat in the middle gallery.[49] Evidently his thrifty behaviour at the theatre exposed middling status, too low for her to entertain a marriage proposal.

However, when scrutinized more closely, these confident ascriptions of playhouse cum social placement also betray possible contradiction. What, for example, was Dudley Ryder, the second son of an upper-middling London linendraper and a law student at the time, doing in a prominent box-seat? Ideally the box-keepers, to maintain proper social order, should have shown him to the middle gallery. Ryder had a penchant for gatecrashing social events that were,

[45] 6 November 1716, in W. Matthews (ed.), *The Diary of Dudley Ryder 1715–1716* (London, 1939), 360. Other references to taking a box-seat include: 1 November 1715; 16 October 1716; 15 November 1716, in *ibid.*, 128, 348, 364.

[46] 16 March 1719 and 10 January 1719, in Wright and Tinling, *London Diary*, 244, 217–18.

[47] 5 May 1725 and 14 January 1726, in R. Parkinson (ed.), *The Private Journal and Literary Remains of John Byrom* (Chetham Society, Manchester, old series, 1854), vol. XXXII, 129, 190.

[48] J. Leigh, *Kensington Gardens* (1720), i, 6–7.

[49] See also H. Payne, *Morning Ramble* (1673), ii, 24; W. Wycherley, *Country Wife* (1675), i, 14; Crowne, *English Frier*, iv, 32. Seat prices for the various sections of the playhouse fluctuated during our period, often depending on whether the play was a new production or not. Common price ranges were as follows: stage (+6*s*.); boxes (4–5*s*.); pit (2*s*. 6*d*.–4*s*.); middle gallery (1*s*. 6*d*.–2*s*.); upper gallery (free–1*s*.). See J. Milhous, 'Company Management', in R. D. Hume (ed.), *The London Theatre World, 1660–1800* (Carbondale, 1980), 17–18.

strictly speaking, above his status. These included dances where he mingled with people whom he also encountered at the playhouse. After one such occasion he expressly noted that he was at first refused entry, 'but as I appeared like a gentleman and told them plainly I came only to dance they let me in'.[50]

Yet Ryder's behaviour was not that unusual, at least as far as the playhouse was concerned. For although the middle sort/middle gallery equation was oft-repeated, just as noticeable were those spectators who chose to ignore it. Some scorned them for doing this, whilst others blithely accepted or positively encouraged the flouting of social decorum. In one of his essays, Richard Steele proposed setting up a review committee drawn from the audience which was to comprise, among others, 'Three Substantial Citizens for the Pit'. In the front boxes, Lucinda, daughter of the merchant citizen Mr Sealand, was one notional candidate for three 'gentlewomen' to be drawn thence.[51] Given Steele's willingness to grant merchant citizens social parity with 'genteel' landowners, his apparently innocent description is actually a loaded one. He had made a similar point when imagining a visit by *The Tatler*'s gentleman eidolon, his sister, and her upper-middling merchant husband to the theatre. They were to sit in a box where 'all who shall be at the Play will allow him to have the Mien of a worthy *English* Gentleman, her that of a notable and deserving Wife'.[52] An ambiguous social trajectory was also apparent on the part of the citizen family featured in Elkanah Settle's *City-Ramble*. The cit characters were placed in the middle gallery before being brought on to the stage to mingle with the gentle spectators and continue their performances.[53] Similar movement had already been forecast by one of the citizens featured in Thomas Rawlins's *Tom Essence* from 1677. To avoid a repeat of the mere suspicion of her infidelity (and presumably all that we have been arguing this represents metaphorically), Tom the milliner requests his wife must now take a box-seat when at the theatre, keeping away from the 'bawdery' of both gallery and pit.[54] Yet we should not be at all surprised to find that the matter was never left to rest, that any resolution was temporary. Hence, only a few months later, an epilogue for an Aphra Behn comedy at the same theatre thrusts the citizens firmly back in their middle-gallery places. What is more, the proclamation is made by the cit who *has* certainly been cuckolded this time around.[55] In other words, situating the cit character on the far side of the genteel divide tallied, not coincidentally, with the placement of erstwhile middling spectators from the City.

50 29 October 1715, in Matthews, *Diary of Ryder*, 127.

51 *Theatre*, no. iii (9 January 1720), ed. J. Loftis (Oxford, 1962), 10.

52 *Tatler*, no. 184 (13 June 1710), vol. III, 7.

53 E. Settle, *City-Ramble* (1711), i, 2.

54 T. Rawlins, *Tom Essence* (1677), v, 66–7. Cf. also the behaviour of Mrs Striker, the haberdasher's wife, in T. Shadwell, *Humorists* (1671), i, 10; Shadwell, *Lancashire Witches* (1682), epilogue.

55 A. Behn, *Debauchee* (1677), epilogue by 'E.R.'. The exact performance dates for the two plays are uncertain, though there is reasonable evidence that both debuted during the 1676–7 season of the Duke's Theatre.

In a not dissimilar manner, the pit might also witness scenes of social ambivalence. Censuring instances of non-genteel and uncivil behaviour, a conduct book, *The Man of Manners*, assumed that its readers were so familiar with the type of confusion found here that it could be adduced as a shorthand explanation of more intimate social *faux pas*. In relation to observing the niceties of status at meals by arraying guests according to their precedence, it complained that 'Families of Tradesmen, of a great Worth and Account, who make very considerable Figures in their Coffee-Houses and Warehouses . . . shew little or no regard to the seating themselves at Table, but all run promiscuously into the Dining-room, as into the Pit at a Playhouse.'[56] Other literature was even more telling on the matter of how the pit might prompt awkward questions concerning social priority. For example, a guide to Restoration London claimed that the pit was one of the best places for elite males to be seen. Further, it contrasted the rakish knight who might acquire a mistress there with the gentleman who would encounter his future wife. Yet the groom-to-be sounded suspiciously like a citizen whose marriage would prove anything but monogamous: 'If you be but a meer *Fleetstreet* Gentleman . . . assure your self . . . you are the first and principal man in election to begin the number of *We three*.'[57]

In the eyes of John Macky gender was apparently just as important as status in determining who sat in the middle gallery, for his early eighteenth-century observations on the playhouse found only 'Citizens Wives and Daughters' there. He implies that City fathers and sons are to be found in the pit, yet he concluded that this area 'contains the *Gentlemen* on Benches'.[58] A decade or so later, James Ralph, sometime travelling companion to a young Benjamin Franklin, was more forthright.[59] Referring to the pit, he wrote of 'substantial, plain, sober Tradesmen' and then rather pointedly included these people among 'the Quality from *Cheapside, Ludgate-Hill, Covent-Garden*, or the *Strand*'.[60] The use of the term 'quality' suggests the view that these particular City inhabitants were somehow on a par with those who were well-born, the gentlemen and -women with whom the citizens were sharing this space in spite of the stricture that the pit be exclusively for the genteel.

56 E. Jones, *The Man of Manners* (1737), 7–8.

57 S. Vincent, *The Young Gallant's Academy* (1674), 57. Vincent appears to have cribbed the phrase 'meer Fleet-street Gentleman' from Thomas Dekker's *The Guls Horne-booke* (1609), 29. Yet, literary similarities aside, Vincent does seem to have been aware of a changed social dynamic within the later seventeenth-century playhouse since Dekker was originally referring to the situation among a smaller number of stage (not pit) spectators.

58 Macky, *Journey through England*, 171. *Emphasis added.* A similar gender bias is implicit in Anon., *Whitsun-tide Ramble*, 7.

59 For their visits to the playhouse and reading aloud of plays during 1725–6, see L. W. Labaree, R. L. Ketcham, H. C. Boatfield, and H. H. Fineman (eds.), *The Autobiography of Benjamin Franklin* (New Haven, 1964), 95–8.

60 Ralph, *Touch-Stone*, 139.

Perhaps attempting to play both sides and raising issues that we will discuss further, *The Spectator* published a letter which contemporaries identified as being from a prominent (and living) wholesale linen-draper. A social dissonance similar to Ralph's use of the term 'quality' is evoked by the contradictory nature of the opening lines. On the one hand, they note the absence of the gentleman's weapon from the hip of the present writer, which, the syntax suggests, is an accessory of those who dominate the playhouse (i.e. the gentle). On the other hand, our citizen is on a level with the 'gentlemen' in the pit by the very act of being present at the theatre:

I do not wear a Sword, but I often divert my self at the Theatre . . . I was in the Pit the other Night, (when it was very much crowded) a Gentleman leaning upon me, and very heavily, I very civilly requested him to remove his Hand; for which he pulled me by the Nose. I would not resent it in so publick a Place, because I was unwilling to create a Disturbance; but have since reflected upon it as a thing that is unmanly and disingenuous, renders the Nose-puller odious, and makes the Person pulled by the Nose look little and contemptible.[61]

Incidentally, this kind of dislocation may explain why 'gentlemen' were so intent on asserting their right to be onstage during the performance. The other elite precincts of the playhouse had been infiltrated by well-heeled urban types or, at least, this was a common impression.

Such disconcerting experiences for individuals like Ryder and the 'quality' from City suburbs like Cheapside (to say nothing for those like Byrd who came from the periphery of Britain's growing empire where they made their fortunes from both land and trade and were positioned as elites in these colonies,[62] or Pepys's 'Lord Berkly and his Lady' who actually had extensive, multiple ties to the City[63]) demonstrate that as much as the playhouse space attempted to endorse a status hierarchy, the theatre's bottom line was quite literally a matter of class. The theatre's position in the marketplace meant that money rather than pedigree ultimately decided where one sat in the auditorium, and fostered a dawning perception that society was, or should be, more often divided along lines of current material inequality than distinctions inherited at birth.

It is therefore misleading, on the one hand, to argue that playhouse tariffs simply 'imposed rigid social distinctions'.[64] The question is what kind of social

61 *Spectator*, no. 268 (7 January 1712), vol. II, 544–5.

62 See K. A. Lockridge, 'Colonial Self-Fashioning: Paradoxes and Pathologies in the Construction of Genteel Identity in Eighteenth-Century America', in R. Hoffman, M. Sobel, and F. J. Teute (eds.), *Through a Glass Darkly. Reflections on Personal Identity in Early America* (Chapel Hill, 1997), 274–339; M. J. Rozbicki, *The Complete Colonial Gentleman. Cultural Legitimacy in Plantation America* (Charlottesville, 1998).

63 *Pepys*, vol. X, 27.

64 H. W. Pedicord, 'The Changing Audience', in R. D. Hume (ed.), *The London Theatre World, 1660–1800* (Carbondale, 1980), 243; also J. Loftis *et al.* (eds.), *The Revels History of Drama. Volume V: 1660–1750* (London, 1976), 18.

distinction was usually paramount. On the other hand, the suggestion that commercial entertainments like the comic drama 'dissolved society's class distinctions' is equally vague.[65] In a very important sense the playhouse made class differences painfully evident, and promoted an alternative ordering of society on the basis of wealth rather than simply mimicking a pre-existent ordering by status: structuration by pedigree alone. Royal proclamations often captured a strong trace of this ambiguity, which they attempted to resolve by commanding that

> no Person of what Quality soever, presume to stand behind the Scenes, or come upon the Stage, either before or during the Acting of any opera or play : And that no Person come into Either of Our Houses for Opera or Comedy without paying first the Established Prices for their respective places.[66]

The first injunction assumes a place for everyone on the basis of inherited degree, the implication being that not even titled gentlemen of the realm can claim a prerogative which interferes with the evening's production. This certainty slips away with the second prohibition, efforts to retrieve it ('their respective places') proving a dead letter in the face of a market-driven order ('Established Prices').

It was distinctly possible for the audience to experience status anxiety, a dissonance akin to that represented onstage by the citizen cuckold scenario. The equivocal nature of the theatre space encouraged a peculiar type of social knowledge. Some comic dialogue made a point of tweaking this social nerve in no uncertain terms, broaching the idea that the playgoing experience rehearsed potentially contradictory lines of social differentiation because wealth edged out lineage; cash confounded the accepted status distinctions of the theatre space. Thus *The Humour of the Age* gave voice to a disconcerting situation which must have been rehearsed time and again within the social arena of the late Stuart playhouse. Drawing the parallel with churchgoing that we noted earlier, and referring once again to the anomalous power of the City, it ran:

> LUCIA: . . . I have seen a fat City Lady tawdrily dress'd in the Year of her Shrievalty, elbow into the Box, as if she had a Prerogative of Place, because she claims it in the City; and wou'd rather pay a double Price, than not have the Front Seat.
>
> RAILTON: Nay, some go to Church too only to be seen. I knew a Proctor's Wife of the Commons us'd to send her Footman every Sunday to keep her a Front-Seat in the Box at *Pauls*.
>
> WILSON: I wonder, the Play-house is not divided here as the Theatre at *Rome* us'd to be, where every one sat according to his respective Quality, and not as he was able to pay.[67]

[65] J. Brewer, *The Pleasures of the Imagination. English Culture in the Eighteenth Century* (London, 1997), 74; also Knif, *Gentlemen and Spectators*, 197, 215.

[66] Order of 13 November 1711 cited in A. Jackson, 'The Stage and the Authorities, 1700–1714 (as Revealed in the Newspapers)', *RES* 14 (1938), 61. A similar example from 1704 is quoted on 59.

[67] T. Baker, *Humour of the Age* (1701), iv, 49–50.

Although it almost certainly exaggerated the social differences elided by the purchase of particular seats, *The Female Tatler* presented an even more outspoken discussion of the matter as it vented spleen at the social discrepancy and discomfort which one could experience whilst at the theatre. Responding to *The British Apollo*, a rival paper, the editorial railed against

> their saying, *All Ranks of People are received at Plays on equal Terms*, 'tis so lame an excuse for their ridiculous *Consort*, that they ought eternally to blush for't. The *Theatre* has *Pit*, *Box*, and *Galleries* for Distinction, and when the meaner sort have the assurance to crowd into the best Places, how they are jostl'd and ridicul'd; at *Consorts* of Note the Prices are extravagant, purposely to keep out inferiour People; but as their Tickets are to be delivered *gratis* to each Subscriber, ev'ry Purse-proud Ale-Wife thinks her self as good as Quality, and as she does 'em as much Service, expects as forward a Seat; and what Woman o' Fashion will lessen her Character, or care to have her Cloaths sullied by sitting *Jig* by *Jole* with *Apollo's* Taplashes.[68]

Note especially the juxtaposition of social terms. Ideally settled on the basis of their status, people of 'rank' and 'quality' are crowded out by individuals of a particular 'sort'. Although branded 'meaner', it is clear that this last grouping has assumed social priority on the basis of their relatively greater wealth instead of their birth.[69]

The last quotes also suggest that a brief but informative contrast may be drawn from late Stuart representations of theatres in the ancient world. These rather wistful portrayals assume a golden age when Graeco-Roman spectators were 'seated in decent Order' and so relieved of a 'promiscuous' or 'disagreeing' audience like that confronting the early modern playgoer. At least one such comparison depended heavily on the incorrect assertion that no money changed hands at classical venues.[70] In related fashion, both John Evelyn and Andrew Marvell were ruffled by the Court's inability to enforce strict protocols of precedence and exclusion that were meant to obtain when a theatre company gave a command performance at a royal residence.[71] Evelyn blamed this situation on the 'scandalous' novelty of people paying for admission.[72]

68 *Female Tatler*, no. 25 (31 August–2 September 1709), [2]. For the proverbial hostility to alewives, their socio-economic potential, and possible similarities with other City wives, see J. M. Bennett, 'Misogyny, Popular Culture, and Women's Work', *HWJ* 31 (1991), 168, 172, 177.

69 For a less vituperative example of a similar logic underwriting a description of the theatre audience, see *Review of the State of the English Nation*, no. 128 (26 October 1706), book 8, 512.

70 These quotes come respectively from representations of ancient drama found in *Examiner*, no. 12 (14–21 February 1711), vol. II, [1] (also repeated in *British Journal*, no. 26 (13 July 1728), [1]); Ralph, *Touch-Stone*, 150; *British Journal*, no. clxxix (12 February 1726), [1], which makes the point about paying for the entertainment.

71 Details of the kind of order that court audiences faced, and probably insisted on themselves, may be found in a case-study that focuses on another court production of the same year, E. Boswell, *The Restoration Court Stage (1660–1702) with a Particular Account of the Production of Calisto* (Cambridge, MA, 1932), 182–4.

72 29 September 1675, *Evelyn*, vol. IV, 75.

Marvell concurred, though he beat Evelyn to the punch by some two months when he explained to his correspondent that 'all Sorts of People flocking thither, and paying their Mony as at a common Playhouse; nay even a twelve-penny Gallery is builded for the convenience of his Majesty's poorer Subjects'.[73] Once again, the choice of a particular social language ('sorts', 'common') implies that it was not the absence of order *per se* but, instead, the presence of a different, partially remodulated hierarchy, and its conflicted inequalities, that these men found unnerving.

Marvin Carlson has advised that theatre is an event embedded in a complex performance matrix of social concerns and actions, all of which contribute to meaning.[74] Just as London's playgoers could attend the theatre and have a particular vision of society brought to their attention, it was almost as though its constant reiteration by various texts worked at cross-purposes and actually led to the expectation of social dissonance once they had arrived. Some perhaps went looking for places where the grid had failed. While attempting to inscribe a status hierarchy the drama's social integrity was put to the test by countervailing tendencies of the medium. Enmeshed in particular modalities of commercial production, the comedies often mediate a fundamental social discrepancy which the larger theatrical experience itself helped to generate and make manifest, subsequently allowing for a critical perspective on the dominant socio-cultural construction known as gentility. Hence the act of attendance could be crucial for making sense of the action being performed, the oft-repeated centrepiece of the citizen's riding.

The reverse was also true, that comic plots relied on the theatre as episteme for their inspiration and their making of meaning. Thus some comedies looked to the theatre as social microcosm and found it wanting, the prosperous middling urbanite appearing, from one point of view, out of place in the gallery and more like those occupying the higher-status pit or even the boxes. Some tried, apparently in vain, to rework either the language of social ascription or the accepted status hierarchy of the theatre space so as to make for a better degree of fit. For instance, Behn's *Luckey Chance*, in the context of commenting on the City (in particular an alderman's daughter), thought in terms of 'Ladys of Quality in the middle Gallery'.[75] Adopting the alternative, an epilogue for Mary Pix's *Innocent Mistress* toyed with what the auditorium might look like if only London's citizens were present:

> Rich Sparks with broad-brim-hats and little Bands,
> Who'll clap dry Morals till they hurt their Hands;
> Nice Dames? who'll have their Box as they've their Pew,
> And come each Day, but not to ogle you:

[73] Marvell to William Popple, 24 July 1675, in H. M. Margoliouth (ed.), *The Poems and Letters of Andrew Marvell* (Oxford, 1952), vol. II, 320.
[74] M. Carlson, *Places of Performance. The Semiotics of Theatre Architecture* (Ithaca, 1989), 204–6.
[75] A. Behn, *Luckey Chance* (1687), iv, 49.

No, each side Box shall shine with sweeter Faces;
None but Chains, Gowns and Coifs shall have their Places,
Their Chit-chat News, Stockjobbing, and Law-Causes.
The Middle-Fry shall in the Gall'ry sit,
And *humh* whatever against Cuckold's Writ.
And City Wives from Lectures throng the Pit.[76]

Fifteen years later, and still trying to settle the audience, Charles Shadwell's *Humours of the Army* took up a more subtle tack when identifying the 'middle Gallery . . . fill'd with the middle Part of the City', while it silently begged the question of what to do with the 'upper' part of the City, the prosperous types who were so often ridden onstage.[77]

Citizens could turn out to watch the cit's riding with the smug satisfaction that they were not like *those* people onstage. Might they gradually have been able to garner confidence that they were also as good as the genteel spectators they sat next to? If, that is, they successfully avoided any social *contretemps* over the course of the evening. The next two chapters will consider this possibility and its implications for our understanding of the late Stuart audience.

76 M. Pix, *Innocent Mistress* (1697), epilogue by P. Motteux. *Italics reversed.*

77 C. Shadwell, *Humours of the Army* (1713), i, 4. A similar point was made by the epilogue to T. Durfey's *The Old Mode and the New* (1703).

5 Excluding the riff-raff

> And at the request of many of the Nobility (who have taken Tickets) 2 Benches of the Pit will be Rail'd in, for more Conveniency. And to prevent any Disappointment, by coming late, 'tis desir'd that their Servants may be sent by 2 a Clock with the Tickets to keep Places.
>
> Advertisement (Drury Lane, 12 February 1708)

It might be argued that a status–class contradiction was neither personally nor commonly experienced at the late Stuart playhouse. If the well-born were also the well-heeled, the standard price of a box-seat (five or six shillings) was presumably trifling for a genteel playgoer. Such logic makes for the conclusion by one scholar of the Restoration theatre that the audience was socially 'balanced'. An orderly cross-section of the social hierarchy can be largely assumed from the graduated price schedule.[1] In the final analysis, this chapter begs to differ. While the audience as a whole might have represented virtually all social levels it did so neither proportionately (it was top-heavy, weighted in a genteel direction) nor in any straightforward manner (criteria for defining and arranging social levels were disputed). We need to keep in mind the impact of some interrelated variables that had the potential to complicate the composition of the late Stuart audience. Like the business of buying a ticket or token, these variables were connected with the marketplace and further tangled the knot of social ambiguity often drawn taut at the metropolis's patent theatres, come each season of comic entertainment.

The aim of any new comedy was to make money, to pack the house and, in particular, to fill those seats in box and pit that fetched the higher prices. Indeed, in some instances, the pit was combined with the boxes as a flimsy justification for inflating ticket prices and profits.[2] As far as the playwright was concerned, the original target audience was those with deep pockets.[3] Performances had to

1 A. R. Botica, 'Audience, Playhouse and Play in Restoration Theatre, 1660–1710', unpublished DPhil dissertation, Oxford University (1985), 12, 110.

2 Defoe notes door prices as high as 6 shillings. Subscribers or 'stage-sitters' may have paid even more for their places, particularly if they had to tip playhouse employees to provide this concession, *Review of the State of the English Nation*, no. 128 (26 October 1706), book 8, 512; below p. 117.

3 J. L. Styan, *Restoration Comedy in Performance* (Cambridge, 1986), 7.

pique the interest of the genteel in order to make a capital gain. This contention, and the corollary that the audience for London's theatre was not of a boundless social depth, can be supported by several items of circumstantial evidence.

First, as Anthony Masters once pointed out, a key reason for the Crown's licensing of a maximum of two theatres with limited seating capacity was the preservation of the value of its monopoly over a finite clientele willing to pay good money to be amused.[4] The *combined* capacity of the late Stuart theatres could not even muster half that of Shakespeare's Globe but, then again, early eighteenth-century managers were not much interested in trying to profit from the accrued pittances of mass, pedestrian audiences. Given the main demographic they aimed for, such a marketing strategy might well have been counterproductive. Hence John Downes, long-time book-keeper and prompter for the Lincoln's Inn company (1662–1706), could recall that their move to the spacious Queen's Theatre in the Haymarket did not make for an equally expansive patronage:

> The Audiences falling off extremly with entertaining the Gentry with such old Ware, whereas, had they Open'd the House at first, with a good new *English* Opera, or a new Play; they wou'd have preserv'd the Favour of Court and City, and gain'd Reputation and Profit to themselves.[5]

Second, if William Byrd's diary is any indication, many members of this early eighteenth-century audience were theatre *habitués*. That is to say the same people returned to the playhouses again and again, night after night.[6] Byrd himself attended the theatre an average of six or seven times a month, about once every three to four acting days.[7] He went to the playhouse not only to be 'diverted', as he put it, but also to see, meet and talk with people whom he knew. These people included titled men and women, members of well-established landed families, some individuals with connections to the City

4 A. Masters (ed. S. Trussler), *The Play of Personality in the Restoration Theatre* (Woodbridge, 1992), 89.

5 J. Downes, in M. Summers (ed.), *Roscius Anglicanus* (New York, 1929), 48.

6 A factor generally observed by Botica, 'Audience', 153–4. See also the London social schedule outlined by Lady Montagu to Alexander Pope, 17 June 1717, in R. Halsband (ed.), *The Complete Letters of Lady Mary Wortley Montagu. Volume I: 1708–1720* (Oxford, 1965), 367.

7 It should be noted that the published transcript of Byrd's London diary, L. B. Wright and M. Tinling (eds.), *William Byrd of Virginia. The London Diary (1717–1721) and Other Writings* (New York, 1958), is incomplete in two respects. First, the original manuscript is extant only for the last twenty-three months of his stay (mid-December 1717 to late November 1719). Byrd evidently arrived in London during the spring of 1715 and was soon joined in his social round by his wife who, tragically, was to contract smallpox and die in 1716. Second, the diary's editors do not index the majority of entries where Byrd records that he visited the playhouse. I count some 110 possible instances occurring across approximately fifteen months of theatre productions, also bearing in mind that the theatres operated on an absolute maximum of twenty-six days a month. The theatres were closed during their season for all Sundays; Wednesdays and Fridays during Lent; throughout Passion Week; on national days of mourning, fasting or thanksgiving.

where Byrd had familial and business ties. Only a handful of times did he make it explicit that he had been to the playhouse and *not* seen someone he recognized.[8] This state of affairs implies that the core of many an audience could readily afford multiple tickets and further reinforces the view that the audience was quite socially circumscribed for much of the theatre season. It was this relative intimacy that allowed Byrd to have seemingly chance encounters with friends and associates at the playhouse, time and again. Earlier, in 1676, it meant that William Cavendish, future duke of Devonshire, had incurred 'great scandal by dayly frequenting [the] theater' following his wounding of Lord Mohun, then critically ill, in a duel.[9] Yet that same theatre season also demonstrates that a lordly retinue (if such had attended Lord Cavendish to the theatre) was not required to proclaim the presence of a prominent few to an anonymous, more promiscuous many. The Royal Society's principal technician, Robert Hooke, had been pointed to and tittered at when he attended *The Virtuoso*, Thomas Shadwell's satire on the natural philosophers of the Society.[10] It appears even Hooke could not escape into a faceless crowd but, rather, was embarrassed by a well-informed, fairly exclusive audience. Similarly, Samuel Pepys was sometimes worried about being recognized at afternoon performances because this might be taken as a dereliction of his official duties.[11] Yet perhaps his concern was misplaced. There is some evidence to suggest that playhouse door-keepers, the more attentive ones at least, could learn to identify particular patrons on sight, telling enquirers whether individuals were in attendance that evening and relaying messages to the said parties.[12]

Third, given this genteel mode of regularly visiting the playhouse, novelty was at a premium.[13] New productions were therefore 'puffed' wherever possible, in newspapers and periodicals, on printed bills, by word of mouth about other places of fashionable resort. As more than one social commentator observed, a key selling-point was precisely the promise that the stage entertainment *and* those attending it would be socially superior or 'genteel'.[14] Plays

[8] Entries for 16 January 1718 and 20 October 1719, in Wright and Tinling, *London Diary*, 66, 330.

[9] Charles Hatton to his brother Christopher, 30 December 1676, in E. M. Thompson (ed.), *Correspondence of the Family of Hatton* (Camden Society, London, 1878), vol. XXII, 143.

[10] Entry for 2 June 1676, in H. W. Robinson and W. Adams (eds.), *The Diary of Robert Hooke M.A., M.D., F.R.S., 1672–1680* (London, 1935), 235. The master watchmaker Thomas Tompion and a City JP accompanied Hooke. The trio met a City Surveyor at the theatre.

[11] 7–8 December 1666, *Pepys*, vol. VII, 399 and 401; 1 April 1668, *ibid.*, vol. IX, 144.

[12] See, for example, the sequence in G. Etherege, *She Wou'd If She Cou'd* (1671), iv, 51. Or, indeed, the remarks of Pepys himself, 30 December 1667, *Pepys*, vol. VIII, 598–600.

[13] The present chapter therefore broadly agrees with the recent account of early eighteenth-century production values offered by K. W. Scheil, *The Taste of the Town. Shakespearian Comedy and the Early Eighteenth-Century Theater* (Cranbury, NJ, 2003), esp. 87ff. However, the following pages offer a different explanation of the clientele said to have sponsored these values.

[14] See *Female Tatler*, no. 69 (12–14 December 1709), [2] (and advertisements using the presentation of 'genteel' costumes as an additional attraction); *Review of the State of the English Nation*, no. 129 (29 October 1706), book 8, 515–16; K. Crouch, 'The Public Life of Actresses: Prostitutes

were marketed as having been requested by 'persons of quality', 'several ladies or gentlemen'.[15] Playwrights solicited the attendance of their patron, and his or her kith and kin.[16]

Fourth, genteel correspondents writing to and from diverse locations typically considered the offerings and happenings of the London playhouses to be noteworthy, even when the 'town' was otherwise 'empty of' or there was 'noe news'.[17] At the same time these writers assumed detailed prior knowledge of dramatists and their plays.[18] This was particularly true when their letters enclosed copies of the latest satiric verses or pamphlets ridiculing prominent contemporaries because these texts frequently alluded to comedic characters in order to score points against their targets.[19] Indeed, the letters themselves could lampoon on the basis of extensive familiarity with the offerings of London's stage and the assumption that their recipients shared such knowledge. Hence, in late September 1708, Anne Clavering commented to her brother about the political position of two MPs: 'Should that happen and some farsess again played in the House it should be the marriage-hater match and he play the part of Solon and Tom Titt that of Byass.' His sister assumed that Sir James would recall two characters from Thomas Durfey's *Marriage-Hater Match'd* (1693).[20] Likewise, in reporting the transient religious position of the Swedish king to

or Ladies?', in H. Baker and E. Chalus (eds.), *Gender in Eighteenth-Century England. Roles, Representations and Responsibilities* (London, 1997), 68.

15 For facsimile examples, see L. R. N. Ashley (ed.), *A Narrative of the Life of Mrs. Charlotte Charke* (Gainesville, 1969), 55b, 169a. It was also possible for bills and newspaper notices to claim that the advertised play had been substituted for by another because these same patrons demanded it. For instance, J. Milhous and R. D. Hume, 'Revision of *The London Stage. Part II 1700–1729*', 24 and 26 October 1702 (Drury Lane). See too A. Jackson, 'Play Notices from the Burney Newspapers 1700–1703', *PMLA* 48 (1933), *passim*, including similar marketing strategies employed by the purveyors of printed playbooks.

16 For example, the correspondence of Leonard Welsted and Lewis Theobald from 1726–7 to the earl and countess of Oxford respectively, HMC, *Portland* 29, 6 (1901), 17, 20.

17 Lady Mary Bertie to Katherine Noel, 2 January 1671, HMC, *Rutland* 24, 2 (1889), 22; Lord Granville to Sir William Leveson, 5 May 1688, HMC, *Fifth Report* 4, 1 (1876), 197.

18 See the series of letters about attendance by the Berties (1670 and 1685–6) in HMC, *Rutland* 24, 2 (1889), 22–3 and 99–106, 119; the letters of Lady Irwin to Lord Carlisle (1728–9) in HMC, *Carlisle* 42, 1 (1897), 54–7. See also correspondence which announced the forthcoming attraction of playhouse satire, for instance Marvell to Edward Harley, 17 November 1677, in H. M. Margoliouth (ed.), *The Poems and Letters of Andrew Marvell* (Oxford, 1952), vol. II, 330.

19 For letters featuring comedic allusions and references see the likes of Dr William Stratford to Edward Harley, 26–31 October 1720 and 23 August 1724, HMC, *Portland* 29, 7 (1901), 280–1 and 382 (blends reference to Jonsonian and Shadwellian characters to voice dislike of certain people); Sir Michael Warton to Lord Dartmouth, 10 August 1710, HMC, *Dartmouth* 20, 1 (1887), 296 (snubs former Treasurer Godolphin by describing him as 'Sieur Volpone' – Warton's version of the nickname derived from Ben Jonson's much revived play *Volpone*); Richard Horsey to Sir Robert Rich, 9 October 1688, MS X.d.451(136), Folger Shakespeare Library (which alludes to Thomas Shadwell's recent *Squire of Alsatia* to show up their rival opinions on William of Orange).

20 Anne to Sir James Clavering, 23 September 1708, in H. T. Dickinson (ed.), *The Correspondence of Sir James Clavering (1680–1748)* (Surtees Society, Durham, 1967), vol. CLXXVIII, 14. Last performed on 8 March 1708 at Drury Lane.

Lord Harley, Matthew Prior saw the lighter side of things by comparing the Scandinavian monarch to the cit character from Edward Ravenscroft's *Citizen Turn'd Gentleman* (1672), also prepared to deny his faith in favour of political expediency.[21] With more seriousness and sentiment, Mary Pierrepont referred to late Stuart drama in her epistolary courtship with Wortley Montagu.[22] If estate libraries and archives, or the advertisements of genteel periodicals,[23] are anything to go by, these packets of correspondence also included series of playbooks, dramatic anthologies and, increasingly, a range of genteel paraphernalia that aimed to cash in on the drawpower of leading actors and favourite scenes by depicting them in quite expensive prints fit for the parlour wall or porcelain for the dressing table, on playing cards used for gambling or fans carried to assemblies.[24]

If we lack the quantitative evidence to show statistically that the main audience demographic comprehended those who claimed gentility, we can at least demonstrate how a superior social profile was a key aim for those scripting and producing the comedies. Writers, actors and managers fully expected their audiences to be mainly genteel and simultaneously did their best to *create* this social profile.[25] To encourage an equally plebeian presence in-season would only tarnish the lustre of refinement they worked so hard to achieve.

Yet despite their efforts to strike an elevated social tone, it is equally true to say that the comedy's producers hoped for too many spectators rather than too few. They wanted crowds of several hundred and then some (a surplus) to ensure that the playhouse was filled to capacity for maximum gain. Therefore, in the case of much-anticipated performances like *The Conscious Lovers*' initial run, or plays which had been requested by influential patrons, it is very likely that a ticket was not all a person required to secure one of the limited number of spaces available.[26] If purchased in advance, tickets noted the section of the playhouse one had paid to enter but it was not yet customary for them to designate a specific position within the aforesaid section. Nor was there always a clear limit on the

[21] Prior to Lord Harley, 22 June 1721, HMC, *Bath* 58, 3 (1908), 505. With no revival since 1700 recorded.

[22] Lady Mary to Wortley, *c*.22 August 1710 and 26 February 1711, in Halsband (ed.), *Montagu. Volume I: 1708–1720*, 55, 84.

[23] See *The Tatler*'s promotion of new playbooks in advertisements from first editions (e.g. no. 308, 27–29 March 1711) and the scores for the songs from comedy (e.g. no. 152, 28–30 March 1710).

[24] For playbooks (and their possible use for amateur performances) see the examples mentioned in J. T. Cliffe, *The World of the Country House in Seventeenth-Century England* (New Haven, 1999), 161–7; the case of Nicholas Blundell mentioned in chapter 6. For related prints see T. Clayton, *The English Print 1688–1802* (New Haven, 1997), 60, 91. For playing cards see Lord Boyle from Brittwell to Counsellor Kempe near Covent Garden, 24 December 1726, in E. C. Boyle (ed.), *The Orrery Papers* (London, 1903), vol. I, 67. For the rising trend of representation on personal accessories, see R. B. Gorrie, 'Gentle Riots? Theatre Riots in London 1730–1780', unpublished PhD dissertation, University of Guelph (2000), 183ff.

[25] Suggested by L. Hughes, *The Drama's Patrons. A Study of the Eighteenth-Century London Audience* (San Antonio, 1971), 81–2.

[26] See n. 15 and also the opening scene of act iv in T. Shadwell's *True Widow* (1679).

total number of tickets sold.[27] Seating assignment took place on the night and disputes were conceivably resolved in favour of the more convincing claim to social precedence.

Certainly in the event of debuts, final appearances of favourite players before their retirement, the promised attendance of a foreign envoy and his or her exotic entourage, or offerings that simply had the good fortune to be all the rage, we can speculate that the theatre venue became something like a modern, trendy night-club. On these occasions it may not have been as simple as paying to get through the lobby doors. It became more a matter of being first in the queue and enough 'in fashion' to be ushered to the place for which one had paid and for which several other people might be competing on that same night. If a particular performance was in demand, success could depend on a string of contingencies: whether a token had been purchased in advance; a servant had been sent ahead to mark an individual spot; the door-keepers chose to acknowledge both tokens and servants, or, more often than not, discriminate in favour of those who presented themselves as regular, socially superior (and perhaps suitably grateful) patrons; a spectator could defend their claim against those who came later (other spectators, servants or keepers) and insisted that room be made for somebody more important.

Often, final payment or 'settlement' for one's seat did not take place until the entertainment had begun in earnest. From those who had not purchased tickets in advance or who had managed to take a higher-priced spot than their ticket's face value, the keepers demanded money. Alternatively, the keepers refunded the money of those compelled to shift to cheaper places or who chose to leave the theatre before the main feature was underway. Furthermore, a form of scalping was possible for actors who sold tickets for their own performances to patrons falling over themselves to make a show of their generosity and also ensure the best possible seat. Hence the treasurer of Drury Lane, Zachary Baggs, explained how the veteran actor Thomas Betterton had pocketed an incredible windfall for his lead role in a rendition of William Congreve's *Love for Love*:

> But the Boxes, Pit and Stage, being laid together on his Day, and no Person admitted but by his Tickets, the lowest at half a Guinea a Ticket; Nay he had much more; for one Lady gave him Ten or Twenty Guineas, some 5 Guineas, some 2 Guineas, and most one Guinea, supposing that he designed not to act any more, and he deliver'd more Tickets out for Persons, than the Boxes, Pit, and Stage could hold; 'tis thought he clear'd at least £450 over and besides the said £76 4*s*. 5*d*.[28]

[27] Cf. the rather unusual advertisements cited in relation to a performance of the opera *Fairy Queen*, for 1 February 1703 (Milhous and Hume, 'Revision'). An added but eminently marketable degree of both exclusivity and civility was promised by high ticket prices (6*s*.); opening of the boxes into the pit; the managers' pledge that there would be only 400 places and all were to be sold in advance.

[28] This was the same performance that *The Tatler* reviewed, see above p. 97. Cited from Milhous and Hume, 'Revision', 7 April 1709. Other near-contemporary examples of players selling tickets at inflated prices can be found for 24 February and 3 March 1709.

So even for people whose social privilege went virtually without saying it could be quite a jumble, as the equally confused negatives of Lady Hervey, in relation to what would have been her second viewing of Addison's tragedy *Cato* in less than a fortnight, will attest:

I dont know a mortal that is not gone to the Play that coud get places, either in boxes, pit or gallery. I was to have gone with the Dutchess of Bolton; though it is allways as full as it can hold, yet there is more rout to day than ordinary, for my Lord Tr[easurer] and [Lord Chancellor] are to be there; tis I find made a mighty party business.[29]

Rather more definitive had been the report of Peregrine Bertie to his cousin, the countess of Rutland, in 1685: 'Yesterday was acted *The Committee*. The King and Queen were there and all the whole Court went to see it, but coming a little after it was begun, [I] could not get any roome.'[30]

Informal vetting occurred and braving it like Dudley Ryder might be called for. For instance, when writing to a friend about a musical entertainment held at Dorset Garden at the turn of the century, Congreve happened to note that the 'boxes and pit were all thrown into one; so that all sat in common: and the whole was crammed with beauties and beaux, not one scrub being admitted'.[31] A few years later, when commenting on the tyranny of fashions (in belief, but dress incidentally too), Jonathan Swift's *Tale of a Tub* imagined the social detraction experienced by three gentlemen who could not afford to buy the latest in modish shoulder-knots: 'If they went to the *Play-house*, the Door-keeper shewed them into the Twelve-peny Gallery.'[32] In other words, because of their unfashionable attire the gentlemen's status goes unrecognized and they are, as 'scrubs', assumed fit for only the cheapest of places. Similarly, *The Female Tatler* pointedly recalled the possibility of *ad hoc* sumptuary discrimination by theatre staff when it described a woman who might be of use to the playhouse impresario, Christopher Rich. This individual

never comes from *Church* but has all the Ladies and Gentlemen's *Apparel* as readily at her Fingers Ends as the *Text*. Not a Ribbon to a Cane, a Knot, or a Fan escapes her, and her Memory is so very Good, that by running over the Names of those that compose the Audience there, she would be of excellent Use in all probability to Mr *Rich*, (if ever he opens House again) to tell Noses for him in the Play-house.[33]

Evidently, those without servants to arrive at the theatre two or three hours prior to the main event in order to warm places for their employers (or the

29 Lady Hervey to John Hervey, 25 April 1713, in S. H. A. Hervey (ed.), *Letter-Books of John Hervey, First Earl of Bristol* (London, 1894), vol. I, 370.

30 Bertie to Katherine (*née* Noel), 31 December 1685, HMC, *Rutland* 24, 2 (1889), 100.

31 Congreve to Joseph Keally, 26 March 1701, in J. C. Hodges (ed.), *William Congreve. Letters & Documents* (London, 1964), 20.

32 J. Swift, *A Tale of a Tub* (1704), in H. Davis (ed.), *The Prose Works of Jonathan Swift* (Oxford, 1939), vol. I, 49.

33 *Female Tatler*, no. 29a, 9–12 September 1709, [2].

spare time to do this themselves),[34] or a clean shirt to go with a smart coat or a stylish mantua and petticoat, besides numerous other personal accessories, or the horsepower, hired or owned, to get there in the fading light (thus avoiding the dirtying of fine lace and linen, the dishevelment of modish wig), just might find themselves out of place as the curtain lifted between five and six o'clock – a time established, incidentally, in order to prevent 'Inconveniency to the Gentry'.[35]

We should not exaggerate the social depth of the first audiences of the comedies we have been discussing. The majority of late Stuart spectators were genteel and moneyed. Or could at least make it appear that this was the case. It was often claimed that certain young gentlemen in the boxes, having paid the incidental expenses of attendance out of their annual allowances, sought to avoid paying for their seats by pretending they had already done so and banking on their superior social front or 'presence'. Thus Charles Shadwell's *Humours of the Army* maintained that 'our rakely young Fellows, live as much by their Wits as ever; and to avoid the clinking Dun of a Box-keeper, at the End of one Act, they sneak to the opposite Side 'till the End of another; then call the Box-keeper saucy Rascal'.[36] Their behaviour was also contrasted explicitly with that of the prosperous citizens who had time and ready money to spare. Trading on the City exchange closed mid-afternoon and business or professional schedules were quite flexible.[37] Hence Thomas Pitt, governor and East India merchant of Madras, could playfully chide a London business associate after a particular deal had not been as profitable as expected:

> I cant but take notice your letter is very short, at which I cant be much concern'd when I am told you are so deeply engag'd dayly at the Play house with our ffriend Roger and Bowridge, to both whom give my service, and tell 'Em 'tis reported here that now being thoroughly accomplish'd they are coming out for the top employs of India.[38]

Similarly, the extant months of an almanac diary kept by a successor to Samuel Pepys as a commissioner for the Navy, Dennis Lyddell, indicate that even he could make an exception to the whirl of business involving politicians,

[34] A timetable evident from R. Burridge, *A Scourge for the Play-Houses* (1702), 2; Anon., *Memoirs of the Life of Robert Wilks, Esq.* (1732), 29.

[35] See, for example, the notice published in *Post Boy* (5–7 December 1700), cited from Milhous and Hume, 'Revision'. In the early Restoration years, performances had usually begun between three and four o'clock.

[36] C. Shadwell, *Humours of the Army* (1713), i, 4. For similar references to this behaviour, see Farquhar, 'A Discourse upon Comedy', 147; T. Baker, *Tunbridge-Walks* (1703), ii, 22; J. Leigh, *Kensington Gardens* (1720), i, 6.

[37] E. Ward, *The Wealthy Shop-keeper* (1700), 12; T. Brown and E. Ward, *A Legacy for the Ladies* (1705), 110, 115.

[38] Pitt to Sir Charles Eyre, from Fort St George, 29 September 1702, in H. Yule (ed.), *The Diary of William Hedges, Esq., . . . III* (Hakluyt Society, London, first series, 1889), vol. LXXVIII, lxxvii.

officers and merchants which often, but not always, kept him 'at the office all afternoon'.[39] Any constraints on one's time were of even less concern to the citizen's family, their leisured wives and children. So the epilogue to John Crowne's *Henry VI* mischievously recalled their behaviour on days when sell-out crowds were expected:

> Boxes i'th' Morning did with Beauty shine
> And Citizens then in the Pit did Dine.
> The Wife with her good Husband did prevail,
> To bring the Sucking Bottle full of Ale.
> Then on her Knees cold Capon-legs were seen,
> Her Husbands Capon-legs I do not mean.[40]

In a similar vein, Daniel Defoe remarked on the presence of 'young Citizens' in the 'Pitt and Boxes', or, less charitably, Peter Motteux disparaged them as 'City Fry . . . Who came by Three to sit on that First Row'.[41] Indeed, representations of the boxes and pit gave as much, if not more, attention to presumptuous City women as they did gentlewomen. *The British Journal* maintained that the '*City Lady* adorns the Play-House Box out of pure Love to be *Modish*'.[42] Likewise, the character of Lady Dainty in William Burnaby's *Reform'd Wife* was assigned dialogue that might have caused some squirming in the boxes when spoken:

> My great Diversion is to turn my Eyes upon the Middle Gallery; – or when a Citizen crowds her self in among us, 'tis an unspeakable Pleasure to contemplate her Airs and her Dress – And they never escape me; for I am as apprehensive of such Creatures coming near me, as some People are when a Cat is in the Room.[43]

Finally, one periodical essay described a young woman who left the theatre in her own coach, speeding by some gentlemen-beaux from the boxes who were on foot.[44] The writer's parting comment implies this indecorum was due to the fact that the woman was not really a gentlewoman but a City heiress who knew no better: 'Some say this lively Image resides near *Temple-Bar*; but I think *John* the Coachman drove towards *West-Smithfield*.'[45]

[39] D. Lyddell, 'Diary', 1706, Add. MS 74,642, f.46^r, British Library. Lyddell noted attending a performance of *Henry IV* at the Haymarket on 26 October 1706 (with an as yet unidentified associate, Mr Sergison).

[40] J. Crowne, *Henry VI. Part i* (1681), epilogue. Similar comment was made by Sir Charles Sedley's *Mulberry-Garden* (1668), i, 9; Congreve's prologue for G. Powell, *Very Good Wife* (1693).

[41] *Review of the State of the English Nation*, no. 128 (26 October 1706), book 8, 512; P. Motteux, epilogue to A. Boyer, *Achilles* (1700).

[42] *British Journal*, no. cxxxv (17 April 1725), [1].

[43] W. Burnaby, *Reform'd Wife* (1700), iii, 27.

[44] For an excellent treatment of the importance of the coach as status symbol at this time, see S. E. Whyman, *Sociability and Power in Late-Stuart England. The Cultural World of the Verneys 1660–1720* (Oxford, 1999), 100–7.

[45] *Visions of Sir Heister Ryley*, no. 44 (29 November 1710), 180.

Whilst London's playhouses were not without humble spectators, a plebeian presence (lower-middling and below) at an evening's feature presentation was conditional and usually in the minority. This much may be inferred, for instance, from the quite limited social range of comedic personae. Servants in employ were the main plebeian type portrayed onstage. Some attempt had to be made to keep the interest of employees whilst they waited on their superiors for several hours at a time. In contrast, roles of labourers, artisans or lesser tradesmen are scarce. The costs we have outlined generally militated against a sustained and sizeable 'popular' presence like that encountered at some London playhouses a century earlier.[46] One early eighteenth-century playbook even printed an epilogue that included its own explanatory note for an allusion to the more socially inclusive contours of the Jacobethan theatre ('the first Audience were the Common People'). The writer evidently considered that the contemporary spectator would not grasp the point if he or she thought in terms of the socially superior and more exclusive nature of many an audience *c.*1700.[47] A similar contrast was made by one of the period's most experienced playwrights, Elkanah Settle, an individual who catered for diverse tastes when scripting items for the patent theatres, City pageants and metropolitan fairs.[48]

In any event, further obstacles stood in the way of a sizeable or routine plebeian attendance. Although London's social geography was variegated, and the case has recently been made for the West End theatre district gradually losing some of its social sheen by the close of the seventeenth century, many ordinary working men and women would still have needed to travel a fair distance to the playhouse.[49] As satire directed at the humbler spectator who did finally make it to the entertainment relished pointing out, this usually meant 'trudging' a long way.[50] By this time quite a few of those who had paid full price may well have been preparing to leave the venue, if they had not already done so. As the maddeningly sparse jottings of Byrd or the future duke of Chandos attest,

[46] I have found much of the work on the Jacobethan theatre thought-provoking, although the debate about the nature of these earlier audiences has only recently begun to consider some of the issues raised in the following pages. Key contributions are A. J. Cook, *The Privileged Playgoers of Shakespeare's London, 1576–1642* (Princeton, 1981); M. Butler, *Theatre and Crisis 1632–1642* (Cambridge, 1984); A. Gurr, *Playgoing in Shakespeare's London* (Cambridge, 1987, second edition 1996).

[47] A. Chaves, *Cares of Love* (1705).

[48] E. Settle, *A Defence of Dramatick Poetry* (1698), 9, 89. See also J. Wright, *Historia Histrionica* (1699), 5; C. Gildon, *The Life of Mr. Thomas Betterton the Late Eminent Tragedian* (1710), 143–4; Anon., *The Stage: A Poem Inscrib'd to Joseph Addison, Esq.* (1713), 4.

[49] H. Love, 'Who Were the Restoration Audience?', *Yearbook of English Studies* 10 (1980), 36, demonstrates that the environs of Drury Lane were 'predominantly humble'. For the argument of a slow shift over time, see the conclusion of A. J. Potts, 'The Development of the Playhouse in Seventeenth-Century London', unpublished PhD dissertation, Cambridge University (1999), 209.

[50] For example, J. Dryden, *Cleomenes* (1692), prologue spoken by Mr Mountfort; S. Centlivre, *Platonick Lady* (1707), epilogue by T. Baker.

putting in an appearance for only the first act(s) of a play that one had previously seen in its entirety sometimes resembled a kind of dramatic connoisseurship cum social hauteur.[51] Byrd termed such behaviour 'looking in' or 'calling at' the playhouse, as if the theatre were the fashionable London lodgings of a genteel acquaintance.[52] On a given evening he might visit both of the capital's theatres and he occasionally noted sitting out a whole evening's entertainment as if this were somehow unusual for the drama in question.[53]

Certainly there were ways and means for the common individual to watch London's late Stuart comic drama, smaller economies of spectatorship. These included coming to view only the closing act or two, and the 'afterpieces' which followed the main feature, at nine or even ten o'clock at night. Thus the dedication to Congreve's *Way of the World* referred to the 'Multitude; such, who come with expectation to Laugh out the last Act of a Play, and are better entertain'd with two or three unseasonable Jests, than with the artful Solution of the *Fable*'.[54] Arriving late to the entertainment meant that the ticket cost was halved and, by this time, London's gainfully employed lower sort would have finished work for the day, many trades still being in full-swing when the comedy's prologue was being presented to those able to enjoy leisure time from the late afternoon onwards.[55] Another possibility was attending at points in the season where genteel spectators were expected to be thin on the ground: when the rival house or other social event was sure to draw off most of the theatre's regular patrons; nights when leading roles were played by novices and prices cheaper; or, as Pepys's nettled and well-known responses to this vulgar presumption imply, during the Christmas–New Year holidays when the *beau monde* tended to leave the metropolis for its manorial holdings in the provinces.

[51] The Huntington Library, California, holds the diary of James Brydges for 1697–1702 (future duke of Chandos), Stowe 26, vols. I–II. I owe this reference to the work of Steve Snobelen on the manuscript. While the peripatetic nature of Brydges's theatre patronage has been noted in the past (L. Hook, 'James Brydges Drops in at the Theater', *Huntington Library Quarterly* 8, 3 (1944–5), 306–11), his journal warrants reassessment in light of more recent scholarship and for what the text might reveal about playgoers other than Brydges himself. Incidentally, similar behaviour was either encouraged or attested by *Tatler*, no. 120 (14 January 1710), vol. II, 215; T. Cibber, *The Lives and Characters of the Most Eminent Actors and Actresses of Great Britain and Ireland* (1753), 69.

[52] For example, 4 October 1718 and 1 April 1719, in Wright and Tinling, *London Diary*, 181, 251.

[53] For instances of the former, see 31 January 1718 and 20 January 1719, in *ibid.*, 73, 221. For the latter, see 14 May 1718 and 19 September 1719, in *ibid.*, 121, 319.

[54] W. Congreve, *Way of the World* (1700; 1735 edition) dedication to Ralph, earl of Mountague, sig. A4^v.

[55] See, for instance, Baker, *Tunbridge-Walks*, prologue. Scheduling was even more restrictive prior to 1700 since performances could begin one or even two hours before five o'clock. The practice of half-price admission has an ambiguous history in the Restoration (25 November 1661, *Pepys*, vol. II, 220 versus 22 May 1667, *ibid.*, vol. VIII, 232; D. Thomas (ed.), *Restoration and Georgian England, 1660–1788. Theatre in Europe: A Documentary History* (Cambridge, 1989), 179–80), yet appears to have been conceded, once more, by theatre management from the 1690s (see Gorrie, 'Gentle Riots', 148ff.).

Yet it is worthwhile stressing one feature of Pepys's discomfiture at perceiving a noticeably common element at the playhouse, a feature which is actually the plebeian exception proving the genteel rule of the late Stuart audience's overall profile. To begin by quoting the most extensive of Pepys's descriptions for the benefit of those readers not already familiar with them:

> Home with great content with my wife; only not so well pleased with the company at the house today, which was full of Citizens, there hardly being a gentleman or woman in the house, but a couple of pretty ladies by us, that made sport at it, being jostled and crowded by prentices. So home . . .[56]
>
> And then abroad with my wife to a play at the Duke of York's House; the house full of ordinary citizens; the play was *Women pleased*, which we had never seen before; and though but indifferent, yet there is a good design for a good play. So home . . .[57]

In using his remarks as evidence that the later seventeenth-century London theatre was a relatively inclusive institution, commentators have disregarded Pepys's compulsion to qualify heavily his use of the term 'citizen' when disparaging what, in any case, he implies is an atypical intrusion by a non-genteel crowd.[58] His elaboration that it was '*ordinary* citizens' upsetting the social tone of entertainment and the pleonastic phrase, 'there hardly being a gentleman or woman in the house', following on from the seemingly straightforward disparagement, 'only not so well pleased with the company at the house today, which was full of Citizens', which must itself be further qualified by reference to tightly packed groups of apprentices,[59] altogether suggest that there was another species of citizen whose presence at the theatre was routine and imminently acceptable. In a word, the citizen who figured himself *genteel* and above the ordinary. A number of Pepys's theatregoing friends and colleagues, to say no more for Pepys and his wife Elizabeth, potentially fell into this very category.

A last indication that the lower sort were a minority at the late Stuart playhouse may be found in the hundreds of pages of anti-theatrical or theatre reform literature which began to pour from the presses in the late 1690s and continued in a fairly steady stream through to the early decades of the next century. Although we should not let it bear absolutely, the manifest lack of paternalistic concern for how the theatres might corrupt London's working population is deafening by its absence. As we shall see in part IV, most anti-theatrical literature was preoccupied with the theatre's effect on the 'gentry' and no more.[60] We expect that strident opposition to the theatre, which deduced some very tenuous social

[56] 27 December 1662, *Pepys*, vol. III, 295–6. [57] 26 December 1668, *ibid.*, vol. IX, 401.
[58] Cf. Botica, 'Audience', 108ff.; Potts, 'Development of the Playhouse', 121–2.
[59] A qualification perhaps also at work on 1 January 1668, *Pepys*, vol. IX, 2.
[60] This bias is clear from R. Blackmore, 'Preface to Prince Arthur, An Heroick Poem' (1695), in J. E. Spingarn (ed.), *Critical Essays of the Seventeenth Century. Volume III: 1685–1700* (Oxford, 1908), 234; Burridge, *Scourge*, 20.

ill-effects from the operation of the playhouses, would have leapt at the chance to argue that the theatre encouraged profligacy and crime among the city's lower sort. Yet, apart from noting the sorties of prostitutes and pickpockets who cruised the theatre precincts for (presumably) well-paying clients and bulging 'bungs' (well-stocked purses to steal), those who opposed the theatre did not even pretend that there was an otherwise notable plebeian presence at Lincoln's Inn Fields or Drury Lane. After a lull in the late 1710s and early 1720s theatre reform made a comeback that included a distinctly new theme, the social condescension which had been virtually absent from the earlier polemic. By this time a new theatre at Goodman's Fields was being established.[61] This playhouse, unlike the theatres of Drury Lane and Lincoln's Inn, was in the heart of working east London,[62] much more accessible in terms of the costs of attendance and times of performance. Its management consciously tried to attract a mainly plebeian clientele with knockdown ticket prices and later curtain calls. Only now was the theatre condemned for promoting idleness amid the labouring population and frowned upon for putting ideas that were above their social station into humble heads.[63]

London's patent theatres at the turn of the century neither catered for nor solicited the custom of the meaner sort to any great extent. Physical restrictions on 'mass' capacity that were only very slowly removed and the financial highs and lows of the companies (when suddenly faced with a season of offerings that failed to appeal to a limited pool of patrons who just as easily afforded the rival amusements of promenade, dance, musical assembly or scientific demonstration) indicate that the playhouses could not really hope to rouse a sizeable, alternate demand further down the social scale even if they had wanted to. Hence Robert Jennens could note

> There has been for four or five days together at the play house in Lincolns Inn Fields acted a new farce . . . the Shame [*sic*] Doctor . . . well enough done and pleases the town extremely. The other house has no company at all, and unless a new play comes out on Saturday revives their reputation, they must break.[64]

61 R. D. Hume, *Henry Fielding and the London Theatre 1728–1737* (Oxford, 1988), 39–44.

62 See G. D. H. Cole and D. C. Browning (eds.), *Daniel Defoe. A Tour Through the Whole Island of Britain* (London, 1962), part i, 328.

63 These crude arguments are readily apparent in such printed literature as Anon., *A Letter to the Right Honourable Sir Richard Brocas Lord Mayor of London. By a Citizen* (1730); *Grub Street Journal*, no. 155 (14 December 1732), [1]; [S. Richardson], *A Seasonable Examination of the Pleas and Pretensions of the Proprietors of, and Subscribers to, Play-houses, Erected in Defiance of the Royal Licence* (1735). See the equally discriminatory notice of an earlier attempt to establish a theatre in Goodman's Fields which concluded: 'This will be a great Ease to the Ladies of Rag-Fair, who are now forc'd to Trudge as far as Lincolns-Inn-Fields to mix themselves with Quality' (The *Observator* cited by Milhous and Hume, 'Revision', 30 October 1703).

64 Jennens to Thomas Coke, 19 November 1696, HMC, *Cowper* 23, 2 (1888), 367.

The most optimistic modern estimate of the size of the plebeian presence at the early Hanoverian playhouse, lower middling *et al.*, is one-third.[65] This may seem a reasonably large number, but many of these people were there at the behest of their employers and the playhouse managers gave them free but second-rate places that would not otherwise sell as a means to attract the custom of their masters and mistresses. Furthermore, about three-quarters of London's general population could be described as lower sort, but, proportionately, they purchased far fewer places at the patent theatres on any given night.

Establishing that the social scope of the late Stuart theatre was usually not plebeian suggests its dominant focus must have tended towards the genteel and upper-middling (or would-be genteel) instead. Assessing the usually limited social reach of the late Stuart playhouse, even if this is done largely in negative terms, as here, is crucial if we are to understand the nature of and reasons for the theatres' contribution to issues of elite stratification and problems concerning gentility.

[65] H. W. Pedicord, *'By Their Majesties' Command'. The House of Hanover at the London Theatres, 1714–1800* (London, 1991), 28.

6 Profiles of the genteel and rich

> A new and numerous gentry has risen among us by the Return of our fleets from sea, of our Armies from the Continent, and from the wreck of the South Sea. All these will have their Diversions and their easie partiality leads them against their own palpable interest to the Hundreds of Drury. They goe not thither because tis Just and Reasonable, but because tis become a Fashion.
>
> J. Dennis, *Causes of the Decay and Defects of Dramatick Poetry* (*c*.1725)

If the comedy's main audience claimed gentility we still need to put more of a face to it. Compared with tracing the outer bounds of the theatre's social field, recovering precise details of most of those inside it is beset by a lack of extensive, hard evidence. We can at best deduce the finer lines of the audience's character, an exercise that most studies choose not to attempt since it lacks empirical rigour. This is unfortunate because some quintessential features of the audience profile for new comedies from the later seventeenth and early eighteenth centuries have gone largely unremarked.

The absence of a strong plebeian element at least hints that many of the audience made a plausible claim to be 'gentry'. The presence of rural, ruling landowners at the London playhouse is not difficult to explain. Quite simply, the season had brought them to the metropolis. Autumn and winter were traditionally the busiest times for all kinds of urban institutions, particularly the law-courts, schools, legislature, government departments and, of course, the theatres.[1] Samuel Pepys, for example, noted the influx of members of parliament at the playhouse once the term had started in early November.[2] Their presence at the theatre probably helps explain high levels of absenteeism from afternoon sessions of the Commons.[3] Later observations also capture the attendance of groups of civil officials, and military officers on winter leave, as well as other professionals (doctors, lawyers) with time on their

[1] Peter Clark provides an evocative sketch of these broad patterns of urban sociability in his history of voluntary societies of the period, *British Clubs and Societies 1580–1800. The Origins of an Associational World* (Oxford, 2000), esp. 141–93.

[2] 2 November 1667, *Pepys*, vol. VIII, 516.

[3] For this absenteeism and proposed solutions, see M. Knights, *Politics and Opinion in Crisis, 1678–81* (Cambridge, 1994), 86, 118–19; J. Spurr, *England in the 1670s. 'This Masquerading Age'* (Oxford, 2000), 222.

hands.[4] Like the fairly ordinary Thomas Smith, Esq., from Wiltshire, gentlemen made their way to the capital to complete various kinds of transactions.[5] They also came merely for the sake of pleasure. Improved facilities and services, ranging from suitable accommodation to readily available medical care, made the company of other family members increasingly common.[6] Breaks from study at Cambridge apparently permitted Edward Browne to come up to London on a fairly regular basis and thus take advantage of the recently revived playhouses of the Restoration.[7]

A genteel presence was perhaps most obvious when one exceptionally important form of family business – marriage – was to be concluded. Courtship was the staple plot-line of late Stuart comedy, the playhouse a possible venue for its conduct as at least one gentleman-tradesman, John Verney, found in 1679, or the gentleman of quality Lord Stawel in 1691.[8] It was a less successful arena for William Byrd, as we shall see below, and a welcome diversion for the Lancastrian gentleman Nicholas Blundell, visiting London during early May of 1703 in order to conclude legal negotiations connected with his forthcoming nuptials.[9] Attending the theatre on subsequent journeys to the metropolis,

4 J. Ralph, *The Touch-Stone* (1728), 141, 163.

5 Smith records making two journeys to London in the early 1720s, attending a play each time after taking care of matters relating to his personal investment in stocks and the installation of a new cleric for the local parish, in Anon. (ed.), 'Diary of Thomas Smith, Esq. of Shaw House', *Wiltshire Archaeological Magazine* 11 (1867), 90 (3 May 1721) and 209 (20 February 1722). See also J. M. Rosenheim, *The Emergence of a Ruling Order. English Landed Society 1650–1750* (London, 1998), 68–88.

6 For instance, see the visits by Sir John Reresby and family during the 1670s, in A. Browning (with M. K. Geiter and W. A. Speck) (ed.), *Memoirs of Sir John Reresby. The Complete Text and a Selection from His Letters* (London, 1936, second edition 1991), 75, 85, 95, 110, 152; the terse but suggestive expenses of Sir John Nicholas for May 1668 and 1674, V.a.419–20, Folger Shakespeare Library.

7 R. D. Hume, 'Dr. Edward Browne's Playlists of "1662": A Reconsideration', *Philological Quarterly* 64 (1985), 69–81.

8 S. E. Whyman, *Sociability and Power in Late-Stuart England. The Cultural World of the Verneys 1660–1720* (Oxford, 1999), 118. John Verney was the younger son, and later heir, of Sir Ralph Verney. His courtship was successful. Whyman notes that he married the 'middling' Elizabeth Palmer soon after (61). But compare M. M. Verney (ed.), *Memoirs of the Verney Family from the Restoration to the Revolution 1660 to 1696* (London, 1899), 161 (where another woman was proposed partly on the basis that she was 'never bred to Playes nor Parkes') and her *Memoirs of the Verney Family during the Commonwealth* (London, 1894), 176 (where appearing fine at a play was a sign of the riotous behaviour of John's scapegrace uncle Tom in the 1660s). For Lord Stawel, see the countess to the earl of Nottingham, 17 February 1691, HMC, *Finch* 71, 3 (1957), 19.

9 Entries for 7 and 10 May 1703, in F. Tyrer and J. J. Bagley (trans. and ed.), *The Great Diurnal of Nicholas Blundell of Little Crosby, Lancashire. Volume I: 1702–11* (Record Society of Lancashire and Cheshire, Liverpool, 1968), no. CX, 35. See also Lady Elizabeth Berkeley to Lady Hatton, 14 February ?1677, in E. M. Thompson (ed.), *Correspondence of the Family of Hatton* (Camden Society, London, 1878), vol. XXII, 143. Notes the clandestine marriage of the daughter of the third earl of Northampton to the eldest son of Sir Edward Hungerford under a pretence that she was attending the theatre with Mrs Katherine Grey.

journeys occasioned by business and the education of their daughters, was *de rigueur* for the Blundells.[10] Their desire to see *The Conscious Lovers* and *Love for Love* was no doubt encouraged by the habit of reading playbooks and organizing amateur performances when at home in the north.[11]

Comedic texts themselves often drew attention to the various aspects of this annual migration by addressing London's genteel visitors in verse. Thus Francis Manning's *All for the Better* began with Robert Wilks pronouncing:

> REjoyce the Stage – All Rural Sports are fled,
> Fields cast their Green, and Trees their Beauty shed.
> Nature is chill'd abroad with Winter's Rage,
> And n[o]w looks only pleasing on the Stage.
> Rejoyce ye *Beaux*, for now the Season comes
> To hush *Bellona*, and to Silence Drums.
> The Troops for Winter-quarters now come in,
> And now your brisk Campaigns at home begin.[12]

Some simply referred to the phenomenon in dialogue with one such remark, typical of many, being: 'Winter is the gay, the happy Season: I hate a Solitary Rural Life, as if one were at variance with the World . . . Give me the shining Town, the glittering Theatres.'[13] Others featured scenarios that relied on travel to London from the counties by gentlefolk, John Vanbrugh's *Provok'd Husband* being the classic example. One particularly prominent gentleman even wrote to the playwright Thomas Southerne and likened himself to the central character of Vanbrugh's comedy:

[10] Entries for 19 December 1715 and 16 August 1717, in F. Tyrer and J. J. Bagley (trans. and ed.), *The Great Diurnal of Nicholas Blundell of Little Crosby, Lancashire. Volume II: 1712–19* (Record Society of Lancashire and Cheshire, Liverpool, 1970), no. CXII, 154, 207; entries for 14–28 September 1723, in their *The Great Diurnal of Nicholas Blundell of Little Crosby, Lancashire. Volume III: 1720–8* (Record Society of Lancashire and Cheshire, Liverpool, 1972), no. CXIV, 115–16.

[11] Blundell's diary is replete with terse notes which provide fascinating clues as to the life of drama beyond London including: the reading aloud of playbooks; performances by members of the household, local community, and troupes of strolling players; the formative years of what were to become permanent theatres in provincial centres like York and Liverpool.

Such activity is also evidenced in HMC, *First Report* 1 (1870), 49 (note of a book of manuscript poems belonging to Sir P. Leycester which includes an 'Epilogue to Taming of the Shrew, acted at Nether Tabley, by the servants and neighbours there at Christmas, 1671'); Ralph Palmer to Lord Fermanagh (John Verney), 3 December 1705, HMC, *Seventh Report* 6, 1 (1879), 506 (reports on the conversion of Lord Wharton's stable at Chelsea for a performance by the duke of Southampton's servants); entry for 9 June 1721 in Anon., 'Diary of Thomas Smith', 93; the examples given in S. Rosenfeld, *Temples of Thespis. Some Private Theatres and Theatricals in England and Wales, 1700–1820* (London, 1978), 10–11, 109. These pastimes created ever-wider networks of cultural familiarity and further help explain the importance of theatre to genteel society's making sense of itself.

[12] F. Manning, *All for the Better* (1703), prologue by G. Farquhar. *Italics reversed.*

[13] Colonel Blenheim in T. Baker, *Fine Lady's Airs* (1708), i, 4.

If I was not sure to see you and some more Freinds in Town, I should begin to be sorry that the Time of my Departure hence approaches. I must leave these Bowers the beginning of next month, and like Sir Francis Wronghead take a journey to London for the Good of my Country . . . I shall also view the poetical Works of our fellow Labourers in the Pen . . . But the Splendour will be so great, and the Beauties so numerous, that perhaps they will turn the Brains of a Rustick, and I may come back hither in a lac'd Coat and a Solitaire.[14]

And conduct books addressed to gentry did not always look askance at the theatre. The turn-of-the-century *Country Gentleman's Vade Mecum* had a section on visiting the playhouse as a way to 'fill up the idle Intervals'. Depicting the auditorium (apart from the upper gallery) as having 'three other different and distinct Classes', it promptly conceded that certain cits broke the rules by buying tokens for the genteel preserves of box and pit.[15]

For a certain part of the year, the Town, the area between the City and the precincts of Westminster, was the central point of convergence and contact between 'established' and 'new' social elites.[16] If the density of its commercial language and imagery is any indication, the comedy assumed that its genteel patrons were quite familiar with London's commercial world. If gentry families did not necessarily lodge cheek-by-jowl with prosperous upper-middling citizens (although several comedies do feature citizens moving from the City proper to London's fashionable western suburbs where they encounter both resident and visiting gentry),[17] they were never too far away. The theatre space closed this distance even further and forced particular social questions into the limelight. The Town as entertainment and pleasure district, and so its playhouses, comprehended spaces for social and aesthetic performances that were 'liminoid'.[18] That is, places where power was negotiated, the limit(ation)s of socio-cultural definitions were rendered visible and held up for scrutiny and possible revision. Much of the theatre's dubious attraction was the experience of this thrill of ambivalence or its rehearsal of cultural instability in the social order, both onstage and in seats. Never mind that comedy after comedy ultimately achieved a semblance of social (re)integration onstage, and affirmed the dominant understanding of gentility as elite social structuration on the basis of birth by the time the play's epilogue was being delivered. Many of the intervening

[14] Fifth earl of Orrery (John Boyle) at Marston to Thomas Southerne, 26 November 1733, in E. C. Boyle (ed.), *The Orrery Papers* (London, 1903), vol. I, 126.

[15] Anon., *The Country Gentleman's Vade Mecum* (1699), 50, 39.

[16] J. Powell, *Restoration Theatre Production* (London, 1984), 11ff.; A. J. Potts, 'The Development of the Playhouse in Seventeenth-Century London', unpublished PhD dissertation, Cambridge University (1999), 195–6, 209–11.

[17] For example, T. Dilke, *City Lady* (1697); C. Cibber, *Double Gallant* (1707).

[18] For this anthropological concept applied to drama, see R. Schechner, *Performance Theory* (London, 1977, revised edition 1988), 168ff.

scenes had at least raised questions and the possibility of transformation. It was largely these elements which made the frequent repetition of the citizen cuckold scenario (and the presentation of the fop figure as we shall see in part III) both necessary and appealing. Quite simply, it spoke to the immediate experience of many in attendance.

Yet, at one and the same moment, this liminality admits of the most perplexing contradiction which silently dogs study of early modern theatre audiences. As the players were readying themselves for a performance so too were the spectators. In other words, theatregoing was a prime tool of self-fashioning.[19] It involved recursive social positioning in the sense that not only did gentlemen and -women form the late Stuart theatre's core audience, but the act of attendance also made for genteel identity, the self-acclamation and, subsequently, the confirmation or interrogation of a superior social position by the audience at large. We are left then, as Patrick Joyce has remarked in the context of nineteenth-century English music-hall, to perform a 'hermeneutic operation upon a hermeneutic operation that was the audience's'.[20] This is not to suggest that the audience was strewn with social impostors but to recognize the importance of the theatre as involving the assertion and counter-assertion of social identity; as an event which did not simply reflect a rock-solid social position already achieved, and previously acknowledged, outside of the auditorium.

Specifically, the competing socio-economic parameters of the theatre space allowed the urban upper-middling, the likes of a Ryder or a Pepys, to claim or even discover a social identity which was at least parallel to that of a Reresby or a Blundell, thereby questioning the integrity of gentility as the cultural construction which was meant to divide early modern society cleanly in two. Dudley Ryder, for one, considered the potential of the drama from the point of view of learning the traits suitable for the genteel individual he was intent on becoming: 'Went to the playhouse. Stayed almost an Act in the side-box. I believe it would have a very good effect upon me to learn me a good manner of speaking to go there often.'[21] Or as *The Young Gallant's Academy* sarcastically advised the young gentleman: 'Hoard up the finest Play-scraps you can get, upon which your lean Wit may most favourly feed for want of other stuff.'[22] Even less accepting was Deputy Driver, the cuckolded citizen annoyed that when not at Hampstead Heath his wife was 'in Town . . . [where] she must be Box'd up at

[19] In an extreme case, at least one opera was to conclude with the lowering of a bridge from the pit to the stage to allow for a masquerade ball. *Freeholder's Journal*, no. iv (21 February 1722), 22.

[20] P. Joyce, *Visions of the People. Industrial England and the Question of Class 1848–1914* (Cambridge, 1991), 225.

[21] Entry for 16 October 1716, in W. Matthews (ed.), *The Diary of Dudley Ryder 1715–1716* (London, 1939), 348. For similar sentiment, see *Censor*, no. 9 (29 April 1715, second edition 1717), 65.

[22] S. Vincent, *The Young Gallant's Academy* (1674), 59–60.

the Play e'ery Night – A pretty Sound, indeed, to have *King* and *Lovelace* bawl out, Mrs. *Driver's* Man! – And because I won't let her have a Footman, she sends the Prentice to keep her a front Seat.'[23]

Did being announced by the playhouse doorkeepers and sitting in a prominent box mark Mrs Driver as a 'gentlewoman', or perhaps even make her one? Driver's fictive, self-effacing remark indicated to the audience it should do neither, but hinted, at one and the same time, that the experience was typically far more ambiguous. This uncertainty is further evident from the irony of descriptions that claim to detect the erasure of social distinctions wrought by the theatre within the space of the playhouse itself. For instance, *Remarques on the Humours and Conversations of the Town* feigned an inability to distinguish the countess from a City wife when describing the amorous attention that each had received from a young gallant cruising the pit.[24] Likewise, a correspondent to *The Universal Spectator* promised to censure 'Citizens . . . in Scarlet, and Cockades, with other Excrescencies of Dress worn by Persons not entitled thereto'.[25] Precisely how these citizens 'disguised' as gentlemen were to be detected was evidently something of a moot point.[26]

This extensive flexibility of social identity, which followed right the way along the immediate upper and lower margins of the genteel/non-genteel faultline, was brought home to the comedy's audiences in several ways and, furthermore, has four main consequences for the established historiography of the late Stuart theatre. We can begin by pointing out two shorter revisions, since much of their supporting evidence has already been adduced in the preceding pages, then move on to examine at greater length two further ramifications for the audience whose profile meant so much to the meaning of the action about to be performed.

First, it is difficult to overemphasize our points about the persistent presence of 'gentry' at the playhouse and theatre as a predominantly 'genteel' occasion. Much of the scholarly literature concerning the nature of the later seventeenth-century London audience ultimately founders on preconceptions of the early modern social order and lack of attention to the question of how the theatre was itself deeply implicated in social delineation. Gentlemen and -women, the gentry at the theatre, have received scant attention. Lumped together with courtly, 'aristocratic patrons' they oppose the 'middle classes'. Hence the all-important and contested ground of gentility drops out of the theatre's social

[23] T. Baker, *Hampstead Heath* (1706), i, 4.

[24] Anon., *Remarques on the Humours and Conversations of the Town. Written in a Letter to Sir T. L.* (1673), 124.

[25] *Universal Spectator*, no. ccxiii (4 November 1732), [1].

[26] The letter printed implies a sequel giving more details. Unfortunately, I have been unable to locate the second letter among extant numbers of *The Universal Spectator*. Perhaps its promise was no more than that.

framing as interpreted (artificially imposed would not be too strong a characterization) by modern-day literary scholars and theatre historians. Given the recursive importance of gentility to both the social action onstage and the acting offstage, this is something we should avoid if we are to appreciate either performance.

Second, it has been said of the Restoration theatre (*c*.1660–1710) that the spectators who mattered were visible, seated in the boxes and pit. This meant 'inhabitants of the middle and upper galleries were socially invisible in a status ridden society', out of sight and, perhaps, out of mind when it came to deciding what kind of entertainment to offer.[27] Our evidence suggests this may be too firm a distinction or, just as likely, that times were changing by the turn of the century. The theatre's field of social view routinely comprised box, pit and middle gallery *together*. Inside this field of vision, the scripted cordon running between pit and gallery was often the focal point for the simple reason that social distinctions were not only brought into the theatre but also made and remade there. Hence, in 1699, Charles Hatton could regale his brother with the unhappy tale of Lady Compton. Thought to be at private devotions, she had slipped away to take in a play from the middle gallery. Her up-market disguise probably drew initial attention as being too modish for a middling spectator before, that is, disapproving frowns turned to wry smiles of recognition for those who already knew her as both the daughter of financier Sir Stephen Fox and wife to the fourth earl of Northampton.[28]

The auditorium space was alive with social contests. Partly because these were so obvious to the original spectators they have, paradoxically, not received much modern scrutiny. They will repay closer attention, for a good many of these rivalries stemmed from the social differentiation which is our principal concern. The playhouse of late seventeenth-century London has previously been characterized as a rather uncomplicated, relaxed and sociable arena. For example, Allan Botica maintains that 'writers of the period were generally struck by the tension between the freedom with which all people interacted within the playhouse and the clear social distinctions which existed beyond [it]'.[29] However,

[27] A. R. Botica, 'Audience, Playhouse and Play in Restoration Theatre, 1660–1710', unpublished DPhil dissertation, Oxford University (1985), 25. A view shared to an extent by P. Holland, *The Ornament of Action. Text and Performance in Restoration Comedy* (Cambridge, 1979), 13; D. Roberts, *The Ladies. Female Patronage of Restoration Drama 1660–1700* (Oxford, 1989), 74–80. A recent exception, supportive of the argument made here, is R. B. Gorrie, 'Gentle Riots? Theatre Riots in London 1730–1780', unpublished PhD dissertation, University of Guelph (2000), 100ff.

[28] Charles Hatton to his brother Christopher, 30 December 1699, in Thompson, *Hatton Correspondence*, vol. XXIII, 244. Cf. C. G. A. Clay, *Public Finance and Private Wealth. The Career of Sir Stephen Fox, 1627–1716* (Oxford, 1978), 333, and for a related tale of a royal maid of honour, 21 February 1665, *Pepys*, vol. VI, 41.

[29] Botica, 'Audience', 38. A similar assessment may be found in Roberts, *Ladies*, 67–9, 82–3.

there were numerous occasions when the opposite was equally true, common enough for defenders of the theatre to feel obliged to redress their occurrence and for dramatists fond of irony to include them in their plots.[30] Competing social perceptions and contested social identifications fuelled dispute and, all too often, potentially lethal confrontation.

On the issue of frequency, it is critical to realize that there must have been many occasions where social tensions were momentarily high but, because they subsided with equal speed, they have left no extant record. This said, in support of a third revision to the current orthodoxy, we still have plenty of reported instances of swords being drawn and duels being fought as a result of altercations at the theatre. For example, the Newdigate family, Warwickshire gentry stock, had several correspondents in London from the last quarter of the seventeenth century. It is remarkable how these different writers each considered events from London's theatre world, and particularly social rivalries that might involve participants otherwise unknown to the correspondents, as being newsworthy for people living in the provinces.[31] For instance, it was reported that the Queen's Guard had intervened to prevent a 'duell [which] was Intended to be fought between the D[uke] of Richmond & Mr Lenners [Leonard] for Some Quarrell between them the night before at the Play house'.[32] The following year it was recorded that

> on Sunday Morning one Mr Young concearned in the riott in the Haymarkett & Mr Carew the son of a Hamps[shire] Gentl[eman] upon a Quarrell about a woman at the Playhouse the Night before fought a duell in Hide Parke where the former was Left mortally wounded.[33]

Incredible as it may seem, this type of one-upmanship could reach the point of no return within the playhouse itself and in the company of many eyewitnesses. Thus in 1667, Sir Ralph Verney received news that Henry Killigrew had overstepped his mark whilst at the play. Killigrew had wanted to send a challenge to the Duke of Buckingham after the duke had scorned Killigrew's 'scurvy language' (directed first at the countess of Shrewsbury and then at the duke himself) and told him to 'govern his tongue and his face better'. Failing to find an evidently foolhardy second to back his confrontation with a peer of the realm, Killigrew, would-be courtier and rakish son of Thomas the dramatist, was said to have

[30] See, for example, Anon., *Stage Acquitted*, 145; the preface to R. Steele, *Conscious Lovers* (1723); Selfish in T. Shadwell, *True Widow* (1679), v, 68.

[31] Subsequent reference will be to the transcriptions available in J. H. Wilson, 'Theatre Notes from the Newdigate Newsletters', *Theatre Notebook* 15, 3 (1961), 79–94; P. Hines, jr., 'Theatre Items from the Newdigate Newsletters', *Theatre Notebook* 22, 2 (1985), 76–83.

[32] 30 June 1694, in Hines, 'Newdigate', 79.

[33] 25 June 1695, in *ibid*.

stroke [*sic*] the Duke twice on the head with his sword in the scabbard, and then run away most nobly over the boxes and forms, and the Duke after him, and cut him well favouredly, he crying, 'Good, your Grace, spare my life,' and fell down, some say to beg for his life, but certainly the Duke kicked him. The Duke lost his wig in the pursuit for a while.[34]

Genteel playwrights were not exempt from first-hand experience of failed brinkmanship and social bravado. In 1673 Edward Ravenscroft, lawyer and future author of *The London Cuckolds*, crossed paths with George Hewitt, the 'young gallant' who was soon to be known as a 'beau' and held by some contemporaries to be the main inspiration for the character of Sir Fopling Flutter.[35] Recollection of their dispute is typically prolix, with spectators trying to reconstitute in words a protracted social calculus that had been worked through in the half-silent medium of sudden, terse and dangerously self-assured gestures. Of course this self-assurance and the failure to draw back from violence is our good fortune because it produced an outcome worthy of record. Sir Joseph Williamson received the following account from Henry Ball, his London agent, who later supplied details of the duel's aftermath:

The quarrell on Monday att the King's Theatre was occasioned thus: one Mr. Ravenscroft having half a yeare since received an affront from Sir George Hewitt in the play-house, and having ever since studyed retalliation, came that day to the play, where finding him there, beate him with his cane and so went away; presently after which my Lord Buckhurst and Capt. Bulkley going out with intentions to the other play-house, were followed by chance by Coll. Strode, so that all three being at the doore and Mr. Ravenscroft and company going by, and my Lord by chance blaming the action, Mr. Ravenscroft presently fell to words, and then they all drew. My Lord was hurt in the body, Capt. Bulkley in the necke, and the Collonell in his hand and eare.[36]

In 1675 John Verney ensured that his father, Sir Ralph, continued to receive word of the drama from London's theatres. 'Mr. Scrope' and 'Sir Tho. Armstrong' had quarrelled as they vied for the attention of 'Mrs. Uphill, the player, who came into that house maskt . . . so a ring was made wherein they fought'. Sir Thomas later claimed that his now dead adversary had instigated the quarrel as he 'owed him a grudge a long time, and happening to sit by each other

[34] Dr William Denton to Verney, 25 July 1667, HMC, *Seventh Report* 6, 1 (1879), 486. Cf. 22 July 1667, *Pepys*, vol. VIII, 348–9. For the eventual resolution of the dispute and Killigrew's return to court see the newsletter of 14 September 1669 in HMC, *Le Fleming* 25, 1 (1890), 66.

[35] For the relationship between the characters of gallant, fop and beau see chapter 7. For further discussion of Hewitt see 'The Town Life' (1686), in G. M. Crump (ed.), *Poems on Affairs of State. Augustan Satirical Verse, Volume IV: 1685–1688* (New Haven, 1968), 63.

[36] Ball to Williamson, 4 July 1673, in W. D. Christie (ed.), *Letters Addressed from London to Sir Joseph Williamson While Plenipotentiary at the Congress of Cologne in the Years 1673 and 1674* (Camden Society, London, new series, 1874), vol. VIII, 87. For the political fallout, see *ibid.*, 94, 100. It was also Ball who had described Hewitt as a 'young gallant', see *ibid.*, 67.

in the play house, struck him over the shins with a cane twice'.[37] When writing to the Caribbean in 1684, Christopher Jeaffreson, son of a West Indian planter made good and sometime London broker for this region's trade, thought it noteworthy that 'Sir James Hackett, lieutenant-colonell to the Lord Dunbarton's regiment, was wounded in the thigh by one Mr. Potter in the playhouse; of which he has since died.'[38] Some months earlier the Newdigates were informed that a 'Mr Vaughan & Mr Charles Deering fought this week & the last dangerously hurt – on the playhouse stage.'[39]

Little had apparently changed towards the end of our period of interest. In December of 1702, for example, Narcissus Luttrell observed that 'last night Beau Feilding was dangerously wounded in the play house by one Mr. Goodyer, a Herefordshire gentleman'.[40] Both public print and private letters carried similar details.[41] Only a few years later we find Peter Wentworth explaining to his brother how the intervention of those in livery had prevented swordplay on the part of their betters.[42] Letters were still being sent to the Newdigates that detailed how, for example, 'Coll. Churchill & Cornet Pope had last Night a Quarrell at the play House in Drury Lane & Challeng'd Each other, but a Guard was Sett to prevent fighting',[43] while in 1719 *Applebee's Original Weekly Journal* reported that restraint had been impossible and a 'Quarrel happening in Drury-Lane Play-House, betwixt a Gentleman and an Officer, they immediately drew their Swords, and the latter was wounded in the Arm'.[44]

The ritualized confrontation of the duel was understood as the preserve of well-born males and its catalysts ranged from apparently trivial, almost incomprehensible slights (such as who had been first to procure the services of a particular prostitute for the evening, or careless disposal of the remains of a snack[45]), to aspects of the theatregoing experience which had a ready capacity

37 John to Sir Ralph Verney, 30 August 1675, HMC, *Seventh Report* 6, 1 (1879), 465. See also HMC, *Le Fleming* 25, 1 (1890), 121 (newsletter of 31 August 1675); Charles Hatton to his brother Christopher, 2 September 1675, in Thompson, *Hatton Correspondence*, vol. XXII, 121.

38 Jeaffreson to Colonel Hill (governor of St Christopher's Island), 29 October 1684, in J. C. Jeaffreson (ed.), *A Young Squire of the Seventeenth Century* (London, 1878), vol. II, 144.

39 29 April 1682, in Wilson, 'Newdigate', 80.

40 N. Luttrell, *A Brief Historical Relation of State Affairs from September 1678 to April 1714* (Oxford, 1837), vol. V, 247. Also recounted in [E. Curll], *Faithful Memoirs of the Life, Amours and Performances, of That Justly Celebrated, and Most Eminent Actress of Her Time, Mrs. Anne Oldfield* (1731), 70–1.

41 See *Flying Post* cited in J. Ashton, *Social Life in the Age of Queen Anne* (London, 1911), 392; Lord Coventry to [unknown correspondent], 17 December 1702, HMC, *Beaufort* 27, 1 (1891), 96.

42 Peter Wentworth to his brother, 18 January 1709, in J. J. Cartwright (ed.), *The Wentworth Papers 1705–1739* (London, 1883), 71.

43 14 February 1713, in Hines, 'Newdigate', 82.

44 *Applebee's Original Weekly Journal*, [unnumbered] (6 June 1719), 1448.

45 See comments in both a Newdigate letter of 12 December 1695, in Hines, 'Newdigate', 79, and HMC, *Laing* 72, 1 (1914), 480–1 (1695 petition of John Young to His Majesty regarding a duel

to bring matters of social precedence directly to the boil. For instance, refusing to give up a seat potentially functioned in much the same way as taking (or not taking) the wall on London's streets, the perceived lack of an anticipated degree of either civility or deference testing society's lines of domination and subordination.[46] Rows of seats were referred to as 'degrees' and the social grid of the theatre could be scaled down to ever-finer social nuances within the broader contours we traced earlier.[47] Hence some descriptions spoke in terms of boxes 'of the third Class' and, even further, of being 'condemn'd to a Fourth' row *within* one of these boxes.[48] So, admitting that he had 'never seen the gentleman to my knowledge before in my life', Sir John Reresby, ever-attuned to the punctilios of status in an autobiographical narrative designed partly to instruct the next generation in the same, recounted an incident at the playhouse during 1678:

> As I sate in the pit a gentleman whos name I afterwards heard to be Mr. Symons came and placed himself next to me, and not content to rest ther, after a while desired me to give him my seat, or to exchange with him (pretending he was to speake to one of his acquentance on the other side). I had noe mind to quitt my seat, which was better to see then his. Besides, he haveing been drinking, his manner of askeing was not altogather soe gratefull, insomuch as I denyed it. Hereupon he said I was uncivil, and I tould him he was a rascall; upon which words we were both prepared to strike one another, had not a gentleman that sate near us . . . put his hand between us to prevent it.
>
> After a while (when I saw noebody observed us) I whispered him in the ear to followe me out, telling him I would stay for him at the out door. But before I gott thether, one (that observed by speakeing to him and going out upon it) acquainted the captain of the guard, who was accidentally at the play, with what had passed, and that we should certainly fit if not prevented, who sent one after me and another to him to secure us by a guard.[49]

Within the following two years Reresby narrowly averted a similar confrontation between two other gentlemen and, by manipulating his courtly patrons with due obeisance, endeavoured to acquire the wind-fallen estate of a peer 'run through' whilst at the theatre![50]

sparked by incivility received at the Dorset Garden playhouse); for that involving orange peel in 1671 between Lord Rochester and the heir of Lord Newport, see J. Orrell, 'A New Witness of the Restoration Stage', *Theatre Research International* 2 (1977), 90.

46 For contests of social deference beyond the playhouse compare *Tatler*, no. 256 (28 November 1710), vol. III, 298–9.

47 See the text of an agreement for carpentry work dating from November 1697 transcribed in J. Milhous and R. D. Hume (eds.), *A Register of English Theatrical Documents, 1660–1737* (Carbondale, 1991), vol. I, 327.

48 These phrases can be found in *Visions of Sir Heister Ryley*, no. 42 (24 November 1710), 166–7; M. Pix, *Different Widows* (1703), ii, 18. See also J. J. Hecht, *The Domestic Servant Class in Eighteenth-Century England* (London, 1956), 201, for a particularly rich example from the 1740s.

49 19 March 1678, in Browning *et al.*, *Memoirs of Sir John Reresby*, 137.

50 *Ibid.*, 168, 213.

Although giving or accepting the challenge of a duel may be considered a matter prescribed for gentlemen, it is distinctly possible that some participants in these playhouse affrays were out to assert their very right to be acknowledged as 'gentlemen' in the first instance, the challenger perhaps responding to the provocation that he 'was no Gentleman'.[51] Indeed, the two men just mentioned, Sir John Reresby and Mr Symons, ended up exchanging verbal thrusts which protested that the other was something less than well-born and bred. This small detail is a further reminder that the confrontations being examined here, even if they were sparked by the most farcical of disagreements or instigated before any playhouse *rencontre*, turned on issues of social distinction for those who looked on or took part. The paradox at the centre of any duel was that each participant believed himself on the right side of the genteel divide. Either duelist, or both, may have been correct, yet correctness did not matter if they were to thrust and parry. The broader cultural significance of these contests was, ironically, that they rehearsed both this divide *and* its potential uncertainty.

We might anticipate that the division was reinforced but its gradual renegotiation cannot be ruled out. After all, some upper-middling citizens did don the sword as genteel status symbol when out on the Town. Ryder, for example, proudly noted the purchase of a new one.[52] In similar fashion, Defoe's Moll Flanders wanted to marry a

> Tradesman forsooth, that was something of a Gentleman too; that when my Husband had a mind to carry me to the Court, or to the Play, he might become a Sword, and look as like a Gentleman, as another Man; and not one . . . that should look as if he was set on to his Sword, when his Sword was put on to him.[53]

The Tatler or *The Touch-Stone* preferred to be a trifle cynical about citizens advancing a claim of gentility in this manner, suggesting that the swords were only borrowed for the evening with the motive of threatening to draw them as a risky means of social assertion.[54] Given the social sympathies of Richard Steele or James Ralph, it is tempting to read this cynicism against the grain. Perhaps the ultimate message of their descriptions was brave it as a gentleman at the playhouse but beware rival claimants who might be equally prepared to make their mark in blood.

As the previous paragraphs have hinted, the social circumspection and exclusivity of London's theatres was mainly worked out by countless less grand, less

[51] *Review of the State of the English Nation*, no. 7 (28 March 1704), book 1, 44. For protocols and their motivation see V. G. Kiernan, *The Duel in European History. Honour and the Reign of Aristocracy* (Oxford, 1988), and, more recently, M. Peltonen, *The Duel in Early Modern England* (Cambridge, 2003), 35ff.

[52] 14 October 1715, in Matthews, *Diary of Ryder*, 119.

[53] D. Defoe, *The Fortunes and Misfortunes of the Famous Moll Flanders* (Wordsworth edition, Ware, 1993), 54–5.

[54] See *Tatler*, no. 26 (9 June 1709), vol. I, 199; Ralph, *Touch-Stone*, 140.

violent gestures: bows, salutes, deferrals. The ultimate and unfortunate consequence of their very repetition, ordinariness and apparent facility is that they have left behind relatively few traces. The historian falls victim to the very success of the process, social structuration, under examination. However, we have come to expect more of a cultural institution that so densely embodied particular social relationships. Even innocuous rituals enacted in the course of the evening, like the social ceremonies of entering or leaving the theatre building, have a textual residue.[55]

Recently widowed and looking to make a good match before he returned to Virginia, Byrd read his participation in the gendered formality of 'handing' or 'leading' the female company from the playhouse as a sign of his chances for being accepted as husband to the daughter of a substantial Lincolnshire gentleman: 'I went to Will's and my Lord Orrery desired me to go with him to the play in Lincoln's Inn Field, where I saw dear Miss Smith and led her out in spite of the old fellow that offered his hand.'[56] In a *billet-doux* he pined to his intended 'Sabrina' (i.e. Miss Smith) that 'I cou'd not bear another shou'd hand you out of the Playhouse.'[57] Yet several weeks later a similar gesture was forbidden after an evening at the opera, a premonition of the rebuff that was to come at the behest of an elite patriarch who did not consider the colonial 'gentleman' a suitable son-in-law.[58] Following a similar socio-cultural logic, an old associate of Byrd's, John Percival, by now first earl of Egmont, was to note with some satisfaction:

> This evening my son came home from the play, where he sat in the stage box with Mrs. Delmee and her brother, and after an easy conversation with both, led her out to her coach, which confirmed what her uncle, Mr. Macham, told him at dinner; that Mr. Delmee had been with him the night before, to tell him that my son had made very honourable proposals to his sister and had proceeded very honourably so far with respect to her; that he had heard a very good character of me, and every one of our family.[59]

[55] Schechner, *Performance Theory*, 169–73.

[56] 7 February 1718, in L. B. Wright and M. Tinling (eds.), *William Byrd of Virginia. The London Diary (1717–1721) and Other Writings* (New York, 1958), 76. See also *Tatler*, no. 145 (14 March 1710), vol. II, 325; *ibid.*, no. 262 (12 December 1710), vol. III, 328.

[57] 'To Sabrina', 28 February 1718, in M. H. Woodfin and M. Tinling (eds.), *Another Secret Diary of William Byrd of Westover for the Years 1739–1741. With Letters and Literary Exercises 1696–1726* (Richmond, VA, 1942), 320.

[58] 22 March 1718, in Wright and Tinling, *London Diary*, 96. The woman in question was Mary Smith, daughter of John Smith, Esq., then Commissioner of the Excise. She was soon to wed Sir Edward Des Bouverie, second baronet of Wiltshire and, ironically enough, the son of a Levant merchant who had only just withdrawn from his father's trade, see H. J. Habakkuk, *Marriage, Debt, and the Estates System. English Landownership 1650–1950* (Oxford, 1994), 428; P. Gauci, *The Politics of Trade. The Overseas Merchant in State and Society, 1660–1720* (Oxford, 2001), 31.

[59] 7 December 1733, in HMC, *Manuscripts of the Earl of Egmont. Diary of Viscount Percival Afterwards First Earl of Egmont. Volume I: 1730–1733* 63, 1 (1920), 458–9.

Unfortunately, Egmont's optimism was also premature. Less than two weeks later, the family of the City heiress in question were asking hard questions about the financial prospects of Egmont's heir. Rumour had it that the 'estate is too small for the lady's fortune' and, of at least equal importance, all parties knew that the lordship was Irish. Each party probably suspected the other of trying to use this last fact to influence a marriage settlement which had, in the first instance, to reconcile status with class. Never mind the petty ethnic prejudices that may also have been at work. Mrs Delmee herself protested that the quality of her suitor (superior to her own but still deemed provincial) did not matter, yet her family informed the Egmonts that the young couple should not be seen in public, together at the playhouse for example, until these issues were resolved.[60]

When push came to shove, matters could easily escalate once again.[61] Hence it was reported to the Newdigates (and simultaneously referred to no less a person than James II for arbitration, as the dispute involved two peers of the realm) that 'this weeke Vice Admirall Herbert comeing to the Playhouse Conceived that he was affronted by the E[arl] of devonshires Coachman whome he desperately wounded. My Lord told him it was not his business to Correct his Coachman.'[62] Five years later, another affront to one of its own, the Lord Longueville, saw the House of Lords debating whether the playhouses should be suppressed once and for all.[63] It is important to recall of such incidents that both social distinctions and their mutability were driven home not only for the likes of a hapless coachman, but also for a wider audience of playgoers.

Comic dialogue evidently tried to find the humorous side of what were further social flashpoints sparked by conflicting answers to questions of social differentiation. For example, the character of Sir William Mode complains how the ceremony of escorting a gentlewoman from the theatre had gone awry:

> One Night after Play, I waited on a Lady from the Box to her Coach, comes a clumsy Cit, with a paultry Mask out of the Gallery, rush'd against me, threw down the Ladies Page, brusht all the Powder out of my Wig, then cry'd ha, ha, ha, we have ruin'd the Beau; had I been a Lord, I wou'd have run him through the Guts, but to be try'd by a *Middlesex*-Jury is the Devil.[64]

By referring to an urban legal forum in which the participation of stern middling householders was proverbial, the punch-line explicitly redacts issues of relative power similar to those we encountered earlier as part of the cit's charivari.

60 18 December 1733, in *ibid.*, 465–6. The pair did not marry, see Habakkuk, *Marriage*, 197.
61 Cf. K. Wilson, 'Citizenship, Empire, and Modernity in the English Provinces, *c.*1720–1790', *Eighteenth-Century Studies* 29, 1 (1995), 76.
62 6 November 1686, in Hines, 'Newdigate', 77. Also registered in the Verney correspondence, Verney, *Restoration to the Revolution*, 416.
63 Edward to Sir Edward Harley, 23 December 1691, HMC, *Portland* 29, 3 (1894), 485.
64 S. Centlivre, *Beau's Duel* (1702), ii, 13.

Moreover, comic slapstick aside, the scene bears at least coincidental resemblance to Elizabeth Freke's recollection of how a 'substantiall cittyzen' was run through after he made the presumptuous error of 'takeing place' of a gentleman 'leading' a lady one evening.[65]

To suggest our final revision to current historiography, the social ambiguity which pulsed through the late Stuart playhouse makes it difficult to sustain the related ideas that the theatre audience comprehended a social cross-section which had bulged in the middle by the early eighteenth century if not before;[66] and that ever-expanding numbers of 'middle-class' spectators were coming to see a distinctly middling *mentalité* represented onstage.[67] Dudley Ryder, we recall, apparently believed that impossibly protean acts of theatregoing would rid him of traits considered revelatory of his common if wealthy roots.[68] By the dominant definition of the day Ryder was, on the one hand, of mean, ungentle birth. On the other, the theatre as social event allowed that very definition to be put under considerable stress. The socio-political rhetoric of gentility could be reappropriated as a result, used to figure a compensatory superiority grounded in recent 'middling' prosperity if the truth be told. Of course, we only know this happened because we have a backstage pass in the form of his diary. Without it we might be inclined to simplify, categorize Ryder as a 'middle-class' patron and so ignore vital aspects of theatregoing's social constituency *and* its attendant contingency.

While the presence of a fundamental tension between birth and money, status and class, is certainly suggestive of shifting social depth in the audience, the echoes are often too imprecise for us to second-guess the exact dimensions or chronology of that change. Even less can we assume a distinct social consciousness or new middling preponderance when many of those involved, following the example of Pepys or Ryder, were attempting to equalize socially in the heady, genteel atmosphere of the playhouse. John Dennis's petulant essay of 1725 or thereabouts, *The Causes of the Decay and Defects of Dramatick Poetry, And of the Degeneracy of the Publick Tast[e]*, incidentally captures a last example of this perpetual flux of social disparity and fusion, or, speaking broadly,

[65] Entry for 28 February 1713 (though the exact geography is unclear), in R. A. Anselment (ed.), *The Remembrances of Elizabeth Freke 1671–1714* (Camden Society, London, fifth series, 2001), vol. XVIII, 287.

[66] Cf. H. Love, 'Who Were the Restoration Audience?', *Yearbook of English Studies* 10 (1980), 29, 39; R. W. Bevis, *English Drama. Restoration and Eighteenth Century, 1660–1789* (London, 1988), 118–19; E. Howe, *The First English Actresses. Women and Drama 1660–1700* (Cambridge, 1992), 6.

[67] L. Hughes, *The Drama's Patrons. A Study of the Eighteenth-Century London Audience* (San Antonio, 1971), 120–1; E. A. Langhans, 'The Theatre', in D. Payne Fisk (ed.), *The Cambridge Companion to English Restoration Theatre* (Cambridge, 2000), 5.

[68] For a comprehensive assessment of Ryder's attempts at achieving a genteel politeness, see P. Carter, *Men and the Emergence of Polite Society, Britain 1660–1800* (London, 2001), 164–75.

the still-incomplete transition from status to class as the dominant principle of social structuration. Dennis rails at the decline in dramatic standards since the 1660s and 1670s, putting much of the blame on those who have spoilt the refined, courtly milieu since they had

> risen among us by the Return of our fleets from sea, of our Armies from the Continent, and from the wreck of the South Sea. All these will have their Diversions and their easie partiality leads them against their own palpable interest to the Hundreds of Drury. They goe not thither because tis Just and Reasonable, but because tis become a Fashion.[69]

But just when we seem to have definitive proof of a straightforward 'middle-class' take-over from an informed pen, we notice the delightfully ambiguous phrase employed to describe these upstart patrons, 'a new and numerous *gentry*'.[70] What is more, an earlier piece by Dennis condemning the 'decline' of London's theatre audiences had also found fault with a 'great many younger Br[o]thers, Gentlemen born', the very individuals out to cuckold prosperous citizens. Dennis even seemed to imply that the reason these people's attendance detracted from the drama as elite preserve was because they lacked the necessary education and refinement which should have been theirs by birth, a deficiency due to economic problems facing England's larger but heavily taxed landowners.[71]

Unlike some modern commentators, Dennis did well to realize that the gap left by the withdrawal of significant courtly patronage was not filled simply and completely by middling Londoners. He also knew intuitively that London's playhouses, although an urbane institution to the bone, had a far more extensive catchment area, each season netting sizeable numbers of gentry from the provinces. If middling London *had* collectively and unequivocally shifted the theatre's constituency in its favour, City skimmington would surely have been a far rarer spectacle and what fun would that have been?

69 In E. N. Hooker (ed.), *The Critical Works of John Dennis* (Baltimore, 1943), vol. II, 278. (A similar point seems to be made more obliquely by Gildon, *Betterton*, 12–13.)

70 Hooker, *Critical Works*, *emphasis added*. See also Dr William Stratford to Edward Harley, 2 March 1722, HMC, *Portland* 29, 7 (1901), 314, which describes recent election candidates as a 'new sort of people . . . They are generally, it is said, the new gentry, that have been raised by the late bubbles.'

71 J. Dennis, *Comical Gallant* (1702), dedication to George Granville, Esq., unpaginated.

Part III

Gentility as culture

7 The fop as social upstart?

> Wherever I go, all the World cryes that's a Gentleman, my life on't a Gentleman; and when y'ave said a Gentleman, you have said all.
>
> J. Crowne, *Sir Courtly Nice* (1685)

This chapter's epigraph is indicative of declarations that followed it, declarations by comic characters that they are manifestly what they appear to be, namely, gentlemen. Yet these characters are not so readily acknowledged as such by the society of the stage. Rather, they are just as frequently identified as 'fops'. Throughout the seventeenth century, the term 'fop' had served to dismiss a person as foolish. This usage continued into our period. In the heat of the moment a few citizen cuckolds are so described, for instance.[1] But to a turn-of-the-century audience the term had more recently come to identify a particular sort of comedic character, a certain kind of fool. This fop had made his debut on the Restoration stage and rapidly become a stock figure, most notably in the wake of Sir George Etherege's *Man of Mode; or Sir Fopling Flutter* (1676).[2] As if not entirely happy with the potential ambiguity of the term 'fop', contemporaries were also elaborating an increasingly intricate web of synonyms like 'beau',[3] 'coxcomb',[4] 'pretty

[1] T. Durfey, *Love for Money* (1691), ii, 22; Anon., *Apparition* (1714), iii, 31.

[2] Advising a correspondent about marriage choices, the *Athenian Mercury* succinctly summed up for its readers the shifts and links between 'fool', 'fop' and 'beau', the key terms of this chapter, in no. 30 (9 July 1692), vol. VII, question 1. See also R. B. Heilman, 'Some Fops and Some Versions of Foppery', *ELH* 49 (1982), 363–5.

[3] See, for example, the comment of Anon., *Mundus Foppensis* (1691), [25], which defines 'beau' as 'A Masculine French Adjective, signifying fine; but now naturaliz'd into *English* to denote a sparkish dressing Fop'; [M. Astell], *A Farther Essay Relating to the Female-Sex* (1696), 105, 'three parts Fo[p], and the rest Hector'; [W. Darrell], *A Gentleman Instructed in the Conduct of a Virtuous and Happy Life* (1704, fourth edition 1709), 42, 'a *Heterogeneous* Race of Gentlemen some call Fops, and others Beaus'; G. D. H. Cole and D. C. Browning (eds.), *Daniel Defoe. A Tour Through the Whole Island of Britain* (London, 1962), part i, 127, where 'fops, fools, beaus, and the like' at Tunbridge are compared to 'persons of honour and virtue'.

[4] This term seems to have undergone contraction similar to the word 'fop', making the two synonymous. For their association, see [M. Evelyn], *Mundus Muliebris* (1690), sig. A2^{v}; J. Dennis, *The Usefulness of the Stage* (1698), 107; Anon., *The Stage: A Poem Inscrib'd to Joseph Addison, Esq.* (1713), 6; J. M. Evans (ed.), *An Apology for the Life of Mr. Colley Cibber, Comedian* (New York, 1987), 77.

gentleman'[5] and 'fine gentleman'.[6] If the fop had become a certain kind of fool, the apposition of these terms implies that the fop's links with questions of elite social structuration were growing consistently tighter across our period of interest. The primary task of this chapter will be to trace the relationship between gentility and the fop character, to show how the two were very closely connected.

What was a fop? How did an early modern audience recognize one? If the various fop characters of late Stuart drama have a common denominator it is their concern to be in fashion. In relation to this definitive aspect, it is worth pointing out that the advent of the 'fop' and the 'beau' in the last quarter of the seventeenth century was a re-christening for an earlier parody of the well-dressed gentleman, the 'gallant'. This transition was captured by Samuel Pepys when he referenced a print of the gallant, first published in 1646, as 'The London-Beau about the Year 1660' in his library catalogue, a retrospective ascription itself dating from *c.*1700.[7] Similarly mature contemporaries would also continue to think in terms of 'gallants' and their 'gallantry' even as the 'fop' or 'beaw' and his 'foppery' became the preferred nomenclature for this particular social caricature. Thus Pepys's friend John Evelyn explained how the son of Sir Edward Seymour had been killed in a duel

> caused by a slight affront given him in St. Ja: Parke, by one that [was] envious at his Gallantry, for he was a new set-up vaine young fopp: who made a greate Eclat about the Town by his splendid Equipage, not setting any bounds to his pompous living; an Estate of 7000 pounds a yeare falling to him, not two years before, all which he left at about 2 or 23 years of age, to another Brother at Oxford: The general dissolution & Corruption & Atheisme of this period was now in as greate height in this nation among both sexes, as anywhere in Christendome.[8]

Although particular clothes and words might come into or fall out of favour, the comic fop represented an individual who was preoccupied with displaying his gentility, with appearing 'janty'.[9] This much is suggested by one of the few

[5] See the description of Beau Maskwell in *Female Tatler*, no. 34a (21–23 September 1709).

[6] For example, Henry Bulkeley to John Wilmot, ?May–June 1676, in J. Treglown (ed.), *The Letters of John Wilmot, Earl of Rochester* (Oxford, 1980), 125; J. Dennis, *A Plot, and No Plot* (1697), iv, 52; Evans, *Apology of Cibber*, 130.

[7] See A. Aspital (ed.), *Catalogue of the Pepys Library at Magdalene College, Cambridge. Prints and Drawings. Volume III, Part i: General* (Woodbridge, 1980), 35.

[8] 15 June 1699, *Evelyn*, vol. V, 331 (and compare *ibid.*, 280). Evelyn also provides a representation of the gallant before the character's redefinition as a dashing suitor, now devoid of most of his earlier negative traits which the fop figure appropriated and redeveloped, in his *Tyrannus* (1661), esp. 16ff. See also [J. Bulwer], *Anthropometamorphosis* (1653), 529ff.; C. Ellis, *The Gentile Sinner* (Oxford, 1660), 9ff.; Anon., *Characters, Or Wit and the World in Their Proper Colours* (1663), sigs. B2^{v}ff.; Anon., *An Address to the Hopeful Young Gentry of England in Strictures on the Most Dangerous Vices Incident to Their Age and Quality* (1669), 28–36.

[9] The term 'genteel' was an anglicized form of the French term, 'gentil', or 'janty' as here. See M. Manley, *Lost Lover* (1696), iv, 24. It came into vogue, like much else that was French in origin, during the later seventeenth century.

5 'C. Cibber Esq. as the character of Ld. Foppington', by G. Grisoni, before 1719

extant, most detailed graphic testimonies we have of how the character appeared in stage performance, *c.*1700 (see Figure 5). Of all our period's newly scripted fop figures, Colley Cibber's Sir Novelty Fashion, seen here as the recently ennobled Lord Foppington, was arguably the most famous. It is rather difficult to know with what aspect of the fop's presentation an early modern spectator might have first identified, for most of the fop's signature accoutrements are visible:

the ludicrously full, full-bottomed wig, the carefully knotted lace steinkirk, the yards of gold trim, the plethora of buttons, the overly large pockets, the carefully hung sword. With his upper body, Foppington balances his hat (kept underarm lest it spoil the fop's other, superior headgear), a snuff-box so shiny that its outer lid reflects the fop's fine phiz (more usually his face was mirrored by a looking-glass on the inside of the box's cover), and gloves. He further postures his gentility, even at bodily expense. The right little finger disjointed by a heavy gold and diamond ring; forefinger bent to thumb-tip in an affected gesture which signs his languid pronunciation of o's as a's and is about to send another pinch of snuff into his cranium. The slender fingers of his right hand are almost dislocated from the rest of the torso which is covered in competing shades of tyrian purple and martial scarlet. He is beardless and pale-faced, the 'blade-less' hilt of the gentleman's weapon of choice offering the suggestion of a protruding posterior in an otherwise slim, straitened figure unaccustomed to physical labour or the duel. Hidden from public view is Foppington's lower body – perhaps because his high-heeled shoes and the stockings which were meant to show off fine slender legs had been sent back to their maker – and the trace of a mincing step.

The neatly blocked inscription in the bottom left corner of Cibber's portrait is a small but pertinent addition. It impresses on us a critical distinction that this chapter's argument will try at all times to maintain: fops were, first and foremost, fictive creations. This is to say that fops, contrary to some influential modern commentary, did not exist in complete independence of the theatre world. Contrasting the fop character with the cit figure provides initial grounds for this fine but necessary point. 'Fop' is phonetically similar to 'cit' in that both functioned as pejorative expletives. However, 'fop' was not a contraction of a social label like the term 'cit', from 'citizen', which normatively identified a distinct social locus and was used in contexts other than comedic discourse. 'Fop', certainly as used by the early eighteenth century, was a cognate of the noun 'foppery' meaning toy.[10] 'Foppery' dismissed objects invested with great importance as being, on the contrary, of little substance or no consequence. Foppish characters, and their later manifestations known as 'beaux' etc., were those guilty of placing too much emphasis on certain things, modish clothes, practised gestures, pampered bodies, as signs of their status.

Fops were objects of fun quite literally and they were defined in performance before making 'their' way offstage and into the wider world. The fop character was frequently and ironically returned to ground zero, to the theatre and the socially prominent box-seat or a place on the stage itself. Susanna Centlivre's Sir William Mode and his description, a soliloquy that sees Mode mimic his

[10] *Oxford English Dictionary*.

aristocratic companion, may stand for the intimate association of playhouse and beau:

> Oh 'tis an unspeakable Pleasure to be in the side-box, or crowd to the Stage, and be distinguish'd by the Beau's of Quality; to have a Lord fly into ones Arms, and kiss one as amorously as a Mistress: Then tell me aloud, that he din'd with his Grace, and that he and the Ladies were so fond of me, they talk'd of nothing else. Then says I, my Lord, his Grace does me too much Honour – Then my Lord, – Pox on this Play, 'tis not worth seeing; we han't been seen at t'other House to-night; and the Ladies will be disappointed, not to receive a Bow from Sir *William*. He, he, he, says I, my Lord, I'll wait upon your Lordship. Then says my Lord, Lead the way Sir *William*. Oh, pray my Lord, I beg your Lordships Pardon – Nay, Sir *William* – Pray my Lord –.[11]

Constantly being defined or subtly redefined by comedy, the term 'fop' could then be applied to real individuals who were also deemed to be behaving foppishly.[12] Thus stigmatized, the foibles of particular people might conceivably have made it back on to the stage. The things they particularly overvalued, such as the gesture of familiar deference made by a peer to Sir William Mode, were incorporated by the satirical playwright as a further accretion to the definition of foppery. At different times, various men were said to have inspired particular stage-fops. Audiences were expected to draw such inferences and manuscript or print lampoons actively encouraged identifications of the moment.[13]

This insistence on the comedic contingency of the fop may all seem an exercise in hair-splitting but it is important, particularly in light of some of the interpretive assumptions underlying earlier readings of the fop caricature. For instance, Susan Staves states that fops are a 'historical phenomenon not simply a theatrical convention' and, by writing of 'satire on fops' (as we shall see, satirical figure *of* the fop would be more appropriate), comes fairly close to suggesting that a group of people who identified themselves as fops walked the streets of the metropolis.[14] Yet fops were not a social type to be hunted down. They represented a particular kind of social typing which derived its primary impetus from the theatre. 'Fop' censures certain people. Fops 'themselves' cannot be censured. Fops were not simply discussed but, instead, discoursed

[11] S. Centlivre, *Beau's Duel* (1702), ii, 11.

[12] For use of the term 'beau' as a description of 'real people', see Sir William Chaytor to his wife and daughter, 17 January 1701; and 27 January 1701; Anne to Sir William Chaytor, 7 February 1701, in M. Y. Ashcroft (ed.), *The Papers of Sir William Chaytor of Croft (1639–1721)* (North Yorkshire County Record Office Publication, no. 33, Northallerton, 1984), 79, 84, 91.

[13] See, for example, chapter 6, n. 35.

[14] S. Staves, 'A Few Kind Words for the Fop', *SEL* 22 (1982), 414, 428. See also Heilman, 'Some Fops', 388–9; P. Carter, 'Men about Town: Representations of Foppery and Masculinity in Early Eighteenth-Century Urban Society', in H. Baker and E. Chalus (eds.), *Gender in Eighteenth-Century England. Roles, Representations and Responsibilities* (London, 1997), 31–57; Carter, 'An "Effeminate" or "Efficient" Nation? Masculinity and Eighteenth-Century Social Documentary', *Textual Practice* 11, 3 (1997), 429–43; Carter, *Men and the Emergence of Polite Society, Britain 1660–1800* (London, 2001), 124–62.

into existence as fictive characters that both inscribed and interrogated gentility in specific ways. As we shall see, terming someone a 'fop' recognized his claim to be a gentleman at the same time as it raised questions about the ultimate integrity of that identity.

Previous interpretations have tended to view the fop in the context of two sets of issues: early modern social hierarchy and mobility or, alternatively, gender and sexuality. Otherwise disparate, these lines of interpretation have similar limitations. Namely, lack of attention to the fop's claim of gentility and the assumption that the character is a reflection on (or of) certain identities: either an upwardly mobile individual from the middling sort or a male homosexual. In both instances identity precedes representation, reality is simply reflected by dramatic 'literature'. Chapters 7 and 8 will critique these two lines of thought in turn. For the crux of the fop's significance was its exploration of the relationship between representation and elite identity. The fop character articulated how early modern English society's dominant human subjects, its 'gentlemen', were as much shaped by, or subjected to, discourse as vice versa; equally reliant on the cultural presentation of their superiority and any basis it had in material experience. In other words, a person who believed himself superior by birth, heir to a pedigree announced by a finer physique and splendid equipage, was liable to ridicule as a 'fop' for not recognizing the role of (excessive) cultural refinement in making him appear to embody an inevitable, natural superiority.

Let us begin by re-evaluating the social position of those most commonly represented as foppish. Deployed satirically, the pejorative label of 'fop' tended to adhere to figures on a specific social trajectory. In order to recover the fop's meaning we need to retrace this represented trajectory with care. Given the fop's tendency to 'dress up', it is perhaps no surprise that most commentators are inclined to view the fop as a comic representation of upward social mobility. In her signal article, Staves argued that a key aspect of the fop's contemporary importance was the character's ability to articulate 'class tensions peculiar to the period' and to express 'anxiety that people were crossing class barriers'.[15] More recent studies have concurred. For instance, arguing on a grand scale that the fop character functioned as something of a hermeneutical sounding-board for two rival philosophies (Hobbesian versus Lockean), William Taliaferro still has resort to unquestioned terms of reference like 'social mobility' and writes of fop figures who 'substitute the style of gentility for its substance'.[16] Likewise, in her study of the commodification of early modern literature, Laura Rosenthal

[15] Staves, 'Kind Words', 428, 426. See also P. Gill, 'Gender, Sexuality, and Marriage', in D. Payne Fisk (ed.), *The Cambridge Companion to English Restoration Theatre* (Cambridge, 2000), 202–5.

[16] W. R. Taliaferro, 'The Fop and Fashion in Restoration Comedy', unpublished PhD dissertation, University of California-Berkeley (1989), 93, 106.

views Cibber's famous fop creation as a 'class upstart' attempting to 'inhabit a class position for which he possesses the money but not the "true gentlemanliness"', therefore representing the 'potential[ly] promiscuous and illicit mixing of classes through an unstable market'.[17] Andrew Williams has argued independently that the fop was the 'embodiment of social pretension'. Enjoying the 'luxury of wealth', the stage beau seeks to cover his 'social inferiority' by 'artificial claims to cultural refinement'.[18] At this point one suspects that critics of the drama take comfort in the coincidence of their readings with related historiography. For Philip Carter the fop measures the 'discrepancy between assumed image and actual identity', a discrepancy symptomatic of 'new forms of wealth and status . . . challenging traditional sartorial indicators of identity and social order', and the character therefore articulated the perceived ill-consequence of a 'debilitating search for novelty and self-improvement through the superficial imitation of social superiors in an anonymous and amoral urban culture'.[19]

Judging by the fop, as the wider orthodoxy concerning the figure's social significance runs, a newly enriched bourgeoisie now had the financial resources to wear genteel fashions, to participate in elite institutions like the theatre, or, in short, to emulate the gentry's culture and live as if gentlemen and -women. This phenomenon creates social uncertainty, threatens class exclusivity, in an increasingly fluid metropolitan environment as would-be gentlemen ('fops') try to climb into the company of ('real') gentlemen by means of socio-cultural imitation. Comedy centred around this character implicitly cathected and then released built-up social tensions as the pretentious Londoner was cuffed or kicked into submission, often humiliated by trick marriage to a cast mistress or lowly chambermaid during the play's closing scenes.

However, there are several flaws in this view of the fop as a social upstart. Even putting aside larger questions about class and the nature of its presence in early modern society, the view that the fop represents and satirizes individuals trying to move from a middle to an upper social stratum, crossing over the (non-) genteel divide, fails to explain how so many of the fop characters from the late Stuart period present as gentlemen on account of their status.[20] Relying on a small sample of dramatic texts, the fop figure in the studies

[17] L. J. Rosenthal, *Playwrights and Plagiarists in Early Modern England. Gender, Authorship, Literary Property* (Ithaca, 1996), 200–1; also Rosenthal, 'Masculinity in Restoration Drama', in S. J. Owen (ed.), *A Companion to Restoration Drama* (Oxford, 2001), 103–4.

[18] A. P. Williams, *The Restoration Fop. Gender Boundaries and Comic Characterization in Later Seventeenth Century Drama* (Salzburg, 1995), 40–3.

[19] P. Carter, 'Mollies, Fops and Men of Feeling: Aspects of Male Effeminacy in Early Modern England, c.1700–1780', unpublished DPhil dissertation, Oxford University (1995), 110, 175.

[20] An observation shared by M. E. Casey, 'The Fop – "Apes and Echoes of Men": Gentlemanly Ideals and the Restoration', in V. K. Janik (ed.), *Fools and Jesters in Literature, Art, and History. A Bio-Bibliographical Sourcebook* (Westport, CT, 1998), 207–14.

mentioned above begins to sound like nothing more than a cit in fine new clothes. While they might indeed be characterized as social butterflies flitting about fashionable areas of London, we are often a long way from matching many fop portrayals with the upward social trajectory assumed of them by modern scholars.

Given the fop's scrupulous self-presentation and adherence to social punctilios, especially his offering servile flattery to persons of status even higher than his own, we should acknowledge an element of mobility but strictly in terms of *political* advancement. The fop was linked to place-seeking within a courtly milieu. Etherege himself used foppery in precisely, and perhaps exclusively, this sense rather than to infer a broader notion of social elevation. Etherege, the fop character's 'author' if ever there was one, was later sequestered to a diplomatic posting at Ratisbon. From here, in a series of letters to English friends, he used foppery to ridicule the overbearing formality of his official duties or, tongue-in-cheek, to lament the uncultured nature of the wider social scene when compared with the refinements of Whitehall he had left behind. Thus:

> Yet I must confess I am a Fop in my heart; ill customes influence my very Senses, and I have been so us'd to affectation that without the help of the aer of the Court, what is naturall cannot touch me. You see what we get by being polish'd, as we call it.[21]

We shall return to this political dimension of foppery later but, for now, we can suggest that fops were generally viewed as being in no way parallel to the upper-middling citizen. Usually it was just the opposite: fops and cits were juxtaposed. For instance, while he is sometimes the overreached comic butt, there is evidently no inconsistency in Sir Harry Wildair, the 'beau baronet' from *The Constant Couple*, putting a merchant citizen, Smuggler, in his properly subordinate place:

> SMUGGLER: Pardon Sir, well Sir, that is satisfaction enough from a Gentleman; but seriously now if you pass any more of your Jests upon me, I shall grow angry.
> WILDAIR: I humbly beg your permission to break one or two more (*striking him*).
> SMUGGLER: O Lord, Sir, you'll break my Bones: are you mad Sir; Murder, Felony, Manslaughter (*Wildair knocks him down*).[22]

An exchange between a citizen, Sir Solomon Sadlife, and a typically idle fop in a play of Cibber's makes the same point from the opposite perspective:

21 Etherege to Edmund Poley, 12 January 1688, in F. Bracher (ed.), *Letters of Sir George Etherege* (Berkeley, 1974), 170. See also Etherege to the earl of Middleton, 19 January 1686, in *ibid.*, 22. For a similar example of the link between courtliness and the beau from 1715, see the letter of Lord Dalrymple transcribed in J. Black, 'Fragments from the Grand Tour', *Huntington Library Quarterly* 53 (1990), 338–9. Compare, generally, *Pepys*, vol. VII, 201 (note 5).

22 G. Farquhar, *Constant Couple* (1700), ii, 21.

SIR SOLOMON: O sweet Mr. *Nothing-to-do*! –

SAUNTER: Know, Sir, that the Noble Family of the *Saunterer's* shall never be stain'd with the base Blood of a Put, Sir; and so your Servant again, Sir. (*Exeunt*)

SIR SOLOMON: Ha! ha! ha! Well, I see there are other Monsters in the World beside Cuckolds, and full as ridiculous.[23]

The fop was not a *parvenu* stereotype. Only a handful of fop figures are depicted as citizens whose industry allows them to jump straight over the counter and into the playhouse side-box of the beaux.[24] Even when citizens are represented in this position, it is noteworthy how the syntax of their description mirrors that of the phrase 'gentleman-tradesman' which we earlier encountered in relation to the cuckolded merchant. Thus the character of Arabella in *Hampstead Heath* describes her liking for the 'Play in a Mobb, where one's entertain'd with such Variety of low Humour, more ridiculously diverting than a modern Comedy. First comes a nice City Merchant, a Creature made up of Beau and Business.'[25]

In the majority of the sixty-five or so new comedies from 1690 to 1725 in which a fop appears there are obvious indications of established, elite status. The briefest of surveys finds gentlemen fops with hereditary titles: the Lords Stately, Brainless, Malepert, Froth, Promise and Absent.[26] There are no indications that we are meant to think of these titles as recently acquired, as the product of 'new money'. And while Cibber's Lord Foppington may be a new peer as the result of a well-placed *douceur*, in his earlier incarnation as Sir Novelty Fashion he is a member of the 'middling gentry' who might claim the title of knight or baronet and be represented as having inherited a substantial landed estate with potentially high income.[27] For instance, Eliza Haywood's fop figure, Toywell, has 3000 pounds per annum; Susanna Centlivre's Sir William Mode 4000; George Farquhar's Wildair as much again.[28] We are also faced with the likes of Sir Nicholas Dainty, Sir John Shittlecock, Sir John Airy, Sir Amorous

[23] C. Cibber, *Double Gallant* (1707), i, 14. For similar appositions, W. Taverner, *Faithful Bride of Granada* (1704), prologue; [T. Brown], *The Works of Mr. Thomas Brown, Serious and Comical, in Prose and Verse* (1720, eighth edition, Dublin, 1778–9), vol. IV, 178.

[24] The most elaborate and unusual instance is the stock-jobber, Witling, in C. Cibber, *Refusal* (1721). Otherwise, see the character of the war profiteer, Biskett, in C. Shadwell, *Humours of the Army* (1713), v, 58; the sons of citizens (sometimes of 'cadet' gentry stock) in M. Pix, *Deceiver Deceived* (1698), i, 2; C. Bullock, *Woman Is a Riddle* (1717), i, 7; Dennis, *Plot*, see below.

[25] T. Baker, *Hampstead Heath* (1706), ii, 18.

[26] Respectively, J. Crowne, *English Frier* (1690); T. Durfey, *Marriage-Hater Match'd* (1692); T. Southerne, *Maid's Last Prayer* (1693); W. Congreve, *Double-Dealer* (1694); W. Burnaby, *Modish Husband* (1702); W. Taverner, *Artful Wife* (1718).

[27] As alluded to by C. Johnson, *Wife's Relief* (1712), i, 15; *Female Tatler*, no. 5 (15–18 July 1709), [2].

[28] E. Haywood, *Wife To Be Lett* (1724), i, 11; Centlivre, *Beau's Duel*, i, 8; Farquhar, *Constant Couple*, ii, 15.

Courtall, Sir Nicholas Empty and Sir Philip Modelove.[29] Less obviously, the list extends to gentlemen characters that go by the names of Gooseandelo, Vaunter, Mockmode, Flash or Tinsel.[30] And those fops presented as down on their luck, seeking to recoup their losses by marrying a rich heiress or widow, still claim 'Family', or social domination on the basis of their superior lineage. Hence Sir Noisy Parrat must 'raise up Issue to my Fore-Fathers' and courts a young lady whom he intends to 'breed up in my house in the Country, and instruct her to carry her self in Company'.[31] Similarly, Squire Empty from Essex rather defensively tells his intended wife: 'All the Country knows I'm a Gentleman bred and born, and have all the good Qualities belonging to a Gentleman, for I can drink Claret and Stale-Beer, and play at Bowls and take Snuff as well as any Side-Box Beau of them all.'[32]

These last examples, presenting fops as rural dwellers visiting London, serve to reinforce our point that original audiences cannot have shared the modern view of the fop as a dyed-in-the-wool urbanite, much less an uppity 'pseudo-gentleman'.[33] While it is certainly true that fops and beaux were customarily associated with the Town as followers of its fashions, they were gentlemen born to landed estates. It was this emphasis on their pedigree, their social more than their geographic location, which accounts for the range of foppish characters, from provincial gull come to the capital for the first time through to the modish, metropolitan *habitué*. Hence even the most urbane of beaux, who considered the country a rustic backwater, could command that he leave the city *post mortem*:

> My body I commit to th' Tomb,
> Which all my Ancestors perfume,
> With strict injunction, that it may
> Be never mixt with vulgar Clay.[34]

Beaux also tended to be thought of as younger males on the threshold of elite adulthood, uncertain of their place in life. As eldest sons expecting to inherit, some bided their time amid London's pleasures, all the while demanding to be recognized as socially superior adults. One broadsheet representation of the beau character elaborated:

29 Appearing in T. Shadwell, *Volunteers* (1692); J. Crowne, *Married Beau* (1694); G. Granville, *She-Gallants* (1696), a character by the name of Airy also appears in P. Motteux, *Love's a Jest* (1696); Manley, *Lost Lover*; D. Crawfurd, *Love at First Sight* (1704); S. Centlivre, *Bold Stroke for a Wife* (1718).

30 See T. Dilke, *Lover's Luck* (1696); Granville, *She-Gallants*; G. Farquhar, *Love and a Bottle* (1699); C. Johnson, *Gentleman Cully* (1702); J. Addison, *Drummer* (1716).

31 H. Higden, *Wary Widdow* (1693), i, 4; v, 51.

32 W. Taverner, *Maid the Mistress* (1708), iv, 37.

33 See also material like Anon., *A Rod for Tunbridge Beaus, Bundl'd Up at the Request of the Tunbridge Ladies, to Jirk Fools into More Wit, and Clowns into More Manners* (1701), esp. 23.

34 [M.S.], *The Beau in a Wood* (1701), 10. See also the likes of 'To My Lord Abingdon at His Country House' and 'The Sketch. A Satyr, Part I', in R. Gould, *The Works* (1709), vol. I, 130 (lines 154ff.); *ibid.*, vol. II, 332 (esp. lines 166ff.).

His only Prayers, are, that his Father may go to the Devil expeditiously, and the Estate hold out to keep himself and his Miss in a good Equipage . . . By these Extravagancies does he signalize himself above common Mortals, and count all other Dunghill-spirited Fops, that are not as madly wild and wicked as himself. Thus is Civility, Vertue and Religion hooted out of the World, and Folly and Atheism exalted and promoted: For this is the Bell-weather of Gallantry, whom our younger Fry of Gentlemen admire for a Hero.[35]

Thinking of beaux as heirs-in-waiting might also start to explain two seemingly incompatible variations of the stereotype. Sometimes beaux were referred to as 'old', past forty years of age.[36] This snicker seems to have commented on those who had to wait years for their fathers to 'go to the Devil expeditiously'; to die so that the beaux, themselves well into adulthood, could end their extended period in limbo as 'boyish' sons and, finally, start to live as gentlemen. Conversely, a premature inheritance, especially one that involved the transfer of political office to the young and inexperienced gentleman, may have been signalled dismissively with the term 'upstart'.

With its connotations of a gendered ageism arising from the uncertain timing and direction of proprietary descent, rather than the upper-class snobbery we might have anticipated, 'upstart' also hints at how the figure of the beau sometimes engaged with an even more pressing and pervasive social anomaly: the uncertain situation of the younger gentry son. Like his elder brother, he too demanded that his familial origins be recognized. Yet his problems really began after his parent's demise, his father leaving him 'nothing to maintain his Gentility, when thrust abroad'. Although his father, when alive, had 'hated . . . that his Son should be a Tradesman, though of never [so] Gentile a Calling, for fear of murthering his Gentility', the younger brother had to confront the tension between a superior pedigree and the need to become part of the gainfully employed majority.[37] Without a landed income or substantial legacy, it was common knowledge that (younger) gentry sons might turn to urban trades or professions as life alternatives of a rather ambiguous kind. For instance, *The Athenian Mercury* was repeatedly asked whether these alternatives detracted from gentle status.[38] The chance that they might was enough for a 'sufficient Spanish merchant' to refuse Lord Fauconberg's nephew as apprentice in the

[35] [T.O.], *The True Character of a Town Beau* (1692), 1–2.

[36] See J. Wilmot, *Valentinian* (1685), prologue spoken by Mrs Cook; T. Southerne, *Sir Anthony Love* (1691), epilogue spoken by Mrs Botelar; J. Dryden, *Cleomenes* (1692), epilogue spoken by Mrs Bracegirdle; A. Boyer, *Achilles* (1700), epilogue written by P. Motteux. See also C. Phipps (ed.), *Buckingham: Public and Private Man. The Prose, Poems and Commonplace Book of George Villiers, Second Duke of Buckingham (1628–1687)* (New York, 1985), 199.

[37] The quotes are from [J.W.], *Youth's Safety* ([second edition], 1698), 64.

[38] See, for example, *Athenian Mercury*, no. 26 (5 May 1694), vol. XIII, question 4; *ibid.*, no. 19 (19 February 1695), vol. XVI, question 6. For Lord Fauconberg's attempts to apprentice his nephew to a substantial City merchant see HMC, *Various* 55, 2 (1903), 171–5 (the quote comes from a letter to the boy's father, Lord Castleton, 23 October 1683, 175).

early 1680s. The merchant was understood to be '"bogled" at the boy's quality', that is, unsure of how the boy's superior birth could be reconciled to the orderly subordination required on the warehouse floor. In contrast with some rather glib generalizations, the fop's continued stage presence would tend to suggest that the broader issue had not been settled definitively by the early eighteenth century.[39] Perhaps, given the nature of gentility argued for in the preceding pages, we should not expect it to have been otherwise. Three decades after the *Athenian* had pronounced on the issue, a correspondent prompted *The Plain Dealer* to do the same. The editor may have reached a similarly positive conclusion (i.e. trade did not derogate from the superiority of one's lineage and its privileges), but what is perhaps more significant is the question's reiteration.[40]

That the comedy took a hand in this repetition further complicates the established explanation of the beau's represented social trajectory and suggests a need for caution when interpreting any association of foppery with the 'bourgeois' City. In our period a number of fops are portrayed as being from an urban background, one-time apprentices in what were considered the more respectable City trades or enlisted in the professions. Witness Clincher, the trainee merchant in the highly acclaimed *Constant Couple*, or Apish the Covent Garden mercer's apprentice from the more obscure *Vice Reclaim'd*.[41] However, we should not think these characters part of a middle (or lower) social stratum just because they are identified as apprentices. On closer inspection they present as the sons of gentlemen, at once well-born but also-rans in terms of what they might expect from patrilineal bequest.[42] We also find fops like Witwoud in *Way of the World*, originally put to an attorney as a gentleman-commoner from the Inns of Court, and a gentleman naval officer, Mizen, in Charles Shadwell's *Fair Quaker of Deal* from 1710.[43]

As we saw in our rereading of the citizen cuckold, the gentleman's younger son might become a cuckolding libertine onstage. Equally, he might turn beau,

39 Cf. P. Earle, 'Age and Accumulation in the London Business Community, 1665–1720', in N. McKendrick and R. B. Outhwaite (eds.), *Business Life and Public Policy. Essays in Honour of D. C. Coleman* (Cambridge, 1986), 53.

40 *Plain Dealer*, no. 85 (11 January 1725), [1–2]. See also, for example, *Spectator*, no. 108 (4 July 1711), vol. I, 447–9.

41 Farquhar, *Constant Couple*, see below; R. Wilkinson, *Vice Reclaim'd* (1703), iii, 28.

42 See S. Staves, 'Resentment or Resignation? Dividing the Spoils among Daughters and Younger Sons', in J. Brewer and S. Staves (eds.), *Early Modern Conceptions of Property* (London, 1995), 194–218. For an exemplary case-study, S. E. Whyman, *Sociability and Power in Late-Stuart England. The Cultural World of the Verneys 1660–1720* (Oxford, 1999), 43–54.

43 W. Congreve, *Way of the World* (1700), iii, 46–7. In a laudatory poem Swift was to contrast Congreve with those young gentlemen who, 'country-bred', had only pretensions to wit since they were: 'Adjourned from tops and grammar to the inns; | Those beds of dung, where schoolboys sprout up beaux | Far sooner than the nobler mushroom grows', in P. Rogers (ed.), *Jonathan Swift. The Complete Poems* (Harmondsworth, 1983), 70. For the character of Mizen, see further comment below.

or, as a quizzical one-liner in *The Fine Lady's Airs* put it, 'Has a Tradesman a Fop Prentice, that airs out his Horses, and heats his Wife'?[44] In ongoing research, Paul Seaver is uncovering fascinating details of early modern London's youth subculture.[45] Yet the character of the apprentice as fop suggests a contrast with his initial conclusions. One of this subculture's possible conflicts, investigated by Seaver through the disciplinary sanctions of the London guilds, was between apprentices who claimed gentle status and their citizen masters to whom they were nominally inferior by the terms of their indentures. As far as his records are concerned, Seaver concludes that this tension was inconsequential. However, demographic research suggests that the phenomenon of genteel apprentices may have been on the increase by the turn of the century and, if contemporary conduct literature is any indication, well-born apprentices probably refused subservience. They enacted their resistance by holding on to symbols of their well-born status: refusing to cut their hair, wearing intricately laced clothes or modishly long wigs, and generally living higher than the demands of their masters or shop discipline could afford.[46]

The immediate impetus for such foppery is variously represented. Some gentle apprentices have merely skipped work or, more seriously, torn up their contracts. Others are depicted as having recently come into unexpected wealth. Clincher, for example, inherits his father's Hertfordshire estate and 'beaus' it about Town, only to receive the following rebuke from his low-born master:

> SMUGGLER: I knew, Sir, what your Powdering, your Prinking, your Dancing and your Frisking wou'd come to.
>
> . . .
>
> Ay, Sir, you must break your Indentures, and run to the Devil in a full Bottom Wig, must you?
>
> . . .
>
> Ay, you must go to Plays too, Sirrah: Lord, Lord! What Business has a Prentice at a Play-house, unless it be to hear his Master made a Cuckold, and his Mistriss a Whore.[47]

The citizen's tirade is to little effect. In the play's sequel, *Sir Harry Wildair*, the foppish Clincher derogates trade as beneath a gentleman born to better things.[48]

44 T. Baker, *Fine Lady's Airs* (1708), i, 2.

45 P. S. Seaver, 'Declining Status in an Aspiring Age: The Problem of the Gentle Apprentice in Seventeenth-Century London', in B. Y. Kunze and D. D. Brautigam (eds.), *Court, Country, and Culture. Essays on Early Modern British History in Honor of Perez Zagorin* (Rochester, NY, 1992), 129–47.

46 Claims of gentility made in company records are themselves problematic. See M. J. Kitch, 'Capital and Kingdom: Migration to Later Stuart London', in A. L. Beier and R. Finlay (eds.), *London 1500–1700. The Making of the Metropolis* (London, 1986), 246; C. Brooks, 'Apprenticeship, Social Mobility and the Middling Sort, 1550–1800', in J. Barry and C. Brooks (eds.), *The Middling Sort of People. Culture, Society and Politics in England, 1550–1800* (London, 1994), 61, 64, 68, 78–82.

47 Farquhar, *Constant Couple*, v, 49.

48 G. Farquhar, *Sir Harry Wildair* (1701), iv, 29.

When compared with the experience of the irascible citizen, some fop characters figured the resulting social strain as a kind of inverted status inconsistency. For there were always some people willing to believe that 'without question the being an apprentice, according to our custom . . . is a blott at least in every man's scutchion'.[49] So, again, how was one to reconcile illustrious pedigree with a working life?

Although we have accounted for one apparent association of foppery with social aspiration, there are others to resolve. On the face of it, some late Stuart plays saw decidedly humble characters behaving foppishly. Valets assume the airs of their masters and become self-ascribed 'gentlemen's gentlemen'. Apprentices or semi-professional types of no higher than lower-middling status brush off their best linen for holiday excursions to genteel leisure resorts. And, perhaps most difficult to figure of all, outright social imposters pretend to be gentlemen and come off as fops or, in fact, double for fops *per se*. Here the fop initially presents as the lower sort trying to achieve a higher, elite social orbit. Yet even in these instances, a careful rereading complicates any easy association of the beau with a phenomenon of outright social mobility and emulation.

For, time and again, fop and gentleman were thought one and the same. Hence the foppish knight Sir William Mode is heard to complain that there is 'not a formal Cit, or awkard Lawyers Clerk, that won't Court the Cook-wench a quarter for Oil and Flower enough to garnish out his Wig for a day, that he may Impudently mimick a Beau; if 'twere not beneath me, I cou'd kick such Animals to a Jelly'.[50] Or, in what is probably the most telling condemnation of all, Sir Thomas Reveller remarks: 'P'shaw, pox, these are bastard *Beaux*, Councellors Clerks kept by their Mistresses, and palm'd upon us at *Epsome*, and these places for Gentlemen.'[51] The reference to bastardy drives home the idea that 'real' fops or 'true' beaux were meant to have some claim on being gentlemen by reason of their superior birth. Thus the son of a rich City merchant is condemned with others of his ilk as 'every pretending aspiring Fop is a Knave as well as a Fool'.[52] If foppery had been synonymous with social pretension how could an already wealthy heir of a citizen pretend to it? In what sense could he aspire to social prominence if his father had 'arrived' before him? Likewise, how does the interpretive paradigm of upward class mobility explain that it is not plain beaux but the '*City* Beaus' whom one can 'scarce distinguish . . . from Gentlemen'?[53] Not to belabour the alternative but resolution lies with lineage.

[49] Sir Thomas Baines from Pera to Lord Chancellor Finch, 20 June 1676, HMC, *Finch* 71, 2 (1922), 32.

[50] Centlivre, *Beau's Duel*, ii, 12. Similar associations are clearly operative in the likes of Anon., ['By a young Gentleman'], *The Character of the Beaux, in Five Parts* (1696), cf. 16, 31.

[51] W. Mountfort, *Greenwich Park* (1691), iv, 44. [52] Dennis, *Plot*, ii, 23.

[53] *London Spy* (April 1699), part vi, 14. *Emphasis added.* See also 'History of Insipids' (1674), in G. de F. Lord (ed.), *Poems on Affairs of State. Volume I: 1660–1678* (New Haven, 1963),

Beaux claim gentility on account of their birth; the 'bastard' or 'City' beau imitates behaviour associated with that claim and, as a consequence, it is initially hard to tell them apart from the well-born as beau. The same twist applied to comedies featuring nefarious social imposters. Their disguises are equally those of gentleman or gentleman *as* beau.[54]

It was conventional for fops and beaux to enjoy superior status. This was the assumption when they were described at second-hand (rather than presented onstage as fully developed characters).[55] And it was a logic grasped by at least two foreign observers when they attempted to make sense of London's cultural scene in the 1720s. A French visitor described beaux simply as 'Young Men of Quality'. Meanwhile a young Scotsman imagined he might have been a Sir Fopling Flutter 'if both Nature and fortune had been indulgent to me and made me a rich finish'd Gentleman', that is, if he had been both well-born and possessed the wherewithal to flaunt his pedigree.[56]

If fops were not intended to satirize *nouveaux riches* buying their way to genteel style and acquaintance, how do we explain key descriptives applied to them, such as 'affectation' or 'artifice'? In what sense could society's elite be perceived as affected? How are we to explain the opening verse of William Mountfort's *Greenwich Park* referring to the beau as 'By Art endeavours Nature to out-do'?[57] As a final case in point, Varnish the gentleman-templar from *Kensington Gardens* is ridiculed as a 'cringing, affected, self-conceited Fop'.[58] What, precisely, is the social discrepancy being suggested by these opaque but derogatory terms?

Rather than encompass a reaction to, or clash between, an 'assumed [understand genteel] image and actual [understand middling] identity', as previous readings would have it, the significance of the gentleman-as-beau character lies elsewhere. What follows will explain the terms of reference we have just noted by arguing that the fop figure articulated concern over the nature

249 (lines 121ff.); 'The Soldiers Glory or the Honour of a Military Life', in W. G. Day (ed.), *The Pepys Ballads (*Cambridge, 1987), vol. V, 67; R. Ames, *Islington Wells* (1691), 7 (lines 131ff.); T. Durfey, *Rise and Fall of Massaniello. Part I* (1700), prologue by Mr Pinkethman; E. Ward, *A Step to the Bath With a Character of the Place* (1700), 8; Anon., *Belsize House* (1722), 7. Anon., *Whipping-Tom: Or, a Rod For a Proud Lady* (fourth edition, 1722), spoke not just of any fops but '*inferior* Fops' whom it identified, simultaneously, as '*Sham*-Gentry', working people who were impudent enough to copy the genteel habit of taking snuff, 9.

54 Compare the character of Dick Amlet in J. Vanbrugh's *Confederacy* (1705), with that of Sir John Roverhead in M. Pix, *Beau Defeated* (1700).

55 For instance, the descriptions of Lord Tiffletops in C. Cibber, *Woman's Wit* (1697), i, 4; the Court in Baker, *Hampstead Heath*, ii, 19.

56 Respectively, B. L. de Muralt, *Letters Describing the Character and Customs of the English and French Nations* (1725, second edition 1726), 33; Thomson to William Cranstoun, 11 December 1724, in A. D. McKillop (ed.), *James Thomson (1700–1748). Letters and Documents* (Lawrence, KS, 1958), 1.

57 Mountfort, *Greenwich Park*, prologue.

58 J. Leigh, *Kensington Gardens* (1720), i, 7.

and integrity of the 'gentleman' as a social identity *per se*.[59] Staging the fop figure was the equivalent of critiquing the supposedly natural superiority (and therefore legitimate dominance) of the gentleman. His presented behaviour put into question the notion that gentility necessarily comprehended an inherited, native pre-eminence which passed seamlessly from generation to generation, the implication being that gentility as pedigree was susceptible to a lingering uncertainty. That uncertainty stemmed from the fact that no gentleman's lineage could actually be shown to be unbroken. No matter how many quarterings of arms he had, how long the parchments tracing his genealogy, how smooth his complexion, how perfect his physiognomy, the gentleman's origins were not capable of irrefutable proof.

The incessant second-guessing of a naturally successive social superiority that the fop comprehended may be retraced in a trio of Restoration pamphlets. The centrepiece of this series is a rare pamphlet from 1675, *News from Covent-Garden, Or, The Town Gallants Vindication*, itself a tongue-in-cheek rejoinder to an earlier pamphlet of the same year, namely, *The Character of a Town Gallant; Exposing the Extravagant Fopperies of Some Vain Self-Conceited Pretenders to Gentility and Good Breeding*. *News from Covent-Garden* imagines the nominal targets of the earlier squib, the foppish town gallants, striking back at their initial depiction in *The Character of a Town Gallant*. These 'Men of Birth' dismiss *The Character*'s author, agreeing amongst themselves that they

> knew by the Title, he had not a drop of Bloud in his Veins, nothing in him of a Gentleman, nor indeed of Sense: Would any Fellow in his Wits, offer to abuse and Laugh at the most Glorious Imbelishments in Nature, Attainments which alone instile us to a place in the Boxes, or Pit . . . Tis all the Interest we pay to Fortune, for those Transcendent Endowments which she has confer'd upon us above Common Mortals: But this should not discourage us from pursuing the Liberty of our own exalted *Genius*.[60]

The gallants' self-important condemnation of *The Character* ironically serves to reiterate the derisive treatment of their particular social perspective (as 'foppery') that had already appeared in the earlier text. The gallants' insistence that their superiority is innate, their genteel style and poise the result of an inherited 'genius', may even have been penned by the author of *The Character* as (s)he played devil's advocate. In other words, *both* pamphlets condemn these gentlemen as 'fops'. Both pamphlets satirize the gallants' belief that their 'attainments', such as their ability to insist on taking precedence at the play-house, are evidence of their naturally superior pedigree rather than a cultural achievement, an acquired 'imbelishment', that is less than definitive proof of their ancestry, of their blood being better than that of common mortals.

59 For the quote, see Carter, 'Mollies, Fops and Men of Feeling'.
60 Anon., *News from Covent-Garden, Or, The Town Gallants Vindication* (1675), 4–5.

Yet this seemingly conclusive exposure of the gallants' foppery hides a deeper ambivalence. Where does this leave others who believe their gentility rings true and is also demonstrated by their assuming priority at the theatre, for instance? It puts them in precisely the same position: liable to accusations of foppery, to doubts about a lineage that it is ultimately impossible to verify. For while scions of gentry families had every reason to believe in their descent, and so their social pre-eminence as individuals, there could be no conclusive evidence of a sustained blood-line, much less the natural succession of an innate superiority ('genius') from parents to heir. They might claim a socially transcendent position but, in the absence of a test for pedigree, they could not make it completely transparent. They had perforce to rely on cultural substitutes like dress and with this reliance came the immanent doubt that any well-dressed 'gentleman' might possibly be a commoner dressing as if he were well-born.

Contemporary moral tracts worked according to an inverse logic, as shown by our third Restoration pamphlet. It steadfastly assumed that certain individuals were, without any question, born to rule on account of their clearly illustrious and irreproachable lineage. Therefore dressing to dazzle inferiors was superfluous precisely because the gentleman's superior birth would shine through without such finery. As *Englands Vanity* explained:

> What need such to swell, that are so *Great* already, or to aspire to a sublime Height when they are born on the Hills of *Excellency*, and break into life . . . with a Diademe of Honour on their forheads, and whom the first light salutes into the World as happy, as Great . . . That as you are fixed by the Generous and only distinguishing bounty of God . . . in the highest Orbe, and to a more abstructed Degree of Happiness and State in the World, than were others.[61]

In other words acting foppishly, paying too much attention to the smoothness of one's complexion or depth of one's bow, was redundant if one believed oneself (along with one's fellow gentry) to be both naturally superior on account of possessing a noble soul and transparently made of something better than 'vulgar clay'. It was the task of the comedic staging of foppery to deflate this very concept, to ask how we tell the gentleman apart from common mortals.

That early moderns were, in certain circumstances, so hesitant about the nature of a fundamental, self-evident 'truth' of their society might seem too close a reading of foppery's significance. Yet question lineage they did, and not just by means of the fop caricature. For example, Isaac Bickerstaff, *The Tatler*'s authorial persona, recounted a dream in which the mark of fantasy was everyone's ability to recognize their true parentage.[62] Similarly, we find

[61] Anon., *Englands Vanity, or the Voice of God* (1683), 25.
[62] *Tatler*, no. 100 (29 November 1709), vol. II, 117.

this riddle of a would-be duellist among the witticisms noted in Sir Robert Southwell's commonplace book:

> The Blade that would not take Son of a Whore for an Affront till he asked his mother, who gave him but a doubtful answer. But when he returned and was called forward then said he I am sure you lye.[63]

The comedy's gentleman-turning-to-beau contemplated the same basic conundrum. People needed to acknowledge the gentleman's superior birth yet his lineage was, by necessity, culturally manifested. However, recognition of his *je ne sais quoi* made gentility prone to imitation and, therefore, in need of constant cultural innovation.

Fops of the stage rebutted the notion that gentle pedigree could ever be beyond cultural construction. They showed that it was necessarily always rhetorical, the function of language, or what Defoe called 'this Family *Jargon*'.[64] The fops' primary significance is not whether the humbly born can gather upward social momentum by pretending to be genteel but how one can ever know the well-born *ipso facto* at a period in time when there was no test for paternity. This chapter's opening quote of the foppish Sir Courtly Nice captures what was at stake in the gentleman-as-beau's representation: 'Wherever I go, all the World cryes that's a Gentleman, my life on't a Gentleman; and when y'ave said a Gentleman, you have said all.'[65] When absent from his ancestral seat Sir Courtly thinks his very person will manifest his descent when, in fact, his gentility relies on others conceding that he *appears* well-born, and their believing that the claim to status signified by his carriage, his dress, his sword, his speech, or the very title of 'gentleman', is sufficient demonstration of his alleged parentage. The irony is that 'all' this is never really enough. His avowal of superior birth can never exceed the bounds of discourse and there is always more than can be said (including the counter-accusation that he was *not* well-born). We only ever have his word(s) for it and, as we shall detail further, the reason why a gentleman like Sir Courtly could be laughed at and considered a 'fop' was his fanciful perception that society could, and always did, accept the gentleman's word as final and definitive; that a natural superiority ('my life'), uncompromised by culture, was not only possible but plain for everyone to see.

Therefore, the fop character is profoundly ironic. Having to pronounce what he believes requires no comment in the first place, that he is a born gentleman, the likes of Sir Courtly Nice, with his excessive and even naive attention to a

63 R. Southwell, 'A Diary of some things fitt to be remembered, May, 1674', Egerton MS, 1,633, f.28^{r}, British Library.

64 D. Defoe, 'A Plan of English Commerce' (1728), in J. McVeagh (ed.), *Political and Economic Writings of Daniel Defoe. Volume VII: Trade* (London, 2000), 129. *Emphasis added.*

65 J. Crowne, *Sir Courtly Nice* (1685), iii, 20.

swag of status symbols, opens the way for rival voices to denounce his gentility as nothing more than a subjective, cultural assertion; a possible fiction woven by manipulation of these same cultural signs rather than an objective truth. The explanatory paradigm of the fop-as-parvenu suitably revised, the following chapter will account for how the sexually suspect behaviour of the stage character made sense within this context of questioning allegedly native social difference.

8 Suspect sexuality and the fop

> . . . change the Features and Complexions that God has given them, into artful Countenances: So that the Sr. *Foplin Flutters*, and Sr. *Courtly Nices*, are no sooner met, but there is such tiffling of Wigs.
>
> E. Ward, *The Secret History of Clubs* (1709)

Probably the primary reason why the relationship between the fop figure and questions of elite status has been mishandled is because historians and literary critics are preoccupied with how the fop speaks to issues of gender and sexuality in the late Stuart period. The represented sexual behaviour of the fop has long attracted diverse comment. Much of this discussion once argued that we, like early eighteenth-century contemporaries, were meant to think of the fop as 'homosexual'. Later, critics objected that for much of the early modern era there was no distinct homosexual identity and, therefore, we must exercise caution when interpreting the significance of the fop's links with sodomitical behaviour. Most recently, however, in a counter-revisionist move, it has been suggested that the fop character's development in the late Stuart period fortuitously coincides with this all-important transition, the advent of the third gender or the effeminate male homosexual. Writing from different disciplinary perspectives, Randolph Trumbach and Laurence Senelick have argued that during the early eighteenth century the fop becomes a corroborative reflection of the rise of a distinct homosexual identity, otherwise manifested by the so-called 'molly subculture' recovered from legal and journalistic narratives.[1] The stage beau is meant to mirror the various cultural reconfigurations upon which this new identity depended.

We will refute this latest reading of the fop's significance by paying careful attention to the nature and possible meaning of three features of the stereotype which have, so far, allowed it to be adduced as evidence for a cultural

[1] For a sketch of this thesis, see R. Trumbach, 'The Birth of the Queen: Sodomy and the Emergence of Gender Equality in Modern Culture, 1660–1750', in M. B. Duberman, M. Vicinus, and G. Chauncey, jr. (eds.), *Hidden from History. Reclaiming the Gay and Lesbian Past* (New York, 1990), 133–5. For its fuller and, at times, more nuanced development in relation to comic drama, see L. Senelick, 'Mollies or Men of Mode? Sodomy and the Eighteenth-Century London Stage', *Journal of the History of Sexuality* 1, 1 (1990), 33–67.

diversification of sexual identities. These terms are sodomy, effeminacy and hermaphroditism. As with our discussion of gender and sexuality in relation to the ridden citizen, the current digression should permit a fuller understanding of the character's significance for gentility. Perhaps even more than before, we need to consider the possibility that gendered and sexually freighted terms were a means to speak figuratively about issues of culture and power rather than plain, direct comment on actual behaviour. There is no disputing that fops were linked with sodomy, described as 'effeminate' and labelled 'hermaphrodites', but we need to unravel each of these associations because the current orthodoxy ignores the equally important issues of social differentiation with which the fop's rehearsal was bound up. We will consider the possibility that alleged sexual misbehaviour allowed late Stuart audiences to think about gentility in a distinctly *pre*-modern and metaphorical way.

The advent of the homosexual molly required a redefinition of sodomy as behaviour involving only adult men. In other words, the new identity necessarily excluded bisexuality (that adult male sodomites might also engage in what we would describe as heterosexual relations with women) as well as other understandings of sodomy (that the adult male could bugger a woman, a boy or an animal). Yet it is not at all clear that the stage figure of the fop matches with this newly exclusive sexual profile. In the relatively small number of scripts where fop characters exhibit homoeroticism they presume the dominant sexual role in the hoped for encounter. By contrast, Trumbach seems to suggest that the molly was typically the subordinate partner in an adult relationship.[2] Yet the fops in question solicit partners with terms of endearment like 'Ganymede', an ephebe from Graeco-Roman legend, thereby foreshadowing a man–boy not an adult male–male relationship which places the fop as the dominant of the pair.[3]

If anything, the blustering stage fop sounds more like a hold-over from the days of the courtly libertine. That is, the superior and powerful male who did not consider sleeping with a younger male as compromising either his masculinity or his status but, instead, saw it as a positive proof of both which functioned in much the same way as rampant 'heterosexual' behaviour.[4] The importance of

[2] For the most recent summary, see R. Trumbach, *Sex and the Gender Revolution. Volume I: Heterosexuality and the Third Gender in Enlightenment London* (Chicago, 1998), 5–9. See also Trumbach, 'Sex, Gender and Sexual Identity in Modern Culture: Male Sodomy and Female Prostitution in Enlightenment England', in J. C. Fout (ed.), *Forbidden History. The State, Society, and the Regulation of Sexuality in Modern Europe* (Chicago, 1992), 91, 94.

[3] See T. Dilke, *Lover's Luck* (1696), v, 46. A similar situation also seems to be implicit with the fop's swearing 'by Jupiter', see C. Bullock, *Woman Is a Riddle* (1717), i, 11; G. Farquhar, *Sir Harry Wildair* (1701), iii, 27.

[4] Trumbach has himself traced the contours of the Restoration libertine subculture well into the eighteenth century and highlighted the importance of Graeco-Roman history to this subculture, *Sex and Gender Revolution*, 86ff. See also J. G. Turner, 'The Properties of Libertinism', in R. P. Maccubbin (ed.), *'Tis Nature's Fault. Unauthorized Sexuality during the Enlightenment* (New York, 1987), 82.

the foppish character's 'homo'-eroticism was sometimes complicated, perhaps deliberately, by the fact that the represented intercourse (that is, verbal banter as sexual invitation) was between a man and a female player acting the opposite male role. Witness, for instance, that the much-noted homoerotic interlude between Coupler and Young Fashion, Lord Foppington's beau-ish brother in John Vanbrugh's *Relapse*, originally featured Mary Kent as Young Fashion.[5] Such ambiguity suggests that what was more important about the fop's represented sexual behaviour was not the object choice but the appearance of a rake-hellish and distinctly non-procreative promiscuity. Of course, the conjectured male–male liaison was consistent with the fop's supercilious claim to be well-born. As we shall elaborate below, the precise nature of that claim was subject to ridicule because it was, in a sense, considered to be less than definitive. Rather than being the straightforward reflection of a novel gender identity, the fop's passing association with sodomy was one way to cross-examine a particular conception of elite selfhood.[6]

Moreover, we may observe here that a similar social logic applies to much-cited non-dramatic representations of the fop, such as the late seventeenth-century satire *Mundus Foppensis*, in which the association of the fop with sodomy is stark. Often glossed over is the fact that all the named sodomitical pairings of this poem involve elite individuals.[7] Conversely, Ned Ward's well-known representation of the mollies in his *Secret History of Clubs* underscores the inferior status of this group of men, a 'Gang' of 'Wretches'.[8] Although there are some very, very faint echoes of his earlier chapter on the up-market 'Society' of the beaux, not once does Ward label the mollies as 'foppish' or the beaux as 'mollies'. It is also noteworthy that those few foppish characters from drama which have been described as 'homosexual' usually do not fit the standard 'gentleman-by-birth-branded-as-fop' profile we traced in chapter 7. For instance, Senelick draws particular attention to the behaviour of the servant Bardach in John Leigh's *Kensington Gardens*, but he has very little to say about the gentleman-fop characters of Sir Vanity Halfwit and Varnish from the same play. Most of the men who were publicly identified and persecuted as 'mollies' seem to have been of humble status,[9] yet little consideration has been given to the possibilities that the 'molly' identity was circumscribed by status or that sodomitical behaviour was differently valorized for disparate social groupings.[10]

5 J. Vanbrugh, *Relapse* (1697), i, 15ff.

6 A similar point about the fop and libertinism is made by G. E. Haggerty, *Men in Love. Masculinity and Sexuality in the Eighteenth Century* (New York, 1999), 45–7.

7 See I. McCormick (ed.), *Secret Sexualities. A Sourcebook of Seventeenth- and Eighteenth-Century Writing* (London, 1997), 124–5.

8 E. Ward, *The Secret History of Clubs* (1709), 284.

9 See McCormick, *Secret Sexualities*, 148, where the robustness of the condemned molly's body may be contrasted with the debility of the fop's.

10 For a general critique of the Trumbach–Senelick thesis, see C. McFarlane, *The Sodomite in Fiction and Satire 1660–1750* (New York, 1997), 12–17, 60–8; Haggerty, *Men in Love*, 5, 53, 57–8.

The equation of the fop with the molly rests squarely on the presence of 'effeminacy', the exhibition of behaviour described as 'effeminate'. However, the readings of 'effeminacy' by Senelick and Trumbach prove rather evasive. Their studies elide important aspects of the meaning of 'effeminacy' in the early eighteenth century and, as a result, the significance of its application to the fop character. Trumbach maintains that 'effeminate' individuals in the seventeenth century were mainly those men deemed to be hyper-sexual (excessively attracted to women) or, secondarily, adolescents who took adult men as their dominant partners, perhaps cross-dressed for them, and were unattracted to women.[11] Of these diametrically opposed definitions Trumbach argues that the first fell into relative disuse by the next century, leaving the second to become synonymous with adult male sodomy. Henceforth, the 'effeminate' were men who behaved like women with other men. Senelick adds that the comic discoursing of the beau's effeminacy was a respectable way to cloak overt reference to sodomy in a public milieu which was experiencing an '*embourgeoisement*', a theatre at the 'forefront of a new bourgeois gentility'.[12]

Once again, it is difficult to reconcile many fop characters with this line of thinking. The discrepancy is largely due to the lack of attention paid to some very important shades of meaning for 'effeminacy' in the late Stuart period. As Susan Shapiro has observed, 'effeminacy' might just as easily refer to a perceived weakness or debility resulting from luxurious and idle living which had little sexually specific connotation and did not necessarily reference cross-gender behaviour.[13] The 'effeminate' gentleman-fop clearly owes something to this definition since most fops present as being preoccupied with gentlemanly attire and manners, many with the impact their modishness will have on the gentlewomen they are courting.[14] Indeed, Alexander Pope was categorically to define beaux and fops as the 'fools of Women'.[15] As far as the fop is concerned, this preoccupation with dress and other status symbols brings us within range of one of the most unremarked but important understandings of 'effeminacy' in the early eighteenth century.

Stepping back for a moment to the earlier issue of the fop's 'affectation', some of our contextual materials shed further light on what it meant to be 'affected' and suggest, in turn, that we need to rethink the significance of the term 'effeminacy' as part of the fop's representation. 'Affectation' referred

[11] Trumbach, 'Birth of the Queen', 133. [12] Senelick, 'Mollies', 46–7.

[13] S. C. Shapiro, '"Yon Plumed Dandebrat": Male "Effeminacy" in English Satire and Criticism', *RES* 39 (1988), 400ff. Also M. Cohen, *Fashioning Masculinity. National Identity and Language in the Eighteenth Century* (London, 1996), 36–40; P. Carter, 'An "Effeminate" or "Efficient" Nation? Masculinity and Eighteenth-Century Social Documentary', *Textual Practice* 11, 3 (1997), 429–35.

[14] For instance, F. Boyle, *Several Discourses and Characters Address'd to the Ladies of the Age* (1689), 31–2.

[15] Pope to John Caryll, 8 November 1712, HMC, *Ninth Report* 8, 2 (1884), 471. See also *Spectator*, no. 536 (14 November 1713), vol. IV, 413.

to the privileging of signifier over signified.[16] Hence Charles Gildon, in his manual for actors, could advise that players achieved no effect by shouting their words because the 'Sound will convey no more to the Understanding, than the Roaring of a Bull, or any other Beast. This proceeds from an Affectation.'[17] Similarly, William Byrd recorded an anecdote in his commonplace book about a 'formal Fellow, who usd to pronounce all his words very distinctly', adding the underlined comment that the individual concerned was a 'distinct Fop'.[18] In the drama fops, as affected individuals, are those who make a point of enacting the postures and gestures, the signs, associated with the 'gentleman'. Believing these signs reflect an inherited and intrinsic superiority, fops are 'all sound and no Sence' as one comedy phrased it.[19] Of course the fop is eventually placed in situations where his signs do not correspond, are not answerable to what is taken as signified. For example, the fop reckons that wearing a sword exhibits his honour and registers an innate right to power. However, time and again, fops refuse to deploy their swords in the gentlemanly combat of the duel. In other comedies, the exposure of the gentleman's affectation might be played out in his misreading the signs of other characters, the genteel finery of a chambermaid being mistaken for the natural superiority held to belong to the woman of illustrious lineage. The result of the fop's affectation, excessive or maladroit manipulation of signs, is effeminacy, or the emptying of signs (specifically elite status symbols) of their substance.

Effeminacy marks the presence of semiotic instability and epistemological uncertainty. Gentlemen did not have to present as mollies, dress in women's clothes and have sex with other adult males in order to be thought of as 'effeminate fops'. The fop's 'effeminacy' referred instead to a lack of correspondence between signifier and signified. Thus John Dennis complained of the rise in 'soft, luxurious, effeminate Arts' among the gentry and then contrasted this state of affairs with a time when 'their Habits, and the rest of their Customs and Manners were such, as very *fairly distinguish'd* their Birth, their Age, their Sex, and their Country'.[20] Now, with the rise of fashion and fall of sumptuary legislation, it seemed one could not tell the English man of quality apart from others of different nationality, gender or status. Similarly, John Evelyn recalled a conversation over dinner with Samuel Pepys and Sir Anthony Deane, naval commissioner, about design modifications to warships. Strangely prescient of a stage figure like Mizen from Charles Shadwell's *Fair Quaker of Deal; or the*

16 In my thinking about the significance of affectation and effeminacy, the following have proven particularly influential: M. G. Ketcham, *Transparent Designs. Reading, Performance and Form in the Spectator Papers* (Athens, GA, 1985), 30–55; D. M. Kuchta, *The Three-Piece Suit and Modern Masculinity. England 1550–1850* (Berkeley, 2002), 26ff.

17 C. Gildon, *The Life of Mr. Thomas Betterton the Late Eminent Tragedian* (1710), 100–1.

18 K. Berland, J. K. Gilliam, and K. A. Lockridge (eds.), *The Commonplace Book of William Byrd II of Westover* (Chapel Hill, 2001), 119.

19 M. Pix, *Beau Defeated* (1700), v, 39.

20 J. Dennis, *An Essay upon Publick Spirit* (1711), 10. *Emphasis added.*

Humours of the Navy (1710), Deane argued that these changes were 'nothing but to gratifie Gentlemen Commanders who must have all their Effeminate accommodations, & for pomp'.[21] Preoccupation with hollow status symbols allegedly weakened the commanders' capacity to do precisely the duty that they claimed their superior birth, as announced by their empty display, already guaranteed, namely, distinguish themselves as effective leaders. In both the narrow context of protracted naval warfare as well as the wider socio-political milieu of the day, the association between one's purported pedigree and a natural capacity or right to rule did not always ring true. The fop character, guilty of affectation and effeminate as a consequence, pointed to questions like: can we trust that an individual wielding the symbols of gentility, wearing a sword and sleeves with gold brocade, riding in a blazoned coach, or bearing the very name 'gentleman', is truly capable and justifiably superior? Actually, the figure promoted the disconcerting possibility that the born gentleman's superiority was nothing more than a cultural conceit, a tissue of signs that papered over a sameness, a lack of social difference, or even weakness, beneath.

Making a seemingly straightforward complaint about fops, *Satyr Unmuzzled* provides additional insight into the significance of the gentleman's finery turned 'foppery'. A verse re-creation of the character, the poem necessarily voices otherwise unspoken assumptions made about the fop by theatre audiences as they read the silent but meaningful presentation of gesture and costume. Fops were:

> All golden outsides with false tinsel hearts,
> They only make a show of worthy parts.
> The name of gentleman's grown odious now,
> It is become great honor's overthrow;
> Full as reproachful to the men we find
> As common whore is to all womankind.
> Here the whole race of gentry are at stake;
> The guiltless suffer for guilty's sake.
> Pity it is that men of noble fame
> Should lose their honor merely for the name.[22]

A little less explicitly, the prologue to a tragedy of Mary Pix further remarked:

> But Trifles still with you have most Success,
> And rise in Value as in Emptiness:
> That Undesigning Thing they call a Beau,
> The pretty Gentleman of Cringe and Bow;
> None e'er believ'd the Ladies strive to win him
> For any thing, alas! that is within him.[23]

21 7 March 1690 , in *Evelyn*, vol. V, 10.
22 'Satyr Unmuzzled' (1680), in E. F. Mengel, jr. (ed.), *Poems on Affairs of State. Volume II: 1678–1681* (New Haven, 1965), 216 (lines 134–43).
23 M. Pix, *Czar of Muscovy* (1701), prologue.

The comedy suggests that even when all the signs are present (from wig and coat of arms to fair complexion) there is no guarantee that they will mean what they signify. Is the fop the superior individual he proclaims himself to be by nature, by virtue of his bluer blood as one of the 'whole race of gentry', and merely reflected by these signs? Or are these signs really a series of useless trifles, indeterminate of true descent and, even less, real superiority? Such doubt suggests that rather than discourse a subject's specific gender identity, the beauish character's 'effeminacy' gestured towards deeper problems of elite subjectivity in signification.

Similar strictures apply to the import of the third apparently sexual term that one finds associated with the fop, namely, the word 'hermaphrodite'.[24] Trumbach has argued that this term underwent a shift in meaning similar to that of 'effeminacy'. As far as late Stuart men were concerned it no longer signalled, *a priori*, a biological ambiguity but the deviance of those who were 'both active and passive in the sexual act' with other men.[25] Once again, this line of thinking ignores an enduring shade of meaning in the early modern period, a shade which complemented the fop's 'effeminacy' and with which the character was also heavily and distinctly painted.

Anna Jones and Peter Stallybrass have argued that the early modern figure of the hermaphrodite was a means to connote 'boundary transgressions' rather than a reality of 'anatomical doubleness'. They explain: 'The hermaphrodite recurs . . . as the site of fixation where there is an imperative to categorize without one single normative system by which such categorization can be made.' The common corollary of such transgressions was the realization that there was no fixity of categories or identities; or, in the case of pedigreed social distinctions, their constant impersonation in the absence of absolutely definitive proof.[26] Referring to a situation which we will be examining at greater length in chapter 11, James Ralph seems to have grasped this very point when he described the beaux as

24 See Sir Quibble Quere in T. Durfey, *Richmond Heiress* (1693), iii, 29. Analogues may be found in T. Shadwell, *Volunteers* (1692), ii, 17; W. Burnaby, *Reform'd Wife* (1700), i, 3; S. Centlivre, *Beau's Duel* (1702), i, 7.

25 R. Trumbach, 'London's Sapphists: From Three Sexes to Four Genders in the Making of Modern Culture', in G. Herdt (ed.), *Third Sex, Third Gender. Beyond Sexual Dimorphism in Culture and History* (New York, 1994), 115.

26 A. R. Jones and P. Stallybrass, 'Fetishizing Gender: Constructing the Hermaphrodite in Renaissance Europe', in J. Epstein and K. Straub (eds.), *Body Guards. The Cultural Politics of Gender Ambiguity* (London, 1991), 102, 105. See also T. A. King, 'The Hermaphrodite's Occupation: Theatricality and Queerness in Seventeenth- and Eighteenth-Century London', unpublished PhD dissertation, Northwestern University (1993), 58ff. (Although the present study finds much to recommend in King's study, it would, however, beg to differ on the socio-political motivation for the fop's rehearsal.)

> *Hermaphrodites* of the Theatre; being neither Auditors nor Actors perfectly, and imperfectly both; I mean those Gentlemen who pass their Evenings behind the Scenes, and who are so busy in neglecting the *Entertainment*, that they obstruct the View of the AUDIENCE in the just Discernment of the Representation; and are a prodigious Hindrance to the Actors, in the Exactness of Performance, the Beauty of which often depends upon a small *Nicety*.[27]

Evidently appreciating that it could be taken the wrong way, Ralph seems at pains to ensure that his use of the term 'hermaphrodite' bears connotations neither of biological hybridity nor of ambiguous sexual preference, deliberately clarifying things by identifying the beaux as men smitten by the actresses. Ralph gestured towards the idea that individuals who insist on presenting to society what they claim as their native superiority, their gentility, risk being caught in a conundrum. That is, having their identity recognized as mutable and only as good as its repeated performance, its next enactment as a culturally constructed distinction and social subjectivity.[28]

Indeed, beaux were often likened to actors in a specific way. Ned Ward sarcastically described their propensity to

> change the Features and Complexions that God has given them, into artful Countenances: So that the Sr. *Foplin Flutters*, and Sr. *Courtly Nices*, are no sooner met, but there is such tiffling of Wigs . . . and managing of Faces, as if they were so many Stage Players patching up stern Looks and Heroick Phizes, for Plumes, Buskins, and *Roman* Mantle, that they might Rant and Strut, till they were soundly clap'd by some of the Box Ladies.[29]

Ward here mocked the gentleman-fop for strutting like the virtuous gentleman-hero of tragedy, for presenting himself as superior when he was, as far as anyone could tell, well-born in name (and wig etc.) only. Of course, much of the humour stemmed from an implicit contrast in perspective. On the one hand, there was the fop's blind insistence that his name was all he needed and that his superiority was self-evident, naturally embodied. On the other, there was the reader considering that gentle birth was, at best, artificially established by means of a cultural semiotics of bodily perfection which relied on practices ranging from cosmetic enhancement (use of make-up, perfume, breeches padded with prosthetic muscles) to studied deportment (formal modes of address and repartee,

[27] J. Ralph, *The Touch-Stone* (1728), 145.

[28] The concept of 'performativity' has most often been used to describe the nature of gendered subjectivity in discourse, but it can be of equal use in the discussion of other social identities as cultural constructs. For the former, see J. P. Butler, *Gender Trouble. Feminism and the Subversion of Identity* (New York, 1990); the introduction to A. Parker and E. K. Sedgwick (eds.), *Performativity and Performance* (New York, 1995). See too H. Guest, '"These Neuter Somethings": Gender Difference and Commercial Culture in Mid-Eighteenth-Century England', in K. Sharpe and S. N. Zwicker (eds.), *Refiguring Revolutions. Aesthetics and Politics from the English Revolution to the Romantic Revolution* (Berkeley, 1998), 178–9; C. Lowenthal, *Performing Identities on the Restoration Stage* (Carbondale, 2003), 26–7 and *passim*.

[29] Ward, *Clubs*, 139–40.

learned movements of bow and dance, clothes neatly arrayed). As John Wilmot, earl of Rochester, sniped at the earl Mulgrave, a 'baffl'd fop':

> Against his stars the coxcomb ever strives,
> And to be something they forbid, contrives.
> With a red nose, splay foot, and goggle eye,
> A ploughman's looby mien, face all awry,
> With stinking breath and every loathsome mark,
> The Punchinello sets up for a spark.
> With equal self-conceit, too, he bears arms,
> But with that vile success his parts performs
> That he burlesques his trade, and what is best
> In others turns, like Harlequin, to jest.[30]

The gentleman-as-beau was conjectured as hermaphroditic because he represented a social identity always liable to be snared between nature and culture. His attempts at enacting his parentage are deemed awkward, theatrical failures rather than effortless, native successes such that he is said to be playing at being well-born and is *perhaps* meanly descended instead.

A recent study has shown how sodomy was often used in the early modern period to discourse the presence of 'performative excess'. As buggery was literally perceived as a perverse act, 'a kind of playing', which denied a supposedly natural and universally human inclination towards procreative sexual behaviour, so it functioned as metaphor for the more fundamental denial of one's true, God-given identity.[31] It is this identity that the gentleman's foppish behaviour (which was not exclusively about a specific kind of sexual relationship) is seen to jeopardize. Foppery meant attending narcissistically and lavishly to the empty punctilios of status at the expense of demonstrating one's true metal, exercising the generous soul one had inherited from genteel ancestors. The apparent denial of natural character ('what they're made for shun', see below p. 184) was known to early moderns as the sin of Sodom and Gomorrah and manifested by a spectrum of transgressive behaviours ranging from idle self-indulgence to idol-worshipping, from profanity to sexual debauchery.[32] Collectively, the

[30] J. Wilmot, earl of Rochester, 'Lord All-Pride' (1677), in G. de F. Lord (ed.), *Poems on Affairs of State. Volume I: 1660–1678* (New Haven, 1963), 414 (lines 13–22).

[31] King, 'Hermaphrodite's Occupation', 5ff. A point also suggested by McFarlane, *Sodomite*, 41, where 'art', or culture, rather than 'nature', is quoted in an early eighteenth-century pamphlet as producing both hermaphroditism and sodomitical lusts. McFarlane also reads sodomy as symbolic of the discursive structuring, the performativity, of the social, 21, 26, 58–9; as does J. Goldberg, *Sodometries. Renaissance Texts, Modern Sexualities* (Stanford, 1992), 17–20, 117–22.

[32] The quote comes from an extended verse description of the fop, 'The Town Life' (1686), in G. M. Crump (ed.), *Poems on Affairs of State. Augustan Satirical Verse. Volume IV: 1685–1688* (New Haven, 1968), 63 (line 44). See A. Bray, *Homosexuality in Renaissance England* (New York, 1982, revised edition 1995), 21ff.; G. Rousseau, 'The Pursuit of Homosexuality in the Eighteenth Century: "Utterly Confused Category" and/or Rich Repository?', *Eighteenth-Century Life* 9, 3 (1985), 132–68.

sins of Sodom connoted uncertainty about the relationship between someone's outer person and their true, inner character. Language and its constant potential for disjunction of sign and signified, for culture to refract rather than simply reflect nature, was the ultimate cause and effect of this ambivalence about the integrity of identity.

In branding the gentleman as fop, by condemning as foppery the constant play of genteel status symbols, the comedy gave expression to an abiding uncertainty over how anyone was to discern pedigree. Those preoccupied with demonstrating their reputedly superior descent to the world by, for instance, cultivating an ever-finer physiognomy (see Figure 6) were suspected of committing the sins of Sodom. Obsessively and hubristically trying to manifest or impersonate their status, they seemed guilty of not resting satisfied with a providentially bestowed identity. This overreaching rendered their original identities illegible (effeminate), and therefore possibly theatrical (hermaphroditic) rather than essentially natural. As a gentlewomen's conduct book warned its readers of the fluttering fop:

> They wou'd never be so sottish as to imagine, that he who regards nothing but his own brutish Appetite, shou'd have any real affection for them, nor ever expect Fidelity from one who is unfaithful to GOD and his own Soul. They wou'd not be so absurd as to suppose, that man can esteem them who neglects his Maker; for what are all those fine Idolatries, by which he wou'd recommend himself to his pretended Goddess; but mockery and delusion from him who forgets and affronts the true Deity?[33]

Simple as the suggestion may sound, we need to work our way back to the biblical connotations of 'sodomy' and its links to questions of selfhood rather than assume that the term, much less the drama's often fleeting allusions to male–male sexual behaviour, heralds a newly exclusive sexual identity. Early moderns would have been very aware of these quite traditional resonances and wrung from them a richer and deeper significance which we cannot afford to ignore in favour of a focus on still faint, future meanings.

That the late Stuart fop's ambiguous sexual reputation spoke to issues of theatricality and identity, rather than marked a male homosexuality, can also be seen by tracing two intersecting cultural logics of the day. One is the early modern association of theatre with sodomy, the other the possibility of a female equivalent to the gentleman-beau.

The first of these connections can be instanced briefly here, as we will return to it in chapter 11. When Daniel Defoe's *Review* spoke of rehabilitating the stage, so the playhouse might become a 'School of Honour', such reform was held to mean that the theatre would present only

[33] Anon., *A Serious Proposal to the Ladies For the Advancement of Their True and Greatest Interest* (1694), 163–4. For absence of the soul and the beau see also *Spectator*, no. 211 (1 November 1711), vol. II, 326.

6 Frontispiece from [M. Astell], *An Essay in Defence of the Female Sex* (1696, second edition, 1696)

what in its own Nature best suits the Being of a Man, and the Character of a Man of Honour – That Lewdness of Speech, that Sodomy of the Tongue, and of Gesture, that Degeneracy even of [obscured, 'fine'?] Manners, shall be as odious to general Acceptation, as it is unmanly in its Nature.[34]

Defoe's initial complaint was that the drama's elite characters were made to behave in ways not consonant with how real men of honour would naturally act. Yet, despite first impressions, he is not denouncing the theatre merely for its presentation of sexually explicit behaviour and considers a far more extensive drawback. By impersonating elite social identity, theatre dissolves the given correspondence between sign and self and, with it, any certainty of character. Being or acting in the world may not arise from one's nature but, instead, be a contrived impression created by the arbitrary association and manipulation of signs, what Defoe condemned with the phrase 'Sodomy of the Tongue'. Defoe's ultimate problem with the theatre was that it denied the transparency of any essential identity, suggesting that society consisted only of cultured appearances. It is this absence of a divinely ordered correspondence, and with it a stable, essential identity, which makes the drama (and the fop character) lewd and sodomitical.

Since we have been arguing that the fop character articulated a fundamental uncertainty about elite identity, an interrogation which might incorporate but was neither confined to nor primarily about issues of male gender identity and sexuality, a further test would be to investigate whether womanly, genteel identity could be similarly questioned. This is chiefly because the interpretive line initiated by Trumbach regarding the molly persona (and its alleged theatrical representation by the beau) relies on there being no discrete lesbian identity (matching the male homosexual identity said to be reflected by newly exclusive male terms like 'sodomy') until the late eighteenth century.[35] Yet read enough comedies from the early years of the century and one finds that similar terms, 'hermaphrodite', 'effeminacy', 'sodomy' and 'foppery' (or variants thereof) were indeed applied to *female* characters.

Gentlewomen figures could be labelled as 'hermaphrodites' or so described using broadly synonymous phrases. In the comic drama, this imaging seems to have been used in respect of the well-born wives of our cuckolded and henpecked citizens.[36] Hence Sir William Rant mocks a female relation, who has recently married a City alderman, as his 'He-Aunt'.[37] As with the gentleman-fop, these terms suggest the collision of an original, natural selfhood with an enacted, assumed role and raise the question of whether all social differences

[34] *Review of the State of the English Nation*, no. 129 (29 October 1706), book 8, 515.
[35] Trumbach, 'Sapphists', 117.
[36] See, for example, T. Baker, *Tunbridge-Walks* (1703), ii, 15; Burnaby, *Reform'd*, v, 45.
[37] T. Shadwell, *Scowrers* (1691), ii, 19.

are impersonations. Are no social identities providentially fixed, absolute and therefore knowable?[38] Need we be reminded, City wives were meant to be both 'naturally' submissive – subjected – as married women and, at the same time, 'naturally' superior to their middling husbands on account of their birth. One comedy, the premiere of Durfey's *Love for Money*, seems to have used transvestism to make this same point. The production featured the actor Anthony Leigh in the role of Lady Addleplot, a widowed gentlewoman now married to deputy Nicompoop.[39]

Another comedy considered that men were not the only ones who might be guilty of 'effeminacy'. Following his avoidance of a duel with two young gentlewomen dressed in breeches, the eponymous character from *The Beau's Duel*, Sir William Mode, is chided by Colonel Manly for not acting like the gentleman that his sword etc. signal him to be. Notice how the condemnation of this behaviour as 'effeminency' is distinct from the idea that Sir William should, in future, relinquish the habit of the gentleman and yet equally applicable to the blustering, cross-dressed gentlewomen who have just hounded him and his second, the foppish Ogle:

> COLONEL MANLY: . . . Take this for a Rule, the less regard you have for your Honour the more you sink in the Esteem of your Mistress, for all Women hate a Coward; you ought to be forbid the Habits of Men, who can be guilty of Effeminency [*sic*] *that even Women would blush at*.[40]

Effeminacy will be eliminated once signs correspond to 'natural', self-evident identities. Thus Sir William must exhibit the innate fortitude of the gentleman-born or he will be stripped of the symbols for genteel masculinity. Equally, the gentlewomen must put off their manly signs and resume the blushing modesty and petticoats of the 'inherently' weaker vessel. As semiotic instability, 'effeminate' behaviour was not clearly gender-exclusive, something only men could do. Indeed, associated pamphlet literature often implied that women were more

38 See Jones and Stallybrass, 'Fetishizing Gender', 100–1.

39 T. Durfey, *Love for Money* (1691), dramatis personae, and also the recollection of Thomas Bruce, second earl of Ailesbury, in W. E. Buckley (ed.), *Memoirs of Thomas, Earl of Ailesbury Written by Himself* (Roxburghe Club, London, 1890), vol. II, 390–1. Compare an advertisement for a 1701 performance of Thomas Baker's *Humour of the Age* 'to which will be added an Interlude of City Customs, by several aldermen's Ladies. To be performed by Mr Cibber, Mr Bullock, Mr Norris, and others', cited in A. Jackson, 'Play Notices from the Burney Newspapers 1700–1703', *PMLA* 48 (1933), 824; notice of an entertainment to follow another Baker comedy, *Tunbridge-Walks*, to be known as '*Visiting Scene of 4 Aldermens Ladies*, perform'd by 4 Men Comedians', quoted by J. Milhous and R. D. Hume, 'Revision of *The London Stage. Part II 1700–1729*', 3 April 1707.

40 Centlivre, *Beau's Duel*, iii, 31. *Emphasis added*. The blushing may be symbolically important, see chapter 11.

predisposed to be effeminate than men, prone to manipulating signs so that they lost all meaning.[41]

Finally, we encounter instances of 'female-' or 'she-' fops, even reference to a 'beauess'.[42] Thus Baker's *Humour of the Age* concluded with the marriage of the virtuous gentlewoman Tremilia, who had professed austere Quaker beliefs, and Mr Freeman. Part of the scene went as follows:

TREMILIA: I have been so us'd, Mr. *Freeman*, to this plain Garb, I fancy I shall appear so awkard otherwise, you'll be asham'd of me; I must intreat *Lucia* to instruct me in her modish Airs.

LUCIA: You have a natural Gentility, too refin'd to want Instruction.

TREMILIA: I'll endeavour to be decent, that I may'nt disgrace you, Sir, but you must excuse me, if I am not the greatest Beauess of the Age.[43]

Given both his familiarity with the figure of the beau and the fact that modish gentlewomen were typically referred to as 'belles',[44] Baker's neologism draws a pointed distinction and thus achieves a firm resolution in the play's closing lines. Notice how Baker, via the comment of Lucia, finally takes an innate and obvious female superiority for granted by rejecting the critique of gentility encapsulated by the juxtaposed figure of the 'beauess'. What these female characters had in common with the gentleman-beau was that they too were represented as claiming a dominance by reason of their lineage, even as they insisted on tricking their bodies with fine clothes and artful gestures as symbols of an always already native superiority.[45] Such behaviour by women was condemned in *England's Vanity* as 'Sodomitical Impudence', a description not of sexual deviance but of their apparent refusal to rest content with what God had bestowed upon them:

41 R. Allestree, *The Ladies Calling* (Oxford, 1677), 13, 'the Effeminacy and Niceness of women'; the entry for 'cosmeticks' in [M. Evelyn], *Mundus Muliebris* (1690), 17; Anon., *The Levellers. A Dialogue between Two Young Ladies, Concerning Matrimony . . .* (1703), reprinted in *The Harleian Miscellany* (1745), 419–20. See the related discussions of J. Lichtenstein, 'Making Up Representation: The Risks of Femininity', *Representations* 15 (1987), 77–87; F. E. Dolan, 'Taking the Pencil out of God's Hand: Art, Nature, and the Face-Painting Debate in Early Modern England', *PMLA* 108 (1993), 224–39; T. A. King, 'Displacing Masculinity: Edward Kynaston and the Politics of Effeminacy', in A. P. Williams (ed.), *The Image of Manhood in Early Modern Literature. Viewing the Male* (London, 1999), 119–40; W. J. Pritchard, 'Outward Appearances: The Display of Women in Restoration London', unpublished PhD dissertation, University of Chicago (1998), 14, 51ff.

42 For 'she-fop', see J. Leigh, *Kensington Gardens* (1720), iv, 53; for 'female-fop', see the title character of Sandford's comedy of the same name (1724).

43 Baker, *Humour*, v, 65.

44 For example, Steele's prologue to J. Vanbrugh, *Mistake* (1706); Lady Mary to Philippa Mundy, 6 February 1712, in R. Halsband (ed.), *The Complete Letters of Lady Mary Wortley Montagu. Volume I: 1708–1720* (Oxford, 1965), 115.

45 For instance, E. Ward, *Adam and Eve Stript to Their Furbelows* (1714), 72ff., offers a feminine equivalent of Sir Courtly in the form of 'Madam *Nice*'.

namely, a stable, legible and essential identity.[46] The figure of the 'female fop' who identifies herself as a 'gentlewoman born', like the more common fop who profusely proclaims himself a 'gentleman', was intended to question the assumption that there was such a thing as a transparent and substantive pedigree prior to representation and, therefore, beyond cultural contestation.

'Pornographic' representation of 'polymorphic' sexual behaviour in this period was avowedly political, often intent on questioning the nature of social differences.[47] If the drama could not be so explicit or quite as graphic, the comedy does seem to encode the beginnings of a similar chain of thought. The double-edged connection between the sodomitical act as a possible expression of social superiority,[48] on the one hand, and the sexually suspect beau representing the critique of that superiority as something other than inherent, knowable and therefore naturally legitimate (i.e. discursive, ambiguous and contestable instead), on the other hand, is evident from the description of a gentleman made in a verse satire on the royal Court during the final months of James II's reign:

> 'Tis strange, Kildare, that refin'd *beau garçon*,
> Was never yet at the Bell Savage shown,
> For 'tis a true and wonderful baboon.
> It therefore wisely was at first design'd
> He ne'er should like to propagate his kind;
> . . .
> No learn'd philosphers [*sic*] need strive to know
> Whether his soul's *extraduce*, or no;
> He has none yet, nor ever will, I fear –
> No soul of sense would ever enter there;
> Though Talbot, that young sodomite, they say,
> With tarse and carrot well enlarg'd the way.[49]

The poem, attributed to the earl of Dorset by its modern editors, likens the foppish courtier to a performing baboon that would make for good entertainment.[50] Dramatic dialogue itself often compared the gentleman-fop to a lesser primate,

[46] Anon., *England's Vanity, or the Voice of God* (1683), 97.

[47] See the editorial introduction to L. Hunt (ed.), *The Invention of Pornography. Obscenity and the Origins of Modernity, 1500–1800* (New York, 1993), 44.

[48] Haggerty has recently highlighted the sexuality of power and the politics of sodomy, *Men in Love*, 6–11, 27, 30–3.

[49] [C. Sackville, earl of Dorset], 'A Faithful Catalogue of Our Most Eminent Ninnies' (1688), in Crump (ed.), *Poems on Affairs of State*, 201–2 (lines 196–200 and 207–12). The brief exegesis following the quotation is based partly on the excellent critical apparatus that accompanies the modern transcription of the original manuscript. For Sir Courtly, see *ibid.*, 210 (line 392); for male–female sodomy, see *ibid.*, 196 (lines 88–90).

[50] We should note too that the satire as a whole acknowledged its dramatic heritage, by later referring to the stage fop Sir Courtly Nice, and made similar derogatory mileage out of other courtiers who engaged in sodomitical behaviour with women (and not just male adolescents as here).

suggesting both a lapse of human reason often associated with semiotic instability and apish, learned behaviour which erased any original identity.[51] The courtier is considered reluctant to continue his much-vaunted lineage but the nature of his lineage is immediately, significantly and more seriously undercut by the accusation of sodomy and the accompanying suggestion that this is itself an indication of the gentleman not being '*extraduce*'; of his lacking a noble, divinely ordained soul, begotten by and inherited from his elite father, which would avoid such bodily excess.[52]

At this juncture, the reader may require some reassurance that, by rehearsing the fop character, the drama could indeed be so critical of the core assumption of the early modern social hierarchy (lineage). The reassurance is not hard to find. A number of periodical essays sought to explain the gentleman's superiority and its 'nature'. If they did not always present entirely consistent arguments, some none the less concluded that lineage guaranteed a legitimate domination. Like an issue of *The Universal Spectator*, they maintained that superiority was in the blood and clear for all to see.[53] Others were more searching, more ambivalent. An essay featured in *The Plain Dealer* during 1724 considered lineage the 'Invention of industrious Policy' by which means certain individuals continued to exercise power until their superiority was 'esteem'd inherent, in their very Nature', and, therefore, lineage should be considered little more than a '*Cypher*' resulting in a 'Nobility that consists in *Sound* . . . an empty, and chimerical, Grandeur'.[54] With the paper's masthead featuring a significant quote from comic drama, the very same words of Sir Courtly Nice which introduced chapter 7, *The Prompter* hedged towards a broadly similar recognition a decade later by means of a Swiftian-esque fable.[55] We should note too that mock replies to this essay's critical stance included letters from an offended gentleman-born (the epistle bore the foppish autograph of 'Gawdy') and, even more significantly in light of the preceding paragraphs about 'hermaphroditic' gentlewomen, correspondence from a froward City wife ('Margery Turn-Penny') who had cuckolded her husband.[56]

51 R. A. Zimbardo, 'At Zero Point: Discourse, Politics, and Satire in Restoration England', *ELH* 59 (1992), 791. See, for example, G. Granville, *The She-Gallants* (1696), iv, 57; Baker, *Tunbridge-Walks*, ii, 16; Dilke, *Lover's Luck*, ii, 12; C. Molloy, *Perplex'd Couple* (1715), ii, 17; C. Cibber, *Provok'd Husband* (1728), v, 88. Also the related comment of E. Hickeringill, *The Ceremony-Monger* (1689, third edition 1696), 10, 'Of Brutes, none are *so loathsome* as the Ape, Wanting Man's Soul, he only has *Man's Shape*.'

52 Although the next chapter argues for more immediate political triggers, the foppish beau probably echoed, on some level, the searching philosophical debates surrounding identity and the human soul in this period. The key contours of this wider questioning have been ably charted by the late Roy Porter's *Flesh in the Age of Reason* (London, 2003), esp. 62–79.

53 *Universal Spectator*, no. ccxii (28 October 1732), [1–2]. But compare earlier issues of the same paper, such as no. lxxi (14 February 1730), [1].

54 *Plain Dealer*, no. xxxviii (31 July 1724), [1].

55 *Prompter*, no. cxxi (6 January 1736), [1].

56 *Ibid*., no. cxxx (6 February 1736), [1–2].

The fop's rehearsal on the London stage represented lineage as a potential illusion, expressing a lingering ambivalence about its trustworthiness as the basis for social distinction and inequality. Thus *Remarques on the Humours and Conversations of the Gallants of the Town* complained of the 'Comical Fop', he 'unravel[s] the richest Imbroideries of antient generosity and Prudence'.[57] The operative word here is potential, for the character drew its comic energy from a persistent but shifting tension between what, at first, seemed to be 'natural' on the one hand, and 'cultural' on the other. By establishing only to collapse the difference between nature and culture, the drama kept the audience guessing on the question of how one was to discern the truly well-born and their pedigreed but always just elusive *je ne sais quoi*. What appears naturally finer one moment becomes a cultural refinement the next, and vice versa. For example, the foppish Lord Stately's overly acute sense of hearing, as a trait revealing his paternity, seems to endorse his generosity until it is suggested that his behaviour is somewhat akin to a tic, a nervous idiosyncrasy rather than congenital marker of a finer, inherited sensibility.[58] Similarly, taking snuff is meant to show off gentle, well-born hands unsullied by labour yet it is a gesture that requires much practice and may even involve a compulsive scrubbing of palms.[59]

The fop ultimately relies on an audience to interpret his embodiment of lineage, to endorse his (re)presentation of fine surfaces, his manipulation of signs, as constitutive proof of the 'gentleman', the existence of an elite selfhood. Hence the epilogue to Susanna Centlivre's *The Wonder* could toy maliciously with the gentlemen-beaux, suggesting that a shock awaited them if it became possible to test paternity and therefore the integrity of the inherited dominance claimed by the eclat of their equipage:

> How many tip top Beau's have had the Fate,
> T' enjoy from *Mamma's* Secrets their Estate.
> Which if Her early Folly had made known,
> He'd rid behind the Coach, that's now His own.[60]

In other words, they might prove the sons of obscure footmen, not gentlemen. A contemporary periodical, *The Grumbler*, tried to go one better. Having argued that inherited honours did not necessarily make for a virtuous and legitimate elite, it advertised a special pair of spectacles which allowed their wearer to distinguish the truly virtuous individual, or, as the editor described them, 'these Glasses are so contrived, as to shew a *Beau* without his Dress or Equipage'.[61]

[57] Anon., *Remarques on the Humours and Conversations of the Gallants of the Town. Two Letters by a Person of Quality* (1673), 80–1.
[58] J. Crowne, *English Frier* (1690), ii, 12.
[59] See the beau Mr Littlegad in J. Carlile, *Fortune-Hunters* (1689), i, 4.
[60] S. Centlivre, *The Wonder* (1714). *Italics reversed.*
[61] *Grumbler*, no. xii (26–29 April 1715), [2].

With at times dizzying recursiveness, there was often a last twist to the fop's presentation of gentility as being ultimately rhetorical. For example, Vanbrugh's *Relapse* began by suggesting that inherited titles were like modish clothes, signs making for an assumed social role rather than simply marking an assured, inherent identity:

TAYLOR: I think I may presume to say, Sir, –

FOPPINGTON: My Lord – You Clawn you.

TAYLOR: Why, is he made a Lord – My Lord, I ask your Lordships Pardon my Lord; I hope my Lord, your Lordship will please to own, I have brought your Lordship as accomplishe[d] a Suit of Cloaths, as ever Peer of *England* trode the Stage in; my Lord; will your Lordship please to try 'em now.[62]

Yet as the tailor's apology hints, the fop's enactment could also comprise an understanding that the discursive dependence of the identity of 'gentleman', and rather less frequently 'gentlewoman', extended even to dramatic discourse itself. In other words, by its very staging of a Lord Foppington or his ilk, the theatre was simultaneously acknowledging its own ambiguous place in the impersonation of genteel lineage. The theatre signalled gentility as rhetorical performance even as its key social function was exactly that, to allow people to enact their pedigree in front of an audience (see parts II and IV).

Hence the Hillaria character of Colley Cibber's *Love's Last Shift* is warned about the threat posed to her virtue (and so her native superiority) by Sir Novelty Fashion. Like his later incarnation, Lord Foppington, Fashion's theatricality is highlighted when he is described as being 'as full of variety as a good Play'. However, further thought on the part of the play's model gentleman (Young Worthy) reveals considerable anxiety about the character's social effect beyond the playhouse. By claiming to have slept with Hillaria, the danger is that Sir Novelty will also reveal the contingent nature of lineage on account of its being a matter for subjective perception, reputation rather than objective proof. Descent may unravel if there are contradictory or dissenting opinions regarding its integrity:

YOUNG WORTHY: O Madam! no Juggler is so deceitful as a Fop; for while you look his Folly in the Face, he Steals away your Reputation, with more Ease, than the other Picks your Pocket.

HILLARIA: Some Fools indeed are dangerous.

YOUNG WORTHY: I grant you, your design is only to laugh at him: But that's more than he finds out: Therefore you must expect he will tell the World another Story: And 'tis Ten to One, but the consequence makes you repent of your Curiosity.[63]

Such reflexivity also explains the irony of the beau in *Tunbridge-Walks* waxing lyrical about what the dedication of a play will mean to him: 'I'me to have a

[62] Vanbrugh, *Relapse*, i, 10. [63] C. Cibber, *Love's Last Shift* (1696), ii, 22, 25.

Dedication next Winter: Well, a Dedication is the prettiest thing – To see one's own Name in the Front of a Book – To the Honourable *Francis Maiden* Esq; – Then to have the World told of one's Airs, and Equipage, and the Valour of one's Ancestors.'[64] The playbook's opening address will literally entail the history of Maiden's pedigree, but the comedy in which Maiden currently features will only serve to show the curious that his innate superiority is discoursed into existence: the product of an elaborate performance which almost (but not quite) convinces the other characters and the audience that Maiden is indeed born to dominate, a gentleman.

In a similar vein, Varnish, the beau character from *Kensington Gardens*, neatly rehearsed the ambivalent nature of the theatre as a site of social production when he, a born gentleman, was mistaken during the onstage action for a lowly player.[65] Of course, Varnish was an actor, John Egleton, playing the role of a gentleman to applause. Yet for those first audiences in the know, the matter of identifying an essential social identity, the key question impelling every fop's performance, redounded even further. For Egleton was represented offstage as an impoverished gentleman who had squandered the revenues of his patrimony and taken to acting as his livelihood.[66] If players could appear 'well-born', how did one know whether the 'well-born' were playing at an identity not innately theirs?

[64] Baker, *Tunbridge-Walks*, iii, 30. [65] Leigh, *Kensington Gardens*, iii, 44.

[66] See Egleton's entry in P. H. Highfill, jr., K. A. Burnim, and E. A. Langhans (eds.), *A Biographical Dictionary of Actors, Actresses, Musicians, Dancers, Managers & Other Stage Personnel in London, 1660–1800* (Carbondale, 1978), vol. V, 44–5.

9 Succession crises and the politics of foppery

> [He] hath a very sharp look, and a very fine, black, piercing eye; that he is very thin, but handsome; and that he is the finest spoken gent. he ever heard, and that he is wonderfully mild and sweet in his temper . . . My lord told me, that the king's picture, for which I was prosecuted, is extremely like the king . . . He said, a very fine gentleman, and a lover of dancing. He said, the king touched many for the evil in his lordship's own house, and that they recovered.
>
> Descriptions of James Francis Edward Stuart, *Reliquiae Hearnianae* (1716)

If the frequency of the fop character's rehearsal during the late Stuart period is any indication, the idea of an inheritable, self-sustaining social superiority, carrying with it the right to exercise authority on the basis of innate worth (to manifest 'virtue'), was the topic of much searching discussion. Here we will be reassessing what the finer details of the fop's presentation might tell us about the impetus behind the interrogation of elite social identity that the figure staged for its first audiences.

Making for the demystification of the gentleman's natural superiority as never capable of being anything more than a cultured but contingent fiction, the late Stuart fop bears traces of the circumstances fuelling disillusionment with the notion that social structuration was always, only and manifestly a matter of one's birth. Perhaps the theatre as an urban institution tended to encourage the perception of such a discrepancy. Gentlemen were ideally to have far more weighty responsibilities than attending the playhouse. They were meant to utilize their inherent ability ('genius') for governing society, not neglect it in favour of flaunting their pedigree about Town. An integral part of the metropolitan season, the theatre was often held to contribute to landlord absenteeism and abandonment of the exercise of an inherited superiority.[1] For instance, one satire complained:

> That men renounce their ease, estates, and fame
> And drudge it here to get a fopling's name;
> That one of seeming sense, advanc'd in years,

[1] See D. R. Hainsworth, *Stewards, Lords and People. The Estate Steward and His World in Later Stuart England* (Cambridge, 1992), 13–17, 75–107.

Like a Sir Courtly Nice in town appears;
Others exchange their land for tawdry clothes
And will in spite of nature pass for beaux.
Indulgent Heav'n, who ne'er made aught in vain,
Each man for something proper did ordain,
Yet most against their genius blindly run,
The wrong they choose and what they're made for shun.[2]

In like manner, John Dennis censured 'others of our Gentry, who have left their Hereditary Seats in the Country to establish themselves in Town . . . endeavour'd to distinguish themselves, and to outvie one another by their foppish Profusion, in Eating, Drinking, Dress, and Equipage'.[3] Opponents of the stage were especially inclined to rehearse arguments that the theatre encouraged the gentry's dissipation. For instance, *The Conduct of the Stage* commented: 'WHAT a Diminution to the Honour of Gentlemen (who by Birth are design'd for Offices of State) to go to Childrens Play, at the Expence of so much Time and Money.'[4] Another critic reckoned it would be 'more Conducing to eternal Welfare, if Gentlemen employ'd their time in Reading, Travailing, and Meditation . . . but most of our Gentry now a Dayes, O! Scandal to our Countrey'.[5] Of course, such activity might possibly be justified as a rare but well-earned diversion from the gentleman's public and social duties, his *vita activa*. There were, however, times when such rationalization was strained. This was noticeably the case for much of our period, a time that saw England engaged in two major wars as well as riven by domestic disquiet from various quarters and in need of vigorous 'gentry' leadership.[6]

Comic drama often contrasted the fop with an active individual (his rank by birth either lower or uncertain until the end of the play resolves it as gentle) who engages in virtuous action (frequently just returned from taking up arms in Europe) rather than spending his days flattering patrons and paying court to eligible women (whose attraction or 'fop-call' is said to be their 'quality'[7]), all the time expecting social recognition and perhaps political sinecure because of his pedigree (because of his claim that he is manifestly who he *is*). Notice, for example, the gentleman-soldier versus fop oppositions of Bellair and

[2] 'The Town Life' (1686), in G. M. Crump (ed.), *Poems on Affairs of State. Augustan Satirical Verse, Volume IV: 1685–1688* (New Haven, 1968), 63 (lines 35–44).
[3] J. Dennis, *An Essay upon Publick Spirit* (1711), 13.
[4] Anon., *The Conduct of the Stage Consider'd* (1721), 33.
[5] R. Burridge, *A Scourge for the Play-Houses* (1702), 20.
[6] A tension also inscribed by the discourse of theatre reform. See, for instance, Anon., *A Representation of the Impiety and Immorality of the English Stage* (1704), 4; Anon., *Conduct of the Stage*, 20–2.
[7] 'Satire on Both Whigs and Tories' (1683), in J. H. Wilson (ed.), *Court Satires of the Restoration* (Columbus, 1976), 126 (line 154).

Gooseandelo in Thomas Dilke's *Lover's Luck* (1696); Standard and Sir Harry Wildair in Farquhar's play from 1701 which takes the beau's name as its title; Merit and Frank Doggrell from *The Wife of Bath* (1713) by John Gay. The most common plot-line sees the pair of fop and active gentleman competing for the hand of a chaste young gentlewoman. The exemplary gentleman wins this contest, his victory symbolizing that gentlemen must, at the very least, emulate the virtue of their ancestors to be considered gentlemen themselves. Asserting a superior birth alone is insufficient; any marks of honour may ring hollow. Lineage makes for neither an unquestioned right to, nor the proper exercise of, power. The likes of Frank Doggrell lose out because they passively claim domination on just that basis and they are tricked into marriage with a humble, unchaste woman by reason of her own empty claims to be of similar 'quality'.

The fop's contrasting with the gentleman-soldier lends initial support to the most common explanation often advanced for the character's currency in the late Stuart period. The potential loss of England's (inter)national interests to France was anxiously and metaphorically figured by the fop's submission to French fashions.[8] It was in this context that a conduct book, *The Gentleman's Library*, redacted both the comic beau and current geopolitical concerns when it counselled gentlemen to act like their ancestors rather than merely parade hollow status symbols earned by their forebears:

> He that depends wholly upon the Worth of others, ought to consider that he has but the Honour of an Image, and is worshipped not for his own sake, but upon the Account of what he *represents* . . . To maintain such indefensible and dangerous Principles of Honour, which not only impose upon our Understandings, but emasculate our Spirits and spoil our Temper, and tend only to the nourishing of Idleness and Pride, is no very Heroical Undertaking.[9]

To be sure, a noticeable feature of the beau stereotype is the recurrent and ironic use of militaristic imagery. The character's languid and selfish lifestyle is mockingly described in terms associated with the patriotic service of the gentleman. The fop's pampered physiognomy does 'killing work' among the women of the *beau monde*.[10] Or, as one prologue elaborated, the beaux

[8] For instance, W. R. Taliaferro, 'The Fop and Fashion in Restoration Comedy', unpublished PhD dissertation, University of California-Berkeley (1989), 57ff.; K. J. Gardner, 'Cultural Anxiety and English Comedy, 1700–1708', unpublished PhD dissertation, Tulane University (1992), 23–6 and *passim*.

[9] [E.P.], *The Gentleman's Library, Containing Rules for Conduct in All Parts of Life* (1715), 361–3. *Emphasis added.*

[10] T. Dilke, *Lover's Luck* (1696), ii, 13.

> from both side-boxes play their Batteries;
> And not a Bullet shot, but burning Eyes:
> Those they discharge with such successful Arts,
> They fire, three deep, into the Ladies hearts.[11]

Alternatively, these gentlemen allow themselves to be abjectly preoccupied with continental modes rather than engage in meaningful action. For instance, attention was often drawn to how fops were 'steinkirked', a pointed reference to the lace cravat named after Steenkerke where English forces had recently been put to rout by the French.[12] Similarly, Sir Novelty Fashion's long sleeves had a rather odd potential:

HILLARIA: Nay, I confess, the Fashion may be very useful to you, Gentlemen, that make Campaigns; for shou'd you unfortunately lose an Arm, or so, that Sleeve might be very convenient to hide the defect on't.

SIR NOVELTY: Ha! I think your Ladiship's in the right on't, Madam. [*Hiding his Hand in his sleeve*].[13]

The beau's deft manipulation of snuff-box or cane could be conceived of as an exercise (un)like that of the weapons drill which early eighteenth-century Londoners might view in Hyde Park.[14]

However, to view the fop as the expression of a francophobic inferiority complex (i.e. English gentlemen becoming frenchified 'fops' spells likely defeat), or perhaps a jingoistic xenophobia (i.e. scorning a foppish delicacy inspires English resolve) may be wide of the mark. It can be argued that the full significance of the beau as francophilic parody has not been appreciated. The social perspectives said to be represented by the fop's enactment (aristocratic and averse to bourgeois mobility; middling and opposed to feckless aristocratic leadership) are simply given an appropriately nationalistic tinge which may miss much of the original impetus behind that enactment.[15] Neither the precise nature of the French threat represented by the fop nor the manner in which this theme meshed so easily with questions of elite social superiority, the character's *raison d'être*, have been traced by modern commentators. We still need to resolve how it was that the fop's insistence on a born superiority rooted in England's past came to be lampooned as a peculiarly 'French' proclivity.[16]

[11] T. Southerne, *Wives Excuse* (1692), prologue spoken by Mr Betterton. *Italics reversed.*

[12] M. Manley, *Lost Lover* (1696), iv, 24; J. Vanbrugh, *Relapse* (1697), i, 12; M. Pix, *Beau Defeated* (1700), v, 45; T. Southerne, *Spartan Dame* (1719), prologue by Mr Fenton.

[13] C. Cibber, *Love's Last Shift* (1696), ii, 21.

[14] J. Crowne, *Darius King of Persia* (1688), epilogue spoke by her that was Barzana; *Spectator*, no. 138 (8 August 1711), vol. II, 46; *Tory Tatler*, no. 2 (27–29 November 1710), [2].

[15] See n. 8; also B. K. Wallace, 'Reading the Surfaces of Colley Cibber's *The Careless Husband*', *SEL* 40, 3 (2000), 474, 477.

[16] For instance, *Universal Spectator*, no. lxxxxii (11 July 1730), [1].

The answer would seem to lie with our first realizing that in one crucial respect the political menace articulated by the beau figure was not, at its core, of completely foreign origin. Rather, the character spoke to a matter at the heart of England's *domestic* politics during the late Stuart period. When the beau was deemed either a 'European monster' or a 'prince', audiences may well have been prompted to think more of the English royal Court in exile across the water at Saint-Germain and not so much of the French elite under a bellicose Louis XIV.[17]

Throughout our period one lineage in particular was an abiding concern, that of the Crown. Its precise nature and form was the source of intense debate and instability. On the one hand, there might appear to be little connection between the vagaries of high politics and the everyday workings of English society at large. Despite some predictions of catastrophe far beyond the upheaval of the mid-seventeenth century and the much-disputed contrivance of a new royal line via the house of Hanover, English society's lesser lines of inherited power remained largely intact amid these constitutional upheavals.[18] On the other hand, it is difficult to imagine the succession crisis not having had some impact at the socio-ideological level and functioning as the primary catalyst for the fop's cultural significance and currency during the late Stuart period.

As this last temporal label hints, England faced prolonged uncertainty over who would inherit its rule and on what grounds, despite the semblance of decisive change in 1688. The remainder of this chapter will show that, at a given moment, accusations of foppery were levelled mainly at those deemed to be on the 'wrong' side of the succession question and its rival solutions. If, by definition, a 'fop' was convinced that socio-political distinctions were obviously natural, went without saying, then both supporters of the exiled Stuarts (jacobites and some tories) and backers of the new regime (mostly whigs) might be liable to the stigma of foppery. For, essentially, the first position relied on the belief that it was possible to discern an enduring line of Stuart inheritance, while the second rested on the perception of a clear but ultimately reparable deviation in that same lineage. However, as a matter of both fortune and design, it was the proponents of a Stuart return from French exile who were most often on the receiving end of the beau's satire.[19] Foppery became a means to dismiss their conviction that the Crown had not followed its manifest, divinely ordained and unbroken line of succession.

17 T. Dilke, *Pretenders* (1698), i, 6; T. Durfey, *Modern Prophets* (1709), ii, 27.

18 J. C. D. Clark, *English Society 1688–1832. Ideology, Social Structure and Political Practice during the Ancien Régime* (Cambridge, 1985), 78, 94–5, 119ff.

19 An argument also broached recently by M. Peltonen, *The Duel in Early Modern England* (Cambridge, 2003), 178ff. The current argument does, however, choose to stress crucial social dimensions.

Certain resonances between partisan polemic and stage satire seem too much to be coincidence. For example, political discourse, aiming to cement allegiance to the monarchy after 1688, increasingly held that the meritorious exercise of authority, virtue, was more important than the absolute claim to authority by birth alone.[20] Tony Claydon has shown in detail how the Court deliberately tried to legitimate the positions of William III and Mary II by lauding their 'virtuous' rule, all but ignoring the rival claim that the Crown had a more direct successor by birth in the person of James 'the Third' as son of the deposed James II.[21] We have already seen how the fop fails to manifest 'virtue' and claims superiority solely on the basis of his pedigree. In a comedy which premiered at a particularly crucial time for England's dynastic politics (1701, on the eve of the Anglo-French battle over the Spanish succession; recognition by France of James III as the true and rightful heir to the British throne; the Act of Succession) the beau baronet Sir Harry Wildair finally resolves: 'Once I was a Friend to *France*; but henceforth I promise to sacrifice my Fashions, Coaches, Wigs, and Vanity, to Horses, Arms, and Equipage, and serve my King in *propria persona*, to promote a vigorous War, if there be occasion.'[22] The key phrase binding political with social concerns is 'in *propria persona*'. Wildair renounces the importance he once gave to his lineage, acknowledging that his superiority should at the very least receive confirmation by virtuous action. His allegedly superior metal must be tested on the European battlefield rather than splendidly brandished down the Mall. At the same time, Wildair's phrase recognizes William III as the right(eous) monarch rather than as the king on account of a disputed line of succession. In another comedy which also concludes with the fop's repentance, the reformed gentleman not only promises to lead virtuously but also swears: 'From this Hour I'll play the Effeminate Fool no more . . . and shew my self a true Hero for my Glorious Queen.'[23] Very possibly the pledge of allegiance to Queen Anne is doubly significant in that it comes from the incongruous figure of Mizen, a naval officer in the armed service widely perceived at the time to harbour pro-jacobite sympathies.[24] Mizen and company may be described as

[20] H. Nenner, *The Right To Be King. The Succession to the Crown of England, 1603–1714* (London, 1995), 193–4.

[21] T. Claydon, *William III and the Godly Revolution* (Cambridge, 1996).

[22] G. Farquhar, *Sir Harry Wildair* (1701), v, 47.

[23] C. Shadwell, *Fair Quaker of Deal* (1710), v, 61.

[24] P. K. Monod, *Jacobitism and the English People 1688–1788* (Cambridge, 1989), 282. There has been considerable disagreement over the definition of jacobitism and, in particular, its relation to tory politics. The term 'jacobite' is used loosely here. It refers not only to those who actively promoted and plotted the return of the 'rightful' heir to the throne, but to passive sympathizers as well. The latter are also described here as 'tory' not so much on the basis of historiography which argues for the synonymity of the terms from studying the political behaviour of certain individuals (see Clark, *English Society*, 32, 143; cf. L. Colley, *In Defiance of Oligarchy. The Tory Party 1714–60* (Cambridge, 1982), 25ff.), but because such conflation was common to satiric discourse.

incongruous because we have seen how most fops were portrayed as shunning the slightest suggestion of public duty, at least until the play's dénouement. The play's author, Charles Shadwell, seems to have been pointing to a similar socio-political crux when he had another character survey the London scene and specifically locate the fops at a tory coffee-house: '*Young Man's* is fill'd with Military Beau's, Sea Gentlemen, and Admiralty Clerks.'[25]

The fop's penchant for swearing evidently becomes deliberately ironic, suggesting a refusal to take the one politically correct oath of the day (i.e. to uphold the new regime) and encoding the phenomenon of seditious words (i.e. oaths condemning the revolution or pledges drunk in favour of the alternative then in exile).[26] Thus Sasaphras, a citizen character from William Mountfort's *Greenwich Park*, snidely describes the fops as 'spruce Tits [who] look as Scornfully and as sour upon a plain dress'd Country-Gentleman as a Grumbletonian upon a Clergy-man that has taken the Oaths'.[27] In related fashion, fops and beaux were often depicted as partial to drinking burgundy and champagne, distinctly French (and contraband) beverages.[28] While in his cups, one such character, Sir Noisy Parrat, was equally ready to sing: '*Oh! There[']s a Difference twixt brisk noble Blood | And the Dull offspring of the Dunghill Brood.*'[29] The added irony of Sir Noisy's remark was that a modest alcohol intake was believed to promote the quality and flow of blood, whilst excessive drinking suppressed both. So for Sir Noisy any 'Difference' was dissolved and, in that event, how was anyone to know if he was well-born?

A parodic dialogue seems to have developed between derisive representations of the gentleman-as-fop and propagandistic depictions of the exiled Stuarts, particularly James 'the Third' who was otherwise known as the 'Pretender' or the 'St. Germain gentleman'.[30] If a fop could be considered a possible 'counterfeit' in terms of his natural superiority then similar doubt surrounded James III. Although he bore all the signs of royal pedigree, many believed that the Pretender so-called was not James II's true heir.[31] From the moment he was born, political invective cast doubt on the child's parentage (that he was really the

[25] C. Shadwell, *Humours of the Army* (1713), i, 4.

[26] Monod, *Jacobitism*, 248–64.

[27] W. Mountfort, *Greenwich Park* (1691), iv, 44. 'Grumbletonian' here referred to those held to belong to the 'Country' opposition.

[28] Sir Noisy (who proposes a health to 'Friends on the other side of the water') in H. Higden, *Wary Widdow* (1693), i, 4; Sir William Mode in S. Centlivre, *Beau's Duel* (1702), ii, 12; Farquhar, *Wildair* (see the choice of Wildair's drink; the play's second beau, Clincher, also proposes a toast to the French settlement of the Spanish succession), ii, 18; iv, 28–9.

[29] Higden, *Widdow*, iii, 28.

[30] [William Greg to Robert Harley from Edinburgh], 12 June 1705, HMC, *Portland* 29, 4 (1897), 195.

[31] R. J. Weil, 'The Politics of Legitimacy: Women and the Warming-Pan Scandal', in L. G. Schwoerer (ed.), *The Revolution of 1688–1689. Changing Perspectives* (Cambridge, 1992), 65, 72–3, 77. Weil's essay has since been presented as part of her *Political Passions. Gender, the Family and Political Argument in England 1680–1714* (Manchester, 1999), 86–104.

7 'Prince James Francis Edward Stuart and his sister Princess Louisa Maria Theresa', by N. de Largillière, 1695

son of a brickmaker, smuggled into Whitehall in a warming-pan and passed off as royal progeny) and conjectured that the heir would need to travel to France where, very much like a gentleman-beau making the grand tour, he might be taught how to body forth the *appearance* of his *alleged* lineage:

> Her arms a sucking Prince embrace,
> Whate'er you think, of royal race
> . . .
> That he should travel did accord;
> To Paris sent to learn grimace,
> To swear and damn with a *bonne grâce*.[32]

Of course, James III's immediate fate proved stranger than poetic fiction. He was soon to spend his youth on an extended *sojourn à la mode* across the Channel. Once there, graphic representations like Nicholas de Largillière's portrait of 1695 served to emphasize James's status and disseminate his dynastic claims (see Figure 7). Putting to one side the allegorical elements (the faithful hound that symbolizes James's legitimacy) and perhaps emblems of nobility (the blue sash of the Garter – though some beaux were represented as aspiring to this honour), signal features of the princely heir's modish dress and precise stance seem reprised to the point of exaggeration by Grisoni's 1715/20 rendering of Lord Foppington. James wears the same type of trim *just-au-corps* and coat, and neat cravat, and, at the tender, smooth-faced age of seven, has the composure to tuck spare glove and hat underarm (making his arm akimbo, a typical gesture of superiority) as well as to stand jauntily in shoes that appear to be red-heeled. Such footwear, though not obvious in the Grisoni portrait, was a hallmark of the beau.[33] Given the twenty-year intermission between the portraits, and the fact that Largillière had also been resident in England as a Stuart Court painter prior to both the 1688 Revolution and Lord Foppington's first appearance, it is tempting to speculate that Grisoni's work (and thus Cibber's performance) was, in some sense, a deliberate travesty of Largillière's portrait and its elite male subject.[34]

Alternatively, we might more cautiously assume that all Grisoni was commissioned to paint was Cibber in his most famous role, perhaps trying to recall its debut in 1696 rather than a performance dating from about the time of the painting's own production, *c.*1720. In this event, Largillière's portrait of the Stuart heir and Foppington's first portrayal *onstage* are so nearly synchronous (1695–6) that they can bear no cause-and-effect relationship. Nor can we be

32 'Tom Tiler, or the Nurse' (1688), in Crump, *Poems on Affairs of State. Volume IV*, 258–9 (lines 10–11; 36–8).
33 *Tatler*, no. 26 (9 June 1709), vol. I, 201; *Spectator*, no. 311 (26 February 1712), vol. III, 126.
34 For Largillière's English connections, see A. Griffiths and R. A. Gerard, *The Print in Stuart Britain 1603–1689* (London, 1998), 236–7.

certain that Grisoni knew Largillière's work. Even so, we are still justified in noting that the Foppington role (1696) may have been as much a forecast of how the Stuart heir would appear in future as the verse satire (1688) which had imagined the weeks-old infant standing with exactly the same genteel poise, the *bonne grâce*, later represented by Largillière. Both satiric projections, poetic and dramatic, were driven by political anxieties that had already been brewing for a considerable time and a blend of well-known artistic conventions. Both fed off the tradition of the naturally fine gentleman and his parodic twin, the culturally refined fop.

Further, we find that the term 'chevalier', a sobriquet of the Pretender's,[35] was also used of fops and beaux.[36] And vice versa. One playwright's description of his foppish character as 'Pretender', suitor to a gentlewoman, seems more than accidental.[37] So too the remarks of Sir William Chaytor, a staunch anti-jacobite, in a letter to his family reporting plans for a Stuart invasion and restoration in early 1701. Having relayed news of the plot he closed by saying of his kinsman, Edward Burdett, 'a lit[t]le time will give him leave to talk of Bell[es] and Beaus'.[38] The remark was very probably sarcastic, since Burdett was a Stuart supporter and Roman Catholic. Chaytor's apprehension over a regime change in the near future was diffused by his risible characterization of its would-be supporters. Even coded ramblings of the tory member of parliament Sir Thomas Cave, in letters written about Stuart forces on the eve of 'The Fifteen' (the Pretender's invasion of England in 1715), continued this immanent association of comedic character with an unsettled succession: 'The dog is young, but ready to go. Name is Beau, born near Cumberland. Now in arms.'[39]

Laudatory verse stressed how the Stuart heir's lineage, and therefore the right to rule, was naturally revealed in his person, particularly by his face. The gaze of the heir was represented as having a mystical power to attract (female) subjects.[40] The gentleman-fop's physiognomy was similarly highlighted and, more importantly, so was the force, the 'darts', of his gaze.[41] Beaux were also linked

35 D. Szechi, *Jacobitism and Tory Politics 1710–14* (Edinburgh, 1984), 17; Monod, *Jacobitism*, 40. Several instances of this usage may be found in Durfey, *Modern Prophets*; P. Bliss (ed.), *Reliquiae Hearnianae. The Remains of Thomas Hearne* (Oxford, 1857), vol. I, 272, entry for 8 September 1712.

36 Anon., *Mundus Foppensis* (1691), [25]; G. Granville, *She-Gallants* (1696), i, 6; Farquhar, *Wildair*, ii, 17; S. Centlivre, *Bold Stroke for a Wife* (1718; 1737 edition), ii, 21.

37 E. Settle, *City-Ramble* (1711), i, 7. Settle's whig allegiance at this time was also well known.

38 Sir William Chaytor to his wife and daughter, 17–18 February 1701, in M. Y. Ashcroft (ed.), *The Papers of Sir William Chaytor (1639–1721)* (North Yorkshire County Record Office Publication, no. 33, Northallerton, 1984), 99.

39 Quoted in S. E. Whyman, *Sociability and Power in Late-Stuart England. The Cultural World of the Verneys 1660–1720* (Oxford, 1999), 175.

40 See Monod, *Jacobitism*, 70–6.

41 For an example of the fop and the lineaments of the gentleman's physiognomy, see J. Addison, *Drummer* (1716), iii, 28. For the force of the fop's gaze see, for instance, the quote from the

in representation with 'idolatry'. They either 'worshipped' themselves and, by extension, their illustrious descent as they preened in front of their mirrors or paid homage to others of the *beau monde* 'who continually lie basking in Frailty; the Chocolate Houses stink of perfum'd Vices, and are full of ungodly Looking-Glasses, that magnify vain Ornaments, and delude, with Idolatry, those that look into them, and occasion Self-Adoration'.[42] The mention of the fop as idol(ater) carried with it associations of popery. Indeed, non-dramatic deployment of the fop figure might pull no punches, one poem likening the beau-gentleman's behaviour to the performance of the Catholic liturgy.[43] The anatomy of beauish fashions in *Mundus Foppensis* got down to finer particulars, describing the fop's 'Rolls', for example, as a 'sort of Dress for the Knees, invented as some say by the Roman Catholicks, for the conveniency of Kneeling'.[44] James II and his heir had been excluded from their birthright because of their Catholic faith and, as Howard Nenner has argued, a means to deny what jacobites continued to proclaim as their natural legitimacy was precisely to taint this insistence with a 'papist' brush; to dismiss divine right and indefeasible hereditary succession as foolish, insubstantial and unsubstantiated superstition.[45] It is certainly little surprise to find that popery (and implicitly high Anglican ritual) could become synonymous with fop[p]ery and vice versa.[46]

The figure of the fop or beau made for blunt and explicit dialogue between what some might consider distinctly socio-cultural issues on the one hand, and narrowly political concerns on the other. For instance, a tract comparing London's two patent theatres had cause to describe a 'flaming full bottom'd Wig' that was, of course, a signature accoutrement of the fop. Yet the description in question ventured that its wearer would 'look like the King's Head peeping out of the Royal-Oak'.[47] This was a pointed allusion to the famed escape of the future Charles II following the royalist defeat at Worcester in 1651. By the eighteenth century, the oak-tree had assumed a prominent place in pro-Stuart

prologue to Southerne's *Wives Excuse* given above; Dilke, *Lover's Luck*, i, 6; W. Taverner, *Artful Wife* (1718), i, 3; J. Leigh, *Kensington Gardens* (1720), ii, 26.

42 G. Farquhar, *Love and a Bottle* (1699), ii, 17; Taverner, *Wife*, iv, 48. Other examples include Tinsel in Addison, *Drummer*, iv, 40; Sir Noisy in Higden, *Widdow*, ii, 17; Sir John in Pix, *Beau Defeated*, iii, 22. See also E. Ward's description of the Beau's Club in *Secret History of Clubs* (1709), 138.

43 'The Town Life', in Crump, *Poems on Affairs of State. Volume IV*, 64 (lines 60ff.). These associations were also rehearsed in periodicals like *Universal Spectator*, no. cclxiv (27 October 1733), [1–2].

44 Anon., *Mundus Foppensis*, [26], 9.

45 This was particularly the case in the matter of the oaths, and the tendency to take them on bended knee, already discussed. See S. Staves, *Players' Scepters. Fictions of Authority in the Restoration* (Lincoln, NE, 1979), 191ff.

46 E. Hickeringill, *The Ceremony-Monger* (1689, third edition 1696), 10ff.; 'The Boast of Great Britain; Or, A Song in Praise of *Mary* Present Queen of *England, Scotland, France*, and *Ireland*', in W. G. Day (ed.), *The Pepys Ballads* (Cambridge, 1987), vol. V, 56.

47 Anon., *A Comparison between the Two Stages* (1702), 63.

symbolism and mythology.[48] More directly, a non-juring apprentice (that is, an individual who has refused to swear allegiance to the new Hanoverian regime and, it is implied, has also rejected the authority of his citizen master)[49] was lampooned as follows:

He's extraordinary Handsome; is of a charming Brown Swarthy Complexion; has a very fine Goggle Eye; Teeth as White as Saffron, and as Sound as a Rotten Pear; his Nose and Chin will make a pretty Pair of Nut-crackers for his *Warming-pan Idol* the *Pretender* . . . He's an Eternal Beau; Wears a Hat without any Button, thereby to be distinguish'd from Honest Men; his Neckcloth thrust thro' a Button-hole in the Form of a Rose, to signifie the Youth and Innocency of his *Baby-King*.[50]

The description of the beau apprentice reads as a bathetic lampoon of the exiled Stuart prince's portrayal then current. Supporters of James III had only awestruck, hushed description and the occasional clandestine picture (sometimes concealed in that indispensable knick-knack of the beau, his snuff-box[51]) to feed their faith that the Pretender was truly his father's son, such as:

[He] hath a very sharp look, and a very fine, black, piercing eye; that he is very thin, but handsome; and that he is the finest spoken gent. he ever heard, and that he is wonderfully mild and sweet in his temper . . . a very fine gentleman, and a lover of dancing.[52]

Although it would be possible to highlight a noticeable predisposition on the part of many playgoers to draw such a conclusion in the wake of 1688, we need not assume all gentlemen-beaux to have been deliberately intended as satirical portraits of specific individuals from among the exiled Stuart court, its domestic adherents (jacobites) or potential supporters (tories). Indeed, verse satires continued to rebuke prominent backers of the Revolution as guilty of foppery. Thus, the earl Mulgrave (John Sheffield, both a 'foppish' victim of Rochester's pen, among others, and a future Lincoln's Inn Fields companion of William Byrd) lashed that 'emptiness of old nobility' William Cavendish (fourth earl of Devonshire and whig grandee) as:

The fop, without distinction, does apply
His bows and smiles to all promiscuously
With an affected careless wave of's wand,
And tottering on, does neither go nor stand:
So humbly proud and so genteelly dull,

[48] Monod, *Jacobitism*, 71–2, 76, 182–3.

[49] As with the identification of 'tory' and 'jacobite', the connection of non-jurancy with jacobitism was complex and unstable. However, such complexity was elided in the case of satire as here. See Clark, *English Society*, 146.

[50] *British Gazetteer*, [unnumbered] (22 December 1716), 607. *Italics reversed.*

[51] M. G. H. Pittock, 'The Culture of Jacobitism', in J. Black (ed.), *Culture and Society in Britain, 1660–1800* (Manchester, 1997), 138.

[52] Bliss, *Reliquiae Hearnianae*, vol. I, 367–8 (entries for 1 September and 2 December 1716 reporting sightings at second hand).

Too weak for Council and too old for trull,
That to conclude with this bilk-stately thing –
He's a mere costly piece of garnishing.[53]

In this event, we need to reconcile two seemingly contradictory tendencies: the undeniable coalescence of anti-Stuart feeling around the fop figure on the one hand and, on the other, the diminishing but not negligible return to be had from counter-deploying the stereotype *against* supporters of the new, post-1688 regime.

We can begin this reconciliation by recognizing that the uncertainty surrounding born superiority, as evidenced by the fop figure, was driven in large measure by the political exigencies of the day. Taking a longer view, the fop was a double-edged figure as far as partisan loyalties were concerned. Anyone advancing a claim to power on the basis of their birth necessarily bodied forth their lineage with cultural symbols. If all pedigrees were cultured, then all were potentially vulnerable to the same foppish critique in the interests of political one-upmanship.

An all too short excursus on verse satire from the decade and a half preceding the Revolution, a period when the dramatic version of the fop character was still in its formative stages, will serve to demonstrate this polemical flexibility. For, prior to the late 1680s, a strong case can be made that those with *whiggish* leanings were far more liable to be branded fops. The signal attributes of such characterization are as they will be after 1688. Yet they tend to relate more to individuals *opposing* the Duke of York (future James II) and his putative heirs and, simultaneously, to those who supported his chief rival, James Scott, Duke of Monmouth. For readers already familiar with the full course of late Stuart politics, the enduring cultural significance of the fop figure beneath the swirling currents of political change will be obvious. The common thread throughout, and so the basic reason for the fop's continued currency, was lineage and the need to prove it in the interests of political legitimation and stability.

Wanting to secure a Protestant succession from the late 1670s, supporters of what would gradually develop from an 'opposition' to a 'whig' faction had, however, to contend with the dubious pedigree of Monmouth. With hindsight his status seems clear enough. He was the illegitimate son of Charles II, from his time in exile during the interregnum, and Lucy Walters. Yet given the high stakes involved we might speculate that any 'reality' probably would not have mattered. In other words, had Monmouth's claim to the throne been more certain, history suggests that this would not have prevented doubts being sown by his opponents (in the same way that the whigs were to instigate rumours about the allegedly spurious James Francis Edward Stuart from the moment

[53] J. Sheffield, 'The Nine' (1690), in W. J. Cameron (ed.), *Poems on Affairs of State. Volume V: 1688–1697* (New Haven, 1971), 196–7 (lines 10–17).

of his birth in 1688). As it was, Monmouth's champions tried their damnedest to corroborate a clandestine marriage between his parents. Meanwhile, some Yorkists went so far as to imply that Monmouth was certainly a bastard of Lucy Walters, but not one sired by Charles II himself.[54]

In this earlier contest for power, pedigree's impersonation became all-important. Rather predictably (given that we have already suggested similar problems, uncertainties and associated tactics would follow upon the next crisis in 1688 when it was the tories on the back foot), supporters argued that Monmouth's right to accession as a true royal heir was obviously written in his person; made manifest by physiognomy and poise; revealed by ability to touch remedially for the King's Evil.[55] Opponents countered by epitomizing Monmouth as the quintessential 'gawdy' or 'gay Fop' and dismissed him as 'such a Fop-King' surrounded by other flattering 'beaus' or 'fine Fop things' who told him what he wanted to hear.[56] In other words, York's supporters mocked Monmouth in ways that would later be visited on his own son as the next 'pretender' to the throne.

Even with the fop as the common denominator, the connections made in the preceding pages between a specific political problem, the Crown's succession, and a wider social uncertainty, a pervasive *malaise* over the legibility of elite lineage, might seem tenuous. However, commentators often did close the seemingly wide socio-political gap between the respective situations of monarch and plain gentleman. Furthermore, the efflorescence of the foppish beau in comic drama after 1690 can be linked to the reversal of partisan fortunes and a (generally) whiggish ascendancy.

The position and rights of possible heirs to the throne were frequently likened to those enjoyed by the heir to an ordinary country estate in common law.[57] If

[54] A ready summary of the charges and counter-charges may be found in R. Clifton, *The Last Popular Rebellion. The Western Rising of 1685* (London, 1984), 77–88.

[55] E. Settle, 'Absalom Senior' (1682), in H. H. Schless (ed.), *Poems on Affairs of State. Volume III: 1682–1685* (New Haven, 1968), 158 (lines 1176ff.); a mock version of the same was 'Letter of the Duke of Monmouth to the King' (1680), in E. F. Mengel, jr. (ed.), *Poems on Affairs of State. Volume II: 1678–1681* (New Haven, 1965), 254–5. See also the critical and satirical appraisal in Anon., *Grimalkin, or The Rebel-Cat* (1681), 4–6.

[56] N. Thompson, *A Choice Collection of One Hundred and Eighty Loyal Songs, All Written since 1678* (1694), 196; Anon., *Old Jemmy: An Excellent New Ballad* (1681); Anon., *Monmouth Degraded Or James Scot, the Little King in Lyme* (1685); Anon., 'Monmouth Routed and Taken Prisoner with his Pimp the Lord Gray. A Song to the Tune of *King Jame[s]'s Jigg*', in Day, *Pepys Ballads*, vol. V, 32. Also Anon., 'A Ballad Called Perkin's Figary' (1679), in Mengel, *Poems on Affairs of State. Volume II*, 122–6; 'The Western Rebel' (1685), in Crump, *Poems on Affairs of State. Volume IV*, 34 (lines 41ff.); Anon., *An Elegy on James Scot, Late Duke of Monmouth* (1685); Anon., *Monmouth's Downfal; Or, the Royal Victory* (1685); Anon., *The Young Bastard's Wish. A Song* (1685).

[57] See the examples cited by Nenner, *Right To Be King*, 31, 136, 140, 148, 153–4, 165; Clark, *English Society*, 83; C. Condren, *The Language of Politics in Seventeenth-Century England* (London, 1994), 68; S. H. Mendelson and P. Crawford, *Women in Early Modern England 1550–1720* (Oxford, 1998), 352–63; Weil, *Political Passions*, 37–8.

one also considered that lineage (and therefore the claim of James II and his male heirs) was the paramount factor in structuring government, resort might then be had to a reciprocal appeal which represented the Stuart monarch as both the 'best Gentleman of the Kingdom', and, at the same time, the 'Fountain of Honour and Gentility'. Here the suggestion was that if the king's lineage (as the nation's 'first gentleman') went unrecognized so would they all. As one opponent of James II's exclusion had it: 'Yours but derived from him; consider therefore seriously what will be your Lot, if your Prince and the Royal dignity should fall to the ground, how can you and your Gentility possibly stand and subsist?'[58] It was here taken as an article of faith that the Crown was the font of gentility, presumably by means of its control over the granting of arms as the prime signifier of elite status. This relationship had always been contentious.[59] Amidst prevailing uncertainty and the eventual solution of the late seventeenth-century succession crisis by means *other* than strict adherence to lineage, it is probably no accident that aphorisms severing the link between the monarch and gentility were current. Hence Daniel Defoe claimed that the 'late King Charles II. of merry Memory . . . usually had that Expression, that he *could make a Knight*, but he *could not make a* GENTLEMAN'.[60]

Political affiliations during our period often prove to be as slippery as social distinctions, but it is worth suggesting that the fop slowly acquired significant meaning (particularly for those of whig sympathies targeted by the citizen cuckold scenario) as satire directed against a tory elite which sometimes flirted with the idea of a second Stuart restoration and did tend to define the gentleman more on the basis of heredity than any other single factor. Obvious examples of this kind of polemical deployment can be found in Thomas Durfey's *Modern Prophets* (1709). Presented in the wake of one of several jacobite invasion scares that dotted the early eighteenth century, this comedy features the character of squire Whimsey who works to establish himself as both a beau and a jacobite supporter.[61] A little more subtle, *The Compromise* presented the frenchified fop, Coupee, as the favoured future son-in-law of the play's provincial and tory squire.[62]

Thanks to the efforts of nineteenth-century historians like Macaulay, we are perhaps accustomed to think of the rough, unpolished country squire as more in keeping with anti-tory humour, to assume that this caricature and the fop character are miles apart in terms of their socio-political targets.[63] Yet these

58 P. Ayres, *Vox Clamantis* (1684), 31. Ayres seems to elide the position of the then monarch, Charles II, with the imminent position of his brother and heir James, duke of York, as king.

59 M. James, 'English Politics and the Concept of Honour 1485–1642', *PP (Supplement)* 3 (1978).

60 D. Defoe, *The Complete English Tradesman* (1727), vol. II, part i, 247.

61 Durfey, *Modern Prophets*, esp. ii, 19, 24; iv, 55; v, 68.

62 J. Sturmy, *Compromise* (1723), esp. v, 74–5.

63 K. C. Sagle, *The English Country Squire as Depicted in English Prose Fiction from 1740 to 1800* (1938, reprint 1971); Colley, *Defiance*, 146–53.

last examples suggest that this was not necessarily the case. So too a remark from the playwright character in George Farquhar's *Love and a Bottle* that the comedy he is writing will feature a gentleman who 'Shams the Beau and 'Squire with a Whore or Chambermaid'.[64] Following a similar logic, country squires who reside for part of the year in London become fops and are labelled 'Town Changelings'.[65] Here they had oaths in common too: 'And *Tory* with Dammees, holds *Whigg* in Derision, | Each Fop would be counted a grave Politician.'[66] The association of tory and jacobite, country squire and town beau, also lends new meaning to the earl of Orrery's comment to Thomas Southerne quoted in an earlier chapter.[67] In light of his Stuart sympathies, Orrery's image of himself as something of a beau might well be facetious in its intent.

Richard Steele's most famous comedy may serve as a particularly rich example of how the two characters, tory squire and gentleman fop, had indeed become two sides of the same political coin by the early eighteenth century. *The Conscious Lovers* features the 'coxcomb' Cimberton as the preferred son-in-law of Mrs Sealand and the action makes clear that Cimberton is a country squire in waiting.[68] Cimberton exhibits classic traits of the stage fop, such as adjusting his attire in front of a mirror at an inappropriate moment.[69] Moreover, a friend of Steele's certainly located Cimberton within this tradition when he imagined Steele thinking

> SURE this is more than CLASSIC Ground I tread,
> All *Pindus* seems to bloom around my Head;
> Wake then, my Muse, what Lyre can lay unstrung,
> In Shades where *Phoebus*, or where *Steel* hath Sung?
> A CIMBERTON each gaudy TULIP shows,
> And each gay Bed is throng'd with Lacquey Beaux.[70]

64 Farquhar, *Love and a Bottle*, iv, 42.

65 P. Motteux, *Love's a Jest* (1696), ii, 22. See also situations like squire Sapless being tutored by the fop Gooseandelo in Dilke's *Lover's Luck*, iv, 34ff; Mockmode as the young squire arrived in London from university in Farquhar, *Love and a Bottle*, ii, 15ff. Similar assumptions are evident in periodical literature like *British Journal*, no. lvii (19 October 1723), [1], and from the survey of anti-tory propaganda by T. N. Corns, W. A. Speck, and J. A. Downie, 'Archetypal Mystification: Polemic and Reality in English Political Literature, 1640–1750', *Eighteenth-Century Life* 7, 3 (1982), 17–24.

66 Anon., *The Cabal: A Voice of the Politicks* (?1690), see Early English Books Tract Supplements, Reel A3 (Ann Arbor, 1998). Christopher Hill notes that proponents of the Stuart cause during the mid-seventeenth-century civil wars were known as 'dammees'. As with the citizen cuckold, this may be a case of an older satiric tradition mutating to fit newer but seemingly related circumstances. See C. Hill, *The World Turned Upside Down. Radical Ideas during the English Revolution* (London, 1972), 162.

67 See p. 129. Colley, *Defiance*, 37; W. A. Speck, *Literature and Society in Eighteenth-Century England. Ideology, Politics and Culture, 1680–1820* (London, 1998), 86.

68 R. Steele, *Conscious Lovers* (1723), ii, 25; iii, 52.

69 *Ibid.*, iii, 49.

70 'Verses Wrote in the Summer-House where Sir Richard Steel[e] Wrote His Conscious Lovers', in J. Whaley, *A Collection of Poems* (1732), 101 (lines 1–6).

Conversely, Steele himself endows Cimberton with a behaviour we might initially associate with the country squire but one which contemporaries interpreted as the author's further attempt to capture and exploit the basic socio-political significance of the fop tradition. With an almost fetishistic gaze directed at Lucinda, the daughter of the Sealands he is courting, Cimberton deems her body a potential vessel for the continuation of his lineage and not sexually attractive of itself: 'He will examine the Limbs of his Mistress with the Caution of a Jockey, and pays no more Compliment to her personal Charms, than if she were a meer breeding Animal.'[71] In other words, the country gentleman treats Lucinda like a thoroughbred brood-mare being vetted for his stables.

A periodical's review of the play provides us with an all-too-rare instance of extended, contemporary response and two considerable supports for our argument concerning the fop's significance. In part, this critique noted:

> Mr. *Cimberton* is a perfect Creature of the Author's; form'd like himself, *ex nihilo*; and . . . has no Being but in the Poet's Imagination. He is a Fool, not of his own, or of Heaven's Making, (as the Epilogue to Sr. *Fopling* has it) but purely the Writer's: A meer Herald's Beast, and therefore a fit Squier or Supporter, to our Mirror of *Chivalry*. Hence . . . his survey of the Lady with the Eye and Phrase of a Jockey . . . is a perfect *Coup da Maitre*.[72]

First, the reviewer reads Steele's Cimberton character as a mockery of the belief that the gentleman's superiority is an innate and manifest inheritance. The gentleman-fop's 'Being', his placement in a genteel lineage and the semblance of superior descent, is no more than a discursive claim elaborated by a particular heraldic lexicon. Second, we should then recognize that the periodical press was as politically partisan as London's theatre. The paper in which this review appeared, *The Freeholder's Journal*, was notably tory in its sympathies.[73] As a result, Steele's critic finally damns him with faint praise. Professing admiration for Steele's skill as a playwright, his ability to script a novel variation on a stock comedic figure, the reviewer quickly turns this commentary into a jibe at the dramatist and a rejection of the socio-political implications of the fop caricature. The reviewer's barbed counter-reply to Steele works like this. The suggestion made by Steele's Mr Cimberton is that an objective, self-evident superiority is elusive, gentility a cultured substitute as revealed by the fop's staging. Steele's critic responds that this suggestion is itself the rhetorical sleight-of-hand, the very concession necessary for someone like Steele, as prominent author, entrepreneur and pro-whig politico of less than impeccable

[71] Steele, *Conscious Lovers*, ii, 24.

[72] *Freeholder's Journal*, no. xlix (28 November 1722), 290 (mispaginated as '284').

[73] H. Erskine-Hill, 'Literature and the Jacobite Cause: Was There a Rhetoric of Jacobitism?', in E. Cruickshanks (ed.), *Ideology and Conspiracy: Aspects of Jacobitism, 1689–1759* (Edinburgh, 1982), 55.

social origin, to claim a social superiority which self-evidently belongs only to those born with it; to 'gentlemen' who are genteel *ipso facto.*

However much the figure might appear a superficial fashion-plate, the fop accrued ever-deeper layers of socio-political meaning by interrogating closely the 'quality' beneath these clothes in response to the protracted succession crisis and the erosion of socio-political consensus within elite society. Thus a character from Peter Motteux's *Love's A Jest* of 1697, on being asked to define and review the beau's heritage, observed that there were several 'sorts' and 'now Beau is every thing: there's your Town, Court, Camp, Sea, Church, and Country Beau'. This met with the reply: 'Methinks 'tis time the Name were abdicated.'[74] Initially, this would seem too capacious a description to support the point we are arguing for here. But double meanings abound: 'sorts' could just as easily refer to social strata; the list of beaux conspicuously eschews reference to the City and the placement of 'Church' with 'Country' promotes ideas of establishment Anglicanism and toryism rather than dissent and its associations with City whiggery; abdication was the fiction forced on James II to allow for the crowning of William and Mary.[75] A pamphlet published only a few months earlier had also identified the different sorts of beau on the grounds that 'there's as much difference between a *Beaux* [*sic*] of *'86*, and a *Beaux* of *'96*'.[76] At the printer's urging that he fill some spare pages, the author conveniently appended some discussion of the sorts of jacobite. While the directness of this comment is virtually unique, it is little surprise to find that even political association has become fashionable and that the same logic (of status and gender) still applies. Women are blamed for turning gentlemen into jacobites as they blur (effeminate) their political loyalties (virtue) by making the men adopt the foppish sartorial and gestural markers of the Stuart follower. Further, the gentility of William's adherents is denied (they are 'Fellows', 'Puppies') by the superior belles and beaux:

A Fourth sort of *Jacobites*, are the *Beaus* . . . Why are they *Jacobites*? why! because 'tis the fashion; the Ladies at t'other end of the Town are generally *Jacobites*; so they are under an Obligation of being so too . . . A modest sober Man minds his interiour parts, more then his exteriour; yet goes neatly, mixt with a little Gentility, though not Extravagancy: No powder'd Coat, Buttons like Tennis-balls; a patch on his Nose, broad Silver Loops, like an Actor in the *Play-House* . . . Women . . . will often start up this

74 Motteux, *Jest*, i, 10.

75 Clark, *English Society*, 128. See also the mock letter, 'From a Beau, dissuading his Brother Beau to go to Flanders', in [T. Brown], *The Works of Mr. Thomas Brown, Serious and Comical, in Prose and Verse* (1720, eighth edition, Dublin, 1778–9), vol. IV, 195, where one beau attempts to console another whose clothes have been soiled by 'reminding him of the inconstancy of human affairs' and 'stories of kings depos'd . . . famous monarchies subverted'.

76 Anon., ['By a young Gentleman'], *The Character of the Beaux* (1696), preface, sig. [A4^{r}]. *Italics reversed.* The pre- and post-revolutionary dates may be far from coincidental. (A muted version of the same argument may be found in Anon., *The Character of a Jacobite* (1690), cf. 1; 21–2.)

question; as, well Sir *Novelty*, Who are you for, King *James*, or King *William*? He having so much Sense to know the Lady's for *James*, placing him first, crys, O Ged, Madam! I'm a *Jacobite*. Ay, indeed Sir, says she, I'm o' your Mind; the *Williamites* are such slovenly Fellows.[77]

A final consideration bearing on the socio-political significance which the comic fop garnered in the late Stuart period is that the incidence of the country squire figure in early eighteenth-century comedy was, relatively speaking, quite low. In light of the strident cross-currents of partisanship that were a feature of London's theatres and clearly manifested in the rehearsal of the cit figure, we come to expect a countering salvo of roughly equal proportion. For three reasons the figure of the country gentleman as a robust but unmannered provincial type does not appear to have been up to this task. First, the persona of the country squire was not unequivocally negative. Witness, for example, the popular figure of Roger de Coverley in the *Spectator* papers of Richard Steele and Joseph Addison. Second, there was also the problem that the squire had earlier been appropriated as part of the whig-opposition ideology – even though the figure was typically used to stress the sturdy independence rather than born superiority of a landowning elite. Third, rather like the character of the rakish libertine, satirical representation of the squire tended to criticize gentlemen as gentlemen and suggest how they should behave. By comparison, the fop questioned 'what' the gentleman was, tested the nature of gentility, and was about as prevalent as the citizen cuckold figure which itself engaged with these same issues.

As gentility was a political weapon, so the struggle to define gentility was fundamentally a political one. Yet, in large measure, that struggle was predicated on the integrity of status as lineage first being placed in doubt. Without some prior questioning of the nature of blood lineage and, in particular, its legibility, the 'gentleman-tradesman' could not be entertained. Cue the fop character and all that this represented, the inability to give definitive proof that social distinctions were nothing more or less than native. We should now realize why claims of lineage became something of a liability and understand the significance of the charge that playwrights scripted fop roles at the behest of influential (whig?) City cuckolds.[78]

77 *Ibid.*, 42–5. 'Sir Novelty' alluded to Cibber's recently debuted signature role of Sir Novelty Fashion, later Lord Foppington. Another equation of foppery with jacobitism is E. Ward, *The School of Politicks* (1691), 23.

78 Anon., *Injur'd Love* (1711), iv, 53.

Part IV

Managing the theatre's social discourse

10 Society and the Collier controversy

And can't they lash the Vice without pointing upon the *Quality*?

J. Collier, *Short View* (1698)

Some of the arguments made about the fop's significance may seem more plausible compared to others. That the figure was politically significant and questioned the integrity of inherited claims to power may now be fairly plain. Interrogating the priority of birth in the structuration of society's elite was not new to the late Stuart period. It is a phenomenon that has been observed at other moments in the social history of early modern England.[1] Perhaps less convincing is the argument made for the extent and depth of the fop's questioning. Namely, that the character could be a densely reflexive representation of the theatre's enactment of gentility and, therefore, gentility's performative nature. To further substantiate these arguments we would need to explore contemporary audience response. Yet traces of such response are scarce, at least as far as the standard sources of diaries, letter-books and even periodicals are concerned. Where are the reviews of Lord Foppington and the theatre's socio-structural potential when we need them? Was it possible for comedy to be so inquisitive of one of early modern society's main assumptions and, most importantly, can we demonstrate contemporary awareness of the drama's critical facility?

Locating late Stuart commentary on the theatre's social power is not difficult. However this material often comes at a price, clouded either by opaque self-righteousness or by satirical hostility. Although formal dramatic critique was still in its infancy, the early eighteenth century was awash with criticism of the theatre. Careful scrutiny of this material reveals not only awareness of gentility's performative nature, but also some understanding of how the drama both made this awareness possible and was itself implicated in the impersonation of gentility. The texts in question are the remnant of a complex dialogue, a messy and at times bewildering tangle of viewpoints. They range from pious ramblings

[1] K. E. Wrightson, 'Estates, Degrees and Sorts: Changing Perceptions of Society in Tudor and Stuart England', in P. J. Corfield (ed.), *Language, History and Class* (Oxford, 1991), 37–41; F. Heal and C. Holmes, *The Gentry in England and Wales, 1500–1700* (Stanford, 1994), 29–30; R. W. S. More, 'The Rewards of Virtue: Gentility in Early Modern England', unpublished PhD dissertation, Brown University (1998), 34, 67.

about the drama's profanity, which refuse to name the scurrilous words at issue even as their censorship is advocated, to brief and bawdy verses, which take prurient delight in exposing the immoral lives of the theatre's personnel yet make no obvious attempt to improve the theatre. Opinions stretched from those that advocated a stricter regulation of London's playhouses to others that argued the theatre had no redeeming features. The discourse of drama's immorality and possible reform variously addressed the theatre's power to (re)structure society at the most fundamental level, with especial attention given to the cultural legibility and legitimacy of a naturally ordained elite.

The recurring themes of this discourse fall into two basic analytical categories: symptoms of the theatre's corruption, particularly its unseemly language and lack of decorum in performance, and causes of the drama's corrupting nature, notably the debauched behaviour of its performers. Ironically, anti-theatrical discourse carries important traces of response to the comedy's most theatrical of characters, the fop. By dissecting the main themes of complaint we can gain further insight into the social implications of the comedy because it was these possibilities, as encapsulated by the gentlemen-beaux, that anti-theatrical discourse was attempting to discipline.

In 1698 Jeremy Collier published his *Short View of the Immorality and Profaneness of the English Stage*, calling for the wholesale reform, if not abolition, of London's commercial theatres. Collier's text prompted many responses. The sustained discourse of theatre reform which followed reveals that drama was indeed perceived by contemporaries as having the power to subject society's structuration to the kind of critique represented by the likes of Lord Foppington. For those who either advocated its sweeping reform or considered that no major intervention was necessary, a main bone of contention was always the matter of how the drama was implicated in the process of social ordering. The debate became preoccupied with the control of a powerful discursive instrument for the (re)making of society and, in particular, the delineation of its dominant group as the 'gentry'.

On the face of it, the *Short View* and its sequels denied any socio-political interest. The same might be said for much of the rather sketchy historiography dealing with what has become known as the Collier controversy. The view persists that the early eighteenth-century debate over the stage was one of 'morality'; that explanation of opposition to the theatre can be found in ethical-religious scruple of a vaguely defined (because seldom questioned) sort. This is the perspective shared by Collier's early twentieth-century bibliographer, the *Short View*'s most recent editor, and the author of the only published monograph on the controversy to date.[2] Those who called for theatre reform in the late Stuart

[2] R. Anthony, *The Jeremy Collier Stage Controversy 1698–1726* (New York, 1937); B. Hellinger (ed.), *A Short View of the Immorality and Prophaneness of the English Stage* (New York, 1987); J. W. Krutch, *Comedy and Conscience after the Restoration* (New York, 1924).

period become 'moralists' and Collier himself emerges as a man of principle, having the courage to voice the sentiments of those for whom the stage was anathema. It comes as no surprise to find the 'middle' or 'merchant class' waiting in the wings, stereotypically sober and opposing the slightest hint of 'aristocratic' licence thanks to Collier's lead, perhaps ready to concede a newly moral drama as long as it reflected the inner worth and ascetic values of the 'bourgeois'.[3] We may be forgiven for thinking that the *Short View* revived the billowing storm of puritan opposition faced by London's playhouses prior to the Civil War. But the echoes are deceptive.[4] Even though the two discourses did share some common ground, there are discrepancies which hint that theatre reform of the eighteenth century was something other than Prynne revisited, or middling morality on the rise.

A major reason for the sudden visibility and impact of the *Short View*'s arguments (for anti-theatrical discourse had always been simmering in the background) was their author's non-jurancy. Collier was a cleric who refused to swear allegiance to the post-1688 regime, to renounce the legitimacy of a seemingly more direct Stuart succession. By this refusal Collier identified himself as a high Anglican, and he was therefore quite removed from the dissenting heirs of mid-seventeenth-century puritanism and their known links to the City. The *Short View* seeks no common cause with the persistent undertow of City opposition to theatre and makes only passing reference to the derogatory citizen scenario.[5] Reading the historiography, we might expect that this stock feature of comic theatre would have met with sustained criticism, particularly in light of its social locus and dubious reliance on sexual innuendo. Collierite tracts reveal no such preoccupation and it is simply not possible to argue that 'in the literature of the Collier controversy there is much stress on the ill effect of plays upon the middle class'.[6] The social sights of the discourse were set squarely and consistently on those of higher status.

Much of the *Short View*'s argument becomes preoccupied with issues relating to elite society. For instance, having complained that dramatic representations of the clergy amounted to slander of their office, Collier digresses to argue for the superior status of England's men of the cloth. The '*Priest-hood* is the profession of a Gentleman' and, vice versa, all clergy are gentlemen by virtue of being God's representatives on earth.[7] Collier's text is also heavily

[3] Krutch, *Comedy*, 132; J. A. Barish, *The Antitheatrical Prejudice* (Berkeley, 1981), 235; E. Burns, *Restoration Comedy. Crises of Desire and Identity* (London, 1987), 230. However, a dissenting opinion is offered by C. Winton, 'The London Stage Embattled: 1695–1710', *Tennessee Studies in Literature* 19 (1974), 9–19.

[4] Cf. M. Cordner, 'Playwright versus Priest: Profanity and the Wit of Restoration Comedy', in D. Payne Fisk (ed.), *The Cambridge Companion to English Restoration Theatre* (Cambridge, 2000), 209–10.

[5] J. Collier, *A Short View of the Immorality, and Profaneness of the English Stage* (1698), 24.

[6] Krutch, *Comedy*, 157.

[7] Collier, *Short View*, 136.

inflected by heraldic rhetoric and this was a feature remarked and sarcastically played upon by those who opposed his arguments, considering them to be about much more than simple Christian morality. Thus one of many similar remarks in Elkanah Settle's *Defence of Dramatick Poetry*, which mocked Collier's 'moral' evaluation of particular dramatists, read as follows: 'Tis true, he singles out one frail Brother of the Quill, *Aristophanes*, and finds a very foul Blot in his Scutcheon.'[8] Likewise, a tract in the form of a dialogue that professed support for the theatre's improvement concluded with a comment signalling not only the superiority of Collier's arguments, but also their interpellation by questions of social domination. The dialogue's main participant was praised with the deference due a gentleman: 'Indeed Sir, – I won't take the Wall of you by no means, – you are Sir *Jeremy's* Back, – pray Sir, Your – most Humble Servant.'[9] Comments like this suggest a need to collapse the moral/socio-political distinction on which modern assessment of the late Stuart discourse of theatre reform is so often based.[10] The social point to this discourse was not merely that the gentry were meant to exhibit *mores* matching their certain social superiority and that the stage, by representing them as behaving dissolutely, instead subverted the social order which their superiority capped.[11] Rather, it was a case of the drama's perceived ability to question the very nature of that superiority being wrong, the theatre's participation in the interrogation of social structuration was itself branded immoral. The discourse of theatre reform was especially concerned with the comedy's inquisition of a manifestly inherent superiority – the gentleman's inherited right and ability to head a natural, divinely ordained social order – as so often represented by the fop.

Listening closely to the voices of those who responded to the *Short View* reveals a further indication that more can be made of the storm over the theatre's reform. For this dialogue conjures what is, at first sight, a nearly incomprehensible but not uncommon image of Collier the non-juring priest and scourge to London's patent theatres. Namely, Collier appears as a modishly dressed beau. For instance, the critic and playwright John Dennis imagined the *Short View*'s

[8] E. Settle, *A Defence of Dramatick Poetry* (1698), 52. Congreve also noted this tendency in his *Amendments of Mr. Collier's False and Imperfect Citations* (1698), 80.

[9] [G. Powell], *Animadversions on Mr. Congreve's Late Answer to Mr. Collier in a Dialogue between Mr. Smith and Mr. Johnson* (1698), 88.

[10] A point also made by R. D. Tumbleson, *Catholicism in the English Protestant Imagination. Nationalism, Religion, and Literature, 1660–1745* (Cambridge, 1998), 129–31.

[11] J. Hopes, 'The Debate on the English Theatre, 1690–1740', unpublished PhD dissertation, University of Newcastle-upon-Tyne (1980), 355ff.; Hopes, 'Politics and Morality in the Writings of Jeremy Collier', *Literature and History* 8 (1978), 164–6. A similar view is broached by R. Russell, 'Dramatists and the Printed Page: The Social Role of Comedy from Richard Steele to Leigh Hunt', unpublished DPhil dissertation, Oxford University (1995), 10–13; Tumbleson, *Catholicism*, 135–7; S. M. Strohmer, '"Every Man an Actor": Performance Theories in the Restoration', unpublished PhD dissertation, University of Michigan (1999), 130ff.

author wearing a 'Sword five Foot long, and a Perruke of three'.[12] Settle elaborated with a mocking reference to Collier's 'false Heraldry' and a 'Modern Beau Wigg, Crevate and Sword'.[13] The satirist Tom Brown pulled out all the stops in his defence of the stage, pointedly formatted like a comic script and entitled *The Stage-Beaux Toss'd in a Blanket*. Here Jeremy Collier was represented by the character Sir Jerry Witwoud whom the dramatis personae introduced as a 'Pert, Talkative, Half-witted, Coxcomb . . . a Noisie Pretender to Vertue . . . he has cast his Gown for the Vanities of a Beau Wigg and Sword'. Sir Jerry's companion is the foppish Lord Vaunt-Title, 'vain of his Quality, a Smatterer in Poetry'.[14] How to explain these images? Collier's opponents were surely not suggesting that the cleric literally dressed as flamboyantly, or manipulated an ornate snuff-box as nimbly, as Cibber's extroverted Lord Foppington. Since his *outré* political views compelled him to lead a quite circumspect life by all accounts, it is likely that those who presented this picture of Collier had never met the man.[15] But if Collier's detractors knew not the man, they were familiar with his arguments. In labelling Collier a 'beau' his respondents were recognizing his polemic, and underlying socio-political perspective, as being of a particular type. Evidently others who subscribed to similar ideas with respect to London's playhouses could not avoid the like aspersion. In general terms, at least, George Ridpath was compared to a 'sharping Beau' by a supporter of the stage.[16] The suggestion was that the socio-political idealism of the discourse of theatre reform (together with its perception of the social power of the theatre) was akin to that represented (and ultimately critiqued) by the comic stage's representation of the fop character. What follows will therefore survey the main themes of this discourse as a means to understand the character's significance for the enactment of claims to gentility.

The *Short View*'s opening chapter comprehends the subject of the 'immodest' language of the stage. Collier criticizes the drama, comedy in particular, for its use of what he terms 'smut' or 'dirty expressions'.[17] He further elaborates this complaint in a second chapter devoted to identifying the 'prophaneness' of the stage, or what we would term dramatic acts of taking the Lord's name in vain, that is, the misapplication of sacred phrases from the scriptural word of God. Worry about possibly rude words broadens to reveal consternation over semiotic instability. After all, innuendo relied on double meanings: 'And when the Sentence has two Handles, the worst is generally turn'd to the Audience. The

[12] J. Dennis, *The Person of Quality's Answer to Mr. Collier's Letter* (1704), 31.
[13] E. Settle, *A Farther Defence of Dramatick Poetry* (1698), 2. See also Anon., *A Vindication of the Stage* (1698), 19.
[14] T. Brown, *The Stage-Beaux Toss'd in a Blanket* (1704), dramatis personae.
[15] Hellinger, *Short View*, x–xvi; R. D. Hume, 'Jeremy Collier and the Future of the London Theater in 1698', *Studies in Philology* 96, 4 (1999), 490.
[16] Anon., *The Stage Acquitted* (1699), 1–2.
[17] Collier, *Short View*, *passim*.

Matter is so Contrived that the Smut and Scum of the Thought rises uppermost.'[18] Likewise, profanity was the misappropriation of divinely ordained and singularly pure language to plural and base ends such that spectators should avoid the theatre 'for fear of learning new Language'.[19] 'Ill-meaning' words were those which lacked stability, or straightforward 'Sence' as the *Short View* repeatedly termed it.[20] They comprised, we might recall, Daniel Defoe's 'Sodomy of the Tongue'.

Collier's text moves rapidly from identifying specific instances of 'smut' to indiscriminately condemning entire plays. So much so that all drama, ancient and modern alike, is fair game. Hence the work of Plautus, the Roman playwright, is dismissed by the following terms: 'And where the Entertainment is Smut, there is rarely any other Dish well dress'd: The Contrivance is commonly wretched, the Sence lean and full of Quibbles.'[21] Quibbles were plays on words, the 'meaningless' manipulation of signs, and a sin often attributed to eponymous fop characters in plays like Thomas Durfey's *Richmond Heiress* (1693) and Thomas Baker's *Hampstead Heath* (1706). We find that it is not only the spoken dialogue, but also the non-verbal communications of gesture and costume which reformers considered opprobrious. Hence *The Conduct of the Stage Consider'd* railed at the theatre's 'Wantoness' of 'Attire, Speech, and Action'.[22] Similarly, Ridpath complained of 'undecent and wanton Gestures, Postures and Actions'.[23] Not only is the drama's dialogue considered 'obscene', it is also branded as 'effeminate' in the same breath.[24] Of course, 'effeminate' was a term crucial to the fop's meaning.

Defenders of the drama responded to the charge of smut and profanity in two ways. First, they argued that the suspect words needed to be interpreted in context. Exclaiming 'by heaven' onstage in the course of a romantic courtship scene was, they argued, distinct from the phrase's meaning when uttered from the pulpit. Second, they charged that the reformers were misinterpreting the phrases in question, deliberately reading meanings that were never intended.[25] Collier was virtually hoist with his own petard, accused of manipulating what he maintained were innocent words or signs in order to achieve perverse, multiple meanings. Hence Durfey complained that Collier's identifications of 'smut' were themselves arbitrary and 'to call 'em *Colliers* would be as significant as any thing'.[26] It is in this regard that we also encounter yet another key term of the fop's representation. In making his arguments, Collier was frequently accused of 'affectation'.[27]

[18] *Ibid.*, 12. [19] *Ibid.*, 23. [20] *Ibid.*, 26–7, 34. [21] *Ibid.*, 18–19.
[22] Anon, *The Conduct of the Stage Consider'd* (1721), 28.
[23] [G. Ridpath], *The Stage Condemn'd* (1698), 85. [24] *Ibid.*, 38.
[25] A position summarized by Tumbleson, *Catholicism*, 137–9.
[26] T. Durfey, *Campaigners* (1698), preface, 11.
[27] See, for example, Dennis, *Person of Quality's Answer*, 30; J. Oldmixon, *Reflections on the Stage, and Mr. Collyer's Defence of the Short View* (1699), preface, unpaginated.

A careful examination of these charges and counter-charges suggests that the point of contention was not simply a matter of whether certain words were rude or not. Rather, the issue was the nature of language *per se* and how the drama both revelled in and revealed its problematic nature. In his mock comedy Tom Brown summed up the position of the drama's opponents when he had his foppish parody of Collier declare: 'I'm for giving every thing its proper Name.'[28] What the theatre's staunch opponents wanted to believe in was a literal language whereby sign corresponded to referent with a one-to-one coherence. Language was supposed to describe, simply to reflect, a preordained material reality. Therefore, criticism from William Congreve, who denied that his work was profane, was itself countered by Collier in the following terms:

> But Mr. *Congreve* says *when they* (the Words of Scripture) *are otherwise applied, the Diversity of the Subject gives a Diversity of Signification.* This is strange Stuff! Has Application so transforming a Quality, and does bare use enter so far into the Nature of Things? If a Man applies his Money to an ill Purpose, does this transmute the Metal, and make it none of the Kings Coin?[29]

While Julie Peters is right to suggest that Collier and his cohorts were preoccupied with the nature and power of language,[30] it can be argued that their concern tended to concentrate on language's capacity for social differentiation. This agenda is manifest in the very terms that the theatre's opponents couched their own descriptions of the unwholesome nature of the drama. They wrote of its 'Rankness' which 'degrades' and 'breaks down the Distinctions between Man and Beast'; how the stage had 'always been out of *Order*, but never to the *Degree* 'tis at present'.[31] And it was this preoccupation, this attempt to deny the socially constitutive power of language in the form of dramatic discourse, that Collier's respondents tried to capture when they imagined him as a beau.

To recap, the beau makes claim to a natural and transparently signified social authority rather than acknowledge that his domination is authored, implicitly no more and no less than the subject of rhetoric. The comedy featured characters who foolishly believed in a literal correspondence: the fops, beaux and pretty gentlemen who manipulated signs (that is, were guilty of 'affectation') to the extent that they stopped meaning at all (that is, until they were emptied of significance or became 'profane' and 'effeminate'). Although fops may profess

[28] Brown, *Stage-Beaux*, 53–4.

[29] J. Collier, *A Defence of the Short View of the Profaneness and Immorality of the English Stage* (1699), 12.

[30] J. S. Peters, '"Things Govern'd By Words": Late 17th-Century Comedy and the Reformers', *English Studies* 68, 2 (1987), 142–53. See also S. Staves, *Players' Scepters. Fictions of Authority in the Restoration* (Lincoln, NE, 1979), 201ff.; R. A. Zimbardo, 'At Zero Point: Discourse, Politics, and Satire in Restoration England', *ELH* 59 (1992), 785–98.

[31] Collier, *Short View*, 2, 6, 127. *Emphasis added.* See also, for example, Anon., *A Representation of the Impiety and Immorality of the English Stage* (1704), 3, 23.

belief in a reality-bound literal language, their very rehearsal gestures towards the opposite conclusion that reality is mediated by discourse.

The theatre's iconoclastic potential was the core issue. However, close attention was given its ability to demystify certain series of symbols as being synonymous with the superior pedigree of the 'gentleman' such that faith in the latter was jeopardized. When Collier argued that the comedy's characters lacked 'decorum' he meant they undermined faith in an inherited and inherent social identity ('Nature') which was proven unproblematically by the corresponding and appropriate signifiers ('propriety'). Furthermore, he specifically charged that genteel characters were assigned dialogue not in keeping with their superior status ('quality') and the associated notion of a finer 'wit' or 'genius':

> Decorum is quite lost . . . Nature must be minded . . . *That Wit has been truly defin'd a propriety of Words and Thoughts. – That Propriety of Thought is that Fancy which arises naturally from the Subject.* Why then without doubt, the Quality, of Characters should be taken care of, and great Persons appear like themselves.[32]

Lack of decorum was actually the thin edge of the wedge. The more troubling subtext of the drama was that it revealed lineage as the basis for social inequality to be the hostage of discourse, necessarily the product of culture. Hence, in siding with the *Short View*, Ridpath argued for 'Simplicity in the inward and outward Man' and condemned the self-fashioning associated with the playhouse that threatened the assumed integrity and transparency of superior lines of descent:

> All those wanton Looks and Gestures, and Postures that be in the Mode are practis'd according to Art, and you may remember you have seen People when dismiss'd from a Play, strive to get that Grace and Meen they saw in the Mimick on the Stage.[33]

Collier also claimed that most of the comedy's genteel characters were 'vicious', meaning that they were made to behave in ways unworthy of or incommensurate with their status. He wanted any such characters to be decorous, exemplary reflections of virtuous, real-life counterparts. He began by opposing the debauchery of the stage libertine as setting a bad example, but he soon expressed as much concern for the negative potential of foppery.[34] His response was not to suggest that the fop might encourage luxurious, idle living. Instead, he rejected the character out of hand as fictive nonsense which was both insulting to society's elite and an impertinence that should not be allowed of playwrights: 'To give them an unlimited Range, is in effect to make them Masters of all Moral Distinctions, and to lay Honour and Religion at their Mercy. To shew Greatness ridiculous, is the way to lose the use, and abate

32 Collier, *Short View*, 185.
33 [Ridpath], *Stage Condemn'd*, 84, 81–2.
34 Collier, *Short View*, 173–4.

the value of the Quality.'[35] 'Moral distinctions' here meant the reflection of a natural or justifiable social order on the basis of lineage. The ridiculous flaws of elite characters in comedy amounted to 'degeneracy',[36] not loose behaviour as we understand it but the loss of a self-evident superiority that was inherited through the *gens* and divinely created.

Those who defended the stage responded that the real problem lay with the notion of a successive, inherent superiority. In the final absence of definitive proof of lineage, one's pedigree was cultivated and those who denied it (instead stressing the gentry's manifest, transparent social distinction) were themselves 'beaux'. To the drama's advocates, the depiction of the gentleman as a fool was entirely legitimate if one did not consider that his superiority was assured solely on the basis of ancestry. Thus James Drake explicitly countered Collier's point of view by writing:

> If Men of Honour and Abilities cou'd entail their Wisdom and Virtues upon their Posterity, then a Title wou'd be a pretty sure sign of Personal Worth, and the Respect and Reverence that was paid to the Founders of honourable Families ought to follow the Estate, and the heir of one shou'd be heir of t'other. But since Entails of this kind are of all kinds the most liable to be cut off, 'tis not absolutely impossible but there may be such a thing in the world, as a Fop of Quality.[37]

Or as John Oldmixon was to reply more succinctly, a 'man may have a Title and not deserve it'.[38]

Those who opposed the playhouse subscribed fervently to the ideal of the intrinsic superiority of the gentleman-born and the theatre's ability to unmask gentility as a contestable process of cultural impersonation was a main motive for Collier and many of his supporters.[39] For all the appearance of morality conveyed by its central term, 'virtue', late Stuart anti-theatrical discourse was as much worried for the social worth, the '*virtu*'(e), of the gentleman and the

35 Collier, *Defence*, 26. A similar point was made in his *Short View*, 140–5.

36 Collier, *Short View*, 175.

37 J. Drake, *The Antient and Modern Stages Survey'd* (1699), 366. See also Settle, *Farther Defence*, 24–6.

38 Oldmixon, *Reflections*, 34.

39 Those familiar with Collier's entire corpus (especially his *Moral Essays* from 1694) might here object that Collier actually downplayed the importance of lineage (a case made by Hopes, 'Politics and Morality') and, therefore, that Collier's position concerning gentility was rather more tortuous. Not wanting to make an already dense argument even more complicated, a few brief observations seem appropriate here. First, gentility was inherently malleable. We should not expect Collier's view (or 'definition') to be entirely consistent. It was in fact contradictory (as Hopes concedes). In the case of the theatre controversy, the quotes given in this chapter show clearly that Collier chose to stress the issue of lineage. Second, whilst Collier might observe in another context that elite parentage did not make a person 'naturally' or even 'virtuously' superior (i.e. all of humanity is fallen; genteel offspring may prove sinful as adults), that superiority in itself was not to be questioned since it was the 'way things were' by the will of God. Third, in any event, such nuance was lost in the heat of debate. To his opponents, Collier's social politics were plainly conservative and could be responded to with studied irony that drew quite deliberately on the fop tradition.

degree to which the drama did or did not subscribe to the idea of an entirely natural social order complete with a legitimately dominant elite. Hence commentators spoke of the drama's relation to 'Virtue and Religion', not 'religion' or 'morality' on their own.[40] Collier clearly believed that such an order existed. Hence *The Occasional Paper* maintained that spectators of the drama 'learn to suspect some of their first and plainest Notions of things. They are now to be taught how they might *Be*, without a Creator; and how, now they are, they may live best without any Dependence on his Providence.'[41] Or as a broadside commentary on a prologue spoken at the opening of the Haymarket theatre in 1705 teased Collier: 'Tho' there are those who reckon your Poets a Set of the most idle and useless Fellows upon Earth, yet we do most religiously assure you that they are all of 'em Creators, Givers of Being, and God Almighties.'[42]

The theatre was deemed 'immoral' because it could raise doubts in the minds of spectators about the legibility of social distinctions. If an indemonstrable superiority, one's lineage, had instead to be delineated by a series of cultural substitutes might these not be used to advance counterfeit claims to the same distinction? As a corollary, assessment of the drama's apparent effect on the spectator was really dependent on one's position regarding the stage's assumed socio-ideological impact. Opponents burdened the theatre with the ruin of genteel lives and estates without any empirical rhyme or reason, condemning it as a debilitating luxury that rendered spectators unfit to meet the inherited responsibilities of a virtuous, 'gentle' rule. In short, it was not so much a question of the extent to which the gentleman was affected by the theatre as the degree to which the theatre effected gentility.

After nearly 300 pages the *Short View*'s objection to the theatre came down to this one complaint, the theatre's immorality (or conversely its morality) relying fundamentally upon evaluation of the extent to which the theatre represented elite social structuration, gentility, either as culturally performative ('Behaviour') or as naturally inherent ('Virtue'):[43]

> To exchange Virtue for Behaviour is a hard Bargain . . . What's Sight good for without Substance? . . . the *Stage* . . . strikes at the Root of Principle, draws off the Inclinations from Virtue, and spoils good Education . . . How *many* of the Unwary have these *Syrens* devour'd? And how often has the best Blood been tainted, with this Infection? What Disappointment of Parents, what Confusion in Families, and What Beggery in Estates have been hence occasion'd?[44]

40 'A Letter . . . to the Author', in P. Motteux, *Beauty in Distress* (1698), preface, ix.

41 *Occasional Paper: Number IX* (1698), 7.

42 Anon., *The Prologue Spoken at the First Opening of the Queen's New Theatre in the Hay-Market . . . The Opening Prologue Paraphras'd in a Familiar Stile, for the Better Conception of the True Meaning, and for the Particular Use of Mr. Jer. Collier* (1705); see Early English Books Tract Supplements, Reel A1 (Ann Arbor, 1998).

43 A point developed from the general observations of S. Shepherd and P. Womack, *English Drama. A Cultural History* (Oxford, 1996), 157. See also Burns, *Restoration Comedy*, 2–3.

44 Collier, *Short View*, 287.

Sometimes the arrangement changed, but almost without fail the early eighteenth-century discourse of theatre reform held to this one particular social chord. Hence a précis of the *Short View* opened by expressing concern for how the 'Disorders of the *Play-House*' affected the spectator but, in all too familiar language, soon had these disorders narrowed down to the drama's propensity to 'taint his Blood, and almost make him disclaim'd at the *Herald's Office*!'[45]

Responsibility for this unacceptable state of affairs was typically laid at the feet of the players. This animosity is readily evident, for instance, in Collier's wide-ranging review of the history of the proscription of dramatic representation, where the *Short View* quotes selectively from decrees of the Roman senate right the way through to recent French legislation.[46] Actors and actresses are repeatedly singled out and condemned because 'their Motion is effeminate, and their Gestures vitious and Significant' (notice, once again, how all these terms were synonymous with the fop).[47] Collier was here recalling his earlier charge that the actions of players comprised 'Lewdness without Shame or Example'.[48] How are we to account for such condemnation? In what ways were their performances either lewd or effeminate? Why was the playwright who produced the script that the players merely performed not usually subject to similar attack? Perhaps given persistent reports of their leading less than exemplary lives, 'their loose way of living' as even one admirer put it,[49] the charge of lewdness levelled at the players was inevitable?

Considerable attention has recently been lent to the representation of players in the later seventeenth and early eighteenth centuries. Late Stuart actresses have usually received more critical attention than their male counterparts. Literary scholars and theatre historians have tended to advance two explanations, often related, for why the late Stuart actress was typically branded a 'whore'; how James Thomson on his first visit to London could consider the Drury Lane star, Anne Oldfield, 'acts very well in comedy but best of all, *I suppose*, in bed'; or what William Byrd might have meant when he described those female players who acted at Bartholomew Fair as a 'frightfull collection of nymphs . . . that one woud swear as the Plain Dealer has it, that they're all citizens daughters lawfully begotten'.[50]

First, it has been argued that actresses were sexually commodified objects, deliberately sent onstage in risqué costumes and alluring roles so as to attract the voyeuristic attention of male patrons. Part of the reason for the female players' alleged promiscuity therefore rests with the idea that women who sold

[45] J. Collier, *Mr. Collier's Dissuasive from the Play-House* (1703), 3–5.

[46] Collier, *Short View*, for example 241, 249, 252. [47] *Ibid.*, 255. [48] *Ibid.*, 13.

[49] P. Bliss (ed.), *Reliquiae Hearnianae. The Remains of Thomas Hearne* (Oxford, 1857), vol. I, 58, entry for 23 November 1705.

[50] Thomson to William Cranstoun, 3 April 1725, in A. D. McKillop (ed.), *James Thomson (1700–1748). Letters and Documents* (Lawrence, KS, 1958), 7, *emphasis added*; Byrd to [Lady Betty Cromwell], 4 September [1703], in M. Tinling (ed.), *The Correspondence of the Three William Byrds of Westover, Virginia, 1684–1776* (Charlottesville, 1977), vol. I, 237.

their bodies to pleasure the (male) gaze were guilty, by association, of selling other more intimate favours. Recently, this argument has been modified. The exact applicability to early modern drama of the concept of the gaze (borrowed originally from the study of cinema) has been questioned.[51] As a result theatre historians have repositioned their initial argument, placing it in the context of research which argues for the rise of a novel economy of specularity in the eighteenth century. The newer argument runs something like this: being a spectacle had earlier been a means to power (e.g. the monarch accrued power by displaying his person), but now it was the spectator who wielded power. Kristina Straub has applied this thinking to the representation of both female and male performers in the Georgian period. She argues that the actor attracted as much (or even more) sexual opprobrium as the actress and was subject to 'homophobic' representation because he made a spectacle of his body, subordinating or 'feminizing' himself within a fundamentally gendered economy of spectatorship where the gaze of the male theatregoer was becoming dominant.[52] Second, because selling oneself on the stage could prove lucrative for some actresses (and actors), it has been suggested that typing the (female) player's commodification as the equivalent of prostitution was a means to 'contain' or 'stabilize' what is vaguely described as the 'class mobility' or 'class anxiety' associated with the acting profession.[53] Imagined sexual incontinence is said to stand for real social promiscuity.

However, the next chapter aims to modify this interpretation by demonstrating that the late Stuart actors' reputation for lewdness had more to do with how they represented social promiscuity *onstage*. The peculiar features of the players' public image registered a lingering ambivalence regarding the theatre's social potential.

[51] For this review of the earlier argument, see D. C. Payne, 'Reified Object or Emergent Professional? Retheorizing the Restoration Actress', in J. D. Canfield and D. C. Payne (eds.), *Cultural Readings of Restoration and Eighteenth-Century English Theater* (Athens, GA, 1995), 18, 30.

[52] K. Straub, *Sexual Suspects. Eighteenth-Century Players and Sexual Ideology* (Princeton, 1992), 32–44, 64–7. Cf. T. A. King, 'Gender and Modernity: Male Looks and the Performance of Public Pleasures', in L. J. Rosenthal and M. Choudhury (eds.), *Monstrous Dreams of Reason. Body, Self, and Other in the Enlightenment* (Lewisburg, 2002), 25–44.

[53] These have become standard terms of reference for much of the research on Restoration and early Georgian players. See, for instance, E. Howe, *The First English Actresses. Women and Drama 1660–1700* (Cambridge, 1992), 30; Straub, *Sexual Suspects*, 153–6; L. J. Rosenthal, '"Counterfeit Scrubbado": Women Actors in the Restoration', *Eighteenth Century: Theory and Interpretation* 34, 1 (1993), 11, 19; Payne, 'Reified Object', 34–5.

11 Caught in the act: promiscuous players and blushing spectators

> A pack of idle, pimping, spunging Slaves,
> A Miscellany of Rogues, Fools and Knaves;
> A Nest of Leachers, worse than *Sodom* bore,
> And justly merit to be punish't more:
> Diseas'd, in Debt, and every moment dun'd;
> By all good Christians loath'd, and their own
> Kindred shun'd.
>
> R. Gould, *A Satyr against the Play-House* (1689)

The early eighteenth-century actor was sexually stigmatized and morally vilified not so much for his or her material social progress from humble beginnings (for only a handful of individuals made a substantial and steady income from acting alone), but rather as a means to scapegoat the cultural potential of his or her performance. The association of playing with sexual debauchery long predated the late Stuart period and, therefore, any novel circumstances of spectatorship. Female and male players were routinely represented in compromising and unnatural positions because of the way that dramatic performance toyed with the nature of early modern society, and disrupted social identities and their attendant inequalities.[1] Specifically, the players' *alleged* promiscuity was recognition of the drama's capacity to question the essential superiority of the gentry by highlighting gentility's performative quality. Several features of the players' public image betray this concern: the prominence of the players' mobility; the socially dangerous and perversely powerful nature of the players' revealed sexuality; the location and disciplining of the players' reputed immorality.

We may begin by addressing the issue of 'class mobility'. The idea that broadcasting the supposedly licentious and dishonourable exploits of the players was a means to deny upward social mobility on their part is difficult to sustain. For the same texts that imagine players as sexually promiscuous also present their subjects, time and again, as passing for gentlemen and -women. It was a commonplace that the theatre's stars were ready and able to mix in genteel social

[1] A similar line of interpretation has recently been signalled by D. P. Fisk, 'The Restoration Actress', in S. J. Owen (ed.), *A Companion to Restoration Drama* (Oxford, 2001), 71.

circles thanks to their popularity among elite spectators, fashionable attire from their own or the theatre's wardrobe, an often-performed and therefore perfected social grace.[2] Thus, *Scourge for the Play-Houses* caustically described rehearsal at Lincoln's Inn Fields where the players had a

> good stock of Impudence . . . no doubt several Scars about them, to testifie they had really been in the Wars of *Venus*; being so Rotten with often Fluxing and Salivating . . . They being full of Breeding, *Good Morrow* was bid to one another . . . Some of 'em were well Accoutred through *Tally-man*'s Faith; and others again, were as bad Cloathed, as a *Taffy* . . . but yet all Sworded, tho' but the meer Scum and Chippings of the Rascality of the People.[3]

Likewise, an issue of *The Female Tatler* devoted to London's thespians hinted at the sexual transgressions of the theatre at the same time as it claimed that '*players* nowadays rise to a mighty Pitch, the *suppos'd Lord* associates with the *real One*'.[4] Represented as encouraging the gentleman to betray his wife, the essay typically reserved more venom for the actress by complaining

> when a modest young Lady shall bring *thirty Thousand Pounds*, and be slighted in a Twelve-Months time, for a flirting conceited Thing, that has neither Mien, Air, Birth, or Education; but allures Mankind with a Spring, a Jett, and a Toss, a sort of *Stage Gentility*, which supposes a wonderful Assurance, and pleases because she's new.[5]

As this last quote suggests, the issue was not so much a matter of class as one of status and the extent to which the low-born player could mirror the superior personage of the born gentleman or -woman and thereby throw the notion of a successive, inherent social dominance into doubt. Charles Gildon began his study of acting by asserting that the actor

> must perfectly express the Quality and Manners of the Man, whose Person he assumes . . . each have their Propriety, and Distinction in Action as well as Words and Language . . . he must transform himself into every Person he represents . . . [which] changes the whole Form and Appearance of him in the Representation, as it does really in Nature.[6]

As much as he lauded the player's skill, the longer Gildon considered theatricality's implications the more unsettled he became. Conceding that 'they are not so agreed in what *Nature* is . . . there seems a Necessity of some Marks, or Rules to fix the Standard of what is *Natural*', he fudged the issue by arguing

[2] Players were often referred to as 'gentlemen' and 'gentlewomen' without any further elaboration. See, for example, Anon., *Poeta de Tristibus* (1682), 4; [T. Cibber], *An Apology for the Life of Mr. T--------- C-----* (1740), 52; C. Gildon, *The Life of Mr. Thomas Betterton the Late Eminent Tragedian* (1710), 16.

[3] R. Burridge, *A Scourge for the Play-Houses* (1702), 1. A point of view also suggested by J. Vanbrugh, *Aesop* (1697), part ii, 4.

[4] *Female Tatler*, no. 6 (18–20 July 1709), [1]. [5] *Ibid.*, [2].

[6] Gildon, *Betterton*, 34.

for the theatre's 'Natural Significancy', its ability to do no more than mimic reality.[7] Colley Cibber adopted a similar position when he praised Anne Oldfield for her portrayal of gentlewomen in comedies, citing her performance as Lady Townly in *The Provok'd Husband* (1728):

> Had her Birth plac'd her in a higher Rank of Life, she had certainly appear'd, in reality, what in this Play she only, excellently, acted, an agreeably gay Woman of Quality, a little too conscious of her natural Attractions. I have often seen her, in private Societies, where Women of the best Rank might have borrow'd some part of her Behavior, without the least Diminution of their Sense, or Dignity.[8]

Cibber's remark might appear harmless enough. He seems to inscribe a distinction between gentlepersons and genteel imposters, socially disqualifying Oldfield because she can only act the elite status she lacks. But in fact Cibber deliberately raises the issue of Oldfield's humble birth as much to achieve the reverse, to interrogate the idea of a clearly innate superiority by subsequently imagining how the actress's genteel spectators might emulate her offstage. The comment appeared in Cibber's account of his own theatrical career, the text shot through with similar social ambiguity. One moment Cibber renounces superiority on the basis of birth to imply that he was a match for any so-called 'gentleman', the next he accepts the claim of the well-born in order to air his own pedigree tongue-in-cheek, showing all the while that he considers such claims to be a matter of impersonation.[9]

In terms of the characteristics of the sexual suspicion that the players attracted, current historiography is limited not so much in what it says but for what it leaves unsaid. In concentrating on this issue, our second main theme, we need to examine more closely both the socially biased character of the players' promiscuity and the contours of its representation. We will begin by reviewing common but neglected features of the representation of female players caught in the act, before turning to their male counterparts. We should be more aware that the alleged debauchery of the theatre was not confined to the players themselves. In other words, it was rarely suggested that stars of the stage shared a bed (and even then the pair in question may have been married), much less that they 'prostituted' themselves to just anybody. The persistent claim is that the players' promiscuity also involved certain members of the theatre's audience. Elite spectators made up the other party in the majority of illicit liaisons said to involve players.

Of course, the prevailing modern interpretation of such rumour is that it was no more than salacious fiction with an agenda of critiquing social mobility. Perhaps we think of the actresses who really did become courtly mistresses,

[7] *Ibid.*, 88, 49.
[8] J. M. Evans (ed.), *Apology for the Life of Mr. Colley Cibber, Comedian* (New York, 1987), 177.
[9] *Ibid.*, esp. 4.

for example of Oldfield and her *de facto* relationship with the whig courtier Arthur Maynwaring, and are tempted to counter that the ill-natured gossip about female players was reporting fact rather than fabricating tittle-tattle. However, closer inspection of this gossip does reveal some significant discrepancy. For instance, *A Comparison between the Two Stages* claimed that Elizabeth Barry had been 'so unfortunate to poor *Anthony*, as the other has been to many *an honest Country Gentleman* . . . In her time she has been the very Spirit of Action every way; Nature made her the delight of Mankind.'[10] Eliding the actress with her role of Cleopatra, and perhaps with incipient racial difference standing in for status inequality, the assertion was that Barry's protean skills extended to her bedchamber and the duping of unsuspecting gentlemen. Yet it was common knowledge that Barry's most conspicuous offstage coupling had been with someone other than a plain and honest gentleman. London society was well aware of Barry's relationship with the flamboyantly libertine courtier John Wilmot, the earl of Rochester, and, incidentally, her straitened financial situation.[11] Such contradiction suggests, in turn, that discourse about players' offstage lives was as ideologically conditioned as (and by) the particular roles they performed when onstage.

The alleged sexual behaviours tend to contemplate the ambiguous effect of the theatre's re-enactment of gentility. In the assignation of the actress with the gentleman-spectator it is actually the spectator who is represented as relinquishing power, not the other way about as current arguments concerning eighteenth-century specularity maintain. Thus, when London's players went on summer tour to Oxford in 1703, William Byrd, who was then enrolled at the Inns of Court, described how 'Mrs. Bracegirdle kills a whole colledge of students every night.'[12] Similarly, a biography of Barry presented in the form of purported letters from her many noble lovers presented these men as 'languishing', 'dying', 'conquered' and 'blasted by the angry Lightning of your Eyes'.[13] Portraying the social power of the theatre in miniature, the seductive spectacle of the actress makes for the suspension or subversion of patrilinearity, the jeopardizing of the gentry's (supposedly) intrinsic superiority. Hence *A Comparison*, presented as a dialogue between three gentlemen, said of an actress, most probably Mary Porter: 'But there is a little Charmer in that House – a Creature so pretty, and yet so Civil; so wanton and so good Natur'd — I have wish'd a thousand times that my other Senses were as well inform'd of her as my Sight; 'gad I'd mortgage

[10] Anon., *A Comparison between the Two Stages* (1702), 18. *Emphasis added in the second line; dialogue attributes omitted.*

[11] See, for example, Henry Savile to the earl of Rochester, 17 December 1677, HMC, *Bath* 58, 2 (1907), 160.

[12] Byrd to [Lady Betty Cromwell], 20 July [1703], in M. Tinling (ed.), *The Correspondence of the Three William Byrds of Westover, Virginia, 1684–1776* (Charlottesville, 1977), vol. I, 223.

[13] A. Smith, *Secret History of the Lives of the Most Celebrated Beauties* (1716), vol. II, 134–6.

some Acres to purchase her Demesne.'[14] Likewise, Robert Gould condemned the female player whose aim was

> To glide into some keeping cully's heart,
> Who neither sense nor Manhood understands
> And jilt him of his Patrimonial Lands.[15]

The actress's gentleman-cully further risked the loss of his 'own good Name' when she fell pregnant and her bastard was falsely 'laid to every one of these Gentlemen'.[16] Hence a genteel conduct book contrasted the 'lewd Divertisements of the Play-house' with 'Conjugal Affections, chaste Conversation, and a legitimate Off-spring'.[17] Rather than being presented as conquering rake-hells, the gentlemen are physically wasted by their encounters with the domineering female imposter, their ability to pass on their pedigree disrupted. For example, a turn-of-the-century lampoon derided the humbly descended Barry for carrying her performance of elite characters too far and leaving behind broken, elite male bodies. Addressing the actor Joe Haynes,[18] the verse shifts constantly between the tragic stage littered with corpses to the perceived social confusion, the shedding of blood, caused by Barry who is anything but a demurely submissive spectacle (here pointedly referred to in her role of Zara from *The Mourning Bride*, a tragic villainess who pretends to be virtuous). Note the perverse use made of the language of inherited predominance:

> And hence has *Zara* all her Thousands
> got:
> Zara! that Proud, Opprobrious, Shameless
> Jilt,
> Who like a Devil justifies her Guilt,
> And feels no least Remorse for all the
> Blood sh'has spilt.
> But prithee Joe, since so she boasts her
> Blood,
> And few have yet her lineage understood,
> Tell me, in short, the Harlot's true Descent,
> . . .
> Her mother was a common Strumpet known
> . . .

14 Anon., *Comparison*, 19.

15 R. Gould, 'A Satyr against the Play-House', in his *Poems, Consisting Chiefly of Satyrs and Satyrical Epistles* (1689), 182. *Italics reversed.*

16 Anon., *Comparison*, 21.

17 J. Graile, *An Essay of Particular Advice to the Young Gentry* (1711), 146–8.

18 See A. Aston, *A Brief Supplement to Colley Cibber Esq.; His Lives of the Late Famous Actors and Actresses* (?1747), 20–3. Haynes himself was nearly arrested for pretending to be an English peer whilst on a visit to France and rumoured to have passed for a gentleman in London on several occasions.

And far surpass'd the Honours of her Line.
As her Conception was a Complication,
So its Produce, alike, did serve the
Nation;
Till by a Black, Successive Course of Ills,
She reach'd the Noble Post which now
she fills.[19]

Similarly, rumours that Oldfield had venereally infected Arthur Maynwaring were so widespread that one of her biographers could then claim the actress had ordered an autopsy of his body to prove the contrary.[20] Disputing Oldfield's right to a pre-eminent position on London's theatre scene, an earlier printed letter tipped its hand concerning the connection between the stage's social politics and the scandal surrounding its personnel. It rehearsed this rumour and then recommended a physician who 'might have *purified* the whole mass of her *blood*, which had been corrupted by a series of complicated distempers, that she need not have been obliged to the very last extremity, of trepanning her skull to effect the Cure'.[21]

If the actress's onstage presence was sexually charged, the representation of her 'private life' was itself equally so. The female player was as much made a sexual object in print as she may have been in performance. Her suspect reputation checked her stage representation and its elision of 'natural' superiority as a matter of cultural impersonation.[22] Hence Kimberly Crouch's study of eighteenth-century actresses passes over the complexity of the presentation of these women as the cultured equals of attractive, young gentlewomen. Crouch argues that such positive images functioned as a '*counterpoint* to the idea that

[19] These lines originally appeared in the 1700 edition of R. Gould's *A Satyr on the Players*, here quoted from P. H. Highfill, jr., K. A. Burnim, and E. A. Langhans (eds.), *A Biographical Dictionary of Actors, Actresses, Musicians, Dancers, Managers & Other Stage Personnel in London, 1660–1800* (Carbondale, 1973), vol. I, 321.

[20] [E. Curll], *Faithful Memoirs of the Life, Amours and Performances, of That Justly Celebrated, and Most Eminent Actress of Her Time, Mrs. Anne Oldfield* (1731), 39–40.

[21] 'A Justification of the Letter to Sir John Stanley, Relating to His Management of the Play-house in Drury Lane' (1712). *Emphasis added.* Retranscribed from an earlier handwritten copy and printed in J. Milhous and R. D. Hume, 'Theatrical Politics at Drury Lane: New Light on Letitia Cross, Jane Rogers, and Anne Oldfield', *Bulletin of Research in the Humanities* 85, 4 (1982), 421.

[22] A point suggested by K. E. Maus, '"Playhouse Flesh and Blood": Sexual Ideology and the Restoration Actress', *ELH* 46 (1979), 604–5; C. Lowenthal, 'Sticks and Rags, Bodies and Brocade: Essentializing Discourses and the Late Restoration Playhouse', in K. M. Quinsey (ed.), *Broken Boundaries. Women and Feminism in Restoration Drama* (Lexington, 1996), 220–1; S. M. Strohmer, '"Every Man an Actor": Performance Theories in the Restoration', unpublished PhD dissertation, University of Michigan (1999), 142ff. Lowenthal's argument has recently been extended in her *Performing Identities on the Restoration Stage* (Carbondale, 2003), 111–43. However, the present study would beg to differ on certain points, particularly by demonstrating that male players did come in for scrutiny.

the actress was treated no differently than the prostitute'.[23] More significant is the entwining of these apparently contradictory assumptions, that female players acted like well-born women onstage and off, that they were as free with their bodies in private as in public.[24]

A reform proposal was caught in this crux when it advocated that all actresses be 'oblig'd by their Articles, to a considerable Forfeiture, upon proof of the abuse of their Vertue, or rather be Expell'd the Theatre; for I think no Woman, after she has play'd the Whore notoriously, can be fancifully receiv'd upon the Stage for a Heroine'.[25] On the one hand, this stricture begins by taking the rumours of the actress's lack of chastity at face value. On the other, it then redacts the associations of virtue with the innate superiority of the gentlewoman, the drama's heroine, and suggests how the actress's sexualized notoriety allowed the gentle person and genteel pretender to be clearly or 'naturally' distinguished by their audiences. Byrd's correspondence, when reporting the death of Susannah Verbruggen, captured an echo of a similar logic at work within the oral culture of London's theatre going *beau monde*:

> She had more of nature in her action than any other player I ever see, & was mistress of so easy, so unaffected a manner, that nothing but the stage coud make one distinguish betwixt the reality & the representation. She had a readiness that never failed her, & an agreableness that never failed the audience.[26]

Byrd recollects Verbruggen's genteel grace in very ambivalent terms. She appears a socially dominant woman by exhibiting refined manners, but, at the same time, is indistinguishable from a courtesan of loose morals (a 'mistress' who has a 'readiness' to please). Offstage she cannot be told apart from the born gentlewoman unless her ambiguous reputation precedes her. And that reputation also had to take account of her much-applauded ability to play the gentleman-beau.[27] Hence *A Satyr on the Players* not only described her as a 'Whore', but also revealed onanistic sexual behaviour which, like sodomy, seemed indicative of an individual who denied her natural self and, instead, revelled in 'personating' a shifting series of identities:

[23] K. Crouch, 'The Public Life of Actresses: Prostitutes or Ladies?', in H. Baker and E. Chalus (eds.), *Gender in Eighteenth-Century England. Roles, Representations and Responsibilities* (London, 1997), 62, *emphasis added*; also 61, 70. A similar argument is made by a case-study of the stage reputation of Anne Oldfield, J. Peck, 'Anne Oldfield's Lady Townly: Consumption, Credit, and the Whig Hegemony of the 1720s', *Theatre Journal* 49 (1997), 397–416.

[24] For a lucid discussion of these assumptions during the 1660s and 1670s see W. J. Pritchard, 'Outward Appearances: The Display of Women in Restoration London', unpublished PhD dissertation, University of Chicago (1998), 94–114.

[25] [G. Powell], *Animadversions on Mr. Congreve's Late Answer to Mr. Collier in a Dialogue between Mr. Smith and Mr. Johnson* (1698), 80–1.

[26] Byrd to [Lady Betty Cromwell], 4 September [1703], in Tinling, *Correspondence*, vol. I, 237–8.

[27] Evans, *Apology for Cibber*, 99.

> *Sue Percival* so long has known the Stage,
> She grows in lewdness faster than ye Age:
> From Eight or Nine she there has Fr-----g been
> So calls that Nature, which is truly Sin.[28]

The main claim made by the publication of the actress's life was that it stripped away her superior artifice (and artificial superiority) to reveal the 'essential', naked truth of the 'natural' baseness, the brutish lust and the social inferiority, beneath. So in the case of Barry it was alleged:

> There's one, Heav'n bless us! by her cursed Pride
> Thinks from the world her Brutish Lust to hide;
> But will that Pass in her, whose only Sence
> Does lye in Whoring, Cheats, and Impudence?
> One that is Pox all o're; *Barry* her Name,
> That mercenary Prostituted Dame,
> Whose nauseous ---- like *Tony's* Tap does run:
> Unpity'd Ass, that can't her Ulcer Shun![29]

Cheap literature and gossip purporting to reveal her secret but real life, and allowing readers to 'see into her Soul, to behold the Vices which lay conceal'd under so fair an Outside', worked to imprint a stable but decidedly plebeian identity on the body of the shape-shifting woman of Drury Lane and Lincoln's Inn Fields.[30] Resorting to lurid probing in order to condemn the contortive effects of performance on what, it insisted, were clearly and originally individuals of mean descent, it finally denied the power of the theatre to fashion social identity. Hence 'People upon the Stage . . . speaking better than those of equal Rank in Life' are branded 'monstrous and unnatural'.[31] Or *A Comparison* represented the protean female player as pregnant but then grotesquely elaborated the consequences of the humbly born appearing genteel:

CRITIC: . . . I have seen one of 'em cramp her Belly so confoundedly with her Stays, to hide it from the Audience, that when the Child has been born, the Jade had mawl'd it into such a deform'd condition, that the good Women have been frighted out of their Wits, and the Midwife her self has mistaken it for a false Conception.

SULLEN: Why shou'd they use so much inhumane art to hide what in time must of necessity be discover'd?[32]

28 Quoted from Highfill *et al.*, *Dictionary of Actors* (1993), vol. XV, 138. Percival was Verbruggen's maiden name.

29 R. Gould, 'Satyr on the Players', in M. Summers (ed.), *Roscius Anglicanus* (New York, 1929), 58.

30 The quote is from an account of Barry's private life in Smith, *Secret History*, vol. II, 140. An extended yet anonymous example of this social 'imprinting' can be found in E. Ward, *Adam and Eve Stript to Their Furbelows* (1714), 88–96.

31 *London Journal*, no. ccclxxxiv (10 December 1726), [1].

32 Anon., *Comparison*, 20–1.

In the representation of actors' offstage lives we encounter similar concerns of power and performance as they related to the 'natural' structuration of society. John Dennis struck the general tone when he vowed to discipline the theatre's male players by 'shewing them what They really are, and by that means rendring them humble . . . that Actors are so far from having the great Qualities of extraordinary Men, that they have not the Understanding and Judgment of ordinary Gentlemen'.[33] To depict or render the actor infirm, as one racked by disease of age, carnality or sybaritic indulgence, was to deny his capacity to reveal the performative nature of born superiority, the gentleman's need to impersonate an allegedly innate social difference.

Put another way, the actor's *dis*-comfort created a comforting distinction between the inherited and so natural poise of the gentleman-born and the learned, artificial and so debilitating pose of the lowly player. Thus it was observed of the senior actor Robert Wilks:

> Every thing told so strongly the involuntary motion of a gentleman, that it was impossible to consider the character he represented in any other light than that of reality – but what was still more surprising, that person who could thus delight an audience from the gaiety and sprightliness of his manner, I met the next day in the street hobbling to a hackney coach, seemingly so enfeebled by age and infirmities, that I could scarcely believe him to be the same man.[34]

Likewise, with quite specific and deliberate attention to the performance of elite characters, Cibber himself captured the functional significance of the less than sober reputation of a bibulous fellow actor: 'Even when he did well, that natural Prejudice pursu'd him; neither the Heroe, nor the Gentleman; the young *Ammon*, nor the *Dorimant*, could conceal, from the conscious Spectator, the True *George Powel*.'[35] Compare Cibber's remark just a few pages later that a 'sensible Auditor would contribute all he could, to his being well deceiv'd, and not suffer his Imagination, so far to wander, from the well-acted Character before him, as to gratify a frivolous Spleen, by Mocks, or personal Sneers, on the Performer'.[36]

The scarring of the actor's body could be mental as well as physical but both were, of course, ultimately textual. When illness forced Barton Booth from his roles as the tragedy's hero and the comedy's gentleman it was bruited as far as Virginia that he had gone mad.[37] Not too remarkable in itself, the gossip appeared more than random fancy when it poignantly suggested that performing

[33] J. Dennis, *The Characters and Conduct of Sir John Edgar* (1720), 6–7.
[34] An anonymous comment from 1729 cited in Highfill *et al.*, *Dictionary of Actors* (1993), vol. XVI, 120.
[35] Evans, *Apology for Cibber*, 141. Ammon was the lead character in Nathaniel Lee's *Rival Queens* (1677); Dorimant the gentleman-libertine in George Etherege's *The Man of Mode* (1676).
[36] Evans, *Apology for Cibber*, 146.
[37] Byrd to Mrs Armiger, 25 June 1729, in Tinling, *Correspondence*, vol. I, 413.

elite roles had gone to Barton's head. In his delirium Booth was said to act the 'Mock-Monarch' over his servants.[38] Booth returned to the 'laborious Business of the Stage', but died a few years later. Even then, there was a continued and morbid fascination with the actor's body. Stressing the amount of mercury (a common treatment for venereal disease) found, the alleged results of Booth's post-mortem were published for the entire world to read.[39]

The critical preoccupation with the actor's sexualized representation has meant that other figurative outlets for this socio-ideological anxiety, which the actor came literally to embody, have been neglected. Such anxiety was just as frequently confronted, possibly dispelled, by the imaging of the actor as a tradesman who sweated for a living and strove to replicate the self-evident and effortless superiority of the well-born.[40] The actor-son of Colley Cibber spilt much ink promoting the contrary idea in the introductory remarks to his own biography of Booth, implying that he was fighting a losing battle. Probably embellishing the social origin of his subject, Theo Cibber insisted that Booth's acting was an art that required 'genius'. Actors were not to be lumped together with 'sad Scrapers' or 'dismal Dawbers' and they were certainly not to be likened to 'mechanics'.[41] However, this kind of redemptive strategy could itself backfire. A common counter-response to sublime, genteel representation was to brand its practitioners idle and lazy, 'Vagabonds' with 'Nauseous Bodies and Souls'.[42]

The reputedly aberrant sexual behaviour of the male player which has received most attention is that involving same-sex relationships.[43] As we noted earlier, this representation has been labelled 'homophobic'. Relying as it does on the wider paradigm introduced by Randolph Trumbach, this characterization needs revision. For if the fop figure was a complex symbol of the cultural performance of gentility, it comes as little surprise that players who enacted genteel identities not their own onstage were represented, in print and by word of mouth, as equally 'beau-ish', sexually suspect and sodomitical, offstage. For example, William Mountfort had shown great promise in elite roles from both comedy and tragedy during the late 1680s. After his violent death in 1692, verses described how he had cut a genteel figure among female admirers and yet he remained subject to rumours of sexual deviancy.[44] Discovering his wife

[38] As reported in T. Cibber, *The Lives and Characters of the Most Eminent Actors and Actresses of Great Britain and Ireland* (1753), 57.

[39] Anon., *Memoirs of the Life of Barton Booth, Esq.* (1733), 13, 19ff.

[40] For examples, see *Tatler*, no. 20 (26 May 1709), vol. I, 161; [E. Curll], *The Life of That Eminent Comedian Robert Wilks, Esq.* (1733), v.

[41] Cibber, *Lives and Characters*, iii, vii–ix.

[42] J. Oldmixon, *Reflections on the Stage, and Mr. Collyer's Defence of the Short View* (1699), 187–8; Anon., *The Whitsun-tide Ramble* (?1720), 8.

[43] Cf. George Harbin to the earl of Oxford, 29 January 1728, HMC, *Portland* 29, 6 (1901), 20 (of ladies and there being 'so much danger of their falling in love with the actors').

[44] A. S. Borgman, *The Life and Death of William Mountfort* (Cambridge, MA, 1935), 160–1.

had found 'beau' Mountfort's charms irresistible, it was widely claimed that a former patron had reasserted his naturally superior prerogatives by force:

> There's a story of late
> That the Chancellor's mate
> Has been f-----d and been f-----d by player
> Mountfort;
> Which though false, yet's as true,
> My Lord gave him his due,
> For he had a small tilt at his bum for it.[45]

Close reading suggests that this episode was more the product of socio-political discourse than the reporting of real events. The chancellor was Lord Jeffreys, the judge infamous for his actions in the wake of Monmouth's rebellion and his later deposition declaring James III to be the true heir. His raping of Mountfort imagined in terms of the duel, the chancellor subordinates the 'base and unmannerly Whig', namely, the impertinent, low-born actor whose party loyalties were well known and whose signature comic role was none other than that of Sir Courtly Nice, the very same fop character who complains that comedies are nauseating because of their being 'sawcy with Quality'.[46]

Similarly, images of a freakish corporeality dogged George Powell, the player who took over several of Mountfort's lead roles:

> Beau *P----ll* shows himself in *Tunbridge* Walks,
> Of strange Amours and Numerous Action talks;
> . . .
> Whores are his Daily Consorts and Delight.
> Is Lewd all Day, but very Chaste at Night.
> Fate may a Stone upon his Grave bestow,
> Tho' Niggard Nature has deny'd him two;
> 'Tis strange that Vice on nature shou'd prevail,
> To fill the Head, and yet forget the Tail.
> Supply his Want of Lewdness with his Wit,
> And make him Boast of Sins he can't Commit.[47]

These representations were persistently ambivalent. On the one hand, they castigated and denaturalized the flawless performance of pedigree by the male

[45] Quoted from G. M. Crump (ed.), *Poems on Affairs of State. Augustan Satirical Verse. Volume IV: 1685–1688* (New Haven, 1968), 72 (footnote).

[46] J. Crowne, *Sir Courtly Nice* (1685), v, 51. Unfortunately there is not sufficient space to investigate further the socio-political dimensions of Mountfort's representation. Mountfort was murdered in 1692, after an attempt was made to abduct the actress Anne Bracegirdle. His death resulted in the trial of Lord Mohun, one of his assailants, before the House of Lords. The trial rivalled the playhouse for its theatricality, and the depositions presenting the last moments of the actor's life rehearse the same socio-political concerns which seem to have become a constant undercurrent of Mountfort's highly publicized career and posthumous reputation.

[47] D. Defoe, *More Reformation. A Satyr upon Himself* (1703), 40–1 (mispaginated as '44–5').

player. On the other, they cannot fully suppress the realization that such performance was only possible if genteel descent was performative, a powerful but necessary spectacle. Once again, the presentation of unnatural acts of sexual subordination should be read in dialogue with the stage's representation of natural domination, the player's uncanny or 'sawcy' ability to reproduce supposedly native social distinctions belonging to those of good birth. Taken together they are a commentary on the performability of gentility. They amount to something other than recognition of the male player's subjection before the all-powerful gaze of the male spectator or a means to resist the player's social mobility. The likes of Mountfort and Powell do not simply make spectacles of themselves. Rather, their imaging in print emphasizes that it is their making a spectacle of gentility onstage which is unsettling. By presenting themselves as elite men to other gentle persons, and having the power to capture the attention and return the gaze of their 'naturally' dominant superiors, they convey the idea that superiority is only in the eye of the beholder. In other words, gentility is a matter of impersonation and subjective perception, not inherited, self-evident perfection. The exquisite performances of these men are deemed excessive; they betray too much of the genteel self to the gentle spectator and, therefore, are considered 'sodomitical' and 'effeminate'. As Robert Gould summed up London's actors:

> A pack of idle, pimping, spunging Slaves,
> A Miscellany of Rogues, Fools and Knaves;
> A Nest of Leachers, worse than *Sodom* bore,
> And justly merit to be punish't more:
> Diseas'd, in Debt, and every moment dun'd;
> By all good Christians loath'd, and their own
> Kindred shun'd.
> . . .
> Now hear a wonder that will well declare
> How extravagantly lewd some Women are:
> For ev'n these men, base as they are and vain,
> Our Punks of highest Quality maintain
> Supply their daily wants (which are not slight)
> But 'tis, that they may be supply'd at night.
> These in their *Coaches* they take up and down,
> Publish their foul disgrace o'er all the Town.[48]

Paradoxically, it is their characterization as 'leachers' or 'beaux' that renders the players' performances watchable. This is because alleging a venereal promiscuity allows for imagining the actor's subordination, breaking the powerful hold of his subversive action onstage. Hence Kristina Straub's conclusion that 'sexuality is a means by which the actor's position as marginal to socially

[48] Gould, 'Satyr against the Play-House', 184.

dominant definitions of class, ethnicity, race, and gender is constructed' requires modification.[49] It would be more accurate to say that the player's represented sexuality was a response to his or her ability to make visible the constructedness at the core of social domination, specifically, the performative nature of gentility as society's key margin of domination and subordination.

The final theme of the representation of the players' immorality worthy of rereading is the incongruous insistence that their lewd behaviour occurred at the playhouse itself. With odd precision, the debauchery of the players is sited at particular places and times within the theatre space. Rather than peep through private keyholes, the discourse of the theatre's imagined immorality mainly pinpointed – and so tried to discipline – two settings for the brazen licentiousness of players and their elite partners. Perhaps more than any other trope, the identification of these two spaces demonstrates how the discourse of theatre reform was leavened with socio-ideological concern.

First there was the acting forestage. This space was deemed to be especially problematic during the delivery of the play's prologue or epilogue. Thus the *Short View* objected vehemently to how the

> *Actors* quit the *Stage*, and remove from Fiction into Life. Here they converse with the *Boxes*, and *Pit*, and address directly to the Audience. These Preliminarie and concluding Parts, are design'd to justify the Conduct of the *Play*, and be-speak the Favour of the Company. Upon such Occasions one would imagine if ever, the Ladys should be used with Respect, and the Measures of Decency observ'd, But here we have Lewdness without Shame or Example . . . And to make it the more agreeable, Women are Commonly pick'd out for this Service. Thus the *Poet* Courts the good opinion of the Audience. This is the Desert he regales the Ladys with at the Close of the Entertainment: It seems He thinks They have admirable Palats! Nothing can be a greater Breach of Manners then such Liberties as these. If a Man would study to outrage *Quality* and Vertue, he could not do it more Effectually.[50]

What riled Collier was not so much the bawdy content of the opening or closing verses but the fact that this part of the theatre's entertainment was presented at all. The versifying player was considered 'licentious' because (s)he deliberately dared to ignore the dramatic frame. Stepping out of the performance (s)he continues to act with natural wit or genteel charm, not simply transgressing innate ('virtuous') social differences belonging to the well-born (the 'quality') but actually collapsing ('outraging') them by suggesting their performability.

The presence of these differences and their dramatic interrogation was commonly represented by the double-edged metonym of the blushing female

49 K. Straub, *Sexual Suspects. Eighteenth-Century Players and Sexual Ideology* (Princeton, 1992), 25.

50 J. Collier, *A Short View of the Immorality, and Profaneness of the English Stage* (1698), 13–14.

spectator.[51] The modest blushes of the well-born ladies in the front boxes, as they witnessed such 'lewd' and 'indecent' performances, figure the reassertion of native superiority ('virtue' and 'quality' again as well as 'blood'), the maintenance of innate but also readily discernible social inequalities ('distinctions', 'distance') in spite of the theatre's potential to challenge these by showing them up as a set of imitable cultural conventions:

> Modesty was design'd by Providence as a Guard to Virtue . . . 'Tis a Quality as true to Innocence, as the Sences are to Health . . . The Enemy no sooner approaches, but the Blood rises in Opposition, and looks Defyance to an Indecency . . . Thus the Distinctions of Good and Evil are refresh'd, and the Temptation kept at proper Distance.[52]

For others the blushing gentlewoman symbolized the exact opposite, the inevitable denaturalization or embarrassing elision of status in performance. Witness Tom Brown's description of the actress Anne Bracegirdle:

> But for a Woman of your *Quality* to first surrender her *Honour*, and afterwards preserve her Character, shows a discreet management beyond the Policy of a Statesman: Your appearance upon the Stage puts the Court Ladies to the *Blush*, when they reflect that a *mercenary* Player should be more renown'd for her *Vertue* than all the Glorious Train of fair Spectators.[53]

Brown's comment relied on the knowledge that Bracegirdle's origins were humble. She was usually described as the daughter of a Northampton coachmaker or coachman.[54] She had no gentle blood in her veins to sully, was not of a 'virtuous' or innately superior degree. Yet Bracegirdle was lauded for (re)creating the illusion that she was indeed well-born. This ability was cause for consternation, the 'truly' well-born ladies proving unable to draw the audience's attention away from Bracegirdle and her enactment of gentility towards its proper focus, the spectacle of their own equally self-fashioned, impersonated superiority. In like manner, a broadsheet depicting Wilks as the beau baronet Sir Harry Wildair (Figure 8) included this pointed, captioned remark on the character's performance: 'And Nature blush'd to see her self outdone.' The social stakes were raised even further when the actor was described as

[51] Cf. J. I. Marsden, 'Female Spectatorship, Jeremy Collier and the Anti-Theatrical Debate', *ELH* 65 (1998), 887.

[52] Collier, *Short View*, 11.

[53] T. Brown, *Letters from the Dead to the Living* (1702, fifth edition 1708), 519 (irregular pagination). *Emphasis added.*

[54] Highfill *et al.*, *Dictionary of Actors* (1973), vol. II, 269. But compare n. 56 below and also Fisk, 'The Restoration Actress', 76, where other contemporary comment apparently considered Bracegirdle 'the offspring of gentry fallen on hard times'. Even if we could, for example, demonstrate an officially registered pedigree for the individuals being discussed here, we must still examine and explain the typically stronger tendency for them to be represented as meanly born. In other words, the players' lives encompass a particularly dense and often ironic sample of gentility's contestability.

8 'Robert Wilks as Sir Harry Wildair', by John Smith, *c.*1732, The Harvard Theatre Collection, The Houghton Library

'ROBERT WILKS Esqr.', placing him among the ranks of the genteel.[55] Against the current of opinion, one biography of Bracegirdle did the same. To side-step the issue of how a low-born individual could perform genteelly, it steadfastly assumed the reverse: 'It is not any Matter of our Enquiry by what Means a

[55] See Figure 8. *Italics reversed.*

Gentlewoman of so good an Extraction came upon the Stage, since the best Families have been liable to the greatest Misfortunes.'[56]

We should pause here to recall certain features of the playhouse space, particularly its intimacy.[57] Despite some alterations during the late seventeenth century, it is generally accepted by theatre historians that most of the performance took place downstage, on a protruding forestage. This practice located the actors much closer to the spectators than to the painted scenes upstage.[58] And as Collier's complaint about the epilogues makes clear, the drama situated not just any spectators but the gentry of box and pit closest to the action. The effect of this familiarity was a failure to achieve the sense of self-contained dramatic illusion we associate with modern drama. In the well-lit theatre space and at a time when it was often still possible to watch the performance from onstage, it was hard to know where or when performance ended and reality began, often conspicuously so.[59] Thus Lord Foppington (or Colley Cibber standing next to the side-boxes and their elite occupants) marks this elision with the densely reflexive comment of the beau that

> my Life, Madam, is a perpetual Stream of Pleasure, that glides through such a Variety of Entertainments, I believe the wisest of our Ancestors never had the least Conception of any of 'em. I rise, Madam, about Ten a-Clock. I don't rise sooner, because 'tis the worst thing in the World for the Complexion; nat [*sic*] that I pretend to be a Beau: But a Man must endeavour to look wholesome, lest he make so nauseous a Figure in the Side-Bax [*sic*], the Ladies shou'd be compell'd to turn their Eyes upon the Play.[60]

Foppington's light remark about ancestors is positively ironic. It points the question, if Cibber personates the born gentleman and competes for attention with the gentlemen gesturing their gentility from the side-box, is their inherited superiority nothing more than a theatrical conception instead of a demonstrably natural creation?[61]

Perhaps a similar effect is more subtly redacted in the picture of Wilks as the beau Wildair. The print positions Wilks in front of the proscenium (notice the contrasting shadow on the stage-floor) and his expression and stance imply

[56] [T. Betterton], *The History of the English Stage* (1741), 26.

[57] The following paragraph is based on the pertinent observations of S. Shepherd and P. Womack, *English Drama. A Cultural History* (Oxford, 1996), 123–5, but also see the more recent remarks by Pritchard, 'Outward Appearances', 84–94.

[58] It has been calculated that the distance from the actor to the back wall of the audience space was just over half that of the distance between the actor and the painted screens or scenery.

[59] J. Roach, 'The Performance', in D. Payne Fisk (ed.), *The Cambridge Companion to English Restoration Theatre* (Cambridge, 2000), 25–6; D. C. Payne, 'Reified Object or Emergent Professional? Retheorizing the Restoration Actress', in J. D. Canfield and D. C. Payne (eds.), *Cultural Readings of Restoration and Eighteenth-Century English Theater* (Athens, GA, 1995), 30.

[60] J. Vanbrugh, *Relapse* (1697), ii, 28–9.

[61] For a contemporary discussion of similar issues which cites the character of Foppington, see *Spectator*, no. 370 (5 May 1712), vol. IV, 393–6.

both detachment from the stage action and engagement with the audience, as if he were a gentleman-spectator making a witty remark on the play. The picture is intended to recall Wilks's presentation of the closing lines of *The Constant Couple*, lines which alluded to the issue of 'virtue' in such a way as to suggest that it was more important than, and not synonymous with, one's lineage in ascertaining gentility.[62] Moreover, Wilks next presented the same play's epilogue, a verse which referred to the practice of addressing the theatre's gentlewomen-spectators that Collier had condemned for its erasure of 'natural' social distinctions. Indeed, this verse seems to have had Collier's criticism specifically in mind. Remembering that he would have spoken the epilogue whilst still in character, Wilks proposed the compromise that spectators applaud his performance and worry about its deeper, more troubling implications later: 'Our Business with good Manners may be done, | Flatter us here, and damn us when you're gone.' Or, as one of the *Short View*'s quoted authorities nervously warned about the risky business of staging society and performing its ideally inherent distinctions: '[We] rate our Degree by our Virtue . . . Sometimes your *Mimicks*, are so Scandalous and Expressing [*sic*], that 'tis almost hard to distinguish between the *Fact* and the *Representation*.'[63]

A similar preoccupation with the integrity and legibility of inherited social superiority and its revelation as a subjective impersonation (because in reproducing it the stage also rendered it reproducible[64]) is manifested by the proscription of a second space of alleged sexual licence, the area known as 'behind the scenes'. For instance, John Oldmixon claimed to dispute the idea that actors were an 'insufferable Generation', denying their lives were any more debauched than those of other people.[65] Then, in an abrupt about-face, he declared in favour of the charge that players were less than morally upright, revealing that much of the sexual stigma attached to the acting profession was a means to redress the social instability incited by the rehearsal of genteel characters. The argument is a lengthy one, but it needs to be quoted in full for the knots of uncertainty it discloses. Of the players Oldmixon wrote:

> Their temptations are not more extraordinary than other mens, unless that their men and women converse behind the Scenes promiscuously, which may tempt 'em to too much liberty . . . The favours which the fair Sex have thrown away on some of the Actors, and the countenance men of Quality have put on the Function, by allowing 'em to be familiar with 'em, have been the occasion of the boldness of the men. They have

62 See G. Farquhar, *Constant Couple* (1700), v, 56. This would mean that the figures upstage are those of Angelica helping the elderly Smuggler. Note also that the picture's caption refers to a 'trip to the Jubilee', the subtitle of this play.

63 Collier, *Short View*, 261.

64 S. Mullaney, 'Discursive Forums, Cultural Practices: History and Anthropology in Literary Studies', in T. J. McDonald (ed.), *The Historic Turn in the Human Sciences* (Ann Arbor, 1996), 176.

65 Oldmixon, *Reflections*, 187.

taken up notions of honour from their company and books, which not being born with 'em, they cou'd not well manage, and have occasion'd several Riots, that may be easily prevented; If Gentlemen were more cautious how they make an acquaintance with 'em, not but that there are some of 'em even now . . . who know very well how to keep within their Character, and make themselves agreeable where-ever they come. The women are ruin'd by the fondness of some Fops to be first in their good graces, and fancying it a high honour to have the smile of a *Roxana* or *Statira*. Let the Scene keepers be charg'd as strictly as they can to suffer no body to come among their Players. Let the Conversation of the Stage be as narrowly watcht as possible; and think on what ways you will to make their men modest and their women chaste.[66]

The import of Oldmixon's injunction to keep the scenes clear, echoing many similar prohibitions, will become apparent once we explore further the significance of the phrase 'behind the scenes' and the perceived impact of the behaviour of particular theatre patrons:[67] namely, the gentlemen (and less typically gentlewomen) who claimed the prerogative of occupying the stage.

As at least one comedy indicated, being behind the scenes did not necessarily mean that the spectator was always tucked away in the green room and hidden from view. Hence the upstart Quibble observed, when he was 'talking to Beau *Smirk*, and giving my self great Airs behind the Scenes, that impudent Fell[o]w *Jack Dapperwit* the Goldsmith's Prentice in *Fleet-street*, had the Assurance to bow to me out of the Eighteen-penny Gallery – I thought I should have dropt down dead.'[68] The phrase 'behind the scenes' implicated the 'gentlemen' who chose to stand or sit alongside the movable screens which comprised the scenery. The screens were slid across (or, later, rolled down) to centre-stage as required, an operation carried out in full view of the main audience and one which would have exposed the presence of stage spectators.[69] Thus a pastiche of Cibber's autobiography and its preoccupation with ridding 'the scenes' of such people claimed mock success in removing 'these Squirts and Puffs of Foplings . . . because Persons then admitted might impede the *Scenery*'.[70] Cibber's own memoir boasted that under his management Drury Lane had been able to 'shut out those idle Gentlemen, who seem'd more delighted to be pretty Objects

66 *Ibid*., 189–90. 'Statira' referred to Anne Bracegirdle and 'Roxana' to Elizabeth Barry, the female leads in Lee's *Rival Queens*. *The History of the English Stage*, attributed to Thomas Betterton, made the intriguing comment that these two tragic roles were the 'perfect burlesque on the Dignity of Majesty [i.e. hereditary monarchy], and good Manners', 19.

67 Examples of official proclamations may be found in A. Jackson, 'The Stage and the Authorities, 1700–1714 (as Revealed in the Newspapers)', *RES* 14 (1938), 59–61; J. H. Wilson, *All the King's Ladies. Actresses of the Restoration* (Chicago, 1958), 28.

68 T. Baker, *Humour of the Age* (1701), iii, 29. A similar suggestion is made in Burridge, *Scourge*, 10.

69 E. A. Langhans, 'The Theatre', in D. Payne Fisk (ed.), *The Cambridge Companion to English Restoration Theatre* (Cambridge, 2000), 9; Langhans, 'The Post-1660 Theatres as Performance Spaces', in S. J. Owen (ed.), *A Companion to Restoration Drama* (Oxford, 2001), 4–14.

70 [T. Cibber], *Life of Mr. T--------- C-----*, 70.

themselves, than capable of any Pleasure, from the Play: Who took their daily Stands, where they might best elbow the Actor, and come in for their Share of the Auditor's Attention'.[71] A print dating from his time as theatre manager, originally entitled 'The Green Room Scuffle', represented some of the chaotic mixing of players and spectators which Cibber claimed to have eliminated (see Figure 9). The Latin motto ('All the world's a stage') perhaps hinted that the problem related more to the revelation of the performative quality of all social identities than to the physical hindrance of the evening's production.[72] For these troublesome playgoers were not always seated quietly in the same place. They might slip from one side of the stage to the other and engage players in conversation as the actors waited for their cues to appear in front of the proscenium.

The scenes then were the second space where genteel social actors and those acting genteel roles collided, where social identities would certainly have been in disarray for the uninitiated. How to tell who were the actors and who the spectators? Or as Joseph Addison's poem 'The Playhouse' advised with ambiguity and *entendre*:

> But next survey the tyring-room and see
> False titles, and promiscuous quality
> Confus'dly swarm.[73]

Were titled individuals being 'false' to their status by dallying 'promiscuously' with humble players? Or base-born players falsely appropriating 'quality' rhetoric? (A rhetoric, we should stress, which extended to a host of non-verbal cues.) The licentiousness of the scenes was not simply a matter of players flirting with gentlemen and -women. This concern was but a symptom of a deeper unease surrounding the theatre's elision of natural social distinctions by a descent into discourse.

Therefore, returning to Oldmixon's injunction, we should ask what did scene-keepers have to do with policing the intimacy of player and spectator? They were, in effect, being enjoined to hold the imaginary line between social impersonation and social reality. Although he toys with the notion that the problem is one of the players maintaining their elite social roles beyond the playhouse, Oldmixon settles most of the blame for this confusion on the genteel theatregoers themselves. This and similar texts referred not merely to gentlemen spectators but, quite specifically, to gullible 'beaus' and conceited 'fops' who,

[71] Evans, *Apology for Cibber*, 340.

[72] A point also recently developed by T. Chico, 'The Dressing Room Unlock'd: Eroticism, Performance, and Privacy from Pepys to the *Spectator*', in L. J. Rosenthal and M. Choudhury (eds.), *Monstrous Dreams of Reason. Body, Self, and Other in the Enlightenment* (Lewisburg, 2002), 47–52.

[73] J. Addison, 'The Playhouse' (1688/9), in G. de F. Lord (ed.), *Anthology of Poems on Affairs of State. Augustan Satirical Verse 1660–1714* (New Haven, 1975), 579 (lines 28–30).

9 'The Green Room Scuffle', by Thomas Booth, *c.*1725

as always, (mis-)took performance for nature.[74] Addison's poem, for instance, espies the actress assuming the signifiers of the elite heroine – 'on her cheeks the blushing purple glows, | And a false virgin modesty bestows'[75] – only to observe with some dismay that 'Her countenance complete, the beaux she warms | With looks not hers, and spite of nature, charms.'[76] Tom Brown went even further, claiming there were 'Affidavits of a multitude of decay'd *Beaux* who have been undone and afterwards laught at by 'em.'[77] The end result is 'conversation' between genteel and non-genteel. 'Conversation' was shorthand for gentility's submersion in performance. It was also a euphemism for sexual intercourse which metaphorically connoted the collapse of lineage, the corruption of natural and immutable lines of power, domination and difference within early modern society.

Spoken by a young girl, the epilogue to *The Cornish Comedy* captured the crux of our argument when, addressing the 'Pretty, Witty Gentlemen call'd Beaus', it observed:

> I've learn'd so much already behind the Scenes,
> I know what a *Billete Doux* and *Ogling* means:
> I know what Man keeps *Somebody*, nay, I know more,
> I know she that will *Kiss* for Money, is a Whore.
> Let the Men-Players leave off when they will,
> Our *Maiden Gentlewomen* will scarce lie still.
> Nay – you may laugh at a young Innocent Creature;
> But I know more than you think tho', of the matter.
> I know the *World's* a *Stage* and do not wrong ye;
> You're better Actors there, than we're among ye;
> Because to act you's not so hard a Task,
> As 'tis for you to act a Vizard Mask.[78]

In short, the exposé of the sexually available player was largely a fiction that tried to confront uncomfortable but fundamental questions concerning the motility of elite social identity as an ongoing process of impersonation. The nagging

[74] An association also readily evident in T. Shadwell, *True Widow* (1679), iii, 45; the 1682 poem, 'On Three Late Marriages', transcribed in J. H. Wilson (ed.), *Court Satires of the Restoration* (Columbus, 1976), 78; 'Satire on Both Whigs and Tories', in *ibid.*, 125; the epilogue to C. Gildon's *Roman Brides Revenge* (1696), cited in Wilson, *Ladies*, 17; Anon., *The Beaus Catechism* (1703), 6; Gould, 'Satyr against the Play-House', 163–4; R. Gould, 'Jack Pavy. A Satyr', in Gould, *The Works* (1709), vol. II, 317 (lines 551ff.); Brown, *Letters from the Dead*, 111; C. Beckingham, *Scipio Africanus* (1718), epilogue spoken by Mrs Bullock.

[75] Addison, 'Playhouse', in Lord, *Anthology of Poems on Affairs of State*, 580 (lines 54–5). As the rest of the poem makes clear, purple signified elite status. Note also the recurrence of the image of blushing.

[76] *Ibid.*, 580 (lines 61–2).

[77] T. Brown, *Amusements Serious and Comical, Calculated for the Meridian of London* (1700), quoted in A. M. Nagler (ed.), *A Source Book in Theatrical History* (New York, 1952), 249.

[78] Anon., *Cornish Comedy* (1696), 47. *Italics reversed.*

doubt was that the drama would reveal 'gentlemen' and 'gentlewomen' were recognizably so in terms only of a perfected performance on the world's stage, rather than of an inherent perfection which went without saying. The promiscuity of the player and genteel spectator was a means to thwart the effect of an actor or actress successfully and commendably impersonating superior birth. This was the main impetus behind sweeping and nonspecific diatribes about the '*Licentious* and *Unbounded Liberty* the Players have taken of late years', the 'shameful *Indignities* put upon Persons of the *Highest Descent* by those of the *Meanest*'.[79] To be forewarned of the players' licentious lives was also, in a sense, to be forearmed. Retailed both by word of mouth and by printed ephemera, this peculiar knowledge of the players which spectators brought with them to the playhouse served as a temporary means of social subordination and placement, reinstating the social distinctions that their genteel performances were about to disrupt, even elide.[80]

[79] Anon., *Some Thoughts Concerning the Stage in a Letter to a Lady* (1704), 12; Anon., *The Occasional Paper: Number IX* (1698), 21.

[80] See too the recent, related discussion in J. G. Turner, *Libertines and Radicals in Early Modern London. Sexuality, Politics, and Literary Culture, 1630–1685* (Cambridge, 2002), 14ff.; T. A. King, 'The Hermaphrodite's Occupation: Theatricality and Queerness in Seventeenth- and Eighteenth-Century London', unpublished PhD dissertation, Northwestern University (1993), 258ff.

12 Rival claims to a genteel authorship

> [Of comedies] . . . the Pharisaical Pride of not being like these, warms us with pleasant Conceptions of our own Worth and Superiority over the greater Part of our Species.
>
> Anon., *Memoirs of the Life of Robert Wilks, Esq.* (1732)

This final chapter has two objectives. First, to address one further dimension of the question, why should late Stuart comedy have been preoccupied with gentility? We will trace how social positioning, and the theatre as an arena for this, was just as important to the comedy's producers as it was for its consumers. In various respects, the rhetoric of gentility was a means of validation for dramatic production. It authorized the cultural importance of playwrights and theatre managers, people who were doing their best to make a profit in an increasingly competitive but potentially lucrative field of cultural endeavour. These individuals had personal experience or, more precisely, often presented themselves and were represented by others as having first-hand knowledge of gentility's contingency. Second, the chapter will then speculate on how gentility's re-enactment conditioned both the development of comic drama and the debate over its management and purpose in the early eighteenth century. Claims for the social disinterestedness of the London stage as 'genteel' entertainment were often special pleading for the appropriation of gentility in dramatic discourse.

Gentility was often at issue for those involved in the theatre as commercial enterprise, particularly for many of the writers. More accurately, we might say that social structuration was made an issue for those scripting comedy. This much is evident from the mere existence of a good many of the texts cited below. Sustained public interest in the careers of these individuals produced biographical dictionaries and commentary, autobiographical dedications and prologues. People wanted to read what they knew (or thought they knew) about writers for the London stage because, almost without fail, the projected or perceived status of a text's producer inflected its authority and, vice versa, the text could allow for the (re)appropriation of gentility.

Just as the cultural activity of comic theatre tended to encompass social evaluation, so that activity was itself socially valued. While that valorization was subject to dispute, a dominant view was that comedy (and the larger cultural field of drama and literature) should be the province of society's elite, gentlemen in particular. The value, reception and authority of any discourse in our period were heavily conditioned by the represented status of its authors. With the advent of the age of party, texts with socio-political pretensions were especially susceptible to such social interrogation because 'gentlemen' asserted the prerogative of public voice and the 'gentry' a collective cultural hegemony. We have only to cast an eye over the authorial personae of some of the most popular periodicals of their day in order to see this principle in action: *The Tatler* was written by 'Isaac Bickerstaff Esquire'; *The Universal Spectator* penned by 'Henry Stonecastle of Northumberland, Esquire'; *The Craftsman*'s by-line read 'Caleb D'Anvers of Gray's-Inn, Esq.', and, of course, *The Gentleman's Magazine* had its 'Sylvanus Urban, of Aldermanbury, Gent.'.[1] Similarly, otherwise 'anonymous' prologues were printed as 'by a Gentleman' in playbooks. The preface to James Ralph's *Touch-Stone* commented facetiously on this link between authorial status and discursive impact by pronouncing: 'I am lineally sprang, by my Father's Side, from *Adam*'s chief Root, the Family of the *Cocks*; and, by my Mother's, from the first *Welsh Kings*: So that the Antiquity and Gentility that run in my Veins, admit of no Dispute, or Rival, in Heraldry', and so on for several more paragraphs.[2]

Naturally enough, gentility as socio-political rhetoric could also be counter-deployed. A means for refuting the position of a rival writer was to deny his (or even more problematically her[3]) status. For example, a pamphlet objecting to John Dennis's views on the state of the theatre remarked in an *ad hominem* attack: 'Thou art really an Owl, and ought to have it for thy Crest, if thou ever had'st a Coat of thy own.'[4] Siding with Dennis's adversary, Sir Richard Steele (who had initiated this particular exchange by publishing a periodical using the gentlemanly pseudonym of 'Sir John Edgar'), the writer thought it pertinent to insist that Steele was well-born, 'of a good Family', but 'preferr'd serving his Country to all the Gifts of Fortune or Birth'.[5] It did not seem to matter that the strict 'reality' of the situation otherwise rendered Steele's claim of elite status little better than Dennis's. Steele's quality was assumed by many to be ethnically compromised by his Irish upbringing, while Dennis's family were quite prominent London citizenry.

1 See too *Female Tatler*, no. 43a (12–14 October 1709), [1], for the genealogy of 'Mrs. Crackenthorpe'.

2 J. Ralph, *The Touch-Stone* (1728), x. *Italics reversed*. For a similar parody, see *Prompter*, no. ii (15 November 1734), [1–2].

3 For a complementary discussion of the intersection of status and gender for women playwrights at precisely this time, see L. A. Freeman, *Character's Theater. Genre and Identity on the Eighteenth-Century English Stage* (Philadelphia, 2002), 66–76.

4 Anon., *An Answer to a Whimsical Pamphlet, Call'd the Character of Sir John Edgar* (1720), 6–7.

5 *Ibid.*, 11.

In her dedication to *The Platonick Lady*, Susanna Centlivre played constructions of femininity and gentility against one another. In order to achieve a vestige of authority, Centlivre maintained that her work had been mistaken for that of a well-educated man when it was in fact from the pen of a well-born woman.[6] She gave priority to her status, foregrounding a calculated yet tenuous claim to pedigree, in an attempt to counter her gendered subordination:

> And why this Wrath against the Womens Works? Perhaps you'll answer, because they meddle with things out of their Sphere: But I say, no; for since the Poet is born, why not a Woman as well as a Man? Not that I wou'd derogate from those great Men who have a Genius, and Learning to improve that Genius: I only object against those ill-natur'd Criticks, who wanting both, think they have a sufficient claim to Sense, by railing at what they don't understand. Some have arm'd themselves with resolution not to like the Play they paid to see; and if in spite of Spleen they have been pleas'd against their Will, have maliciously reported it was none of mine, but given me by some Gentleman.[7]

It is also readily noticeable how dramatic commentators, especially the compilers of literary biographies, sought to reconcile the status of particular authors with their cultural achievements and popularity. For the likes of Sir John Vanbrugh, scion of an elite family and courtier, there was no compelling need to explain further the 'great deal of wit in all his Performances . . . His Dialogue is extremely easy, and well turn'd.' The reason was obvious, at least to Giles Jacob's *Poetical Register* of 1719.[8] Yet representing the life of the author behind what was steadily becoming canonical drama proved more difficult. When considering William Shakespeare, Jacob took the unusual step of vaguely citing historical documents (the text usually just stated 'the facts' categorically) and resorted to lengthy circumlocution (for instance, Shakespeare's occasional stylistic slips were excused by a lack of education which was itself due to Shakespeare senior's large number of children) in an uneasy reconciliation of superior cultural standing with a less than illustrious origin: 'His Family, as appears by the Register and publick Writings relating to that Town, were of good Figure and Fashion there, and are mention'd as Gentlemen.'[9] Clearly, Jacob was preening the feathers of the former upstart crow from Stratford-upon-Avon.

Hegemonies tend by their very nature to be self-justifying, self-perpetuating. Gentlemen were meant to dominate the cultural field of drama and literature on the basis of various rationales. For some, drama was simply an extension of the gentleman's innate superiority, his native 'wit' or born 'genius' making for

[6] C. Gallagher, *Nobody's Story. The Vanishing Acts of Women Writers in the Marketplace, 1670–1820* (Berkeley, 1994), 110ff.

[7] S. Centlivre, *Platonick Lady* (1707), dedication to 'all the *Generous Encouragers* of Female Ingenuity', sig. A2^{v}.

[8] G. Jacob, *The Poetical Register* (1719), 262. [9] *Ibid.*, 226.

refined expression to match his inherent perfection. For instance, in a laudatory preface, Charles Gildon described the chief characters of Thomas Durfey's *Marriage-Hater Match'd* in the following terms: 'The wit of Sir *Philip* and the Widow, like sprightly Blood in youthful Veins, runs through the whole Play, giving it a Noble and vigorous Life.'[10] With William Congreve's first offering for the stage, *The Old Batchelour*, the plaudits relied heavily on the rhetoric of gentility for reflexive confirmation of the work's apparent excellence. In a series of commendatory prologues printed with the first edition from 1693, Congreve was described as the 'heir' of John Dryden; likened to the gentleman steward such that 'you, too Bounteous, sow your Wit so thick'; identified as one who exercised the elite prerogative of hunting (but understand also a predatory, libertine sexuality) as he 'boldly follow[ed] on the Chase'.[11] Towards the end of our period, *The Grub Street Journal* subscribed to the idea of 'Gentlemen-Writers' amongst whom the poet 'cultivate[s] his genius'.[12] Conversely, those who ventured to gainsay the gentleman's literary ability, as the expression of an inherited generosity, were described in socially apposite language. Congreve's critics were branded 'ungenerous' and an 'ill-natured Brood', for example.[13]

Socially conditioned double standards applied to the assessment of originality as well as stylistic skill. At a time when concepts of intellectual property were hardening, identifying the sources appropriated by a particular text became increasingly important.[14] For those writers like Thomas Shadwell, identified by Gerald Langbaine's *Account of the English Dramatick Poets* as a 'gentleman', piecing together a script from earlier works of others was described in language redolent of the construction of a squire's country pile and, therefore, bore mostly positive connotations. In Langbaine's estimation, Shadwell 'builds' on a subject, 'improves the ground' or 'the foundation', and occasionally 'receives a hint'.[15] Compare the evaluation of similar cultural work by Thomas Durfey. His humbler origins are recorded in less than complimentary fashion and, by

[10] T. Durfey, *Marriage-Hater Match'd* (1692), sig. a[r].

[11] The first and third quotes come from a prologue by Thomas Southerne, the second from the pen of Bevil Higgins. All printed as front matter to W. Congreve, *Old Batchelour* (1693). See H. Weber, 'A "double Portion of his Father's Art": Congreve, Dryden, Jonson and the Drama of Theatrical Succession', *Criticism* 39, 3 (1997), 361–9.

[12] *Grub Street Journal*, no. 134 (27 July 1732), [1]. See also R. Blackmore, 'Preface to Prince Arthur, An Heroick Poem' (1695), in J. E. Spingarn (ed.), *Critical Essays of the Seventeenth Century. Volume III: 1685–1700* (Oxford, 1908), 233.

[13] These terms come from the prologue written by W. Marsh in Congreve, *Batchelour*.

[14] L. J. Rosenthal, *Playwrights and Plagiarists in Early Modern England. Gender, Authorship, Literary Property* (Ithaca, 1996).

[15] G. Langbaine, *An Account of the English Dramatick Poets* (Oxford, 1691), 442ff. See H. Love, 'Shadwell, Rochester and the Crisis of Amateurism', *Restoration: Studies in English Literary Culture, 1660–1700* 20, 2 (1996), 119–34; cf. A. Dharwadker, 'Class, Authorship, and the Social Intertexture of Genre in Restoration Theatre', *SEL* 37 (1997), 469ff.

extension, his writing is depicted in a rather different light, as 'alteration', 'borrow'd', or simply 'stoln'.[16]

For other commentators, equal emphasis was placed on the gentleman's superior and liberal (or 'generous') education, particularly his classical learning. Thus Dennis characterized Congreve as being 'of the number of those happy few, who so abound in Hereditary Possessions and in rich returns from *Greece* and from *Italy*, that you always carry some of it about you to be liberal to your Friends of that which you sell to Strangers'.[17] In a similar vein, the cultural field of literature was likened to the home of the Muses, Mount Parnassus. It was said to comprise 'estates' of gentlemen 'freeholders' who, given the associations with manual labour, preferred to describe themselves as 'poets' or 'authors' rather than as 'writers' or 'playwrights'.

When it came to the act of composing for the stage, one line of thought was that the drama served as the natural extension of the gentleman's wider authority. The 'virtuous' governor of society could employ the drama's didactic potential as a selfless and disinterested means to social orderliness and harmony.[18] On the other hand, reading, writing, and watching comedy were leisure activities which potentially detracted from the gentleman's authority and public obligations, unless, of course, they served to re-create him for the better fulfilment of social duties by promoting his own reason and refinement. Giving the 'leisure Hours of Business, and Virtue, an instructive Recreation' as Colley Cibber put it.[19] With the social implications of comedy plainly signalled by use of the term 'Degrees', *The Fine Lady's Airs* was dedicated to Sir Andrew Fontaine on the following terms:

> Amongst other Degrees of Knowledge, I have heard You express some value for Poetry; which, cou'd one imitate Your right Tast of those less profitable Sciences, who permit it but at some Seasons, as a familiar Companion to relieve more serious Thoughts, and prevent an Anxiety, which, the constant Application, You have always been inclin'd to give harder Studies, might probably draw on You, is an Amusement worthy the greatest Head-piece.[20]

[16] Langbaine, *Account*, 179ff.

[17] Dennis to Congreve [?August, 1695], in J. C. Hodges (ed.), *William Congreve. Letters & Documents* (London, 1964), 190. See also the dedication of J. Dennis, *Invader of His Country* (1720), to the duke of Newcastle.

[18] See, for instance, the opening paragraph of J. Swift, 'A Letter of Advice to a Young Poet; Together with a Proposal for the Encouragement of Poetry in This Kingdom', in H. Davis *et al.* (eds.), *The Prose Works of Jonathan Swift* (Oxford, 1948), vol. IX, 327; *British Gazetteer*, no. 122 (9 September 1727), [1].

[19] J. M. Evans (ed.), *Apology for the Life of Mr. Colley Cibber, Comedian* (New York, 1987), 262. See also third earl of Shaftesbury, 'Sensus Communis: An Essay on the Freedom of Wit and Humour in a Letter to a Friend' (1709), in P. Ayres (ed.), *Characteristicks of Men, Manners, Opinions, Times* (Oxford, 1999), vol. I, 67.

[20] T. Baker, *Fine Lady's Airs* (1708), sig. b2^{r-v}.

In the case of scripting comedy the means to authority were paradoxical. The writer adopted a pose of self-effacing modesty and studied nonchalance, asserting that the work in question was nothing more than the casual but witty musings of a gentleman retired to his country seat for all too infrequent respite from the burdens of public responsibility.[21] Yet the dilettante's retirement made for a superior and authoritative discourse, apparently removed from the faction and corruption of a wider world which included the marketplace.[22] Thus in writing the memoirs of his career, Cibber maintained that he was 'for shewing, that the Wisest, or Greatest Man, is very near an unhappy Man, if the unbending Amusements I am contending for, are not sometimes admitted to relieve him'.[23] As Dennis further explained, in terms that recall only to reject those used to describe the jealous merchant-citizen, the gentleman-poet's natural genius and its cultivation were combined with

> due Application, and that likewise includes two things, the one of which is Leisure, and the other Serenity. First, Leisure, for Poetry is of that Dignity, that it requires the whole man. And never any man writ any thing that was admirable, who had any avocations at the time that he writ it. But secondly, to succeed in Comedy requires Serenity. For a Comick Poet is obliged to put off himself, and transform himself into his several Characters; to enter into the Foibles of his several persons, and all the Recesses and secret turns of their minds, and to make their Passions, their Interests, and their Concern his own. Now how should he possibly do this, unless he is absolutely free, and undisturbed by tormenting Passions, which bind him, as it were, and if I may use that expression, chain him fast to himself.[24]

Having a play in production could prove a genteel status symbol. According to biographers of the late Stuart dramatists, a disproportionate number were young men studying at the Inns of Court who penned dramatic scripts in the hopes of obtaining preferment or simply as a means of reinforcing their own sense of social pre-eminence. As one such playwright, Thomas Baker, contended:

> There are others that run mightily upon the Gentility of the matter, and say, Poetry is scandalous to a Gentleman. I must confess, to write a sensible, witty thing, is not the Character of a modern Gentleman. But I believe such Pretenders are rather afraid Poetry shou'd grow more in Fashion, and that Writing a Play should become as Essential a Quality to compleat a Gentleman, as keeping a Mistress.[25]

21 See, for example, Samuel Johnson's verdict on Congreve in R. Montagu (ed.), *Samuel Johnson. Lives of the English Poets* (London, 1965), 251.

22 The work of Steven Shapin, on how the image of the retired country gentleman created a possible validation for scientific discourse, makes for interesting parallels. See the bibliography for further details.

23 Evans, *Apology for Cibber*, 17.

24 J. Dennis, *Comical Gallant* (1702), dedication to George Granville, Esq., unpaginated. *Italics reversed.*

25 T. Baker, *Humour of the Age* (1701), epistle dedicatory to Charles, Lord Halifax, unpaginated.

All the same, there were signs that the relationship between drama and genteel cultural hegemony was under mounting pressure.[26] The repeated rehearsal of the image of the gentleman-poet was itself an indication that status and cultural achievement were out of step. The root causes of this disruption were the increased commercialization of dramatic endeavour and gentility's persistent appropriation. As we suggested in part II, by the early eighteenth century the theatre's economy was driven less by courtly patronage and more by paying spectators and readers. Although the patron–client relationship did not disappear completely, the dramatist had increasingly to play to market demand.[27] Scripted courtly performances, plays written by (elite) individuals primarily for their social cachet, declined in relative importance compared with productions that had a profit (and professional) motive.[28] The days of Buckingham, Boyle, the Howard brothers or Sedley were on the wane. The implications of this shift were complex and not immediately resolved, but there seems little doubt that the reciprocal relationship of social position to dramatic authorship became an increasingly complicated and contested matter from about 1690. Indeed, that many writers from the Restoration seemed to have had relatively unproblematic claims on gentility was to make it all the more likely their successors, whose status was more ambiguous, would set a premium on advancing such claims themselves. William Wycherley's Dapperwit gave an early hint of this transition when he complained

'tis now no more reputation to write a Play, then it is honour to be a Knight: your true wit despises the title of Poet, as much as your true gentleman the title of Knight; for as a man may be a Knight and no Gentleman, so a man may be a Poet and no Wit, let me perish.[29]

In a broader sense the social position of the writer had always been potentially ambivalent. If writing was a work of the intellect appropriate for the well-born, as opposed to the labour of non-gentle hands, who was to say whether the successful but base-born author was not entitled to a basic social equivalence with the gentleman poet? As a contributor to *The British Journal* forthrightly put it: 'I find that writing originally, is the Work of the Mind, and consequently

[26] A. Dharwadker, 'Restoration Drama and Social Class', in S. J. Owen (ed.), *A Companion to Restoration Drama* (Oxford, 2001), 146–9.

[27] For a comprehensive treatment of these issues in relation to non-dramatic literature, see D. Griffin, *Literary Patronage in England, 1650–1800* (Cambridge, 1996). Conversely, this is not to suggest that the early Restoration theatre and its 'courtly' playwrights were totally lacking a commercial impetus, see, for example, N. K. Maguire, *Regicide and Restoration. English Tragicomedy, 1660–1671* (Cambridge, 1992), 18ff., 102ff.

[28] E. Burns, *Restoration Comedy. Crises of Desire and Identity* (London, 1987), 58, 88; P. Kewes, *Authorship and Appropriation. Writing for the Stage in England, 1660–1710* (Oxford, 1998), 12–31.

[29] W. Wycherley, *Love in a Wood* (1672), ii, 26.

a genteel Imployment.'[30] Yet the fact that the same journal was still plugging this line of thought a year later indicates the issue was undecided.[31] Those who tried to maintain a distinction between the work of 'gentlemen poets' and all 'other' writers found their task difficult. Jonathan Swift, for instance, began an essay likening those in the 'Business' of poetry to people who worked at the craft of shoe-making.[32] In the space of a few pages, however, writing becomes a 'noble Profession' more akin to the trade of a prosperous merchant and, however facetiously, Swift closed by referring to 'Gentlemen of the *Quill*'.[33] Like many doctors, lawyers and clergy, genteel and non-genteel writers were apt to meet on the common ground of professionalism if both were reasonably well remunerated. At least this is how writers of humbler origin would have it.[34] More importantly still, some individuals could use their texts, their position as writers, to fashion themselves as 'gentlemen' and 'gentlewomen' even as they sought, simultaneously, a cultural authority for their work on the basis of this very same, self-ascribed gentility.[35]

In the late Stuart period it became possible for a prominent minority of dramatists to attain a 'genteel' level of income – as it had not been in the recent past and was not for writers working mainly in the non-dramatic genres. For instance, a satire on Durfey ridiculed him by putting the following words in his mouth: 'Scarce any of my Profession have made more of the Muse, appeared in the Garb of a Gentleman, kept a privater handsome Equipage, or used better Company than my self.'[36] A satirical print seems to have made a similar mockery of Durfey's social position (see Figure 10), as perhaps had the character of D'Ogrelle in John Gay's *Wife of Bath* (1713). This change was due mainly to the institution of the author's night, playwrights receiving the takings from the performance of their new works if these ran to a third evening (sometimes a sixth and, very occasionally, a ninth). Fingers crossed, dramatists stood to earn several times the amount they might otherwise expect from a publisher for the right to print their scripts, the latter worth perhaps no more than an average of

30 *British Journal*, no. clv (4 September 1725), [1]. Similar comment may be found in *British Gazetteer*, no. 122 (9 September 1727), [1–2].

31 *British Journal*, no. ccxviii (26 November 1726), [1].

32 Swift, 'Letter of Advice to a Young Poet', compare 328, 333, 336.

33 *Ibid.*, 339–41.

34 See, for instance, George Farquhar's assumption that writing for the stage was on a par with other 'Arts and Sciences', in 'A Discourse upon Comedy, in Reference to the English Stage', in his *Love and Business* (1702), 113, 124.

35 For a pertinent case-study of these issues, centred on a polemical opponent of many of the playwrights considered here, see C. Thomas, 'Pope and His *Dunciad* Adversaries. Skirmishes on the Borders of Gentility', in J. E. Gill (ed.), *Cutting Edges. Postmodern Critical Essays on Eighteenth-Century Satire* (Tennessee Studies in Literature 37, Knoxville, 1995), 274–300.

36 Anon., *Visits from the Shades; or Dialogues, Comical and Political* (1704), 80. For similar jibes, see 'The Tryal of Skill; or a New Session of the Poets Calculated for the Meridian of Parnassus, in the Year, MDCCIV', in F. H. Ellis (ed.), *Poems on Affairs of State. Augustan Satirical Verse. Volume VI: 1697–1704* (New Haven, 1970), 684 (lines 65ff.).

10 Catalogued as ‘A Satire on a Poor Author and Poet’, *c.*1730, this print is possibly a satirical portrait of the author and playwright Thomas Durfey

£30.[37] The situation of playwrights who were also placed as theatre managers and investors was better still.[38] When Cibber surveyed the theatrical scene of the early eighteenth century he noted, for instance, the impact of opera for the rival Haymarket theatre in socially redolent terms: ‘Their Novelty, at least, was a Charm that drew vast Audiences of the fine World after them. *Swiney* their sole

[37] S. S. Kenny, ‘The Publication of Plays’, in R. D. Hume (ed.), *The London Theatre World, 1660–1800* (Carbondale, 1980), 310–11.

[38] B. S. Hammond, *Professional Imaginative Writing in England 1670–1740: ‘Hackney for Bread’* (Oxford, 1997), 49–69.

Director was prosperous, and in one Winter, a Gainer by them, of a moderate younger Brother's Fortune.'[39] Cibber himself commanded quite large sums as a playwright and made a killing from his manager's share in Drury Lane, or, as he chose to explain his situation: 'Our daily Receipts exceeded our Imagination: And we seldom met, as a Board, to settle our weekly Accounts, without the Satisfaction of Joint-Heirs, just in Possession of an unexpected Estate, that had been distantly intail'd upon them.'[40] And Tony Aston observed of Cibber's partner, the actor Thomas Doggett: 'While I travell'd with him, each Sharer kept his Horse, and was everywhere respected as a Gentleman.'[41] Theatre could be big business with unsettling social potential for those who ultimately decided what to offer genteel London in the way of comic drama.

In fact, their financial organization meant that London's patent theatres bore some similarity to the single most conspicuous commercial development of the seventeenth century, the rise of the joint-stock company. At least one disgruntled writer, who managed to get his play into print but perhaps not stage production, observed of the Drury Lane management: 'There is a kind of Unity among the *Great Ones*, to preserve the Commerce of the *Stage* to themselves, as our *Companies* in *England* do their *Trade* to *Guinea*, and the *Indies*; and that they Treat any *Upstart*, who Barters his Wit there, like an *Interloper*.'[42] Or John Oldham described the situation thus:

> You've seen what fortune other Poets share;
> View next the Factors of the Theatre:
> That constant Mart, which all the year does hold,
> Where Staple wit is barter'd, bought, and sold.[43]

As tenuous as the connection might seem, we find that the enterprise of writing and producing for the theatre could put dramatists in a social position equivalent to and no less conflicted than that of the citizen engaged in mainstream commerce.

Such parallels were not lost on writers or their contemporaries, particularly those for whom the literary marketplace was anathema.[44] Play-scripts became

39 Evans, *Apology for Cibber*, 226. 40 *Ibid.*, 261.

41 A. Aston, *A Brief Supplement to Colley Cibber Esq.; His Lives of the Late Famous Actors and Actresses* (?1747), 16.

42 W. Walker, *Marry, Or Do Worse* (1704), preface, sig. A2^{r}. Similar comparisons were made in the wake of the South Sea Bubble, *Weekly Journal*, no. 163 (13 January 1722), 978; *ibid.*, no. 170 (3 March 1722), 1018.

43 J. Oldham, 'A Satyr', in his *The Works* (1684), vol. III, 174 (lines 191–4). Oldham's analogy continues for several more stanzas.

44 For example, 'Session of the Poets' (1676), in G. de F. Lord (ed.), *Poems on Affairs of State. Volume I: 1660–1678* (New Haven, 1963), 353; Swift's sarcastic proposal that Dublin's poets should be formed into a city corporation like any other trade, 'Letter of Advice to a Young Poet', 344.

stocks to be promoted and traded;[45] illusive fictions and speculative investments whose value depended on future performance to and valuation by an audience expecting to see a novel, fashionable entertainment.[46] Hence a satire directed at the theatrical dynasty of the Cibbers included this barbed comment about posting bills to promote the plays offered by Drury Lane: 'I comply'd with his Request, and wrote them in such a *promissory Way*, (a Way which has been since call'd *Puffing*) that they engross'd the Attention of the Town.'[47] Dramatists had reputations or 'Credit' to maintain with their audience. In his preface to *Humour of the Age*, Baker complained that a

> Man that thinks, in this Age, to raise his Credit by Writing, exposes his Sense by so hazardous an Enterprize, he may as well expect to raise his Means by buying Stock when 'tis got to the highest Value; for Sense and Wit are as much out of Fashion, as Knavery and Hypocrisie are in.[48]

In a similar vein, Durfey referred to one of his comedies as an 'ill ballass'd Bark . . . [on] an Ocean where most of our Tribe too late find themselves becalm'd with uncertain Applause, or else wrack'd in the storm of ill-natur'd Criticism'.[49] Unsuccessful productions were 'empty Projects',[50] or as one prologue explained to the audience:

> Gallants! behold before your Eyes the Wight,
> Whose Actions stand accountable Tonight,
> For all your Dividends of Profit or Delight.
> New Plays resemble Bubbles, we must own,
> But their intrinsick Value soon is known:
> There's no imposing Pleasure on a Town.
> And when they fail, count o'er his Pains and Trouble,
> His Doubts, his Fears, the Poet is the Bubble.[51]

And, finally, in an image which itself trafficked in ambiguous social differentiation, Cibber questioned that 'while the Theatre is so turbulent a Sea, and so infested with Pirates, what *Poetical Merchant*, of any Substance, will venture

[45] A. Hill, *Fatal Vision* (1716), prologue.

[46] Similar arguments have recently been made for non-dramatic texts of the period by C. E. Nicholson, *Writing and the Rise of Finance. Capital Satires of the Early Eighteenth Century* (Cambridge, 1994); J. S. Peters, 'The Bank, the Press, and the "Return of Nature". On Currency, Credit, and Literary Property in the 1690s', in J. Brewer and S. Staves (eds.), *Early Modern Conceptions of Property* (London, 1995), 365–88; C. Ingrassia, *Authorship, Commerce, and Gender in Early Eighteenth-Century England. A Culture of Paper Credit* (Cambridge, 1998).

[47] [T. Cibber], *An Apology for the Life of Mr. T--------- C-----* (1740), 13.

[48] Baker, *Humour*, dedication to Lord Halifax, unpaginated.

[49] T. Durfey, *Marriage-Hater Match'd* (1692), dedication to the duke of Ormond, sig. A2^{r-v}. *Italics reversed.*

[50] C. Cibber, *Lady's Last Stake* (1708), dedication to the marquis of Kent, sig. A2^{v}.

[51] C. Cibber, *Refusal* (1721). *Italics reversed.*

to trade in it? If these valiant Gentlemen pretend to be Lovers of Plays, why will they deter *Gentlemen*, from giving them such, as are fit for Gentlemen to see?'[52]

The theatre was perceived to be lucrative despite the risks. It became something of a commonplace that the playwright

> from the favourable Success the Town has afforded him . . . may live like a Gentleman of Reputation and Credit, if he manages his stock wisely; yet he must not think this will do always, the Town have their Freaks and Vagaries, and are never long pleased with an Author; and the Muses too are slippery Jades.[53]

But no matter how successful, the low-born cultural entrepreneur remained as socially illegitimate as the merchant-citizen in terms of his status. Indeed, as both projectors and investors, some playwrights had first-hand knowledge of commercial enterprise beyond the theatre.[54] This commercial involvement could make for some odd cultural reverberations. For example, *The Tryal of Skill* began by mocking the wholesale import business of Peter Motteux, as if this was inherently detractive of his literary endeavours which were themselves profit-driven and quite attuned to variable market conditions.

Perhaps most significantly of all, the contradictory social positioning of the playwright sometimes provoked a discursive response which made use of images similar to those associated with the comedic representation of the prosperous man of commerce.[55] It is important to highlight here the simple fact that these socially freighted descriptions of particular authors were penned by individuals who themselves faced possible status inconsistency; who were themselves competing to be heard and, therefore, jockeying to claim gentility as a means of socio-cultural promotion. Thus a mock dialogue set in Hades threatened Cibber in the following terms: 'He'll bastinade your Corps with a Brimstone Ladle, that cou'd it be otherwise, after your arrival thither, you shou'd return to Earth, they might guess by the Marks he'd bestow'd upon you, you'd been only taking a trip to *Horn-Fair*.'[56] In related fashion Durfey was likened to a cuckoo for daring to assert the cultural prerogative of gentlemen, passing off their work (and its associated pedigree) for his own.[57]

Authorial representation, or self-promotion, even extended to the rather dubious rebuttal of images associated with 'mercenary' (but highly successful) hacks like that used to dismiss Cibber just quoted. Hence Congreve's claim of gentility was complemented by his representation as the virile, full-blooded lover in

52 Evans, *Apology for Cibber*, 104. *Emphasis added.* 53 Anon., *Visits from the Shades*, 80–1.

54 See, for example, Richard Steele's business proposal, *An Account of the Fish-Pool* (1718). The dedication to Sir John Ward, then the Lord Mayor of London, redacts many of the ideas at issue in *Conscious Lovers* (1723).

55 S. Shepherd and P. Womack, *English Drama. A Cultural History* (Oxford, 1996), 136–9.

56 Anon., *Visits from the Shades*, 23–4. 57 Langbaine, *Account*, 179.

place of the feeble husband who risked cuckoldry. One of the prologues printed with *The Old Batchelour* suggested

> MOST Authors on the Stage at first appear
> Like Widows-Bridegrooms, full of Doubt and Fear:
> They Judge from the Experience of the Dame,
> How hard a Task it is to quench her Flame:
> . . .
> With utmost Rage from her Embraces thrown,
> Remains convicted, as an empty Drone.
> Thus often, to his Shame, a pert Beginner
> Proves in the end, a miserable Sinner.
>
> As for our Youngster, I am apt to doubt him:
> With all the Vigour of his Youth about him:
> But he, more Sanguine, trusts in one and twenty,
> And impudently hopes he shall content you:
> For tho' his Batchelour be worn and cold,
> He thinks the Young may club to help the Old.[58]

In a not unrelated manner, William Taverner prefaced *The Maid the Mistress* with a comment that refused the profit motive of other writers. Likening the Muses to domineering viragos reminiscent of City wives, or the cit's tempestuous Lady Credit, he instead compared himself to the swaggering gentleman-libertine born with certain prerogatives:

> I am not so Muse-ridden as to suffer any Trifle of this Nature to encroach on my Profession, and tho' Poetry (the Delight and Ornament of the greatest Men in all Ages) shall continue my darling Mistress, my Intention is never to wed her. Interest forbids the Banes [*sic*]. As I never design to bring again on the Stage any more of my scribling, I add not Asseverations which always carry with them an Air rather of Passion than Reason.[59]

Evidently William Burnaby did not have as much confidence in the socio-cultural superiority of the comic playwright, believing his target audience, the Town, was a 'Mrs. that grants her Favours from Humour and her fine Play, is often like her fine Gentleman, a Thing without Wit or Design'.[60]

The very need to engage with this particular set of associations, an engagement repeated by the prologues for both *The Double-Dealer* and *Way of the World* in the case of Congreve, suggests that the status of even a prominent writer was not beyond dispute. Those with the slightest claim to be of pedigree used their superior status (and its positive combination with the images we discussed earlier) as a means to enhance their work's value. Denying their own

[58] See n. 11, 'By an unknown Hand'.
[59] W. Taverner, *Maid the Mistress* (1708), 'To the Reader', unpaginated.
[60] W. Burnaby, *Modish Husband* (1702), preface, unpaginated. *Italics reversed.*

involvement in the marketplace, even as they dismissed other writers as common 'scribblers' and simple 'hacks' who sold their skills for a living, gentility was a means to 'authorial empowerment'.[61] The son of a younger brother of Staffordshire gentry stock, Congreve was reported by the French writer Voltaire to have had

> one Defect, which was, his entertaining too mean an Idea of his first Profession, (that of a Writer) tho' 'twas to this he ow'd his Fame and Fortune. He spoke of his Works as of Trifles that were beneath him; and hinted to me in our first Conversation, that I should visit him upon no other Foot than that of a Gentleman, who led a Life of Plainness and Simplicity. I answer'd, that had he been so unfortunate as to be a mere Gentleman I should never have come to see him; and I was very much disgusted at so unseasonable a Piece of Vanity.[62]

In other words, Congreve sought to present himself as born to a social position above relations of exchange. This despite the fact he had inherited no landed estate and relied on income from his pen, shares in the Lincoln's Inn and Haymarket theatres received as payment for his play-scripts, proceeds from the sale of his collected *Works*, investments in the main public stocks of the day and the salaries of several government commissions.[63] At least one critic, one rival voice, feigned disbelief at Congreve's claims for the genteel authority of his work and did so by bathetically comparing the author to one of his characters, the 'Wittol of Wittol-Hall', a willing or naive cuckold.[64] It did not seem to matter that Congreve never married. The author went on to dismiss Congreve as a mercenary hack and to conflate social with literary miscegenation. Congreve's originality was impugned as much as his status.[65] However, this particular satire also makes plain both the contingency of lineage as impersonation and the diverse, even contradictory ways the drama was embroiled in elite social structuration.[66] For as we shall see below, it was just as easy for this attack on Congreve to *accept* the dramatist's claim to be well-born and thereby open the

61 The phrase 'authorial empowerment' is borrowed from Gallagher, *Nobody's Story*, 34.

62 The comment was made *c.*1726 and is cited from Hodges, *Letters*, 242–3. It appeared originally in *Letters concerning the English Nation by M. de Voltaire* (1733); D. F. McKenzie has recently disputed the statement's significance in '*Mea Culpa*: Voltaire's Retraction of His Comments Critical of Congreve', *RES* 49, 196 (1998), 462. Whilst this essay presents a meticulously supported argument for Voltaire's later retraction of his judgement of Congreve as vain, McKenzie is some way from showing that Congreve never made the initial remark concerning his gentility.

63 Cibber's *Apology* suggests Congreve was offered shares in Lincoln's Inn Fields as payment for *Love for Love*, Evans, *Apology for Cibber*, 115ff.; Hodges, *Letters*, 118, 132, 135.

64 [G. Powell], *Animadversions on Mr. Congreve's Late Answer to Mr. Collier in a Dialogue between Mr. Smith and Mr. Johnson* (1698), 1. *Italics reversed.*

65 *Ibid.*, 9–10ff.

66 For an intriguing reversal comparing the poet to the mistress of both cit and fop, see the epilogue to Nathaniel Lee's *Theodosius* (1680) cited in A. Masters (ed. S. Trussler), *The Play of Personality in the Restoration Theatre* (Woodbridge, 1992), 19.

way for Congreve to be mocked as a failure of gentility in a different way: to brand him a 'fop'.[67]

Bearing in mind our earlier argument that the fop could be used to comment reflexively on the drama's role in constructing gentility, we should not be too surprised to find several comedies which feature foppish gentlemen with pretensions to authorship and a genteel hegemony. Hence D'Ogrelle (or Doggrell), the beau from Gay's *Wife of Bath*, is portrayed as writing 'only for his Diversion, nay, he pays the Bookseller for printing his Works, – and writes the most like a Gentleman of any Man on this side [of] *Parnassus*'.[68] Likewise the foppish Count Insolls in Mary Pix's *Deceiver Deceived* pronounces, 'I write like a man of Quality, to please my self' – and so on.[69] Samuel Johnson condemned Congreve's similar comment to Voltaire, Congreve's insistence that he was of genteel birth and wrote only for his own pleasure, as 'despicible foppery'.[70] And if the satirist who mocked Congreve as a wittol did not explicitly brand the author as 'fop', he certainly pictured Congreve behaving like one. Thus it was maintained that Congreve liked to 'stay and Ogle his Dear *Bracilla*, with sneaking looks under his Hat, in the little side Box' at the playhouse.[71] 'Bracilla' was the actress Anne Bracegirdle with whom Congreve was linked romantically, making him like the other gullible beaux we discussed in the previous chapter. Some understanding of how dramatic discourse might contribute to the impersonation of gentility was evinced by the accompanying accusation that although Congreve's lineage might be rhetorically pure, it was not ethnically so. Pouncing on the rumour that he was of Irish heritage rather than a cadet of lesser Midland gentry, Congreve's detractor sniped that he 'has been regenerated ever since he turn'd Poet, and his *Muse* has had a new *Birth* too . . . What Miracle has made him a *Staffordshire Man*, I know not, but I'm sure his *Muse*, for all his fine Flights, is but a *Bogtrotter still*.'[72]

The depiction of Congreve seated among the gentlemen-beaux spectators at the playhouse starts to bring us full circle. From suggesting a further reason why late Stuart comic drama could engage so knowingly with problems of elite social structuration (personal experience and its cultural expression), we return to the interrelated issues of how the theatre was understood to influence, and

[67] The epilogue to T. Scott, *Unhappy Kindness* (1697) also juxtaposes the poet with both the cit and the beau. More generally, the same kind of social 'double-think' is at work in a poem by John Dunton, 'The Beggar Mounted'. A satire on some 'Mushrome Gentlemen', the poem begins by riding these men as base-born 'mounted cits'. However incongruously, it can also imagine some of them as fops after they 'boast their *Birth*, and *High Descent*'. See J. Dunton, *Athenianism* (1710), 304, 312.

[68] J. Gay, *Wife of Bath* (1713), i, 11. See also the remarks of Sir Vanity Halfwit in J. Leigh, *Kensington Gardens* (1720), iv, 65.

[69] M. Pix, *Deceiver Deceived* (1698), ii, 15.

[70] Montagu, *Samuel Johnson*, 257.

[71] [Powell], *Animadversions*, 'Preface to the Reader', sig. *a* 4^{v}. *Italics reversed.*

[72] *Ibid.*, 3. (Dialogue attributions have been omitted.)

could be influenced by, the identification of society's elite. Different stances on these issues meant that supporters of early eighteenth-century drama were divided in their understanding of the nature and regulation of comedy, their aesthetic concerns socially conditioned.

Those who supported the basic institution of the stage (as distinct from those like Jeremy Collier for whom contemporary theatre, despite denials to the contrary, had virtually no redemptive features or possibilities) were quite consistent in their arguments that theatre be of a didactic strain, subscribing to variations on the Horatian commonplace that the comic drama's basic function was to instruct and delight. Whilst prepared to concede there had been times when the theatre overstepped the bounds of propriety, they retained faith in the moral potential of comedy and considered that past lapses could be remedied to public benefit. However, the theatre's proponents squabbled over how comic theatre was to achieve its mission of edification and who should superintend it. This in-fighting invariably returned to the deeper question of the theatre's social potential, the drama's ability to present a particular (re)vision of society.

Almost as much as the wider breach concerning the theatre's immorality, debate amongst the drama's supporters serves to demonstrate that there was more at stake than either a moral direction, generic propriety, or stylistic nicety. In other words, agreement over the basic form and function of comedy was often fractured by underlying differences concerning the nature of society's elite and who should manage its suitably varied delineation on London's stages.

Turning first of all to the issue of control. On one level the matter was quite simple. There was basic accord concerning the type of person who should ideally oversee London's theatres. Yet, paradoxically, the very existence of such consensus tells us a great deal about why management of the theatre was so hotly disputed. Agreement that 'gentlemen' should regulate the stage was a sure sign that its power to present a particular view of society's most powerful was being contested.

If promoters of the theatre offered ways to reform the theatre, a common absence from these proposals was any direct appeal to the Crown, even though it was the Crown that had final authority over the playhouses as licenser.[73] Instead the stage was consistently identified as property and, to the improvers at least, a particular kind of property, that is, real estate. Figured as such, it was deemed only natural that the drama be placed in the 'disinterested' hands of 'Men of quality', gentlemen, rather than the acquisitive and vulgar clutches of playwrights, actor-managers, or those 'insolent Fellows' as one periodical essay haughtily dismissed them.[74] The latter were to be subordinated as 'tenants' and

[73] M. J. Kinservik, 'Theatrical Regulation during the Restoration Period', in S. J. Owen (ed.), *A Companion to Restoration Drama* (Oxford, 2001), 36–52.

[74] *British Journal*, no. ccxviii (26 November 1726), [1].

'agents'; they were described at best as mere stewards, or, at worst, if one agreed with Dennis, as the 'Rabble and Scum of *Parnassus*' who 'oppress or demolish all whom God and Nature have plac'd above them'.[75] Dennis was here making exaggerated use of social insubordination (and then degradation) to protest, in part, the commercialization of dramatic endeavour which we have already discussed.

If further justification for this intervention in and restructuring of the stage's management was advanced, its key terms are predictable. The theatre's new governors would have the 'Genius', 'Generosity', and 'inborn, and ingenuous Disposition' to see to it that the theatre was presenting the 'right' kind of entertainment.[76] Suitable, socially inflected regulation would make for the theatre's '*Political* Use', as a later essay phrased it.[77] In one sense, regulation would mean the moral and judicious – 'politic' – use of the drama. In another, regulation would allow for correction of the stage's social vision such that society's ordering of power – the 'political' – would appear as natural action and not an ideological act. In this theatre the '*Gentleman*, the *Soldier*, and the *Patriot*, are inspir'd with *Sentiments* . . . productive of Blessings to the People, they are born to *act for*'.[78] If the theatre proved a powerful but unstable site for the enactment of gentility, the discourse of theatre reform could also deploy gentility in a tautological attempt at both acquiring and justifying control of this cultural arena. Arguments which appear to be made from a position of unimpeachable social superiority serve to underscore the fact that it was precisely this dominance which was so often being contested within the theatre. Hence the influential (and possibly lucrative) representation of gentility could only be entrusted, it was often argued, to 'gentlemen'.[79]

There were both winners and losers in this early eighteenth-century contest for the theatre. The most prominent among the former was probably the early Georgian manager of Drury Lane, Richard Steele (in association with the acting trio of Cibber, Wilks and Booth). Surely the most vocal among the latter was John Dennis. For all that they would appear to have had in

[75] [Powell], *Animadversions*, 79–80; J. Dennis, 'Remarks on a Play, Call'd the Conscious Lovers, a Comedy' (1723), in E. N. Hooker (ed.), *The Critical Works of John Dennis* (Baltimore, 1943), vol. II, 251. The idea that the Restoration theatre had been managed by 'gentlemen', but by the early eighteenth century had fallen into the sordid 'Hands of Players', was a constant theme of Dennis's. See also his 'The Causes of the Decay and Defects of Dramatick Poetry, And of the Degeneracy of the Publick Tast[e]' (?1725), in Hooker, vol. II, 277; [L. Milbourne], *A Letter to A. H. Esq. Concerning the Stage* (1698), 2.

[76] *Weekly Register* (5 February 1732), reproduced in J. Loftis (ed.), *Essays on the Theatre from Eighteenth-Century Periodicals* (Los Angeles, 1960), 48–9, 53. Similar terms are used in Anon., *A Letter to My Lord ******* on the Present Diversions of the Town* (1725), 11.

[77] *Prompter*, no. xxxviii (21 March 1735), [1]. [78] *Ibid.*

[79] Instructive parallels might be drawn here with the contest to control print publication during the later seventeenth century as explored by A. Johns, *The Nature of the Book. Print and Knowledge in the Making* (Chicago, 1998), 307–13.

common (upper-middling social origins, educational background, broadly similar political loyalties), these two men engaged in a heated and often very personal dispute concerning the purpose and nature of comedy. Their creative differences were fuelled by opposing views on what the drama's role – if any – should be in relation to the structuring of society.[80] Debate centred on their competing assessments of Etherege's *Man of Mode* (1676), and, subsequently, Steele's own *Conscious Lovers* (1723). As we saw in chapter 1, much has been claimed for Steele in respect of a novel social and moral direction for early eighteenth-century theatre. If his ideas did not always supersede comedic conventions when they went into production, Steele continued to promote several points of his departure from theories of comedy which were in keeping with the 'establishment' views of Dennis. Or, more accurately perhaps, Steele took these theories to new heights, in a dubious socio-ideological direction as far as his most strident critic was concerned.

His vitriol aside, Dennis's essays suggest that his views on comedy were at once conservative and widely shared. As Dennis saw it, Collier's arguments, when taken with several grains of salt, were basically correct. Comic drama had a moral mission. From Dennis's point of view, that mission might best be termed disciplinary. Comedy was to correct society's vices and follies by means of derision: 'But can any Thing but corrupt and degenerate Nature be the proper Subject of Ridicule? And can any Thing but Ridicule be the proper Subject of Comedy?'[81] In subscribing to an essentially Hobbesian theory of humour, Dennis hinted that the principal targets of comedy should be plainly non-gentle, or vulgar. For example, in the dedicatory preface to *The Comical Gallant* (1702) he maintained that 'Humour is more to be found in low Characters, than among Persons of a higher Rank, and consequently that low Characters are more proper for Comedy than high.'[82] Unlike Collier, Dennis did not mean that gentle individuals should necessarily be excluded from dramatic representation altogether. There is, however, the strong implication that genteel characters should be presented mainly as the ridiculers (making witty remarks on the foibles of their social inferiors) and that any mocking of elite characters must not be directed at their superiority *per se* (in the way that the baseness of common folk was a legitimate means to mirth).

By comparison, Steele's views on the nature and function of comedy could be labelled exhortative. He considered that comedy should be used positively and have the 'Effect of Example and Precept': be employed to encourage 'virtue'

80 For a reading of their debate broadly sympathetic to the one offered here, but appearing after this chapter was drafted, see Freeman, *Character's Theater*, 203ff.

81 J. Dennis, 'A Defence of Sir Fopling Flutter, a Comedy Written by Sir George Etheridge' (1722), in Hooker, *Critical Works*, vol. II, 243.

82 Dennis, *Comical Gallant*, dedication, unpaginated. *Italics reversed.*

rather than present salacious satire of often dubious effect.[83] As Dennis had already countered: 'How little do they know of the Nature of true Comedy, who believe that its proper Business is to set us Patterns for Imitation: For all such Patterns are serious Things, and Laughter is the Life, and the very Soul of Comedy.'[84] In Steele's mind the comic drama's social targets were society's leaders, those who should be setting an example as its governors. Of course, the next question was who were the elite, the 'virtuous' whom comedy was meant to instruct? As we saw earlier, Steele's pat response was the 'gentry'.[85] Yet all the while, more radical social side-effects were latent. In Steele's case the applicability of generous language might be widened to include the virtuous merchant, the theatre employed as an influential ideological platform for a (re)construction of gentility that placed new, positive stress on virtue rather than birth. Arguably it was these side-effects which made Steele's views, and their exposition in *The Conscious Lovers*, a bitter pill for Dennis to swallow. Hence, in an oblique remark aimed at Steele and Drury Lane after *The Conscious Lovers*' debut, Dennis wrote of 'vile Wretches . . . arrived to such a Height of Impudence as to pretend to teach Virtue to the rest of the World'.[86]

Yet Dennis could not know of this success when he first crossed swords with Steele in the early 1710s because Steele's exemplary comedy had yet to go into production. Instead, Dennis criticized Steele on the basis of two *Spectator* essays that were themselves critiques of *The Man of Mode; or Sir Fopling Flutter* and, implicitly, presentations of how Steele planned to do things differently.[87] On the face of it, Steele objected to Etherege's classic piece because it glamorized the absence of virtuous behaviour in two gentleman-characters, the rakish Dorimant and the foppish knight of the play's subtitle. But for those familiar with Steele's politics, his remarks were clearly more far-reaching. Steele was suggesting that 'vicious' behaviour should not be left uncriticized, even be lauded, on the basis of a prior claim to superior status (lineage). Steele later put this argument from superiority into the mouth of *The Conscious Lovers*' gentleman patriarch, Sir John Bevil ('What might injure a Citizen's Credit, may be no Stain to a Gentleman's Honour'), in order to negate it.[88] By maintaining instead that the honour of a gentleman should indeed be virtuous, Steele could then broach the notion of the virtuous but humbly born being gentle. The end result was that lineage surrendered its primacy to virtue in early modern social calculus, or, as Steele articulated in the conclusion to his review of *Sir Fopling*

[83] R. Steele, *Conscious Lovers* (1723), preface, unpaginated.
[84] Dennis, 'Fopling Flutter', in Hooker, *Critical Works*, vol. II, 245.
[85] See *Tatler*, no. 8 (28 April 1709), vol. I, 73–4.
[86] Dennis, 'Remarks on Conscious Lovers', in Hooker, *Critical Works*, vol. II, 255.
[87] *Spectator*, no. 65 (15 May 1711), vol. I, 278–80; *ibid.*, no. 75 (26 May 1711), vol. I, 322–5.
[88] Steele, *Conscious Lovers*, iv, 62.

Flutter: 'What I would . . . contend for is, that the more Virtuous the Man is, the nearer he will naturally be to the Character of Gentile and Agreeable.'[89]

At this juncture, we should pause to emphasize what Steele was not suggesting in either his essays or his comedy. We should not think that birth became totally irrelevant or that virtue was entirely synonymous with behaving morally. We have seen time and again that 'virtue' had as much to do with the governing of society and, as the master-stroke in Steele's reconfiguration of gentility, opened the way to a legitimate claim for power on behalf of a prominent minority whom we would describe sociologically as urban, upper-middling. It was his appropriation of the socio-political rhetoric of gentility and the manipulation of established comedic convention to this end that was objected to by Steele's critics, Dennis foremost among them.

In contrast, Dennis's counter-arguments took social precedence on the basis of degree for granted. Etherege's comedy was acceptable to Dennis because he interpreted it as portraying the 'fine gentleman' *qua* gentleman. As far as Dennis was concerned, *Sir Fopling Flutter*'s didacticism went no further than criticizing the gentleman's more extreme 'finery' and did not seek to ask the more searching question of 'who then was the gentleman?' In any event, Dennis's less than forthcoming definition of gentility, as nothing more than refined manners, implicitly removed all such interrogation from the comedy's agenda and denied the theatre a place in processes of social structuration: 'I appeal to every impartial Man, if when he says, that a Man or a Woman are genteel, he means any Thing more, than that they are agreeable in their Air, graceful in their Motions, and polite in their Conversation.'[90] If 'degenerate Nature' was the proper target of comedy, generate Nature, 'all whom God and Nature have placed above them' (that is, above the common people), was strictly off-limits.[91]

The Conscious Lovers was preoccupied with the work of reconfiguring gentility, rehearsing new takes on Dorimant and Sir Fopling. When Dennis finally reviewed the long-awaited premiere, his criticisms were fairly predictable. He attempted to skirt the crucial issue of gentility as impersonation on the basis that there was such a thing as a naturally manifest superiority, an inherent and self-evident elite identity. In terms very reminiscent of another review which we examined closely in chapter 9, Dennis dismissed Steele's foppish character, Cimberton, as 'so very monstrous, that one would not think he could be produced by any thing that had human Shape, and for the Credit of Human Nature ought, like a *Sooterkin*, to be demolished as soon as he appears'.[92] In more muted fashion, the 'virtuous' character of the play's young gentleman

89 *Spectator*, no. 75 (26 May 1711), vol. I, 325.
90 Dennis, 'Fopling Flutter', in Hooker, *Critical Works*, vol. II, 244.
91 See the preceding notes for these quotes from Dennis.
92 Dennis, 'Remarks on Conscious Lovers', in Hooker, *Critical Works*, vol. II, 273.

(who refuses to be ruled by the passions of either blood-honour or self-interest) was rejected as 'made up of Qualities' – one thinks immediately of the alleged, singular 'quality' of the well-born gentleman – 'incoherent and contradictory'.[93]

Ultimately, however, Steele could not be quite so different when it came to his citizen, Mr Sealand. Steele left it more of an open question whether his merchant was a 'gentleman' than either he planned or his critics anticipated. Perhaps the laughing genre could be pushed only so far before it ceased to be comedy and, in that sense, was not as suitable for an unequivocal revisioning of elite society as Steele had once designed. Arguably the broader implications of his reconfiguring of gentility and their positive enactment had to wait another decade to be presented, in 1731, in the form of George Lillo's tragedy, *The London Merchant*.[94] For the informed late Stuart theatregoer well knew that the more elite (in all senses of the word) cultural province was not comedy but tragedy.

93 *Ibid.*, 272.

94 Even then the situation was not necessarily straightforward, see Freeman, *Character's Theater*, 113–22.

Afterword
Some consequences for early modern studies

That both Steele and Dennis should debate the theatre's socio-political potential with reference to the institution's own past is one final indication of gentility's mutability throughout the early modern period. So complex (and incomplete) was gentility's construction that, in one sense, the preceding chapters amount only to a case-study of how elite social structuration worked in a particular time and place, within a certain discourse. Yet this study can claim a broader importance in relation to early modern textual criticism and socio-cultural history.

Turning to textual criticism first of all. Characters from the comic stage obviously found their way into other genres and these texts were also concerned with issues and problems of social ordering. The conclusions of the present book suggest fresh possibilities in our reading of other narratives and their particular themes. For instance, the novelty of Defoe's *Moll Flanders* (in terms of its representation of genteel womanhood) might be revisited with regard to its representation of both gentility and gender. For the tale also comprehends the narrative of another citizen's cuckolding.[1] Our understanding of pictorial satire might be similarly refined, the smaller details of the social politics of print filled in. There would seem to be as yet unremarked shades of meaning in the graphic representation of the beau, for example.[2] In terms of the drama itself, it is clear that the comedy's producers were conscious of working within a particular tradition. While some modern commentators might adjudge many late Stuart play-scripts inferior, their study can only improve our understanding of more canonical works from both the Renaissance and the early Restoration. This is because the characters and plot-lines of late Stuart comedy were themselves interpretations of these earlier plays. In an important sense Sir Novelty Fashion captured something of Colley Cibber's reading of Sir Fopling Flutter, for example. Adopting an even broader view, knowing more about the early eighteenth-century playhouse as a socio-cultural institution contributes

[1] Cf. M. Shinagel, *Daniel Defoe and Middle-Class Gentility* (Cambridge, MA, 1968). See Moll's relationship with the City banker in D. Defoe, *The Fortunes and Misfortunes of the Famous Moll Flanders* (Wordsworth edition, Ware, 1993), 130–85.

[2] Cf. M. Hallett, *The Spectacle of Difference. Graphic Satire in the Age of Hogarth* (New Haven, 1999), 169–95.

to a greater understanding of how the theatre itself functioned as metaphor. If Londoners persisted in their opinion that all their world was a stage, why was this so?

The historiographical implications require a little more explanation. Contemporaries were themselves adamant that the seasonal visit to the London playhouses was exceptional when compared to their more circumscribed existence in the provinces. Yet the capital's theatre was also an exemplar. Even if it refracted the workings of elite society to the point of satirical oversimplification, its study attunes us to the intricacies of those workings in contexts where such magnification is not so readily available. It sharpens our perception of elite composition and its change over time.

By the same token, it no longer seems possible to trace an absolute progression in the ideological fortunes of 'the gentry' and 'their gentility' – to claim that gentility ceased to be a matter of lineage in favour of a turn to practised gestures and refined speech, or that 'the gentry' was a more (or less) open group at a given time. Lineage was itself always a matter of culture, gentility forever susceptible to appropriation as a result. Certainly there were discernible shifts of emphasis and degrees of tractability, depending on the precise context in which people negotiated gentility as a continual process of definition and domination. And we can readily concede that this process was usually far more contingent and unstable in an urban environment. Clearly there were individuals in society whose gentility was, by contrast, more unassuming and ostensibly unassailable. Numerous traces, from stately country houses to witty genteel characters in comedy who are neither fops nor cuckolds, suggest as much. Visits to estate muniments will therefore continue to yield vital insight into the histories of elite individuals from the early modern period. But like some innovative recent work, which is itself based on this more conventional kind of archival research,[3] the foregoing study has argued that the history of these people and their society was more nuanced and dynamic than we have assumed. Beyond the staid walls of the country pile, gentry hegemony was conditional upon, and conditioned by, all kinds of interactions and influences. And we must realize that this domination was by no means as static or self-assured as it might first seem, even within manorial precincts. It required constant impersonation.

Going behind the scenes to focus on moments when the delineation of social superiority faltered should prompt us to be more critical of those times when things seemed all right on the night, when gentility's performance appeared flawless. We have concentrated on representations of the failure or complication of that enactment. The apposition of a Sir Solomon Sadlife and a Sir Harry Wildair, the plainly dressed citizen and the richly attired beau, may stand as

[3] Especially S. E. Whyman, *Sociability and Power in Late-Stuart England. The Cultural World of the Verneys 1660–1720* (Oxford, 1999).

synecdoche for this new-found complexity. Once viewed as the embodiment of the upwardly mobile middling sort mindlessly emulating the 'cult(ure) of gentility', the beau character now reads more like a response to the persistent appropriation of that culture to diverse ends. At the same time, the cit's urbane-but-middling position in that process is far less certain. A position frequently taken for granted in order to argue for change and crises in other relationships of power (gender, sexuality and, to a lesser extent, nationality or ethnicity), we need to be aware of how the latter may have been impacted by questions of status. More importantly still, genteel domination was neither inert nor a foregone conclusion; middling assimilation into a newly cosmopolitan elite was far from seamless.[4] It could not and should not be taken for granted and, in the shorter term at least, was a far from easy or terminal process of social realignment. Nor did the socio-cultural initiative always run one way. However inadvertently, scholarly talk of emulation and gentrification implies that one group, the 'gentle' landowners, took the lead while an urban elite had either to accept or reject this ultimate prominence.[5] This risks missing the contingency masked by the broad yet superficial continuity of generous language. Its hegemonic sway was undeniable. Yet this made gentility not an exclusive property but, instead, the subject of ceaseless negotiation and contest, agency and innovation, by those who would be gentle. The notion of socio-cultural consensus by mere assimilation ignores the loud, sometimes nervous laughter of those perched in box-seats getting their crown's-worth of both cit and fop.

[4] See H. R. French, 'The Search for the "Middle Sort of People" in England, 1600–1800', *Historical Journal* 43, 2 (2000), 277–93; French, 'Social Status, Localism and the "Middle Sort of People" in England 1620–1750', *PP* 166 (2000), 66–99; P. Clark, *British Clubs and Societies 1580–1800. The Origins of an Associational World* (Oxford, 2000), 155ff.

[5] For instance, cf. P. Borsay, *The English Urban Renaissance. Culture and Society in the Provincial Town, 1660–1770* (Oxford, 1989), esp. 202ff.; D. Wahrman, 'National Society, Communal Culture: An Argument about the Recent Historiography of Eighteenth-Century Britain', *Social History* 17, 1 (1992), 43–72.

Bibliography

PRIMARY MATERIAL

(*Note: place of publication is London unless stated otherwise.*)

MANUSCRIPTS

Beinecke Library, Yale University

Disney, J., 'The Institution of the Gentleman In a Letter to a Young Gentleman upon his remove from Cambridge to the Temple', *c.*1699, Essays, Osborn Shelves b 346.

British Library, London

Blenheim Papers, vol. CCCLVI, Add. MS 61,456.

Lyddell, D., 'Diary', 1706, Add. MS 74,642.

North, (Family of), 'Correspondence', Add. MS 32,500.

Southwell, R., 'A Diary of some things fitt to be remembered, May, 1674', Egerton MS, 1,633.

Folger Shakespeare Library, Washington, DC

Nicholas, J., Almanac diaries and accounts for 1668 and 1674, V.a.419–20.

Rich, (Family of), Papers, MS X.d.451 (136).

Houghton Library, Harvard University

'Copyright agreement between Richard Steele and Jacob Tonson for The Conscious Lovers', ?1722, fMS Eng 760(19).

PLAYS

Addison, J., *The Drummer* (1716).

Anon., *The Apparition* (1714).

Anon., *The Cornish Comedy* (1696).

Anon., *The Factious Cit* (1685).

Anon., *Injur'd Love; or the Lady's Satisfaction* (1711).

Anon., *The Woman Turn'd Bully* (1675).

Baker, T., *The Fine Lady's Airs* (1708).

Hampstead Heath (1706).

The Humour of the Age (1701).

Tunbridge-Walks (1703).

Bancroft, J., *Henry the Second* (1693).
[Beaumont, F., and J. Fletcher], *The Beggars Bush; or the Royal Merchant* (1661).
Beckingham, C., *Scipio Africanus* (1718).
Behn, A., *The City-Heiress* (1682).
The Debauchee (1677).
The False Count (1681).
The Luckey Chance (1687).
The Revenge (1680).
The Roundheads (1682).
Sir Patient Fancy (1678).
The Town-Fopp (1677).
Betterton, T., *The Amorous Widow* (1729).
Bourne, R., *The Contented Cuckold* (1692).
[Bowes, G.], *Love the Leveller* (1704).
Boyer, A., *Achilles* (1700).
Brome, R., *The City Wit* (1653).
The Madd Couple Well Matcht (1653).
Bullock, C., *Woman is a Riddle* (1717).
The Per-juror (1717).
Burnaby, W., *The Modish Husband* (1702).
The Reform'd Wife (1700).
Carlile, J., *The Fortune-Hunters* (1689).
Centlivre, S., *The Artifice* (1723).
The Basset-Table (1706).
The Beau's Duel (1702).
A Bold Stroke for a Wife (1718; 1737 edition).
The Man's Bewitch'd (1709).
Mar-Plot (1711).
The Perplex'd Lovers (1712).
The Platonick Lady (1707).
The Wonder (1714).
[Chapman, G., J. Marston and B. Jonson], *Eastward-Hoe* (1605).
Chaves, A., *The Cares of Love* (1705).
[Chetwood, W. R.], *The Stock-Jobbers* (1720).
Cibber, C., *The Careless Husband* (1705).
The Double Gallant (1707).
The Lady's Last Stake (1708).
Love's Last Shift (1696).
The Non-Juror (1718).
The Refusal (1721).
Woman's Wit (1697).
Xerxes (1699).
Congreve, W., *The Double-Dealer* (1694).
Love for Love (1695).
The Old Batchelour (1693).
The Way of the World (1700).
Cowley, A., *The Cutter of Coleman Street* (1663).

Crawfurd, D., *Courtship à la Mode* (1700).
Love at First Sight (1704).
Crowne, J., *City Politiques* (1683).
Darius King of Persia (1688).
The English Frier (1690).
Henry VI, Part i (1681).
The Married Beau (1694).
Sir Courtly Nice (1685).
Dennis, J., *Appius and Virginia* (1709).
The Comical Gallant (1702).
The Invader of His Country (1720).
A Plot, and No Plot (1697).
Dilke, T., *The City Lady* (1697).
The Lover's Luck (1696).
The Pretenders (1698).
Doggett, T., *The Country-Wake* (1696).
Drake, J., *The Sham-Lawyer* (1697).
Dryden, J., *Cleomenes* (1692).
The Kind Keeper (1680).
The Wild Gallant (1669).
Dryden, jr., J., *The Husband His Own Cuckold* (1696).
Durfey, T., *The Campaigners* (1698).
Love for Money (1691).
The Marriage-Hater Match'd (1692).
The Modern Prophets (1709).
The Old Mode and the New (1703).
The Richmond Heiress (1693).
The Rise and Fall of Massaniello. Part I (1700).
The Royalist (1682).
Estcourt, R., *The Fair Example* (1706).
Etherege, G., *The Man of Mode* (1676).
She Wou'd If She Cou'd (1671).
Farquhar, G., *The Constant Couple* (1700).
Love and a Bottle (1699).
Sir Harry Wildair (1701).
Gay, J., *The Wife of Bath* (1713).
Gildon, C., *Love's Victim* (1701).
The Roman Brides Revenge (1697).
Granville, G., *The She-Gallants* (1696).
Haywood, E., *A Wife To Be Lett* (1724).
Higden, H., *The Wary Widdow* (1693).
Hill, A., *The Fatal Vision* (1716).
Howard, R., *The Committee* (1665).
Johnson, C., *The Country Lasses* (1715).
The Female Fortune Teller (1726).
The Generous Husband (1713).
The Gentleman Cully (1702).

The Victim (1714).
The Wife's Relief (1712).
Leanerd, J., *The Country Innocence* (1677).
The Rambling Justice (1678).
Lee, N., *Rival Queens* (1677).
Leigh, J., *Kensington Gardens* (1720).
Manley, M., *The Lost Lover* (1696).
Manning, F., *All for the Better* (1703).
Molloy, C., *The Coquet* (1718).
The Perplex'd Couple (1715).
Motteux, P., *Beauty in Distress* (1698).
Farwel Folly (1707).
Love's a Jest (1696).
Mountfort, W., *Greenwich Park* (1691).
Otway, T., *The Souldiers Fortune* (1681); in J. C. Ghosh (ed.), *The Works of Thomas Otway* (Oxford, 1932), vol. II.
Payne, H., *The Morning Ramble* (1673).
Pix, M., *The Beau Defeated* (1700).
The Czar of Muscovy (1701).
The Deceiver Deceived (1698).
The Different Widows (1703).
The Innocent Mistress (1697).
Powell, G., *A Very Good Wife* (1693).
Ravenscroft, E., *Careless Lovers* (1673).
The Citizen Turn'd Gentleman (1673).
Dame Dobson (1684).
The London Cuckolds (1681).
Rawlins, T., *Tom Essence* (1677).
Tunbridge Wells (1678).
Revet, E., *The Town-Shifts* (1671).
Rowe, N., *The Biter* (1705).
[Sandford, Mr], *The Female Fop* (1724).
Scott, T., *The Unhappy Kindness* (1697).
Sedley, C., *Bellamira* (1687).
The Mulberry-Garden (1668).
Settle, E., *The City-Ramble* (1711).
Shadwell, C., *The Fair Quaker of Deal* (1710).
The Humours of the Army (1713).
Shadwell, T., *Epsom-Wells* (1673).
The Humorists (1671).
The Lancashire Witches (1682).
The Scowrers (1691).
A True Widow (1679).
The Volunteers (1692).
The Woman-Captain (1680).
Shirley, J., *The Gamester* (1637).
Southerne, T., *The Disappointment* (1684).

The Maid's Last Prayer (1693).
Sir Anthony Love (1691).
The Spartan Dame (1719).
The Wives Excuse (1692).
Steele, R., *The Conscious Lovers* (1723).
The Funeral (1702).
Sturmy, J., *The Compromise* (1723).
Tate, N., *Cuckold's-Haven* (1685).
Tatham, J., *The Rump* (1660).
Taverner, W., *The Artful Wife* (1718).
Faithful Bride of Granada (1704).
The Female Advocates (1713).
The Maid the Mistress (1708).
Vanbrugh, J., *Aesop* (1697).
The Confederacy (1705).
The Mistake (1706).
The Provok'd Husband (1728; with C. Cibber).
The Relapse (1697).
Walker, W., *Marry, Or Do Worse* (1704).
Wilkinson, R., *Vice Reclaim'd* (1703).
Wilmot, J., *Valentinian* (1685).
Wilson, J., *The Cheats* (1664).
The Projectors (1665).
Wycherley, W., *The Country Wife* (1675).
The Gentleman Dancing-Master (1673).
Love in a Wood (1672).

SERIALS

(Applebee's) Original Weekly [1719–20].
Athenian Mercury (1691–7).
British Apollo (1708–11).
(Read's Weekly Journal; or) British Gazetteer (1716–[32]).
British Journal (1722–31).
Censor (1715–17, second edition, 3 vols., 1717).
Examiner; or Remarks upon Papers and Occurrences (1710–14).
Female Tatler (1709–10). Like many serials of the period, *The Female Tatler* has a somewhat confused publication history. The confusion stems from the fact that for some of its life two different periodicals were printed under the same masthead. For this reason all quotes are from the Adam Mathew microfilm. Where there are competing editions of the paper, for example issue number 20, I have simply noted the second paper, as it sequenced on the microfilm, as '20a'.
Freeholder's Journal (1722–3).
Gentleman's Journal (1692–4).
Gentleman's Magazine; or Trader's Monthly Intelligencer (1731–[2]).
Grub Street Journal (1730–[2]).
Grumbler (1715).

London Journal (1725–34).
London Spy (1698–1700).
London Terraefilius; or the Satyrical Reformer (1707–8).
Plain Dealer [1724–5].
Prompter (1734–6).
Review of the State of the English Nation (1704–13), ed. A. W. Secord, 22 'books' (New York, 1938).
Spectator (1711–14), ed. D. F. Bond, 5 vols. (Oxford, 1965).
Tatler (1709–11), ed. D. F. Bond, 3 vols. (Oxford, 1987).
Theatre (1720), ed. J. Loftis (Oxford, 1962).
Tory Tatler (1710–11).
Town Talk (1715–16), ed. J. Nichols (1789).
Universal Spectator and Weekly Journal (1728–[35]).
Visions of Sir Heister Ryley (1710–11).
Weekly Journal; or Saturday's Post (1717–33) [subsequently known as *Mist's* and *Fog's Weekly Journal*].

OTHER EARLY PRINTED MATERIAL

Allestree, R., *The Ladies Calling* (Oxford, 1677).
Ames, R., *Islington Wells, or the Threepenny-Academy* (1691).
Anon., *The Academy of Pleasure* (1656).
Anon., *An Address to the Hopeful Young Gentry of England in Strictures on the Most Dangerous Vices Incident to Their Age and Quality* (1669).
Anon., *An Answer to a Whimsical Pamphlet, Call'd the Character of Sir John Edgar* (1720).
Anon., *The Art of Cuckoldom; or the Intrigues of the City-Wives* (1697).
Anon., *The Beaus Catechism* (1703).
Anon., *Belsize House* (1722).
Anon., *The Cabal: A Voice of the Politicks* (?1690). See Early English Books Tract Supplements, Reel A3 (Ann Arbor, 1998).
Anon., *Cambridge Jests, Or Witty Alarums for Melancholy Spirits* (1674).
Anon., *The Censor Censur'd; or the Conscious Lovers Examin'd in a Dialogue between Sir Dicky Marplot and Jack Freeman* (1723).
Anon., *The Character of a Jacobite, By What Name or Title Soever Dignifyed or Distinguished* (1690).
Anon., *The Character of a Town-Gallant; Exposing the Extravagant Fopperies of Some Vain Self-Conceited Pretenders to Gentility, and Good Breeding* (1675, second edition 1680).
Anon., ['By a young Gentleman'], *The Character of the Beaux, in Five Parts . . . To Which is Added the Character of a Jacobite* (1696).
Anon., *Characters, Or Wit and the World in Their Proper Colours* (1663).
Anon., *A Comparison between the Two Stages* (1702).
Anon., *The Conduct of the Stage Consider'd* (1721).
Anon., *The Country Gentleman's Vade Mecum* (1699).
Anon., *The Crafty London Prentice, or, The Cruel Miss Well Fitted* (?1730).

Anon., ['By a Person of Quality'], *A Discourse Concerning the Character of a Gentleman* (Edinburgh, 1716).
Anon., *An Elegy on James Scot, Late Duke of Monmouth* (1685).
Anon., *Englands Vanity, or the Voice of God* (1683).
Anon., *The English Theophrastus; or the Manners of the Age. Being the Modish Characters of the Court, the Town, and the City* (1706).
Anon., *Grimalkin, or The Rebel-Cat* (1681).
Anon., *The Honest London Spy, Discovering the Base and Subtle Intrigues of the Town* (?1725).
Anon., *A Letter of Advice to a Young Gentleman of an Honourable Family, Now in His Travels beyond the Seas* (1688).
Anon., *A Letter to My Lord ******* on the Present Diversions of the Town* (1725).
Anon., *A Letter to the Right Honourable Sir Richard Brocas Lord Mayor of London. By a Citizen* (1730).
Anon., *The Levellers. A Dialogue between Two Young Ladies, Concerning Matrimony, Proposing an Act for Enforcing Marriage, for the Equality of Matches, and Taxing Single Persons* (1703). Reprinted in *The Harleian Miscellany* (1745), 416–33.
Anon., *The London Cuckolds. An Excellent New Song, to an Old Tune &c.* (1682).
Anon., *The London-Libertine* (?1700). See Early English Books Tract Supplements, Reel A3 (Ann Arbor, 1998).
Anon., *Memoirs of the Life of Barton Booth, Esq.; with His Character* (1733).
Anon., *Memoirs of the Life of Robert Wilks, Esq.* (1732).
Anon., *Monmouth Degraded Or James Scot, the Little King in Lyme* (1685).
Anon., *Monmouth's Downfal; Or, the Royal Victory* (1685).
Anon., *Mundus Foppensis: Or, The Fop Display'd, Being the Ladies Vindication, In Answer to a late Pamphlet, Entituled, Mundus Muliebris* (1691).
Anon., *The New Courtier* (?1700). See Early English Books Tract Supplements, Reel A5 (Ann Arbor, 1998).
Anon., *News from Covent-Garden, Or, The Town Gallants Vindication* (1675).
Anon., *The Occasional Paper: Number IX. Containing Some Considerations About the Danger of Going to Plays in a Letter to a Friend* (1698).
Anon., *Old Jemmy: An Excellent New Ballad* (1681).
Anon., *Poeta de Tristibus* (1682).
Anon., *The Prologue Spoken at the First Opening of the Queen's New Theatre in the Hay-Market . . . The Opening Prologue Paraphras'd in a Familiar Stile, for the Better Conception of the True Meaning, and for the Particular Use of Mr. Jer. Collier* (1705). See Early English Books Tract Supplements, Reel A1 (Ann Arbor, 1998).
Anon., *Remarques on the Humours and Conversations of the Gallants of the Town. Two Letters by a Person of Quality* (1673).
Anon., *Remarques on the Humours and Conversations of the Town. Written in a Letter to Sir T. L.* (1673).
Anon., *A Representation of the Impiety and Immorality of the English Stage* (1704).
Anon., *A Rod for Tunbridge Beaus, Bundl'd Up at the Request of the Tunbridge Ladies, to Jirk Fools into More Wit, and Clowns into More Manners* (1701).
Anon., *A Serious Proposal to the Ladies For the Advancement of Their True and Greatest Interest* (1694).

Anon., *Some Thoughts Concerning the Stage in a Letter to a Lady* (1704).
Anon., *The South Sea Ballad, Set by A Lady* (1720). See Early English Books Tract Supplements, Reel A6 (Ann Arbor, 1998).
Anon., *The Stage Acquitted* (1699).
Anon., *The Stage: A Poem Inscrib'd to Joseph Addison, Esq.* (1713).
Anon., *Visits from the Shades: or Dialogues, Comical and Political* (1704).
Anon., *War Horns, Make Room for the Bucks with Green Bowes* (1682).
Anon., *Whipping-Tom: Or, a Rod For a Proud Lady* (fourth edition, 1722).
Anon., *The Whitsun-tide Ramble* (?1720).
Anon., *The Young Bastard's Wish. A Song* (1685).
[Astell, M.], *A Farther Essay Relating to the Female-Sex: Containing Six Characters, and Six Perfections: with a Description of Self-Love : to Which is Added a Character of a Compleat Beau* (1696).
Aston, A., *A Brief Supplement to Colley Cibber Esq.; His Lives of the Late Famous Actors and Actresses* (?1747).
Ayres, P., *Vox Clamantis; or an Essay for the Honour, Happiness and Prosperity of the English Gentry* (1684).
[B. B.], *The Young Gentlemans Way to Honour in Three Parts* (1678).
[Betterton, T.], *The History of the English Stage, from the Restauration to the Present Time* (1741).
Blome, R., *The Art of Heraldry* (1685, fourth edition 1730).
Boyle, F., *Several Discourses and Characters Address'd to the Ladies of the Age* (1689).
[Brokesby, F.], *A Letter of Advice to a Young Gentleman at the University* (1701).
Brown, T., *Letters from the Dead to the Living* (1702, fifth edition 1708).
The Stage-Beaux Toss'd in a Blanket: or Hypocrisie alamode, Expos'd in a True Picture of Jerry – a Pretending Scourge to the English Stage: a Comedy (1704).
[Brown, T.], *The Works of Mr. Thomas Brown, Serious and Comical, in Prose and Verse*, 4 vols. (1720, eighth edition, Dublin, 1778–9).
Brown, T., and E. Ward, *A Legacy for the Ladies; or Characters of the Women of the Age with a Comical View of the Transactions That Will Happen in the Cities of London and Westminster* (1705).
Bulstrode, W., *Essays* (1724).
[Bulwer, J.], *Anthropometamorphosis . . . And an Appendix of the Pedigree of the English Gallant* (1653).
Burridge, R., *A Scourge for the Play-Houses: or the Character of the English-Stage* (1702).
Cavendish, M., *Orations of Divers Sorts, Accommodated to Divers Places* (1662, second edition 1663).
Cibber, T., *The Lives and Characters of the Most Eminent Actors and Actresses of Great Britain and Ireland, from Shakespear to the Present Time* (1753).
[Cibber, T.], *An Apology for the Life of Mr. T--------- C-----* (1740).
Collier, J., *A Defence of the Short View of the Profaneness and Immorality of the English Stage* (1699).
Moral Essays (1694).
Mr. Collier's Dissuasive from the Play-House; in a Letter to a Person of Quality, Occasion'd by the Late Calamity of the Tempest (1703).
A Short View of the Immorality, and Profaneness of the English Stage (1698).

Congreve, W., *Amendments of Mr. Collier's False and Imperfect Citations* (1698).
[Curll, E.], *Faithful Memoirs of the Life, Amours and Performances, of That Justly Celebrated, and Most Eminent Actress of Her Time, Mrs. Anne Oldfield* (1731).
The Life of That Eminent Comedian Robert Wilks, Esq. (1733).
Dare, J., *Counsellor Manners His Last Legacy to His Son* (1673, second edition 1676).
[Darrell, W.], *A Gentleman Instructed in the Conduct of a Virtuous and Happy Life* (1704, fourth edition 1709).
Defoe, D., *The Complete English Tradesman*, 2 vols. (1726–7).
More Reformation. A Satyr upon Himself (1703).
Reformation of Manners. A Satyr (1702).
Dekker, T., *The Guls Horne-booke* (1609).
Dennis, J., *The Causes of the Decay and Defects of Dramatick Poetry* (?1725).
The Characters and Conduct of Sir John Edgar (1720).
A Defence of Sir Fopling Flutter, a Comedy Written by Sir George Etheridge (1722).
An Essay upon Publick Spirit; Being a Satyr in Prose upon the Manners and Luxury of the Times (1711).
The Person of Quality's Answer to Mr. Collier's Letter, Being a Disswasive from the Play-House (1704).
Remarks on a Play, Call'd the Conscious Lovers (1723).
The Usefulness of the Stage, to the Happiness of Mankind, to Government, and to Religion (1698).
Drake, J., *The Antient and Modern Stages Survey'd; or Mr. Collier's View of the Immorality and Profaneness of the English Stage Set in a True Light* (1699).
Dunton, J., *Athenianism: or, the New Projects of Mr. J. D.* (1710).
Ellis, C., *The Gentile Sinner, Or, England's Brave Gentleman Characterized in a Letter to a Friend, Both As He Is, and As He Should Be* (Oxford, 1660).
[E. P.], *The Gentleman's Library, Containing Rules for Conduct in All Parts of Life* (1715).
Evelyn, J., *Tyrannus, or, the Mode in a Discourse of Sumptuary Lawes* (1661).
[Evelyn, M.], *Mundus Muliebris: Or, The Ladies Dressing-Room Unlock'd, And Her Toilette Spread. In Burlesque. Together With the Fop-Dictionary, Compiled for the Use of the Fair Sex* (1690).
Farquhar, G., 'A Discourse upon Comedy, in Reference to the English Stage', in his *Love and Business* (1702).
Gildon, C., *The Life of Mr. Thomas Betterton the Late Eminent Tragedian* (1710).
Gould, R., *Poems, Consisting Chiefly of Satyrs and Satyrical Epistles* (1689).
The Works, 2 vols. (1709).
Graile, J., *An Essay of Particular Advice to the Young Gentry, for the Overcoming the Difficulties and Temptations They May Meet With* (1711).
[Haywood, E.], *Bath Intrigues in Four Letters to a Friend in London* (1725).
Hickeringill, E., *The Ceremony-Monger* (1689, third edition 1696).
Jacob, G., *The Poetical Register; or the Lives and Characters of the English Dramatick Poets* (1719).
Jones, E., *The Man of Manners: or, Plebeian Polished. Being Plain and Familiar Rules for a Modest and Genteel Behaviour, on Most of the Ordinary Occasions of Life* ([third edition], 1737).
[J. W.], *Youth's Safety* ([second edition], 1698).

Langbaine, G., *An Account of the English Dramatick Poets* (Oxford, 1691).
[Lawson, J.], *The Upper Gallery. A Poem. Inscribed to the Rev. Dr. Swift, D.S.P.D* (1733).
Logan, J., *Analogia Honorum; or a Treatise of Honour and Nobility, According to the Laws and Customes of England* (1677).
Mackenzie, G., *Moral Gallantry. A Discourse* (1685).
Macky, J., *A Journey through England* (1714, second edition 1722).
Miège, G., *The New State of England* (1691, fourth edition 1702).
[Milbourne, L.], *A Letter to A. H. Esq. Concerning the Stage* (1698).
[M.S.], *The Beau in a Wood, A Satyr. With His Last Will and Testament: And Also His Elegy and Epitaph* (1701).
Muralt, B. L. de, *Letters Describing the Character and Customs of the English and French Nations* (1725, second edition 1726).
Oldham, J., *The Works of Mr. John Oldham, Together with His Remains*, 4 vols. (1684).
Oldmixon, J., *Reflections on the Stage, and Mr. Collyer's Defence of the Short View* (1699).
Ozell, Mr (trans. and ed.), *M. Misson's Memoirs and Observations in His Travels over England* (1719).
[Powell, G.], *Animadversions on Mr. Congreve's Late Answer to Mr. Collier in a Dialogue between Mr. Smith and Mr. Johnson. With the Characters of the Present Poets* (1698).
Ralph, J., *The Touch-Stone; or Historical, Critical, Political, Philosophical and Theological Essays upon the Reigning Diversions of the Town* (1728).
Ramesey, W., *The Gentlemans Companion; or a Character of True Nobility and Gentility* (1672).
Rémond des Cours, N., *The True Conduct of Persons of Quality* (1694).
[Richardson, S.], *A Seasonable Examination of the Pleas and Pretensions of the Proprietors of, and Subscribers to, Play-houses, Erected in Defiance of the Royal Licence* (1735).
[Ridpath, G.], *The Stage Condemn'd* (1698).
Settle, E., *A Defence of Dramatick Poetry: Being a Review of Mr. Collier's View of the Immorality and Profaneness of the Stage* (1698).
A Farther Defence of Dramatick Poetry (1698).
Smith, A., *A Secret History of the Lives of the Most Celebrated Beauties*, 2 vols. (1716).
Smithurst, B., *Britain's Glory and England's Bravery* (1689).
Steele, R., *An Account of the Fish-Pool* (1718).
Thompson, N., *A Choice Collection of One Hundred and Eighty Loyal Songs, All Written since 1678* (1694).
[T.O.], *The True Character of a Town Beau* (1692).
[Venette, N.], *The Mysteries of Conjugal Love Reveal'd* (1703, eighth edition 1707).
Vincent, S., *The Young Gallant's Academy* (1674).
Ward, E., *Adam and Eve Stript to Their Furbelows* (1714).
The Character of a Covetous Citizen, or a Ready Way to Get Riches (1701).
The Dancing-School with the Adventures of the Easter Holy-Days (1700).
Nuptial Dialogues and Debates, 2 vols. (1723).
The School of Politicks: or, The Humours of a Coffee-House (1691).
The Secret History of Clubs (1709).
A Step to the Bath With a Character of the Place (1700).

A Trip to Jamaica With a True Character of the People and Island ([third edition], 1698).

The Wealthy Shop-keeper; Or, the Charitable Citizen (1700).

Whaley, J., *A Collection of Poems* (1732).

Woolley, H., *The Gentlewomans Companion; Or, A Guide to the Female Sex* (1673, third edition 1682).

Wright, J., *Historia Histrionica* (1699).

MODERN EDITIONS OF MANUSCRIPTS AND EARLY PRINTED BOOKS

Alsop, G., 'A Character of the Province of Maryland (1666)', in C. C. Hall (ed.), *Narratives of Early Maryland 1633–1684* (New York, 1946).

[Anon.], 'Diary of Thomas Smith, Esq. of Shaw House', *Wiltshire Archaeological Magazine* 11 (1867), 82–105, 204–17, 308–15.

Anselment, R. A. (ed.), *The Remembrances of Elizabeth Freke 1671–1714* (Camden Society, London, fifth series, vol. XVII, 2001).

Ashcroft, M. Y. (ed.), *The Papers of Sir William Chaytor of Croft (1639–1721)* (North Yorkshire County Record Office Publication, no. 33, Northallerton, 1984).

Ashley, L. R. N. (ed.), *A Narrative of the Life of Mrs. Charlotte Charke* (Gainesville, 1969).

Ashton, J., *Social Life in the Age of Queen Anne* (London, 1911).

Aspital, A. (ed.), *Catalogue of the Pepys Library at Magdalene College, Cambridge. Prints and Drawings. Volume III, Part i: General* (Woodbridge, 1980).

Axtell, J. L. (ed.), *The Educational Writings of John Locke* (Cambridge, 1968).

Ayres, P. (ed.), *Characteristicks of Men, Manners, Opinions, Times*, 2 vols. (Oxford, 1999).

Berland, K., J. K. Gilliam, and K. A. Lockridge (eds.), *The Commonplace Book of William Byrd II of Westover* (Chapel Hill, 2001).

Black, J., 'Fragments from the Grand Tour', *Huntington Library Quarterly* 53 (1990), 337–41.

Bliss, P. (ed.), *Reliquiae Hearnianae: The Remains of Thomas Hearne*, 2 vols. (Oxford, 1857).

Boyle, E. C. (the Countess of Cork and Orrery) (ed.), *The Orrery Papers*, 2 vols. (London, 1903).

Bracher, F. (ed.), *Letters of Sir George Etherege* (Berkeley, 1974).

Browning, A. (with M. K. Geiter and W. A. Speck) (ed.), *Memoirs of Sir John Reresby. The Complete Text and a Selection from His Letters* (London, 1936, second edition 1991).

Buckley, W. E. (ed.), *Memoirs of Thomas, Earl of Ailesbury Written by Himself*, 2 vols. (Roxburghe Club, London, 1890).

Cameron, W. J. (ed.), *Poems on Affairs of State. Volume V: 1688–1697* (New Haven, 1971).

Cartwright, J. J. (ed.), *The Wentworth Papers 1705–1739* (London, 1883).

Christie, W. D. (ed.), *Letters Addressed from London to Sir Joseph Williamson while Plenipotentiary at the Congress of Cologne in the Years 1673 and 1674* (Camden Society, London, new series, vols. VIII and IX, 1874).

Cole, G. D. H., and D. C. Browning (eds.), *Daniel Defoe. A Tour Through the Whole Island of Britain* (London, 1962).

Cooper, W. D. (ed.), *Savile Correspondence. Letters to and from Henry Savile, Esq., Envoy at Paris, and Vice-Chamberlain to Charles II. and James II. Including Letters from his Brother George Marquess of Halifax* (Camden Society, London, old series, vol. LXXI, 1858).

Crump, G. M. (ed.), *Poems on Affairs of State. Augustan Satirical Verse. Volume IV: 1685–1688* (New Haven, 1968).

Davis, H., *et al.* (eds.), *The Prose Works of Jonathan Swift*, 14 vols. (Oxford, 1939–68).

Day, W. G. (ed.), *The Pepys Ballads*, 5 vols. (Cambridge, 1987).

de Beer, E. S. (ed.), *The Diary of John Evelyn*, 6 vols. (Oxford, 1955).

Defoe, D., *The Fortunes and Misfortunes of the Famous Moll Flanders* (Wordsworth edition, Ware, UK, 1993).

Dickinson, H. T. (ed.), *The Correspondence of Sir James Clavering (1680–1748)* (Surtees Society, Durham, vol. CLXXVII, 1967).

Ellis, F. H. (ed.), *Poems on Affairs of State. Augustan Satirical Verse. Volume VI: 1697–1704* (New Haven, 1970).

Evans, J. M. (ed.), *Apology for the Life of Mr. Colley Cibber, Comedian* (New York, 1987).

Halsband, R. (ed.), *The Complete Letters of Lady Mary Wortley Montagu. Volume I: 1708–1720* (Oxford, 1965).

Hellinger, B. (ed.), *A Short View of the Immorality and Prophaneness of the English Stage* (New York, 1987).

Hervey, S. H. A. (ed.), *Letter-Books of John Hervey, First Earl of Bristol*, 3 vols. (London, 1894).

Historic Manuscripts Commission [HMC]

First Report 1 (1870).

Fifth Report. Part I 4, 1 (1876).

Sixth Report. Part I 5, 1 (1877).

Seventh Report. Part I 6, 1 (1879).

Ninth Report. Part II 8, 2 (1884).

Manuscripts of the Marquis of Bath Preserved at Longleat, Wiltshire.

Volume II 58, 2 (1907).

Volume III (Prior Papers) 58, 3 (1908).

Manuscripts of the Duke of Beaufort, K.G., the Earl of Donoughmore, and Others 27, 1 (1891).

Manuscripts of the Earl of Carlisle, Preserved at Castle Howard 42, 1 (1897).

Manuscripts of the Earl Cowper Preserved at Melbourne Hall, Derbyshire 23, 2 (1888).

Manuscripts of the Earl of Dartmouth 20, 1 (1887).

Manuscripts of the Marquess of Downshire Preserved at Easthampstead Park, Berks. Volume I: Papers of Sir William Trumbull 75, 1 (1924).

Manuscripts of the Earl of Egmont. Diary of Viscount Percival afterwards First Earl of Egmont.

Volume I: 1730–1733 63, 1 (1920).

Volume II: 1734–1738 63, 2 (1923).

Manuscripts of the late Allan George Finch, Esq., of Burley-on-the-Hill, Rutland. Volume II: 1670–1690, and Books c1651–1681 71, 2 (1922).

Volume III: 1691 with addenda 1667–1690 71, 3 (1957).
Manuscripts of Sir William Fitzherbert, Bart. and Others 32, 1 (1893).
Manuscripts of J. B. Fortescue, Esq., Preserved at Dropmore 30, 1 (1892).
Manuscripts of Lord Kenyon 35, 1 (1894).
Laing Manuscripts Preserved in the University of Edinburgh. Volume I 72, 1 (1914).
Manuscripts of S. H. Le Fleming, Esq., of Rydal Hall 25, 1 (1890).
Manuscripts of the Marquess of Ormonde, K.D., Preserved at Kilkenny Castle. Volume IV 36, 4 (1906).
Manuscripts of His Grace the Duke of Portland Preserved at Welbeck Abbey.
Volume II 29, 2 (1893).
Volume III 29, 3 (1894).
Volume IV 29, 4 (1897).
Volume V 29, 5 (1899).
Volume VI 29, 6 (1901).
Volume VII 29, 7 (1901).
Volume VIII 29, 8 (1907).
Manuscripts of His Grace the Duke of Rutland, K.G., Preserved at Belvoir Castle. Volume II 24, 2 (1889).
Manuscripts in Various Collections. Volume II 55, 2 (1903).

Hines, jr., P., 'Theatre Items from the Newdigate Newsletters', *Theatre Notebook* 32, 2 (1985), 76–83.

Hodges, J. C. (ed.), *William Congreve. Letters & Documents* (London, 1964).

Hooker, E. N. (ed.), *The Critical Works of John Dennis*, 2 vols. (Baltimore, 1939–43).

Jackson, A., 'Play Notices from the Burney Newspapers 1700–1703', *PMLA* 48 (1933), 815–49.

Jeaffreson, J. C. (ed.), *A Young Squire of the Seventeenth Century. From the Papers (A.D. 1676–1686) of Christopher Jeaffreson of Dullingham House, Cambridgeshire*, 2 vols. (London, 1878).

Jessop, A. (ed.), *The Lives of the Right Hon. Francis North, Baron Guilford; The Hon. Sir Dudley North; and the Hon. and Rev. Dr. John North by the Hon. Roger North, Together with a Biography of the Author*, 3 vols. (London, 1890).

Keynes, G. (ed.), *The Letters of Sir Thomas Browne* (London, 1931, second edition 1946).

Labaree, L. W., R. L. Ketcham, H. C. Boatfield, and H. H. Fineman (eds.), *The Autobiography of Benjamin Franklin* (New Haven, 1964).

Latham, R. C., and W. Matthews (eds.), *The Diary of Samuel Pepys 1660–1669*, 11 vols. (London, 1970–83, reprint 1995).

Loftis, J. (ed.), *Essays on the Theatre from Eighteenth-Century Periodicals* (Los Angeles, 1960).

Lord, G. de F. (ed.), *Anthology of Poems on Affairs of State. Augustan Satirical Verse 1660–1714* (New Haven, 1975).
Poems on Affairs of State. Volume I: 1660–1678 (New Haven, 1963).

Luttrell, N., *A Brief Historical Relation of State Affairs from September 1678 to April 1714*, 6 vols. (Oxford, 1837).

McCormick, I. (ed.), *Secret Sexualities. A Sourcebook of Seventeenth- and Eighteenth-Century Writing* (London, 1997).

McKillop, A. D. (ed.), *James Thomson (1700–1748). Letters and Documents* (Lawrence, KS, 1958).

McVeagh, J. (ed.), *Political and Economic Writings of Daniel Defoe. Volume VII: Trade* (London, 2000).

Margoliouth, H. M. (ed.), *The Poems and Letters of Andrew Marvell*, 2 vols. (Oxford, 1952).

Matthews, W. (ed.), *The Diary of Dudley Ryder 1715–1716* (London, 1939).

Mengel, jr., E. F. (ed.), *Poems on Affairs of State. Volume II: 1678–1681* (New Haven, 1965).

Milhous, J., and R. D. Hume (eds.), *A Register of English Theatrical Documents, 1660–1737*, 2 vols. (Carbondale, 1991).

Montagu, R. (ed.), *Samuel Johnson. Lives of the English Poets* (London, 1965).

Nagler, A. M. (ed.), *A Source Book in Theatrical History* (New York, 1952).

Parkinson, R. (ed.), *The Private Journal and Literary Remains of John Byrom* (Chetham Society, Manchester, old series, vol. XXXII, 1854).

Phipps, C. (ed.), *Buckingham: Public and Private Man. The Prose, Poems and Commonplace Book of George Villiers, Second Duke of Buckingham (1628–1687)* (New York, 1985).

Priestley, J., 'Some Memoirs Concerning the Family of the Priestleys, Written, at the Request of a Friend, By Jonathan Priestley, Ano. Domini 1696, Aetatis Suae 63', in Anon. (ed.), *Yorkshire Diaries and Autobiographies in the Seventeenth and Eighteenth Centuries. Volume II* (Surtees Society, Durham, vol. LXXVII, 1886), 1–31.

Quarrell, W. H., and M. Mare (trans. and eds.), *London in 1710 from the Travels of Zacharias Conrad von Uffenbach* (London, 1934).

Robinson, H. W., and W. Adams (eds.), *The Diary of Robert Hooke M.A., M.D., F.R.S., 1672–1680* (London, 1935).

Rogers, P. (ed.), *Jonathan Swift. The Complete Poems* (Harmondsworth, 1983).

Rosenfeld, S., *Temples of Thespis. Some Private Theatres and Theatricals in England and Wales, 1700–1820* (London, 1978).

Schless, H. H. (ed.), *Poems on Affairs of State. Volume III: 1682–1685* (New Haven, 1968).

Smith, D. N. (ed.), *The Letters of Thomas Burnet to George Duckett, 1712–1722* (Roxburghe Club, London, 1914).

Spingarn, J. E. (ed.), *Critical Essays of the Seventeenth Century. Volume III: 1685–1700* (Oxford, 1908).

Summers, M. (ed.), *Roscius Anglicanus* (New York, 1929).

Thomas, D. (ed.), *Restoration and Georgian England, 1660–1788. Theatre in Europe: A Documentary History* (Cambridge, 1989).

Thompson, E. M. (ed.), *Correspondence of the Family of Hatton, being chiefly letters addressed to Christopher, First Viscount Hatton A.D. 1601–1704* (Camden Society, London, new series, vols. XXII and XXIII, 1878).

Tinling, M. (ed.), *The Correspondence of the Three William Byrds of Westover, Virginia, 1684–1776*, 2 vols. (Charlottesville, 1977).

Treglown, J. (ed.), *The Letters of John Wilmot, Earl of Rochester* (Oxford, 1980).

Tyrer, F., and J. J. Bagley (trans. and ed.), *The Great Diurnal of Nicholas Blundell of Little Crosby, Lancashire (*Record Society of Lancashire and Cheshire, Liverpool, nos. CX, CXII, CXIV, 1968–72).

Verney, M. M. (ed.), *Memoirs of the Verney Family during the Commonwealth* (London, 1894).

Memoirs of the Verney Family from the Restoration to the Revolution 1660 to 1696, 4 vols. (London, 1899).

Wilson, J. H. (ed.), *Court Satires of the Restoration* (Columbus, 1976).

'Theatre Notes from the Newdigate Newsletters', *Theatre Notebook* 15, 3 (1961), 79–94.

Woodfin, M. H., and M. Tinling (eds.), *Another Secret Diary of William Byrd of Westover for the Years 1739–1741. With Letters and Literary Exercises 1696–1726* (Richmond, VA, 1942).

Wright, L. B. (ed.), *The Prose Works of William Byrd of Westover. Narratives of a Colonial Virginian* (Cambridge, MA, 1966).

Wright, L. B., and M. Tinling (eds.), *William Byrd of Virginia. The London Diary (1717–1721) and Other Writings* (New York, 1958).

Yule, H. (ed.), *The Diary of William Hedges, Esq., . . . III* (Hakluyt Society, London, first series, vol. LXXVII, 1889).

MONOGRAPHS AND ARTICLES

Adair, R., *Courtship, Illegitimacy and Marriage in Early Modern England* (Manchester, 1996).

Amussen, S. D., *An Ordered Society. Gender and Class in Early Modern England* (Oxford, 1988).

Andrew, D. T., 'Aldermen and the Big Bourgeoisie of London Reconsidered', *Social History* 6, 3 (1981), 359–64.

Anthony, R., *The Jeremy Collier Stage Controversy 1698–1726* (New York, 1937).

Barish, J. A., *The Antitheatrical Prejudice* (Berkeley, 1981).

Barry, J., and C. Brooks (eds.), *The Middling Sort of People. Culture, Society and Politics in England, 1550–1800* (London, 1994).

Bennett, J. M., 'Misogyny, Popular Culture, and Women's Work', *HWJ* 31 (1991), 166–88.

Berry, H. M., *Gender, Society and Print Culture in Late-Stuart England. The Cultural World of the* Athenian Mercury (Burlington, VT, 2003).

Bevis, R. W., *English Drama. Restoration and Eighteenth Century, 1660–1789* (London, 1988).

Bond, R. P., *Queen Anne's American Kings* (Oxford, 1952).

Borgman, A. S., *The Life and Death of William Mountfort* (Cambridge, MA, 1935).

Borsay, P., *The English Urban Renaissance. Culture and Society in the Provincial Town, 1660–1770* (Oxford, 1989).

Boswell, E., *The Restoration Court Stage (1660–1702) with a Particular Account of the Production of Calisto* (Cambridge, MA, 1932).

Braddick, M. J., *State Formation in Early Modern England, c.1550–1700* (Cambridge, 2000).

Braddick, M. J., and J. Walter, 'Introduction. Grids of Power: Order, Hierarchy and Subordination in Early Modern Society', in M. J. Braddick and J. Walter (eds.), *Negotiating Power in Early Modern Society. Order, Hierarchy and Subordination in Britain and Ireland* (Cambridge, 2001), 1–42.

Brannigan, J., *New Historicism and Cultural Materialism* (London, 1998).

Braverman, R., *Plots and Counterplots. Sexual Politics and the Body Politic in English Literature, 1660–1730* (Cambridge, 1993).

Bray, A., *Homosexuality in Renaissance England* (New York, 1982, revised edition 1995).

Brenner, R., *Merchants and Revolution. Commercial Change, Political Conflict, and London's Overseas Traders 1550–1653* (Cambridge, 1993).

Brewer, J., *The Pleasures of the Imagination. English Culture in the Eighteenth Century* (London, 1997).

The Sinews of Power. War, Money and the English State, 1688–1783 (London, 1989).

Brooks, C., 'Apprenticeship, Social Mobility and the Middling Sort, 1550–1800', in J. Barry and C. Brooks (eds.), *The Middling Sort of People. Culture, Society and Politics in England, 1550–1800* (London, 1994), 52–83.

Brown, L., *Ends of Empire. Women and Ideology in Early Eighteenth-Century English Literature* (Ithaca, 1993).

English Dramatic Form, 1660–1760. An Essay in Generic History (New Haven, 1981).

Bruster, D., *Drama and the Market in the Age of Shakespeare* (London, 1992).

Bucholz, R. O., *The Augustan Court. Queen Anne and the Decline of Court Culture* (Stanford, 1993).

Burns, E., *Restoration Comedy. Crises of Desire and Identity* (London, 1987).

Bush, M. L., *The English Aristocracy. A Comparative Synthesis* (Manchester, 1984).

Butler, J. P., *Gender Trouble. Feminism and the Subversion of Identity* (New York, 1990).

Butler, M., *Theatre and Crisis 1632–1642* (Cambridge, 1984).

Canfield, J. D., 'Restoration Comedy', in S. J. Owen (ed.), *A Companion to Restoration Drama* (Oxford, 2001), 211–27.

Tricksters & Estates. On the Ideology of Restoration Comedy (Lexington, 1997).

Cannadine, D., *The Rise and Fall of Class in Britain* (New York, 1999).

Capp, B., *When Gossips Meet. Women, Family, and Neighbourhood in Early Modern England* (Oxford, 2003).

Carlson, M., *Places of Performance. The Semiotics of Theatre Architecture* (Ithaca, 1989).

Carter, P., 'An "Effeminate" or "Efficient" Nation? Masculinity and Eighteenth-Century Social Documentary', *Textual Practice* 11, 3 (1997), 429–43.

'Men about Town: Representations of Foppery and Masculinity in Early Eighteenth-Century Urban Society', in H. Baker and E. Chalus (eds.), *Gender in Eighteenth-Century England. Roles, Representations and Responsibilities* (London, 1997), 31–57.

Men and the Emergence of Polite Society, Britain 1660–1800 (London, 2001).

Casey, M. E., 'The Fop – "Apes and Echoes of Men": Gentlemanly Ideals and the Restoration', in V. K. Janik (ed.), *Fools and Jesters in Literature, Art, and History. A Bio-Bibliographical Sourcebook* (Westport, CT, 1998), 207–14.

Castronovo, D., *The English Gentleman. Images and Ideals in Literature and Society* (New York, 1987).

Chico, T., 'The Dressing Room Unlock'd: Eroticism, Performance, and Privacy from Pepys to the *Spectator*', in L. J. Rosenthal and M. Choudhury (eds.), *Monstrous Dreams of Reason. Body, Self, and Other in the Enlightenment* (Lewisburg, 2002), 45–65.

Clark, I., *Comedy, Youth, Manhood in Early Modern England* (London, 2003).

Clark, J. C. D., *English Society 1688–1832. Ideology, Social Structure and Political Practice during the Ancien Régime* (Cambridge, 1985).
Clark, P., *British Clubs and Societies 1580–1800. The Origins of an Associational World* (Oxford, 2000).
Clay, C. G. A., *Public Finance and Private Wealth. The Career of Sir Stephen Fox, 1627–1716* (Oxford, 1978).
Claydon, T., *William III and the Godly Revolution* (Cambridge, 1996).
Clayton, T., *The English Print 1688–1802* (New Haven, 1997).
Cliffe, J. T., *The World of the Country House in Seventeenth-Century England* (New Haven, 1999).
Clifton, R., *The Last Popular Rebellion. The Western Rising of 1685* (London, 1984).
Cohen, M., *Fashioning Masculinity. National Identity and Language in the Eighteenth Century* (London, 1996).
Colebrook, C., *New Literary Histories. New Historicism and Contemporary Criticism* (Manchester, 1997).
Colley, L., *In Defiance of Oligarchy. The Tory Party 1714–60* (Cambridge, 1982).
Combe, K., 'Rakes, Wives and Merchants: Shifts from the Satirical to the Sentimental', in S. J. Owen (ed.), *A Companion to Restoration Drama* (Oxford, 2001), 291–308.
Condren, C., *The Language of Politics in Seventeenth-Century England* (London, 1994).
Cook, A. J., *The Privileged Playgoers of Shakespeare's London, 1576–1642* (Princeton, 1981).
Cordner, M., 'Playwright versus Priest: Profanity and the Wit of Restoration Comedy', in D. Payne Fisk (ed.), *The Cambridge Companion to English Restoration Theatre* (Cambridge, 2000), 209–25.
Corfield, P. J., 'The Rivals: Landed and Other Gentlemen', in N. Harte and R. Quinault (eds.), *Land and Society in Britain, 1700–1914. Essays in Honour of F. M. L. Thompson* (Manchester, 1996), 1–33.
Corns, T. N., W. A. Speck, and J. A. Downie, 'Archetypal Mystification: Polemic and Reality in English Political Literature, 1640–1750', *Eighteenth-Century Life* 7, 3 (1982), 1–27.
Cowley, R. L. S., *Marriage-A-La-Mode. A Re-view of Hogarth's Narrative Art* (Manchester, 1983).
Cressy, D., *Travesties and Transgressions in Tudor and Stuart England. Tales of Discord and Dissension* (Oxford, 2000).
Crouch, K., 'The Public Life of Actresses: Prostitutes or Ladies?', in H. Baker and E. Chalus (eds.), *Gender in Eighteenth-Century England. Roles, Representations and Responsibilities* (London, 1997), 58–78.
Cust, R., 'Honour and Politics in Early Stuart England: The Case of Beaumont *v.* Hastings', *PP* 149 (1995), 57–94.
Dabhoiwala, F., 'The Construction of Honour, Reputation and Status in Late Seventeenth- and Early Eighteenth-Century England', *Transactions of the Royal Historical Society*, sixth series, 6 (1996), 201–13.
De Krey, G. S., *A Fractured Society. The Politics of London in the First Age of Party 1688–1715* (Oxford, 1985).
Dharwadker, A., 'Class, Authorship, and the Social Intertexture of Genre in Restoration Theatre', *SEL* 37 (1997), 461–82.

'Restoration Drama and Social Class', in S. J. Owen (ed.), *A Companion to Restoration Drama* (Oxford, 2001), 140–60.

Dickson, P. G. M., *The Financial Revolution in England. A Study in the Development of Public Credit, 1688–1750* (London, 1967).

Dillon, J., *Theatre, Court and City, 1595–1610. Drama and Social Space in London* (Cambridge, 2000).

Dolan, F. E., 'Taking the Pencil out of God's Hand: Art, Nature, and the Face-Painting Debate in Early Modern England', *PMLA* 108 (1993), 224–39.

Earle, P., 'Age and Accumulation in the London Business Community, 1665–1720', in N. McKendrick and R. B. Outhwaite (eds.), *Business Life and Public Policy. Essays in Honour of D.C. Coleman* (Cambridge, 1986), 38–63.

Eley, G., 'Is All the World a Text? From Social History to the History of Society Two Decades Later', in T. J. McDonald (ed.), *The Historic Turn in the Human Sciences* (Ann Arbor, 1996), 193–243.

Erskine-Hill, H., 'Literature and the Jacobite Cause: Was There a Rhetoric of Jacobitism?', in E. Cruickshanks (ed.), *Ideology and Conspiracy: Aspects of Jacobitism, 1689–1759* (Edinburgh, 1982), 49–69.

Everitt, A., 'Social Mobility in Early Modern England', *PP* 33 (1966), 56–73.

Fisher, W., 'The Renaissance Beard: Masculinity in Early Modern England', *Renaissance Quarterly* 54 (2001), 155–87.

Fisk, D. P., 'The Restoration Actress', in S. J. Owen (ed.), *A Companion to Restoration Drama* (Oxford, 2001), 69–91.

Foucault, M. (trans. R. Hurley), *The Care of the Self. Volume 3 of The History of Sexuality* (New York, 1986).

The Use of Pleasure. Volume 2 of The History of Sexuality (New York, 1985).

Fox, A., *Oral and Literate Culture in England 1500–1700* (Oxford, 2000).

Foyster, E. A., 'Male Honour, Social Control and Wife Beating in Late Stuart England', *Transactions of the Royal Historical Society*, sixth series, 6 (1996), 215–24.

Manhood in Early Modern England. Honour, Sex and Marriage (London, 1999).

Freeman, L. A., *Character's Theater. Genre and Identity on the Eighteenth-Century English Stage* (Philadelphia, 2002).

French, H. R., '"Ingenious & learned gentlemen" – Social Perceptions and Self-Fashioning among Parish Elites in Essex, 1680–1740', *Social History* 25, 1 (2000), 44–66.

'The Search for the "Middle Sort of People" in England, 1600–1800', *Historical Journal* 43, 1 (2000), 277–93.

'Social Status, Localism and the "Middle Sort of People" in England 1620–1750', *PP* 166 (2000), 66–99.

Gallagher, C., *Nobody's Story. The Vanishing Acts of Women Writers in the Marketplace, 1670–1820* (Berkeley, 1994).

Gallagher, C., and S. J. Greenblatt, *Practicing New Historicism* (Chicago, 2000).

Gauci, P., *The Politics of Trade. The Overseas Merchant in State and Society, 1660–1720* (Oxford, 2001).

Giddens, A., *The Class Structure of the Advanced Societies* (London, 1973, second edition 1981).

Gill, P., 'Gender, Sexuality, and Marriage', in D. Payne Fisk (ed.), *The Cambridge Companion to English Restoration Theatre* (Cambridge, 2000), 191–208.

Goldberg, J., *Sodometries. Renaissance Texts, Modern Sexualities* (Stanford, 1992).

Gowing, L., *Domestic Dangers. Women, Words, and Sex in Early Modern London* (Oxford, 1996).

'Women, Status and the Popular Culture of Dishonour', *Transactions of the Royal Historical Society*, sixth series, 6 (1996), 225–34.

Grassby, R., *The Business Community of Seventeenth-Century England* (Cambridge, 1995).

The English Gentleman in Trade. The Life and Works of Sir Dudley North, 1641–91 (Oxford, 1994).

Kinship and Capitalism. Marriage, Family, and Business in the English-Speaking World, 1580–1740 (Cambridge, 2001).

Greenblatt, S. J., *Renaissance Self-Fashioning. From More to Shakespeare* (Chicago, 1980).

Griffin, D. H., *Literary Patronage in England, 1650–1800* (Cambridge, 1996).

Griffiths, A., and R. A. Gerard, *The Print in Stuart Britain 1603–1689* (London, 1998).

Griswold, W., *Renaissance Revivals. City Comedy and Revenge Tragedy in the London Theatre 1576–1980* (Chicago, 1986).

Guest, H., '"These Neuter Somethings": Gender Difference and Commercial Culture in Mid-Eighteenth-Century England', in K. Sharpe and S. N. Zwicker (eds.), *Refiguring Revolutions. Aesthetics and Politics from the English Revolution to the Romantic Revolution* (Berkeley, 1998), 173–94.

Gurr, A., *Playgoing in Shakespeare's London* (Cambridge, 1987, second edition 1996).

Habakkuk, H. J., *Marriage, Debt, and the Estates System. English Landownership 1650–1950* (Oxford, 1994).

Haggerty, G. E., *Men in Love. Masculinity and Sexuality in the Eighteenth Century* (New York, 1999).

Hainsworth, D. R., *Stewards, Lords and People. The Estate Steward and His World in Later Stuart England* (Cambridge, 1992).

Hall, S., 'For Allon White: Metaphors of Transformation', in A. White (ed.), *Carnival, Hysteria, and Writing. Collected Essays and Autobiography* (Oxford, 1993), 1–25.

Hallett, M., *The Spectacle of Difference. Graphic Satire in the Age of Hogarth* (New Haven, 1999).

Hammond, B. S., *Professional Imaginative Writing in England 1670–1740. 'Hackney for Bread'* (Oxford, 1997).

Haynes, J., *The Social Relations of Jonson's Theatre* (Cambridge, 1992).

Heal, F., 'Reputation and Honour in Court and Country: Lady Elizabeth Russell and Sir Thomas Hoby', *Transactions of the Royal Historical Society*, sixth series, 6 (1996), 161–78.

Heal, F., and C. Holmes, *The Gentry in England and Wales, 1500–1700* (Stanford, 1994).

Healy, M., *Fictions of Disease in Early Modern England. Bodies, Plagues and Politics* (London, 2001).

Hecht, J. J., *The Domestic Servant Class in Eighteenth-Century England* (London, 1956).

Heilman, R. B., 'Some Fops and Some Versions of Foppery', *ELH* 49 (1982), 363–95.

Highfill, jr., P. H., K. A. Burnim, and E. A. Langhans (eds.), *A Biographical Dictionary of Actors, Actresses, Musicians, Dancers, Managers & Other Stage Personnel in London, 1660–1800*, 16 vols. (Carbondale, 1973–93).

Hill, C., *The World Turned Upside Down. Radical Ideas during the English Revolution* (London, 1972).

Holland, P., *The Ornament of Action. Text and Performance in Restoration Comedy* (Cambridge, 1979).

Hook, L., 'James Brydges Drops in at the Theater', *Huntington Library Quarterly* 8, 3 (1944–5), 306–11.

Hopes, J., 'Politics and Morality in the Writings of Jeremy Collier', *Literature and History* 8 (1978), 159–74.

Howe, E., *The First English Actresses. Women and Drama 1660–1700* (Cambridge, 1992).

Hughes, D., *English Drama 1660–1700* (Oxford, 1996).

Hughes, L., *The Drama's Patrons. A Study of the Eighteenth-Century London Audience* (San Antonio, 1971).

Hume, R. D., *The Development of English Drama in the Late Seventeenth Century* (Oxford, 1976).

'Dr. Edward Browne's Playlists of "1662": A Reconsideration', *Philological Quarterly* 64 (1985), 69–81.

Henry Fielding and the London Theatre 1728–1737 (Oxford, 1988).

'Jeremy Collier and the Future of the London Theater in 1698', *Studies in Philology* 96, 4 (1999), 480–511.

The Rakish Stage. Studies in English Drama, 1660–1800 (Carbondale, 1983).

Hunt, L. (ed.), *The Invention of Pornography. Obscenity and the Origins of Modernity, 1500–1800* (New York, 1993).

Ingram, M. J., 'Juridical Folklore in England Illustrated by Rough Music', in C. Brooks and M. Lobban (eds.), *Communities and Courts in Britain, 1150–1900* (London, 1997), 61–82.

'Ridings, Rough Music and Mocking Rhymes in Early Modern England', in B. Reay (ed.), *Popular Culture in Seventeenth-Century England* (London, 1985), 166–97.

'Ridings, Rough Music and the "Reform of Popular Culture" in Early Modern England', *PP* 105 (1984), 79–113.

'"Scolding women cucked or washed": A Crisis in Gender Relations in Early Modern England', in J. Kermode and G. Walker (eds.), *Women, Crime and the Courts in Early Modern England* (London, 1994), 48–80.

Ingrassia, C., *Authorship, Commerce, and Gender in Early Eighteenth-Century England. A Culture of Paper Credit* (Cambridge, 1998).

Jackson, A., 'The Stage and the Authorities, 1700–1714 (as Revealed in the Newspapers)', *RES* 14 (1938), 53–62.

James, M., 'English Politics and the Concept of Honour 1485–1642', *PP (Supplement)* 3 (1978).

Jenkins, P., *The Making of a Ruling Class. The Glamorgan Gentry, 1640–1790* (Cambridge, 1983).

Johns, A., *The Nature of the Book. Print and Knowledge in the Making* (Chicago, 1998).

Jones, A. R., and P. Stallybrass, 'Fetishizing Gender: Constructing the Hermaphrodite in Renaissance Europe', in J. Epstein and K. Straub (eds.), *Body Guards. The Cultural Politics of Gender Ambiguity* (London, 1991), 80–111.

Joyce, P., *Democratic Subjects. The Self and the Social in Nineteenth-Century England* (Cambridge, 1994).

Visions of the People. Industrial England and the Question of Class 1848–1914 (Cambridge, 1991).

Kenny, S. S., 'The Publication of Plays', in R. D. Hume (ed.), *The London Theatre World, 1660–1800* (Carbondale, 1980), 309–36.

Ketcham, M. G., *Transparent Designs. Reading, Performance and Form in the Spectator Papers* (Athens, GA, 1985).

Kewes, P., *Authorship and Appropriation. Writing for the Stage in England, 1660–1710* (Oxford, 1998).

'The Politics of the Stage and the Page: Source Plays for George Powell's *A Very Good Wife* (1693) in their Production and Publication Contexts', *Zagadnienia Rodzajów Literackich* 37, 1–2 (1994), 41–52.

Kiernan, V. G., *The Duel in European History. Honour and the Reign of Aristocracy* (Oxford, 1988).

King, T. A., 'Displacing Masculinity: Edward Kynaston and the Politics of Effeminacy', in A. P. Williams (ed.), *The Image of Manhood in Early Modern Literature. Viewing the Male* (London, 1999), 119–40.

'Gender and Modernity: Male Looks and the Performance of Public Pleasures', in L. J. Rosenthal and M. Choudhury (eds.), *Monstrous Dreams of Reason. Body, Self, and Other in the Enlightenment* (Lewisburg, 2002), 25–44.

Kinservik, M. J., 'Theatrical Regulation during the Restoration Period', in S. J. Owen (ed.), *A Companion to Restoration Drama* (Oxford, 2001), 36–52.

Kitch, M. J., 'Capital and Kingdom: Migration to Later Stuart London', in A. L. Beier and R. Finlay (eds.), *London 1500–1700. The Making of the Metropolis* (London, 1986), 224–51.

Klein, L. E., 'Politeness for Plebes. Consumption and Social Identity in Early Eighteenth-Century England', in A. Bermingham and J. Brewer (eds.), *The Consumption of Culture 1600–1800. Image, Object, Text* (London, 1995), 362–82.

'The Political Significance of "Politeness" in Early Eighteenth-Century Britain', in G. J. Schochet (ed.), *Politics, Politeness, and Patriotism. Papers Presented at the Folger Institute Seminar* (Washington, DC, 1993), 73–108.

Knif, H., *Gentlemen and Spectators. Studies in Journals, Opera and the Social Scene in Late Stuart London* (Helsinki, 1995).

Knights, M., *Politics and Opinion in Crisis, 1678–1681* (Cambridge, 1994).

Knutson, H. C., *The Triumph of Wit. Molière and Restoration Comedy* (Columbus, 1988).

Krutch, J. W., *Comedy and Conscience after the Restoration* (New York, 1924).

Kuchta, D. M., *The Three-Piece Suit and Modern Masculinity. England 1550–1850* (Berkeley, 2002).

Langford, P., *A Polite and Commercial People. England, 1727–1783* (Oxford, 1989).

Langhans, E. A., 'The Post-1660 Theatres as Performance Spaces', in S. J. Owen (ed.), *A Companion to Restoration Drama* (Oxford, 2001), 3–18.

'The Theatre', in D. Payne Fisk (ed.), *The Cambridge Companion to English Restoration Theatre* (Cambridge, 2000), 1–18.

'The Theatres', in R. D. Hume (ed.), *The London Theatre World, 1660–1800* (Carbondale, 1980), 35–65.

Laqueur, T., *Making Sex. Body and Gender from the Greeks to Freud* (Cambridge, MA, 1990).

Leacroft, R., *The Development of the English Playhouse* (London, 1973).

Leinwand, T. B., *The City Staged. Jacobean Comedy, 1603–1613* (Madison, 1986).

Lichtenstein, J., 'Making Up Representation: The Risks of Femininity', *Representations* 15 (1987), 77–87.

Lockridge, K. A., 'Colonial Self-Fashioning: Paradoxes and Pathologies in the Construction of Genteel Identity in Eighteenth-Century America', in R. Hoffman, M. Sobel, and F. J. Teute (eds.), *Through a Glass Darkly. Reflections on Personal Identity in Early America* (Chapel Hill, 1997), 274–339.

Loftis, J., *Comedy and Society from Congreve to Fielding* (Stanford, 1959).

Loftis, J., et al. (eds.), *The Revels History of Drama. Volume V: 1660–1750* (London, 1976).

Love, H., 'Shadwell, Rochester and the Crisis of Amateurism', *Restoration. Studies in English Literary Culture, 1660–1700* 20, 2 (1996), 119–34.

'Who Were the Restoration Audience?', *Yearbook of English Studies* 10 (1980), 21–44.

Lowenthal, C., *Performing Identities on the Restoration Stage* (Carbondale, 2003).

'Sticks and Rags, Bodies and Brocade: Essentializing Discourses and the Late Restoration Playhouse', in K. M. Quinsey (ed.), *Broken Boundaries. Women and Feminism in Restoration Drama* (Lexington, 1996), 219–33.

McCrea, B., *Impotent Fathers. Patriarchy and the Demographic Crisis in the Eighteenth-Century Novel* (Newark, 1998).

McFarlane, C., *The Sodomite in Fiction and Satire 1660–1750* (New York, 1997).

McKendrick, N., '"Gentleman and Players" Revisited: The Gentlemanly Ideal, the Business Ideal, and the Professional Ideal in English Literary Culture', in N. McKendrick and R. B. Outhwaite (eds.), *Business Life and Public Policy. Essays in Honour of D.C. Coleman* (Cambridge, 1986), 98–136.

McKenzie, D. F., '*Mea Culpa*: Voltaire's Retraction of His Comments Critical of Congreve', *RES* 49, 196 (1998), 461–5.

McKeon, M., *The Origins of the English Novel 1600–1740* (Baltimore, 1987).

McRae, A., *God Speed the Plough. The Representation of Agrarian England, 1500–1660* (Cambridge, 1996).

McVeagh, J., *Tradefull Merchants. The Portrayal of the Capitalist in Literature* (London, 1981).

Maguire, N. K., *Regicide and Restoration. English Tragicomedy, 1660–1671* (Cambridge, 1992).

Mandell, L., 'Bawds and Merchants: Engendering Capitalist Desires', *ELH* 59 (1992), 107–23.

Manley, L., *Literature and Culture in Early Modern London* (Cambridge, 1995).

Mann, M., *The Sources of Social Power. Volume I: A History of Power from the Beginning to A.D. 1760* (Cambridge, 1986).

Marsden, J. I., 'Female Spectatorship, Jeremy Collier and the Anti-Theatrical Debate', *ELH* 65 (1998), 877–98.

Masters, A. (ed. S. Trussler), *The Play of Personality in the Restoration Theatre* (Woodbridge, 1992).

Maurer, S. L., *Proposing Men. Dialectics of Gender and Class in the Eighteenth-Century English Periodical* (Stanford, 1998).

Maus, K. E., '"Playhouse Flesh and Blood": Sexual Ideology and the Restoration Actress', *ELH* 46 (1979), 595–617.

Mayfield, D., and S. Thorne, 'Social History and Its Discontents: Gareth Stedman Jones and the Politics of Language', *Social History* 17, 2 (1992), 165–88.

Meldrum, T., 'London Domestic Servants from Depositional Evidence, 1650–1750: Servant–Employer Sexuality in the Patriarchal Household', in T. Hitchcock, P. King, and P. Sharpe (eds.), *Chronicling Poverty. The Voices and Strategies of the English Poor 1640–1840* (London, 1997), 47–69.

Mendelson, S. H., and P. Crawford, *Women in Early Modern England 1550–1720* (Oxford, 1998).

Milhous, J., 'Company Management', in R. D. Hume (ed.), *The London Theatre World, 1660–1800* (Carbondale, 1980), 1–34.

Milhous, J., and R. D. Hume, *Producible Interpretation. Eight English Plays 1675–1707* (Carbondale, 1985).

'Theatrical Politics at Drury Lane: New Light on Letitia Cross, Jane Rogers, and Anne Oldfield', *Bulletin of Research in the Humanities* 85, 4 (1982), 412–29.

Miller, S., 'Consuming Mothers/Consuming Merchants: The Carnivalesque Economy of Jacobean City Comedy', *Modern Language Studies* 26, 2–3 (1996), 73–95.

Mingay, G. E., *The Gentry. The Rise and Fall of a Ruling Class* (London, 1976).

Monod, P. K., *Jacobitism and the English People 1688–1788* (Cambridge, 1989).

Montrose, L., *The Purpose of Playing. Shakespeare and the Cultural Politics of the Elizabethan Theatre* (Chicago, 1996).

Morrill, J. S., 'The Northern Gentry and the Great Rebellion', *Northern History* 15 (1979), 66–87.

Muldrew, C., *The Economy of Obligation. The Culture of Credit and Social Relations in Early Modern England* (London, 1998).

Mullaney, S., 'Discursive Forums, Cultural Practices: History and Anthropology in Literary Studies', in T. J. McDonald (ed.), *The Historic Turn in the Human Sciences* (Ann Arbor, 1996), 161–89.

Munns, J., 'Change, Skepticism, and Uncertainty', in D. Payne Fisk (ed.), *The Cambridge Companion to English Restoration Theatre* (Cambridge, 2000), 142–57.

Nenner, H., *The Right To Be King. The Succession to the Crown of England, 1603–1714* (London, 1995).

Newman, K., *Fashioning Femininity and English Renaissance Drama* (Chicago, 1991).

Nicholson, C. E., *Writing and the Rise of Finance. Capital Satires of the Early Eighteenth Century* (Cambridge, 1994).

Novak, M. E., 'Libertinism and Sexuality', in S. J. Owen (ed.), *A Companion to Restoration Drama* (Oxford, 2001), 53–68.

O'Brien, J. F., 'The Character of Credit: Defoe's "Lady Credit," *The Fortunate Mistress*, and the Resources of Inconsistency in Early Eighteenth-Century Britain', *ELH* 63 (1996), 603–31.

Orr, B., *Empire on the English Stage 1660–1714* (Cambridge, 2001).

Orrell, J., 'A New Witness of the Restoration Stage', *Theatre Research International* 2 (1977), 86–97.

Owen, S. J., 'Drama and Political Crisis', in D. Payne Fisk (ed.), *The Cambridge Companion to English Restoration Theatre* (Cambridge, 2000), 158–73.

'Restoration Drama and Politics: An Overview', in Owen (ed.), *A Companion to Restoration Drama* (Oxford, 2001), 126–39.

Restoration Theatre and Crisis (Oxford, 1996).

Parker, A., and E. K. Sedgwick (eds.), *Performativity and Performance* (New York, 1995).

Paster, G. K., *The Body Embarrassed. Drama and the Disciplines of Shame in Early Modern England* (Ithaca, 1993).

'The Unbearable Coldness of Female Being: Women's Imperfection and the Humoral Economy', *ELR* 28, 3 (1998), 416–40.

Payne, D. C., 'Reified Object or Emergent Professional? Retheorizing the Restoration Actress', in J. D. Canfield and D. C. Payne (eds.), *Cultural Readings of Restoration and Eighteenth-Century English Theater* (Athens, GA, 1995), 13–38.

Peck, J., 'Anne Oldfield's Lady Townly: Consumption, Credit, and the Whig Hegemony of the 1720s', *Theatre Journal* 49 (1997), 397–416.

Pedicord, H. W., *"By Their Majesties' Command". The House of Hanover at the London Theatres, 1714–1800* (London, 1991).

'The Changing Audience', in R. D. Hume (ed.), *The London Theatre World, 1660–1800* (Carbondale, 1980), 236–52.

The Theatrical Public in the Time of Garrick (New York, 1954).

Peltonen, M., *The Duel in Early Modern England* (Cambridge, 2003).

Peters, J. S., 'The Bank, the Press, and the "Return of Nature". On Currency, Credit, and Literary Property in the 1690s', in J. Brewer and S. Staves (eds.), *Early Modern Conceptions of Property* (London, 1995), 365–88.

'"Things Govern'd By Words": Late 17th-Century Comedy and the Reformers', *English Studies* 68, 2 (1987), 142–53.

Pittock, M. G. H., 'The Culture of Jacobitism', in J. Black (ed.), *Culture and Society in Britain, 1660–1800* (Manchester, 1997), 124–45.

Pocock, J. G. A., *The Machiavellian Moment. Florentine Political Thought and the Atlantic Republican Tradition* (Princeton, 1975).

Virtue, Commerce, and History. Essays on Political Thought and History, Chiefly in the Eighteenth Century (London, 1985).

Porter, R., *Flesh in the Age of Reason* (London, 2003).

Porter, R., and L. Hall, *The Facts of Life. The Creation of Sexual Knowledge in Britain, 1650–1950* (New Haven, 1995).

Posner, D. M., *The Performance of Nobility in Early Modern European Literature* (Cambridge, 1999).

Powell, J., *Restoration Theatre Production* (London, 1984).

Reay, B., *Popular Cultures in England 1550–1750* (London, 1998).

Reid, G. W. (ed.), *Catalogue of Prints and Drawings in the British Museum. Division I. Political and Personal Satires. Volume II: June 1689 to 1733* (London, 1873).

Roach, J., 'The Performance', in D. Payne Fisk (ed.), *The Cambridge Companion to English Restoration Theatre* (Cambridge, 2000), 19–39.

Roberts, D., *The Ladies. Female Patronage of Restoration Drama 1660–1700* (Oxford, 1989).

Rogers, N., 'Money, Land and Lineage: the Big Bourgeoisie of Hanoverian London', *Social History* 4, 3 (1979), 437–54.

'A Reply to Donna Andrew', *Social History* 6, 3 (1981), 365–9.

Whigs and Cities. Popular Politics in the Age of Walpole and Pitt (Oxford, 1989).

Rosenheim, J. M., *The Emergence of a Ruling Order. English Landed Society 1650–1750* (London, 1998).

Rosenthal, L. J., '"Counterfeit Scrubbado": Women Actors in the Restoration', *Eighteenth Century: Theory and Interpretation* 34, 1 (1993), 3–21.

Playwrights and Plagiarists in Early Modern England. Gender, Authorship, Literary Property (Ithaca, 1996).

Rousseau, G., 'The Pursuit of Homosexuality in the Eighteenth Century: "Utterly Confused Category" and/or Rich Repository?', *Eighteenth-Century Life* 9, 3 (1985), 132–68.

Rozbicki, M. J., *The Complete Colonial Gentleman. Cultural Legitimacy in Plantation America* (Charlottesville, 1998).

Sagle, K. C., *The English Country Squire as Depicted in English Prose Fiction from 1740 to 1800* (1938, reprint 1971).

Schechner, R., *Performance Theory* (London, 1977, revised edition 1988).

Scheil, K. W., *The Taste of the Town. Shakespearian Comedy and the Early Eighteenth-Century Theater* (Cranbury, NJ, 2003).

Scott, J., *Stratification and Power. Structures of Class, Status, and Command* (Cambridge, 1996).

Scott, J. W., *Gender and the Politics of History* (New York, 1988).

Seaver, P. S., 'Declining Status in an Aspiring Age: The Problem of the Gentle Apprentice in Seventeenth-Century London', in B. Y. Kunze and D. D. Brautigam (eds.), *Court, Country, and Culture. Essays on Early Modern British History in Honor of Perez Zagorin* (Rochester, NY, 1992), 129–47.

Senelick, L., 'Mollies or Men of Mode? Sodomy and the Eighteenth-Century London Stage', *Journal of the History of Sexuality* 1, 1 (1990), 33–67.

Shapin, S., '"The Mind Is Its Own Place": Science and Solitude in Seventeenth-Century England', *Science in Context* 4, 1 (1990), 191–218.

'"A Scholar and a Gentleman": The Problematic Identity of the Scientific Practitioner in Early Modern England', *History of Science* 29, 3 (1991), 279–327.

A Social History of Truth. Civility and Science in Seventeenth-Century England (Chicago, 1994).

Shapiro, S. C., '"Yon Plumed Dandebrat": Male "Effeminacy" in English Satire and Criticism', *RES* 39 (1988), 400–12.

Shepard, A., *Meanings of Manhood in Early Modern England* (Oxford, 2003).

Shepherd, S., and P. Womack, *English Drama. A Cultural History* (Oxford, 1996).

Sherman, S., 'Lady Credit No Lady; or, the Case of Defoe's "Coy Mistress," Truly Stat'd', *Texas Studies in Literature and Language* 37, 2 (1995), 185–214.

Shesgreen, S., *Hogarth and the Times-of-the-Day Tradition* (Ithaca, 1983).

Shinagel, M., *Daniel Defoe and Middle-Class Gentility* (Cambridge, MA, 1968).

Speck, W. A., *Literature and Society in Eighteenth-Century England. Ideology, Politics and Culture, 1680–1820* (London, 1998).

Society and Literature in England 1700–60 (Dublin, 1983).

Spurr, J., *England in the 1670s. 'This Masquerading Age'* (Oxford, 2000).

Staves, S., 'A Few Kind Words for the Fop', *SEL* 22 (1982), 413–28.

Players' Scepters. Fictions of Authority in the Restoration (Lincoln, NE, 1979).

'Resentment or Resignation? Dividing the Spoils among Daughters and Younger Sons', in J. Brewer and S. Staves (eds.), *Early Modern Conceptions of Property* (London, 1995), 194–218.

Stevenson, L. C., *Praise and Paradox. Merchants and Craftsmen in Elizabethan Popular Literature* (Cambridge, 1984).

Stone, jr., G. W., 'The Making of the Repertory', in R. D. Hume (ed.), *The London Theatre World, 1660–1800* (Carbondale, 1980), 181–209.

Stone, L., *Broken Lives. Separation and Divorce in England 1660–1857* (Oxford, 1993).

'History and Post-Modernism', *PP* 134 (1991), 217–18.

The Road to Divorce. England 1539–1987 (Oxford, 1990).

Uncertain Unions. Marriage in England 1660–1753 (Oxford, 1992).

Stone, L., and J. C. F. Stone, *An Open Elite? England 1540–1880* (Oxford, 1984).

Straub, K., *Sexual Suspects. Eighteenth-Century Players and Sexual Ideology* (Princeton, 1992).

Styan, J. L., *Restoration Comedy in Performance* (Cambridge, 1986).

Szechi, D., *Jacobitism and Tory Politics 1710–14* (Edinburgh, 1984).

Tague, I. H., *Women of Quality. Accepting and Contesting Ideals of Femininity in England, 1690–1760* (Woodbridge, 2002).

Thomas, C., 'Pope and His *Dunciad* Adversaries. Skirmishes on the Borders of Gentility', in J. E. Gill (ed.), *Cutting Edges. Postmodern Critical Essays on Eighteenth-Century Satire* (Tennessee Studies in Literature 37, Knoxville, 1995), 274–300.

Thompson, E. P., *Customs in Common* (London, 1991).

Thompson, R., *Unfit for Modest Ears. A Study of Pornographic, Obscene and Bawdy Works Written or Published in England in the Second Half of the Seventeenth Century* (London, 1979).

Trumbach, R., 'The Birth of the Queen: Sodomy and the Emergence of Gender Equality in Modern Culture, 1660–1750', in M. B. Duberman, M. Vicinus, and G. Chauncey, jr. (eds.), *Hidden from History. Reclaiming the Gay and Lesbian Past* (New York, 1990), 129–40.

'London's Sapphists: From Three Sexes to Four Genders in the Making of Modern Culture', in G. Herdt (ed.), *Third Sex, Third Gender. Beyond Sexual Dimorphism in Culture and History* (New York, 1994), 111–36.

Sex and the Gender Revolution. Volume I: Heterosexuality and the Third Gender in Enlightenment London (Chicago, 1998).

'Sex, Gender and Sexual Identity in Modern Culture: Male Sodomy and Female Prostitution in Enlightenment England', in J. C. Fout (ed.), *Forbidden History. The State, Society, and the Regulation of Sexuality in Modern Europe* (Chicago, 1992), 89–106.

Tumbleson, R. D., *Catholicism in the English Protestant Imagination. Nationalism, Religion, and Literature, 1660–1745* (Cambridge, 1998).

Turner, D. M., *Fashioning Adultery. Gender, Sex and Civility in England, 1660–1740* (Cambridge, 2002).

'"Nothing is so secret but shall be revealed": The Scandalous Life of Robert Foulkes', in T. Hitchcock and M. Cohen (eds.), *English Masculinities 1660–1800* (London, 1999), 169–92.

Turner, J. G., *Libertines and Radicals in Early Modern London. Sexuality, Politics, and Literary Culture, 1630–1685* (Cambridge, 2002).

'The Properties of Libertinism', in R. P. Maccubbin (ed.), *'Tis Nature's Fault. Unauthorized Sexuality during the Enlightenment* (New York, 1987), 75–87.

Underdown, D. E., 'The Taming of the Scold: The Enforcement of Patriarchal Authority in Early Modern England', in A. J. Fletcher and J. Stevenson (eds.), *Order and Disorder in Early Modern England* (Cambridge, 1985), 116–36.

Wahrman, D., *Imagining the Middle Class. The Political Representation of Class in Britain, c.1780–1840* (Cambridge, 1995).

'National Society, Communal Culture: An Argument about the Recent Historiography of Eighteenth-Century Britain', *Social History* 17, 1 (1992), 43–72.

Walker, G., 'Expanding the Boundaries of Female Honour in Early Modern England', *Transactions of the Royal Historical Society*, sixth series, 6 (1996), 235–45.

Wall, C., *The Literary and Cultural Spaces of Restoration London* (Cambridge, 1998).

Wallace, B. K., 'Reading the Surfaces of Colley Cibber's *The Careless Husband*', *SEL* 40, 3 (2000), 473–89.

Walsh, M. W., 'The Significance of William Mountfort's *Greenwich Park*', *Restoration and 18th Century Theatre Research* 12, 2 (1973), 35–40.

Walter, J., 'Public Transcripts, Popular Agency and the Politics of Subsistence in Early Modern England', in M. J. Braddick and J. Walter (eds.), *Negotiating Power in Early Modern Society. Order, Hierarchy and Subordination in Britain and Ireland* (Cambridge, 2001), 123–48.

Wear, A., *Knowledge and Practice in English Medicine, 1550–1680* (Cambridge, 2000).

Weber, H., 'A "double Portion of his Father's Art": Congreve, Dryden, Jonson and the Drama of Theatrical Succession', *Criticism* 39, 3 (1997), 359–82.

Weil, R. J., *Political Passions. Gender, the Family and Political Argument in England 1680–1714* (Manchester, 1999).

'The Politics of Legitimacy: Women and the Warming-Pan Scandal', in L. G. Schwoerer (ed.), *The Revolution of 1688–1689. Changing Perspectives* (Cambridge, 1992), 65–82.

Whyman, S. E., 'Land and Trade Revisited: The Case of John Verney, London Merchant and Baronet, 1660–1720', *London Journal* 22, 1 (1997), 16–32.

Sociability and Power in Late-Stuart England. The Cultural World of the Verneys 1660–1720 (Oxford, 1999).

Williams, A. P., *The Restoration Fop. Gender Boundaries and Comic Characterization in Later Seventeenth Century Drama* (Salzburg, 1995).

Wilson, J. H., *All the King's Ladies. Actresses of the Restoration* (Chicago, 1958).

Wilson, K., 'Citizenship, Empire, and Modernity in the English Provinces, c.1720–1790', *Eighteenth-Century Studies* 29, 1 (1995), 69–96.

The Sense of the People. Politics, Culture and Imperialism in England, 1715–1785 (Cambridge, 1995).

Wiltenburg, J., *Disorderly Women and Female Power in the Street Literature of Early Modern England and Germany* (Charlottesville, 1992).

Winton, C., 'The London Stage Embattled: 1695–1710', *Tennessee Studies in Literature* 19 (1974), 9–19.

Woolf, D., *The Social Circulation of the Past. English Historical Culture 1500–1730* (Oxford, 2003).

Wrightson, K. E., 'Estates, Degrees and Sorts: Changing Perceptions of Society in Tudor and Stuart England', in P. J. Corfield (ed.), *Language, History and Class* (Oxford, 1991), 30–52.

'The Politics of the Parish in Early Modern England', in P. Griffiths, A. Fox, and S. Hindle (eds.), *The Experience of Authority in Early Modern England* (London, 1996), 10–46.

'"Sorts of People" in Tudor and Stuart England', in J. Barry and C. Brooks (eds.), *The Middling Sort of People. Culture, Society and Politics in England, 1550–1800* (London, 1994), 28–51.

Zammito, J. H., 'Are We Being Theoretical Yet? The New Historicism, the New Philosophy of History, and "Practicing Historians"', *Journal of Modern History* 65, 4 (1993), 783–814.

Zimbardo, R. A., 'At Zero Point: Discourse, Politics, and Satire in Restoration England', *ELH* 59 (1992), 785–98.

'Toward Zero/Toward Public Virtue: The Conceptual Design of Dramatic Satire before and after the Ascension of William and Mary', *Eighteenth-Century Life* 12, 3 (1988), 53–66.

UNPUBLISHED MATERIAL

Botica, A. R., 'Audience, Playhouse and Play in Restoration Theatre, 1660–1710', DPhil dissertation, Oxford University (1985).

Carter, P., 'Mollies, Fops and Men of Feeling: Aspects of Male Effeminacy in Early Modern England, c.1700–1780', DPhil dissertation, Oxford University (1995).

Gardner, K. J., 'Cultural Anxiety and English Comedy, 1700–1708', PhD dissertation, Tulane University (1992).

Glaisyer, N. A. F., 'The Culture of Commerce in England, 1660–1720', PhD dissertation, Cambridge University (1999).

Gorrie, R. B., 'Gentle Riots? Theatre Riots in London 1730–1780', PhD dissertation, University of Guelph (2000).

Harteker, L. M., 'Steward of the Kingdom's Stock: Merchants, Trade, and Discourse in Eighteenth-Century England', PhD dissertation, University of Chicago (1996).

Hopes, J., 'The Debate on the English Theatre, 1690–1740', PhD dissertation, University of Newcastle-upon-Tyne (1980).

King, T. A., 'The Hermaphrodite's Occupation: Theatricality and Queerness in Seventeenth- and Eighteenth-Century London', PhD dissertation, Northwestern University (1993).

Mandy, J. K., 'City Women: Daughters, Wives, Widows, and Whores in Jacobean and Restoration City Comedy', PhD dissertation, Lehigh University (1996).

Milhous, J., and R. D. Hume, 'Revision of *The London Stage. Part II 1700–1729*' (forthcoming from Southern Illinois University Press). The author consulted a digital draft of July 2001, kindly made available by the authors.

More, R. W. S., 'The Rewards of Virtue: Gentility in Early Modern England', PhD dissertation, Brown University (1998).

Potts, A. J., 'The Development of the Playhouse in Seventeenth-Century London', PhD dissertation, Cambridge University (1999).

Pritchard, W. J., 'Outward Appearances: The Display of Women in Restoration London', PhD dissertation, University of Chicago (1998).

Russell, R., 'Dramatists and the Printed Page: The Social Role of Comedy from Richard Steele to Leigh Hunt', DPhil dissertation, Oxford University (1995).

Strohmer, S. M., '"Every Man an Actor": Performance Theories in the Restoration', PhD dissertation, University of Michigan (1999).

Taliaferro, W. R., 'The Fop and Fashion in Restoration Comedy', PhD dissertation, University of California-Berkeley (1989).

Index